THE ROYAL BRITISH LEGION CENTENARY COOKBOOK

COOKING WITH HEROES

Foreword

By Charles Byrne, Director General, The Royal British Legion

It is always inspiring to see how members of the Armed Forces family look after each other. From our beginning 100 years ago, when four veterans' charities from the First World War came together to form an alliance, the Royal British Legion has always fostered partnerships and communities. Working with other charities is the more visible part of our work; it is through the individuals – whether serving, veterans, family, friends or supporters – that our true impact is felt.

This book encapsulates that community spirit entirely. It is the creation of an impressive team of serving and ex-service men and women from across the Armed Forces family, as well as the Legion's own members. It celebrates and commemorates the stories of those from the UK, the Commonwealth and beyond, who have served and sacrificed in the defence of Britain. It is a reminder of the timeless qualities of our Armed Forces who defend our national values and of the Legion's unofficial motto: "Service not Self". The spirit of these awe-inspiring histories is only enhanced by the traditional recipes that readers will discover and enjoy throughout this book.

The Legion has been here for a century to provide support for the Armed Forces community. It has campaigned to governments in the interest of that community and united the nation in publicly remembering their service and sacrifice. We will be here for a century to come. While times may change, our three core missions of upholding the well-being, interests and memory of the Armed Forces community will remain the same. As conflict and difficulty remain in the world, so do the courageous and resilient men and women, prepared to stand in harm's way to defend our country – and the Legion will be at their side.

To me, the military values are personified in so many ways; through the perseverance and strong-will displayed in the most challenging of circumstances; the dedication and support given to your peers through exceptional hardship and the playing of your part as best as you can. It is selfless and delivered without expectation of reward or recognition.

Message of support

From Samuel Asante-Nnuro, Chairman of The Commonwealth Legion

The work that the Royal British Legion has done to support the men and women of the Armed Forces community over the past century is beyond measure, and it is a great honour to be able to congratulate all those associated with it on the occasion of its centenary.

The Armed Forces family spans the UK, the Commonwealth and beyond, and is itself a vital and vibrant part of a wider international community; one that the Royal British Legion does so much to sustain and nurture. The bravery and quiet dedication of those who serve, or have served, can on occasion be taken for granted, but the Royal British Legion ensures that they are never forgotten, and for that it is to be commended and celebrated.

The Royal British Legion has inspired us at the Commonwealth Legion in many ways. Our values of integrity, respect, caring for the disadvantaged, being the voice for the voiceless and providing help to the helpless are woven into everything that the Royal British Legion does. These principles, the culmination of its efforts over the past hundred years, are ones that we at The Commonwealth Legion share with our Royal British namesake.

It is an honour to support and advocate for those who have given so much for our society; an honour that motivates us in all that we do, whether campaigning for the immigration rights of Commonwealth service personnel, or helping ex-service men and women find their feet and overcome the challenges of life beyond the military.

The Royal British Legion has stood shoulder to shoulder with the Armed Forces community for 100 years, and will no doubt continue to do so for many, many more. A selfless commitment to the welfare of others lies at the heart of military service, and the Royal British Legion is a perfect example of that ethos in action.

It only leaves me to congratulate the Royal British Legion and all those involved in the production of this wonderful centenary publication, which heralds the achievements of service men and women from the UK and around the world. What a fantastic way to celebrate our Armed Forces family, and those who do so much to support its past, present and future.

Contents

Chapter one
Starters, soups and snacks

Regions and recipes

Official sponsors

Chapter two
Main courses

Regions and recipes

Official sponsors

Chapter three
Puddings

Regions and recipes

Official sponsors

Appendices

Introduction

By Squadron Leader Jon Pullen, RAF (retired)

Having spent more than 35 years in the RAF, I have seen first-hand the work that the Armed Forces charities do for our military family. A few years ago I realised that the largest of these charities, the Royal British Legion, was heading at pace towards its centenary, presenting a wonderful opportunity to marshal my contacts in the services community and raise some money for this most worthy of causes. In the best traditions of the military it would be a case of Armed Forces personnel supporting Armed Forces personnel.

This was something I have been doing for a while. In 2009 I teamed up with a host of military chefs and volunteers to write *Food For Heroes*, the official Help For Heroes cookbook, a best-selling publication that raised £100,000 for the Help For Heroes charity. Eight years later I worked with the RAF100 Appeal and the publisher St James's House to produce a book that celebrated the Royal Air Force's centenary, a very successful partnership that saw us not only raise around £150,000 for the RAF's charities but also produce *The RAF100 Cookbook*, a really beautiful and unique way of telling the story of the RAF's first 100 years.

The Royal British Legion's centenary would give us a chance to do this again on an even grander scale. Founded on 15 May 1921, the Royal British Legion was the amalgamation of four national organisations of ex-servicemen that had established themselves after the Great War. The main purpose of the Legion was straightforward: to care and campaign for those who had suffered as a result of their service in the First World War. One hundred years later and this bastion of support to the Armed Forces is still helping British servicemen and women and their families by providing vital financial, social and emotional assistance.

In an effort to understand what a fitting celebration for the RBL's centenary needed to be, I spent some hours with a team of volunteers from across the three services, considering the values of the Royal British Legion and the Armed Forces and what both mean to the

nation. The book needed to embody notions like tradition, courage, dependability and determination in the face of adversity. With this in mind we set about the book's concept: we divided the United Kingdom, her Overseas Territories and the Commonwealth into 100 different regions and then, by teaming up with members from across the Royal British Legion, we identified a local hero or heroine to represent each region. The only rule was that it had to be someone nominated by the local RBL members who they thought fitting to represent their region and who had made a significant contribution to the defence of Britain.

We then asked our team of military chefs to choose, research and develop a recipe to represent the food culture of each region in honour of our local heroes. These recipes are often traditional, forgotten or unfashionable recipes brought into the 21st century, using readily available ingredients that can be prepared in a home kitchen. As well as more than 60 serving and veteran military chefs from across the services who have volunteered their exceptional skills, we have also been joined by a virtual who's-who of celebrity chefs who have volunteered their support, including Cyrus Todiwala, James Martin, Melissa Hemsley, the Hairy Bikers, Rick Stein, Ainsley Harriott and Jamie Oliver to name but a few. We are also delighted with the support we have received from so many sponsors joining us in our efforts to raise funds for the Legion: dozens of cake makers, wineries, brewers, bakers, food companies and more have backed our campaign, meaning that the Royal British Legion will receive £5 from the recommended retail price of £19.95.

In total, more than 140 personnel from across the whole military family have contributed to the writing of this book, including serving personnel, family and friends, veterans, reservists, civil servants and even military youth groups. We have had plenty of experience to call upon with the team having served for a total of 1,385 years between us, with 446 separate operational deployments completed over a total period of 2,148 months – not to mention the vast quantities of range stew, egg

"More than 140 personnel from across the whole military family have contributed to the writing of this book, including serving personnel, veterans, reservists, family and friends"

banjos, and cheesy-hammy-eggies consumed. It should also be noted that all of this was undertaken during the pandemic, meaning that, for the best part of a year, the editorial team met every other Tuesday evening for an hour on Zoom to share progress, issues and perhaps a small glass of something. Particular mention needs to go to two individuals: ex-Flight Sergeant Stu Harmer, one of the most capable chefs I've ever known, who was responsible for ensuring the delivery of the recipes, and my friend and colleague Flight Lieutenant Dan Beechey, who had the unenviable task of ensuring the writing deadlines were all met. Others in the team were old friends from my previous books – Lieutenant Commander Andrew "Tank" Murray, Squadron Leader Mal Craig, Flight Lieutenant Samantha Broderick and Sergeant Stefan "Stef" Sewell – along with new friends and colleagues Captain Steve Blanks, Warrant Officer RN "Dixie" Dean, Chief Petty Officer Russ Keitch, Sergeant Sam Cootes and Mrs Kim Beechey, all of whom gave up their time and talents. Finally, a massive thanks to our editor John Lewis and to Robert Hogg-Thompson and the RBL team, who have been so supportive and encouraging in pulling the book together; I will definitely miss our weekly virtual bubble! To you and your teams, a massive heartfelt thanks for your immense efforts; I know you are as proud of what we have produced as I am.

As a team, our journey has been nothing short of astonishing, emotional and inspiring. What became clear as we started our research to identify the Local Heroes with the Legion membership was the challenge of only selecting 100 of these inspirational individuals. At this time when we are scrutinising our nation's record of diversity, I was struck by how many individuals from the Commonwealth and Empire came to aid the fight.

We discovered Captain John Perkins, born a slave in the middle of the 18th century who rose to captain a Royal Navy 32-gun frigate in 1800; we found out about Flying Officer Errol Walton Barrow, who joined the RAF as an aircraftsman in 1940, finished the war as a navigator and went on to become the Prime Minister of Barbados; we learned of the Mauritian national, Lise Marie Jeanette de Baissac, codenamed "Odile", who travelled to England in 1940 and was one of the first two Special Operations Executive (SOE) agents to parachute behind enemy lines. We uncovered stories of the Falkland Islanders of 1982 who stood up to the invading Argentine force; of the Canadian Commander James Campbell Clouston, who took the role of the pier master on the East Mole overseeing the evacuation of 40,000 British servicemen every day during the "Miracle of Dunkirk"; of Squadron Leader Mohinder Singh Pujji who, in 1940, travelled to England from India to join the Royal Air Force as a Hurricane pilot. And there are so many, many more.

Closer to home, we learned how, under the right circumstances, so many ordinary men and women can be so extraordinary. There's Major John Howard, who oversaw and led the assault on Pegasus Bridge as part of the D-Day landings; Lance Corporal Jamie Webb, who was aged only 24 when he was killed while serving in Afghanistan; Elizabeth Webber Harris, who risked her life to nurse cholera sufferers on the North West Frontier and how the officers of the regiment raised the money to present her with a gold "Victoria Cross"; and, perhaps the most poignant of them all, Private Matthew Rooney, who fought in the First World War, earning no great distinctions or honours, who sadly died within weeks of the Armistice. Like so many, they all gave their todays for our tomorrows. These were ordinary people doing extraordinary things.

What all of these individuals have in common is the courage and conviction of purpose, determination and endeavour to do what they could when called upon, often making the ultimate sacrifice in the process. It is these same qualities that draw men and women to serve their country today, many of whom have given of their time and talent to contribute to the book you hold before you in support of the Royal British Legion in its centenary year.

A history of the Royal British Legion

The Royal British Legion has been supporting current and ex-service men and women and their families since 1921

In the years that followed the First World War, millions of families were suffering great hardship. Over six million British men had served in the conflict and more than 700,000 never returned. There were millions of people who had depended on those who had died – wives, children and parents who were often financially dependent on those they had lost in the war. Of those fortunate enough to survive the war, 1.75 million had suffered some kind of disability and half of these were permanently disabled. Britain's economy also plummeted in the years after the war, and by 1921 there were two million people unemployed.

This is why the Royal British Legion was established in 1921 – to help the nation's military family after a devastating war. The Legion united four organisations that had been set up in the previous years with a similar aim but addressing different needs. The National Federation of Discharged and Demobilised Sailors and Soldiers (NFDDSS), an organisation aligned to the Liberal Party that ran soup kitchens for veterans, was formed in 1917. There was also the Labour Party-aligned National Association of Discharged Sailors and Soldiers (formed in 1917), which campaigned for improved pensions, the Conservative Party-aligned Comrades of The Great War (formed in 1917) and the Officers' Association (formed in 1920).

In May 1921, a "unity conference" was held at the Queen's Hall in Langham Place, London and combined to form the British Legion on Sunday, 15 May 1921. Field Marshall Earl Haig, who co-chaired the meeting, served as the Legion's president until his death in 1928. Fred Lister of the NFDDSS became National Chairman, the Liverpool MP and disability advocate Major Jack Brunel Cohen became the first Honorary Treasurer, while Edward, Prince of Wales (later Edward VIII) became the

Legion's Patron. By the end of the year, 2,500 branches of the Legion had been set up in the UK, along with branches in Tanzania, Kenya, Hong Kong, Gibraltar, Paris and Cologne.

By the time the Legion had been formed, the tradition of the "Two Minute Silence" had already been established, initiated by King George V in November 1919. The Cenotaph in Whitehall was built in 1920, as was the Grave of the Unknown Warrior in Westminster Abbey. In 1921, the Legion launched the first ever Poppy Appeal, selling silk poppies to raise funds to help First World War veterans with employment and housing. The poppies sold out almost immediately and raised over £106,000 (nearly £6 million in today's money).

In view of how quickly the poppies had sold, and wanting to ensure plenty of poppies for the next appeal, the Legion's Major George Howson moved production of the poppies from France to London, where it was staffed by disabled ex-servicemen. Today, the factory (now based in Richmond, Surrey) and the Legion's warehouse in Aylesford, Kent produce millions of poppies each year. When Earl Haig's wife Dorothy established the Lady Haig Poppy Factory in Edinburgh in 1926 to produce poppies exclusively for Scotland, their Appeal changed to the Earl Haig Fund (Scotland). Today, over five million Scottish poppies (which have four petals and no leaf unlike poppies in the rest of the UK) are still made by hand by disabled ex-servicemen at Lady Haig's Poppy Factory and distributed by the Poppy Appeal's sister charity, Poppyscotland.

On the evening after Armistice Day in 1927, the Legion organised the first Festival of Remembrance at the Royal Albert Hall. It was broadcast live across the world by BBC radio and featured songs, military bands and an observation of the two-minute silence. After the performance, Edward,

Opposite: Her Majesty The Queen, Patron of the Royal British Legion, amid a sea of ceramic poppies at the Tower of London in 2014. Each of the 888,246 poppies represented a British or Commonwealth life lost in the First World War

> *"For its older veterans, the Legion provides respite nurses for carers and pioneers new approaches to dementia care"*

Prince of Wales led a two-mile torchlit march from South Kensington to the Cenotaph in Westminster. Since then, the Festival of Remembrance has been a regular fixture of the Royal Albert Hall's calendar, still organised by the Legion, attended by senior royalty, and taking place on the Saturday before Remembrance Sunday and broadcast internationally by the BBC. Since 1929, the evening has always culminated with thousands of crêpe paper poppy petals falling from the roof of the hall, each representing a life lost in war.

During the Second World War, the Legion was active in Britain's civil defence, providing officers for the Home Guard (many of them being Legion members who had served in the First World War). Fred Lister, along with his successor as the Legion's Chairman, Colonel George Crosfield, advised the government on postwar planning and providing support for service personnel returning from war. The Legion was also heavily supportive of servicemen with disabilities: it lobbied heavily for the Disability Act of 1944, and supported Dr Ludwig Guttmann in his efforts to introduce sport and physiotherapy to veterans with spinal injuries the National Spinal Injuries Unit at Stoke Mandeville Hospital. Four years later the Stoke Mandeville Games launched to coincide with the London Olympics and subsequently in 1960 the Paralympics was born. The Legion's in-house publication, *Journal* also made it clear that men with mental-health problems should be treated and that there should be no stigma attached to either them or their family. Membership grew rapidly after 1945, reaching 3 million in 1950. The Legion continued to expand as a charitable service, catering for veterans of the First World War, the Second World War and all other conflicts involving British and Commonwealth troops.

King George V granted the British Legion, as it was known then, the first Charter in 1925, while Elizabeth, Duchess of York (later Queen Elizabeth, The Queen Mother), served as a Patron of the Women's Section from 1924 to her death in 2001. But it was only on the occasion of its Golden Anniversary that the Legion formally received its "Royal" appellation, becoming The Royal British Legion on 29 May 1971. In the 50 years since, it has continued to be at the heart of a national network looking after the nation's Armed Forces community. Today, the Legion has 235,000 members across 2,500 branches and maintains the three-fold mission that it established a century ago: to provide for the Armed Forces community in need, to campaign authorities in their interest, and to honour their service and sacrifice.

The ex-services community – comprising veterans and their families – currently numbers 6.2 million people in the UK, and nearly half of them are over 75. Caring for the increasingly complex needs of veterans of all ages falls to a sprawling network of the Legion's teams of advisors, carers and support workers. The Legion has also responded to a changing environment with speed and invention. In response to the returning injured from Afghanistan and Iraq, for instance, it has funded research into blast injuries, operates an adventure training ground and sports centre, and provides support to family and friends joining athletes at the Invictus Games. The Legion has also committed itself to reflecting modern Britain and its Armed Forces with a focus on inclusivity: reaching out to multi-faith and multi-ethnic communities in aspects of its Remembrance and campaigning work, and embedding an inclusive approach to all its operations and services.

It continues to offer employment support to help ex-service personnel transition into civilian life, also providing advice and mentorship on starting new businesses and on finance and tax management. The Legion offers help with getting additional training and education through an employment grant scheme. Many ex-service personnel who have experienced depression and disability have benefited from the Legion's case workers and its Pop In Centres; the Legion has also helped find housing for homeless veterans. For its older veterans, the Legion provides respite nurses for carers, pioneers new approaches to dementia care, and has expanded its capacity for dementia patients in its care homes across the country (in Somerset, Warwickshire, Norfolk, North Yorkshire, East Sussex and Kent). It also helps with day-to-day matters to enable older veterans and their families maintain their independence and stay safe in their homes, assisting with home adaptations, repairs, basic maintenance and the installation of alarms.

Along with its affiliate charities, the Royal British Legion is here to help serving and ex-serving personnel all year round, every day of the week. For members of the Armed Forces, its support starts after seven days of service and continues through life, long after service is over.

Opposite, clockwise from top: Earl Haig and Legion secretary GW Willcox examine wreaths before Armistice Day, 1922; a Chelsea Pensioner selling poppies; the Queen visits the Poppy Factory in Richmond

Chapter one

Starters, soups and snacks

These starters include distinctive soups from Glasgow, Singapore, Malaysia, Jamaica, Cheshire and Northumberland; seafood snacks from Newfoundland, the Antarctic, the Bahamas, Derry, Belize and the Falkland Islands, and plenty of unique regional specialities – from Welsh cawl to Zimbabwean cornmeal bread; from Staffordshire oatcakes to Nepalese pork.

Potato and apple bread

Chief Petty Officer John Potts, Royal Navy (retired)

County Armagh is famous for its apples and, at the time of the Plantations of Ireland in the 16th and 17th centuries, tenants were actively encouraged to plant fruit orchards. Potato bread was a staple for breakfast and snacks in Northern Ireland, so it comes as no surprise that County Armagh has worked its apples into this local speciality. The dish consists of mashed potatoes, flour, apples, sugar, salt and butter and is typically pan-fried until golden brown. It can be served for breakfast with maple-cured streaky bacon, on its own as a snack, or as a desert with vanilla cream or lemon curd.

Armagh

Vegetarian
Preparation time: 20 minutes
Cooking time: 35–45 minutes

Serves 4

INGREDIENTS

500g potatoes, peeled and cut
  into 1cm dice
30g salted butter
80g plain flour
¼ tsp baking powder
20g sultanas
2 Bramley apples, peeled, cored
  and thinly sliced
¼ tsp vanilla paste
40g caster sugar
½ tsp ground cinnamon
Double cream or lemon curd
  to serve

METHOD

• Place the diced potatoes in a medium saucepan, cover with
cold water, season well with salt, bring to a boil and simmer
for 12–15 minutes or until tender.

• Drain the potatoes in a colander and allow to dry out; while
still warm add the butter and mash until smooth.

• Add the flour, baking powder and sultanas and mix
thoroughly to form a dough.

• Divide the dough into two portions, roll one half on a lightly
floured worktop to a 15cm disc, and set aside.

• Toss the apples in the cinnamon, sugar and vanilla paste
until evenly coated.

• Evenly spread a layer of the apple slices on top of the potato
disc leaving a border of about 1cm around the edge; brush
the border with a little water.

• Roll the remaining potato dough on a lightly floured
worktop into a disc about 18cm across (big enough to cover
the top of the first half and the filling).

• Lay this on top of the apples and press the two layers of
dough together to thoroughly seal in the filling.

• Heat a large frying pan over a low heat for 2 minutes, dust
with a little flour and carefully slide the potato cake into the
pan, taking care not to break it.

• Gently cook for 10–12 minutes until golden on one side; slide
it out of the pan and onto a plate, flip this over onto another
plate before returning to the frying pan to cook the other
side for a further 10–12 minutes.

• Once both sides are golden brown, cut into four portions
and serve with double cream or lemon curd.

Rear Admiral Charles Davis Lucas VC

Charles Davis Lucas was born in Druminargal House in Poyntzpass, County Armagh in 1834 into a wealthy, landowning family. He enlisted in the Royal Navy aged 13 in 1848 and by the age of 20 had risen to the rank of mate (nowadays known as sub-lieutenant), seen action in HMS *Vengeance* during the Second Anglo-Burmese War and received the India General Service Medal (Pegu) for his actions.

In 1854, during the Crimean War, Lucas was part of the naval force blockading the Russian Baltic fleet in order to divert resources away from the Crimean front. He was aboard the wooden battleship HMS *Hecla*, alongside HMS *Odin* and HMS *Valorous*, bombarding the fort of Bomarsund off the coast of Finland in the Baltic Sea. British forces were vastly outgunned, having only 38 guns between the three ships against more than 100 entrenched Russian guns.

During the battle a shell landed on the upper deck of Lucas's ship with the fuse still burning. All hands were immediately ordered to lie flat on the deck. However Lucas, with extreme disregard for his own safety, ran forward and hurled the shell into the sea where it exploded before hitting the water. His actions saved anyone from being killed or seriously injured and he was immediately promoted to Acting Lieutenant by his Commanding Officer, William Hall, as this was the only way of recognising bravery for persons of his rank at that time. This and other acts of individual bravery during the Crimean War were well reported and led to parliament requesting "that an Order of Merit to persons serving in the Army or Navy for distinguished and prominent gallantry to which every grade should be admissible". This became the Victoria Cross. Lucas was subsequently awarded the inaugural VC by the Queen on 26 June 1857.

Lucas served on many more vessels throughout his naval service before retiring in 1873 as Captain (and

subsequently being promoted to Rear Admiral while on the retired list). He also served as a Justice of the Peace in Kent and Argyllshire. He died in 1914 and is buried at St Lawrence's Church in Mereworth near Maidstone. A copy of Lucas's medals (as his originals were left on a train carriage and never recovered) are displayed in the National Maritime Museum in Greenwich.

Written by Lieutenant Commander Andrew "Tank" Murray
AFC, Royal Navy

Potted herrings with pink grapefruit

Leading Catering Services Charlie Hall, Royal Navy

For over 200 years, the Northern Irish coast has been home to a thriving fishing industry. It provides a wide range of sustainable fish that directly influences the region's culinary heritage. Belfast Bay has always been at the centre of this marine harvest and is well known for its molluscs, mackerel and, most importantly, herring. Herring was once a reliable, nutritious source of protein back in the 1800s, but over the decades it has become somewhat forgotten. Potted herring is a traditional dish in the Antrim region, with the addition of salt and vinegar having a pickling effect on the fish fillets that extends their shelf life for an extra day or two.

Preparation time: 25 minutes
Cooking time: 30 minutes

Serves 4

INGREDIENTS

4 fresh herrings, filleted and boned
35g plain flour, generously seasoned
 with salt
60g butter
600ml Irish cider vinegar
150ml Calvados
600ml water
1 tbsp black peppercorns
3 cardamom pods, crushed with the
 flat of a knife blade
1 tbsp capers
1 pink grapefruit

METHOD

• Preheat the oven to 200°C.
• Coat both sides of the herring fillets with the seasoned flour, roll up each fillet, from head to tail, and secure in place with a cocktail stick.
• Melt the butter in a frying pan over a medium heat and, when foaming, add the rolled fillets and fry until lightly browned all over, including the rolled ends, then transfer to a baking dish, seam side down.
• Mix the cider vinegar, calvados, water, peppercorns and cardamom pods together and pour into the baking dish to cover about two thirds of the herring rolls.
• Bake in the preheated oven for 30 minutes until the tops of the fish become crispy.
• While the herrings are baking use a citrus zester to peel the grapefruit skin into fine strands then peel and carefully remove the segments with a small sharp knife.
• Char the grapefruit segments in a dry frying pan over a high heat to give them a dark, charred effect.

To serve
• Remove the cocktail sticks from herrings, place two fillets on each serving plate, spoon over a little of the cooking liquor and garnish with the charred grapefruit segments and a scattering of the zest.

Lance Corporal Kylie Watson MC

Born in Ballymena, County Antrim, one of five children, Kylie Watson joined the Army in 2006 and the Royal Army Medical Corps in 2007, having studied battlefield medicine. In 2008 she made her first operational tour, to Basra in Iraq, before continuing her training to qualify as a Class One Medic. Shortly afterwards, in 2010, Watson was deployed to Afghanistan as a fully qualified battlefield medic serving embedded in 9 Platoon, C Company, 1st Battalion the Duke of Lancaster's Regiment, based in Helmand Province.

While on a foot patrol in June 2010, an Afghan National Army (ANA) soldier about 70 metres ahead of her was shot twice in the pelvis. He immediately went into shock and was treated by another member of the patrol, a sniper who was needed for his core role. Watson ran forward at speed, under heavy fire, to provide treatment to the wounded soldier. Despite some Afghan soldiers trying to stop her from treating their severely wounded comrade – they didn't want a woman to provide medical assistance – Watson persevered and stopped the bleeding while splinting the soldier's pelvis ready for evacuation to the advanced medical teams at Camp Bastion.

On another patrol Watson again put herself in mortal danger to attend to another wounded ANA soldier, once again under heavy Taliban fire. The casualty had been hit in the chest and had stopped breathing. This time, however, despite 20 minutes of cardiopulmonary resuscitation (CPR) in exposed ground, Watson was unable to save the life of the injured soldier.

She was awarded the Military Cross on 25 March 2011 for her actions. "Watson's immense courage, willingness to put her own life at risk and absolute bravery saved the life of one warrior and acted as an inspiration to her platoon and their Afghan National Army partners," read the citation.

Lance Corporal Watson is only the fourth woman to be awarded the Military Cross since it was created in 1914: Private Michelle Norris was awarded one for saving the life of a colleague in Iraq in 2006, while Able Seaman Kate Nesbitt and Army medic Sarah Bushbye both received MCs for showing gallantry in Afghanistan.

"We don't know where she gets her bravery from," said her mother, Lorna Watson. "She just takes everything in her stride. We're very, very proud."

Written by WREN Telephonist Tania Murray, Royal Navy (retired)

"Watson's immense courage, willingness to put her own life at risk and absolute bravery saved the life of one warrior and acted as an inspiration to her platoon"

King prawn fritters

Senior Aircraftsman Clint Lashley, RAF

This is my personal take on a traditional Bahamian dish, conch fritters. Since it is incredibly hard to get conch in the UK, I have chosen to use king prawns. These are very easy to get hold of, are full of flavour and stand up well to the different Bahamian ingredients. It is a dish packed with flavour and colour and makes a perfect start to any meal.

Dairy-free
Preparation time: 25 minutes plus
 30 minutes chilling time
Cooking time: 25 minutes

Serves 4

INGREDIENTS

For the fritter filling
200g king prawns, shells removed
200g plain flour
1 green pepper, finely diced
1 red onion, finely diced
50g pineapple, finely diced
1 garlic clove, finely chopped
1 red chilli, finely diced
2 tsp ground allspice
½ lemon, juiced
1 egg, beaten

For the mango dipping sauce
1 mango, peeled and coarsely chopped
50g brown sugar
100ml water

For the pané
60g flour
2 eggs, beaten
100g desiccated coconut

To cook
400ml rapeseed oil
Salt and freshly ground black pepper

METHOD

To make the fritter filling
• Place the prawns into a food processor and blitz to a paste, transfer to a bowl, mix in the remaining filling ingredients until thoroughly combined and season lightly with salt and pepper.
• Mould the filling into 12 even-sized balls, place on a tray, cover and chill in the freezer for 30 minutes until firm.

To make the mango dipping sauce
• Place the chopped mango in a saucepan with the brown sugar and water, bring to a simmer and cook for 10 minutes; purée in a blender, transfer to a small bowl, cover and chill until you're ready to serve.

To pané and cook the fritters
• Heat a suitable pan with enough of the oil to cover the balls over a medium-high heat.
• Place the flour in a bowl, season with a little salt and pepper and place the beaten eggs and coconut into separate bowls.
• Coat the chilled prawn filling balls with the flour, tap off the excess, dip into the beaten egg then roll in the desiccated coconut to coat.
• Once all the balls have been coated, gently lower into the oil and cook, stirring occasionally, until thoroughly cooked through to the centre (75°C if you have a probe thermometer) and lightly browned; finish cooking in the oven if necessary.
• Drain the fritters on kitchen paper to absorb the excess oil.

To serve
• Serve three fritters per portion with a small bowl of the mango dipping sauce.

The Bahamas: Local hero

Sir Alfred Étienne Jérôme Dupuch OBE

Sir Étienne Dupuch is remembered today in the Bahamas as a fiercely independent-minded editor and an astute politician who strove to end racial discrimination. However, many Bahamians are unaware that Sir Étienne saw extensive active service during the First World War and was instrumental in supporting a mammoth Bahamian war drive for the second.

He was born on 16 February 1899 in Nassau, the son of a journalist who founded the *Tribune* newspaper in 1903 using a tiny treadle press and a motto "Being bound to swear to the dogmas of no master". It was a spirit that he championed throughout his life. Schooled at home by his mother, he supported the family by delivering newspapers on roller-skates from the age of five until he joined the Bahamas War Contingent in 1916, aged 17. Serving with the British West India Regiment, Étienne served with distinction on the western front in France. His battalion was redeployed for combat operations in Africa where he survived a severe episode of pneumonia brought on by the variation of temperatures in the Sahara.

After returning to the Bahamas with a victory medal, Étienne became editor of the *Tribune* in 1919, a role he held for 54 years (earning him a place in the *Guinness Book Of Records*). During the Second World War he formed a Bahamian committee that provided significant quantities of essential war materials to the Allies, frequently against protocol and without the knowledge of the islands' wartime governor, the Duke of Windsor. He organised fundraising efforts to support the Allies throughout the war, collected money to buy fighter planes and operated a canning factory to help feed the children of the UK.

As well as editing the *Tribune*, he served as an MP in the Bahamian House of Assembly between 1925 and 1956 before moving to the upper house, the Senate. He and his youngest brother Eugene were driving forces for anti-discrimination legislation: both were part of a delegation to England in 1963 that helped to create the first constitution of the Bahamas, resulting in the islands gaining self-government in 1964.

He was knighted by the Queen in 1964 and presented with a papal knighthood from Pope Pius XII. In 1972 he handed control of the *Tribune* to his daughter Eileen, who is still following in her father's footsteps as the editor 49 years later. Sir Étienne passed away at the age of 92 in 1991 in his Camperdown home, with a lasting legacy in the pages of Bahamian history.

Written by Squadron Leader Andy Mortimer, RAF

"During the Second World War he formed a Bahamian committee that would provide significant quantities of essential war materials to the Allies"

Welsh rarebit with bacon and poached egg

Assistant Chef James Higgins, Royal Fleet Auxiliary

One of the reasons I chose to write a recipe for this dish is because, when it comes to Welsh rarebit, many people think of it as nothing more than cheese on toast but, as you can see, there's a lot more going on to make it blasus (delicious in Welsh). The other reason I chose this dish is because a good friend of mine, Tom Gallagher, with whom I once worked in a restaurant (The Sea Shanty in Anglesey), passed away in July 2020; he was one of the people who inspired me to become a chef. This is one of the most popular dishes we had on our menu so I chose it to honour his memory. The first recorded reference to the dish comes from a 1725 recipe for "Welsh Rabbit"; 300 years later it now has its own national day in the USA – 3 September each year is "Welsh Rarebit Day".

Preparation time: 30 minutes
Cooking time: 30–45 minutes

Serves 4

INGREDIENTS

For the cheese topping
40g lightly salted butter
40g plain flour
200ml Welsh stout
200g extra mature cheddar, grated
1 tbsp wholegrain mustard
2 tbsp Worcestershire sauce
1 tbsp shredded sage
Freshly ground black pepper

For the bacon and eggs
1 tsp olive oil
4 rashers of streaky bacon,
  each cut into four pieces
4 extra-thick slices of white bread
2 tbsp white wine vinegar
4 large eggs

To serve
Balsamic glaze (optional)
Pea shoots

METHOD

For the cheese topping
- Place a roasting tray over a medium heat, half fill with boiling water and keep at a simmer (this is called a bain-marie).
- Melt the butter in a small saucepan over a medium heat, stir in the flour to make a roux and cook, stirring continuously, for a couple of minutes.
- Warm the stout and gradually add to the roux a little at a time, ensuring each addition is thoroughly incorporated before adding more, until you have a thick and smooth sauce.
- Cover the saucepan with a lid and simmer in the bain-marie, stirring occasionally, for 30 minutes, topping up the bain-marie with boiling water if necessary.
- Add the grated cheese, mustard, Worcestershire sauce and sage and stir until the cheese has melted.
- Season with black pepper and set aside to cool.

For the bacon and eggs
- Preheat the grill to high and bring a saucepan of water to a rapid simmer.
- Heat the olive oil in a frying pan over a medium heat, add the streaky bacon and cook on both sides until crispy, remove and drain on absorbent kitchen paper.
- Lightly toast the bread, butter one side and evenly spread the cooled cheese topping over the buttered toast slices.
- Place under the grill for 2–3 minutes until the topping is golden brown and bubbling.
- Add the white wine vinegar to the simmering water, swirl the water to create a whirlpool effect, add the eggs and poach for 2 minutes; remove the poached eggs from the pan with a slotted spoon and allow to drain on a double thickness of absorbent kitchen paper.

To serve
- To serve, drizzle balsamic glaze onto four plates (if using), place the Welsh rarebits in the centre of each plate, place the poached eggs in the middle of each rarebit, top with the crispy bacon and garnish with pea shoots.

Bangor: Local hero

Captain John Fox Russell

John Fox Russell was born 27 January 1893 in Holyhead, the eldest of eight siblings, to Dr William Fox Russell and Ethel Maria Fox Russell. After attending schools in Anglesey and Cumbria he sat an entrance examination to the Royal College of Surgeons in Ireland. However, instead of studying in Dublin, he began his medical studies at the London School of Medicine in October 1909, and also joined the London University Officer Training Corps.

John became associated with the Royal Welch Fusiliers when he was commissioned in December 1913. The following August he attended a camp at Aberystwyth, during which his battalion was mobilised and he was put in command of H Company of the 6th Battalion. He was soon promoted to Lieutenant and then Temporary Captain by January 1915. With the onset of war John was seconded to complete his medical studies, before joining the Royal Army Medical Corps in May 1916. Initially attached to the Royal Field Artillery, he arranged for a transfer to his beloved Royal Welch Fusiliers, becoming their Medical Officer.

John married Alma Taylor in September 1916, and they set up home in Tunbridge Wells before he embarked for the Middle East. He served in Palestine and took part in the First Battle of Gaza on the 26 March 1917, tending to the wounded under heavy fire. He was later awarded the Military Cross.

On 6 November 1917, at Tel-el-Khuweilfeh, north-west of Beersheba, Captain Russell displayed conspicuous bravery in action until the moment of his death. "He repeatedly went out to attend the wounded under murderous fire from snipers and machine guns," according to a citation in *The London Gazette*. "When no other means were at hand, he carried them in himself, though almost exhausted." He was killed while helping his comrades, and was buried in Beersheba War Cemetery, near two other VCs, Alexander Lafone and Leslie Maygar. His wife Alma was presented with the VC by King George V at Buckingham Palace on 2 March 1918. As well as a VC and MC, he was awarded the British War Medal 1914–20, Victory Medal 1914–19 with Mentioned in Dispatches oakleaf, and Territorial Force War Medal 1914–19. All of his medals were donated to the Royal Army Medical Corps Museum (now Museum of Military Medicine) by Alma, who emigrated to New Zealand in 1956 and died in 1990. On 13 November 2017, 100 years after his death, a memorial stone was laid at the cenotaph near John's Holyhead home.

Written by Warrant Officer 1st Class Alun Evans, Royal Electrical and Mechanical Engineers, Army

Aber gold

Aber Falls Distillery, near Bangor, is reviving the age-old whisky-making traditions of North Wales, using entirely local ingredients

www.aberfallsdistillery.com

There hadn't been a whisky distillery in North Wales for more than 100 years until the opening of Aber Falls Distillery in 2017. It is located in the Welsh village of Abergwyngregyn, just across the Menai Strait to Anglesey and on the doorstep of Snowdonia. In nearby Caernarfon Castle you can find the Royal Welch Fusiliers Museum, for which Aber Falls makes a Black Flash whisky, named after the silk ribbons the Fusiliers traditionally wore on the back of their neck.

"It's all part of our plan to make something very special," says Managing Director James Wright (pictured, above). "We are creating a platform for Welsh food and drink that really engages with the consumers and helps the region. Everything is done on site here. We get the grain from local farmers, we mash, ferment distil, age, blend and bottle on site. We are extremely proud to be 100 per cent Welsh."

James and the team bottled the inaugural Aber Falls whisky in spring 2021 and will soon start to produce age-declared whisky and special editions. His big dream is to build the Welsh whisky category, and James is collaborating with other distilleries in the principality to give their whisky its own protection. "Our vision has always been to create great-tasting and sought-after whisky with a distinctive Welsh expression that will eventually gain global recognition, helping drive the Welsh whisky category," he says.

Even before the first whisky hit the shelves, Aber Falls had risen to fame with its production of gins and liqueurs. These provided initial cash flow and created brand recognition, and were acclaimed in themselves winning several awards including a winning Best New British Product at the Great British Food Awards. These gins include a Welsh Dry, Orange Marmalade, Small Batch and Rhubarb & Ginger, along with a Salted Toffee Liqueur, all using locally sourced ingredients wherever possible. Raising the bar, Aber Falls distilled a gin at the top of Snowdon made with botanicals picked from the mountainside – the resulting bottle was given to Wales Air Ambulance to auction, raising £1,080 for the charity, making it Wales's most expensive gin. Following this success, James will continue to produce other limited-edition spirits even after the focus has switched to whisky.

His commitment to the area is absolute. Any waste ingredients from the distillery are returned to Welsh farms or used for green energy, while James hopes to one day harness the power of the nearby waterfalls (after which Aber Falls take its name) to meet the site's energy requirements. Aber Falls has a visitor and business centre, which James wants to use as a springboard for skills training and to help tourists locate the best in local food and drink. The visitor tours offer people the chance to see the distillery and experience first-hand how to make whisky, as well as sample the goods.

"We are very proud to be able to say that we are 100 per cent Welsh and we are very much about community and sustainability," he says. "It is a beautiful setting and North Wales is accessible for many – for example, you can get here on the train in two and a half hours from Euston."

So what's next? "What we are now looking to do is facilitate collaboration that can deliver a more exciting sustainable future for the country's food and drink industry," says James, "helping put Wales on the map – far and wide. Aber Falls is a big part of that."

Belizean smoked salmon empanades

Corporal Chris Scotting, RAF

Many years ago, after leaving school, I got my first job cooking at College Hall, Royal Air Force College Cranwell, where the civilian head chef (ex RAF) often recalled memories of serving in Belize during the 1970s. He fondly reminisced about this superb dish with such passion and delight, and about the beautiful country from which it originated. This, linked with his stories of service life and his time spent travelling the world, inspired me to join the RAF. His expert guidance and culinary enthusiasm ensured that being a chef was the only career I ever wanted to have, and here I am still going strong 16 years later. So, as a thank you for his tutelage, this recipe is dedicated to him, John Baxter.

Preparation time: 50 minutes
Cooking time: 15 minutes

Serves 4 as a starter

INGREDIENTS

For the dough
2 eggs
125ml ice-cold water
1 tsp white vinegar
360g plain flour (plus a little
  extra flour for dusting)
1 tsp sea salt flakes
60g chilled butter
Extra sweet paprika (for dusting)

For the filling
3 Desiree potatoes, peeled
200g smoked salmon,
  coarsely chopped
2 tsp ground cumin
3 tsp extra-sweet paprika
5 pickled jalapeños, diced
1 lemon, juiced
Salt and freshly ground
  black pepper

Belize: Local hero

Flight Sergeant Henry Cassian Waight

Belize, formerly known as British Honduras, became a British Crown Colony in 1840 and hundreds of its subjects volunteered to fight for the Allied cause in the Second World War. These included young men like Orlando Pepitue, Chester Marchand and Charles Egerton-Eves, and the RAF Flight Lieutenant Raymond Lind, who joined Bomber Command and took part in many diversionary raids around Belgium to interfere with German radar. Lind, who was awarded a Distinguished Flying Cross in July 1946, died in July 2017 at the grand old age of 99.

Ray Lind's colleague Henry Cassian Waight, however, was one of these sons of Belize who did not return home. Born in 1912, the son of John Woods Waight and Lottie Evelyn Gladys Waight, Henry joined the RAF in 1941 where, like Lind, he volunteered for aircrew duties. He was trained as a bomb aimer before joining 101 Squadron at RAF Ludford Magna, Lincolnshire. During the bombing campaign against Germany, 101 Squadron flew on more raids than any other but also suffered the highest number of casualties of any RAF unit in the war, with 1,176 aircrew killed in action. One casualty was Lancaster DV 267, which was lost on the RAF's disastrous raid to Leipzig on the night of 19 February 1944, a raid that at that time was the RAF's most costly, resulting in the deaths of 420 aircrew and another 131 being taken captive.

Waight, aged 32, was one such victim. On that fateful night in February 1944 he bailed out from his burning Lancaster DV 267 before it crashed near the town of Leek Tolbert in the Netherlands. His body was found near the town of Noordijk and buried by the town people in the local Protestant Cemetery, where it is the only Commonwealth war grave. In memory of so many young men and women from across the world who gave their lives in the Second World War, every year on the anniversary of Henry's death the local townsfolk of Noordijk hold a remembrance service at his graveside to honour those who gave their lives for others.

Written by Squadron Leader Malcolm Craig, RAF

METHOD

To make the dough

- Separate one of the eggs, put the egg white and yolk in separate bowls, whisk the egg yolk and set aside. Crack the remaining egg into the bowl with the egg white, add the water and vinegar and whisk to combine.
- Place the flour and salt into a bowl and, using your fingertips, rub in the butter until the mixture has a coarse breadcrumb texture. Make a well in the centre, pour in the egg mixture and gradually mix into the flour with a fork, working out from the centre, until a dough is formed; if the dough is too sticky add a little more flour.
- Turn out the dough onto a lightly floured worktop and knead for 2 minutes or until smooth, but do not overwork; wrap the dough in clingfilm and rest it in the fridge for 30 minutes.

To make the filling

- Boil or steam the potatoes until tender, chop into 1cm cubes while still warm (the potato needs to be soft to help bind the filling together) and place in a medium bowl; add the remaining filling ingredients and toss until well combined; season with salt and pepper and set aside.
- Preheat the oven to 200°C and line an oven tray with baking parchment.
- Divide the dough into 16 equal pieces and, using your hands, shape each piece into a ball, then with a rolling pin, roll out each ball to a flat 10cm disc (alternatively roll out and cut into 15 rounds using a 10cm round pastry cutter).
- Put one tablespoon of filling in the centre of each disc, fold over to enclose the filling then crimp and fold the edges to seal and create a wavy edge.
- Put the empanades on the lined baking tray, brush with the reserved egg yolk, sprinkle with a little paprika and bake for 12 minutes or until golden and thoroughly heated through to the centre.
- Serve either warm or cold with a sweet chilli dipping sauce.

VEGETARIAN ALTERNATIVE

Potato and corn empanades

- Follow the above steps, replacing the smoked salmon with cooked sweetcorn.

Antarctic bannocks

Catering Services Gessan Alexander, Royal Navy

British Antarctic Territory

Bannocks are an ancient flatbread predominant in Scotland, Ireland and the North of England that probably date back some 1,500 years. Originally, they were unleavened flat cakes of barley or oatmeal dough; modern bannocks are generally made with wheat flour, sometimes with oats, and leavened with either baking powder or bicarbonate of soda. Bannocks became an important foodstuff for Sir Ernest Shackleton and his men when their ship Endurance sank in Antarctica in November 1915. As a quick way to fuel the body with carbohydrates they could be served with a variety of spreads or used to mop up soups and stews. They were prepared by the ship's cooks, Charles Green and his assistant Able Seaman Perce Blackborow (who was a stowaway on the ship), on improvised stoves fuelled by seal and penguin blubber to nourish Shackleton and his men during their march across the ice in December 1915. My recipe uses the classic bagel filling, smoked salmon and cream cheese, to top the bannocks.

Preparation time: 10–15 minutes
Cooking time: 10 minutes

Serves 4

INGREDIENTS

For the bannocks
150g plain white flour
2 tsp baking powder
1 tsp salt
75ml cold water
40g lightly salted butter

For the topping
100g cream cheese
1 tsp creamed horseradish
1 tbsp lemon juice
2 tbsp chives, finely chopped
100g smoked salmon
Freshly ground black pepper

METHOD

For the bannocks
• Sift the flour, salt and baking powder into a bowl.
• Gradually add enough of the water, adding a little at a time, to form a soft, workable dough; knead the dough for a couple of minutes.
• Divide the dough into four equal-sized pieces, roll each into a ball then flatten and roll out to about 1½cm thick.
• Heat a large frying pan over a low-medium heat, add the butter and, when foaming, add the bannocks and cook slowly until the bottoms are firm and golden brown then flip them over to finish cooking; they may require up to 5 minutes on each side, turn down the heat if the they're browning too quickly.
• Transfer to a wire rack to cool.

For the topping
• Mix together the cream cheese, horseradish, lemon juice and half of the chopped chives and season to taste.
• Spread the cream cheese mix over the bannocks, top with slivers of smoked salmon, scatter over the remaining chopped chives and finish with a twist of black pepper.

Major Sir Ernest Shackleton CVO OBE

Ernest Shackleton was born in Kilkea, County Kildare in Ireland on 15 February 1874 before settling in London. Refusing to follow his father into medicine, he joined the Merchant Navy when he was 16 before becoming a Master Mariner in 1898.

In 1901, Shackleton joined the British National Antarctic Expedition aboard the ship *Discovery*. Although it was not a Royal Navy ship, the captain, Lieutenant Robert Falcon Scott, required the crew, officers and scientific staff to submit to the Navy Discipline Act. So, on 4 June 1901, Shackleton joined the Royal Navy Reserve as a sub-lieutenant as *Discovery* attempted to reach the South Pole. Despite falling ill and having to return home, he gained valuable experience. Bitten by the bug, he undertook his second Antarctic expedition with the ship *Nimrod* on 1 January 1908, getting closer to the Pole, climbing Mount Erebus (Antarctica's second highest volcano) and making many scientific discoveries. He was knighted on his return.

Shackleton's third expedition was in 1914 aboard the *Endurance*, which attempted to cross Antarctica via the South Pole. As conditions grew worse in the South Atlantic, *Endurance* froze into an ice floe. Shackleton quickly realised that there would be no quick escape so ordered the ship to be converted into a winter station. As the ice thawed in October, it became apparent that the hull was seriously damaged and as the ice turned to water the ship began to sink. For the next five months, Shackleton and his party camped on ice floes as they drifted north, hoping to reach solid land. In April 1916, the ice floe began to break apart so Shackleton ordered his crew into three 20-foot-long boats and set sail for Elephant Island, arriving there after five days across treacherous seas. He and his crew spent 16 days crossing 830 miles of South Atlantic Ocean to reach South Georgia before trekking 32 miles solo across the inhospitable island in 36 hours to locate a whaling station. The remaining crew from the *Endurance* were rescued in August 1916, with not a single man lost.

On returning to England in May 1917, Shackleton undertook various roles before being appointed as a temporary major serving with the North Russian

Expeditionary Force where he was awarded an OBE for valuable services as well as being mentioned in dispatches.

In 1922, Shackleton attempted a final expedition circumnavigating Antarctica but, on 5 January in South Georgia, he finally succumbed to an enduring heart condition. At his wife's request he was buried where he died, at Grytviken, South Georgia. History nearly forgot Shackleton in favour of Robert Scott but, in the late 20th century, he became more significant, his name associated with courage, fortitude and determination. In 2002, he was placed 11th in the BBC's popular vote for the 100 Greatest Britons.

Written by WREN Telephonist Tania Murray, Royal Navy (retired)

Mini salt cod fishcakes with sweet chilli sauce

Chief Petty Officer Catering Services Russell Keitch, Royal Navy

Dried and salted cod has been produced for over 500 years in Newfoundland – it's said to have been dried in the sun and wind on the coastal cliffs and rock faces. Images of cod can be found scattered all over Newfoundland, but the fish itself became hard to come by. In 1992, when cod almost became extinct, the Canadian government imposed a 10-year moratorium on cod fishing, which put nearly 30,000 people out of work and led to many Newfoundlanders moving away to seek employment elsewhere. The cod did not return for almost 20 years when, over time, they eventually reverted to their original abundance. My salt cod fishcakes come with a sweet chilli sauce to accompany the salty fish.

Commander James Campbell Clouston

James Clouston was born in August 1900 in Montreal, learning to sail on nearby Lake Saint Louis. He attended McGill University and enlisted in the British Royal Navy in 1918, earning the rank of sub-lieutenant just 16 days before his 24th birthday. Clouston had a successful naval career, being promoted through the ranks until he was assigned Commander to the warship destroyer *Isis* in May 1937.

With *Isis* docked requiring repairs in 1940, Clouston was recruited along with 11 other officers to work under Captain William Tennant to organise the evacuation of the trapped Allied troops following their defeat during the Battle of France. Clouston was allocated as the pier master for the East Mole, a narrow concrete-based wooden walkway that was only wide enough for four men to walk abreast and was not designed to be used by ships. A 16ft tidal rise and rough waters made things even more difficult. However, Clouston demonstrated that it was the best place to evacuate troops. Armed with a megaphone and a small team of soldiers, he manned the pier for five days and five nights with barely a break, evacuating troops while under enemy fire. They expected 45,000 troops to be evacuated, but the "Miracle of Dunkirk" saw more than 338,000 saved.

On 2 June, setting off in a group of two motor launches from Dover, Clouston and his crew were attacked by German dive-bombers while crossing the Channel and ended up in the water. The other motor launch, despite being severely damaged, initially stayed to see if they could help, but Clouston ordered them to carry on and continue to Dunkirk. This selfless act of bravery condemned Clouston but saved the lives of the remaining sailors on the still-functioning motor launch. Clouston's last words were that of encouragement to his fellow sailors in the Channel, imploring them to carry on swimming. He received a Mention in Dispatches for this act of bravery, and also for saving thousands during the evacuation.

He was outlived by his pregnant wife, Gwyneth, and a two-year-old son. Commander Clouston was recognised in 2017 as a Hometown Hero in a ceremony that took place at Lake Saint Louis. A commemorative story panel of his life and courageous acts was installed there, as was a duplicate in Dunkirk's City Hall.

Written by Kim Beechey

"Armed with a megaphone and a small team of soldiers, Clouston manned the pier for five days and five nights with barely a break, part of an operation that evacuated more than 338,000 troops"

Preparation time: 12–24 hours
Cooking time: 30–45 minutes

Serves 4–6

INGREDIENTS

For the sweet chilli sauce
1 tsp cornflour
2 red chillies, finely chopped
1 garlic clove, finely chopped or crushed
10g fresh ginger, finely chopped
100ml white wine vinegar
200g caster sugar
1 tbsp fish sauce
½ tsp sea salt

Salted cod fishcakes
300g salt cod
1 large baking potato, peeled and
  roughly chopped into 3cm dice
1 medium onion, cut into 1cm dice
1 tbsp fresh coriander, finely chopped
1 medium egg, beaten
20g plain breadcrumbs
Ground black pepper
Plain flour for dusting
2 tbsp vegetable oil

METHOD

Advance preparation
• Soak the salt cod for 12–24 hours (depending on the thickness and how salty the cod is) replacing the water and rinsing the fish two or three times during the soaking process.

For the sweet chilli sauce
• Mix the cornflour with a couple of tablespoons of cold water to a thin paste and set aside.
• Add all of the remaining ingredients to a small saucepan, place over a medium-high heat, bring to a boil and simmer rapidly to reduce for 2 minutes.
• Remove from the heat, stir in the cornflour then bring back to a simmer, cook for a couple of minutes, stirring frequently; transfer to a bowl and set aside to cool completely before covering and chilling in the fridge until required.

Salted cod fishcakes
• Gently simmer the salt cod in enough water to cover for 20–25 minutes until it becomes flaky, do not boil or it will become tough; drain and set the cod aside for about 5 minutes until it is cool enough to handle.
• Remove the skin and bones, ensuring all of the bones are removed (there will be a lot of them).
• Boil the chopped potato for about 15 minutes until just soft, tip into a colander and leave to drain and steam dry for 2 minutes before mashing (take care not to overwork).
• Mix the mashed potatoes with the salt cod, onion, coriander, beaten egg, breadcrumbs and enough ground black pepper to season; the mixture should be soft and mouldable.
• Shape the fishcake mix into 16–20 mini fish cakes about 4 or 5cm across.

To cook and serve
• Heat the vegetable oil in a frying pan over a medium heat; don't allow the oil to get too hot or the fishcakes will burn before they're heated through.
• Dust the fishcakes in a little flour and tap off the excess.
• Shallow-fry the fishcakes until golden brown on both sides and thoroughly heated through to the middle.
• Briefly drain the cooked fishcakes on a piece of kitchen paper to absorb any excess oil then serve with a bowl of the sweet chilli sauce on the side.

Asparagus and Cheshire cheese soup with apple and walnut loaf

Senior Aircraftsman James Kerr, RAF

Cheese soup was originally a peasant's dish using cheap ingredients to make a tasty meal; here we use it to celebrate Cheshire cheese, the famous dairy speciality of the region. It is one of the country's oldest recorded cheeses, mentioned as far back as 1580 and claimed to be included in the Domesday Book. Other fantastic produce of the region are asparagus and apples, which are perfect to incorporate into this dish – the crumbly, tangy and salty cheese paired with asparagus makes a wonderful and unique soup that is only enhanced when paired with the wholesome, almost sweet, nutty soda loaf.

Cheshire: Local hero

Lance Corporal Jamie Webb

Lance Corporal Jamie Webb was born on 6 October 1988 and hailed from Handforth, Cheshire. After attending Wilmslow High School and Macclesfield College he enlisted in the British Army aged 18 and joined 1st Battalion The Mercian Regiment (Cheshire) in September 2006 where he became affectionately known as "Webby". Following his initial infantry training, he was posted to B Company who were at the time deployed in Ballykinler, Northern Ireland on Operation Banner.

Following his return from Northern Ireland, Private Webb again deployed on operations, this time to Iraq on Operation Telic 11, spending three months with B Company, undertaking security operations before returning home. He was subsequently deployed with 1st Battalion The Mercian Regiment on two tours of Afghanistan. His first tour in 2010 was as part of Operation Herrick 12: he served as a rifle section second-in-command in the Nahr-e Saraj area operating with the Danish battle group. His performance earned him a promotion to Lance Corporal.

In October 2012 he was deployed for his second tour of Afghanistan on Operation Herrick 17, as part of Transition Support Unit Nad-e-Ali, led by 1 Mercian battlegroup as a company intelligence collator and section second-in-command. Tragically, Lance Corporal Webb was fatally wounded in an insurgent attack on his patrol base at Nad-e-Ali in Helmand province on 25 March 2013. He was 24.

Lance Corporal Webb was a justifiably proud Mercian Regiment soldier, who deployed on four operational tours and developed a reputation for being a highly capable junior commander, earning huge respect from his peers. "Webby was always thinking of ways to make our bond ever stronger and succeeded in strengthening the friendships of those around him," said one comrade. "Living opposite him in our accommodation in camp, he was always someone I could confide in and always had a way of cheering me up; a quality that everyone knows he possessed in abundance. He became a brotherly figure to me. His passing saddens me deeply." Lance Corporal Webb has been remembered in his home town of Handforth, Cheshire by the naming of a local road, Jamie Webb Drive, in his memory.

Written by Corporal Matt Lockwood, RAF, and Jackie Daly, Royal British Legion Membership Support Officer, Cheshire

"Webby was always thinking of ways to make our bond ever stronger and succeeded in strengthening the friendships of those around him"

Vegetarian
Preparation time: 20 minutes for the loaf
  and 15 minutes for the soup
Cooking time: 30–40 minutes for the loaf
  and 30 minutes for the soup

Serves 6

INGREDIENTS

For the apple and walnut loaf
30g self-raising flour
130g wholemeal flour
50g brown sugar
½ tsp bicarbonate of soda
½ tsp salt
50ml olive oil
½ orange, finely grated zest only
1 egg, beaten
150ml tepid milk
2 cooking apples, cored and coarsely chopped
  or grated, with skin
60g walnuts, coarsely chopped
Butter, for greasing the baking tray

For the asparagus and Cheshire cheese soup
1½ litres vegetable or chicken stock
680g asparagus, trimmed and roughly chopped
40g butter
2 tbsp olive oil
1 onion, roughly chopped
2 stalks of celery, roughly chopped
2 cloves garlic, crushed
85g flour
100ml single cream
450g Cheshire cheese, grated plus a few small
  cubes for garnish
Salt and pepper

METHOD

To make the apple and walnut loaf
• Preheat the oven to 180ºC, grease a baking tray with butter
  and dust lightly with flour.
• Place the flours, sugar, bicarbonate of soda and salt into a
  mixing bowl and mix until combined.
• Make a well in the centre of the dry mix, add the oil, orange
  zest and beaten egg and gradually add the milk; mix well,
  by hand or in a stand mixer with a dough hook, until a rough
  dough has formed. Add a little more flour if the dough is
  too wet and sticky, you may not need all of the milk.
• Add the apples and walnuts and knead into the dough
  until it is smooth.
• Shape the dough into a neat round, place onto the tray and
  bake for 30–40 minutes until well browned and crusty;
  transfer to a wire rack to cool.

To make the soup
• Bring three-quarters of the stock to a boil in a large saucepan,
  add the asparagus and cook until tender; drain the asparagus
  reserving the stock.
• Heat the butter and oil in a large saucepan or casserole over
  a medium heat, add the onion and celery and cook, stirring
  frequently, for about 5 minutes until they start to soften,
  add the garlic and continue to cook for a further 2 minutes.
• Stir in the flour, cook, stirring constantly, to a blonde colour;
  add the stock, including the stock reserved from cooking
  the asparagus, a little at a time and cook, stirring constantly,
  until smooth.
• Add the single cream and simmer, stirring occasionally, for about
  10 minutes.
• Pour the soup into a blender (it might need to be blended in a
  couple of batches), add the cooked asparagus and pulse the mix
  a few times before blending until smooth.
• Pour the soup into a clean saucepan, bring to a simmer and stir
  in the grated Cheshire cheese until melted; season with salt and
  pepper to taste.

To serve
• Ladle the hot soup into bowls, sprinkle the top with
  a little diced Cheshire cheese and serve with the warm
  apple and walnut soda loaf.

Hear to eternity

Phonak's state-of-the-art hearing aids offer crisp and natural sound that assists speech recognition and can help to improve emotional wellbeing

www.phonak.com

Hearing loss is a problem that affects many people in later life, but anybody who experiences a loss of hearing in the 21st century has many more attractive solutions than in the past. For decades, a hearing aid invariably took the form of an unsightly so-called "beige banana" wedged behind the ear but now companies such as Switzerland-based Phonak have designed a range of intelligent, comfortable and discreet premium devices.

"When creating our latest Phonak hearing solution, we turned to nature for inspiration," explains Anna McLean, Phonak's UK Director of Marketing. "Hearing is such an intricate part of our existence and fundamental for our overall well-being. Nature is also the source of so many sounds that can soothe, relax and comfort us. What better way to rediscover sound than with a hearing aid inspired by nature itself?"

Phonak begins with the premise that good hearing is closely linked to people's cognitive, social and emotional wellbeing. The belief is that if somebody is able to hear properly, then they will be better equipped to enjoy the full array of life's possibilities and to interact with friends and families. "There is research that links dementia with hearing loss," explains Anna. "If you can't hear people, you can't engage with them and you might start to withdraw." It offers another reason for people to ensure they have their hearing checked if they have any concerns.

If people do feel they are experiencing hearing loss, Phonak has incredible technology to help improve the situation. Its top-of-the-range device is the Phonak Paradise, carefully engineered to provide a crisp, natural sound. Particular attention is spent on improving speech

recognition and reducing noise, rather than simply focusing on sound amplification. The device is discreet, rechargeable and packed with technology that offers a range of benefits for the user and their friends and family.

"People with hearing loss often complain about understanding speech when somebody is speaking softly or from a distance or in loud environments," says Anna. "We have created something called Speech Enhancer which means you can hear better in those situations. We also have personalised noise cancellation and we have something called Target Match, an automated guidance system which means the microphone moves and can be targeted directly at the people who is talking. Then there is Roger technology. This is like an external mic that you place on a table like a receiver and that collects the sound and transmits it direct to the hearing aid. That is really helpful if you are in a group situation." Some users might even give their Roger device to a friend to wear when they are out on a golf course or on a country walk, so they can hear them above the noise of the wind and traffic.

Phonak's hearing devices can be simply controlled via a smart phone or tablet, which acts like a remote control. You can tap the device itself to access Bluetooth, connecting directly to television sets and smart phones so the user can stream music, TV shows or telephone calls direct to their ear. Phonak devices are available through retailers across the UK as well as via the National Health Service. Veterans can access support with their hearing loss through the Veterans Medical Funds programme, details of which can be found on the Royal British Legion's website. "There are funding schemes that are available through the Royal British Legion for hearing loss and we supply the products for those schemes," says Anna.

Pan-fried Irish scallops, black pudding and bacon

Private Carly Hawsden, Army

When given the opportunity to write a recipe for Derry, I immediately thought of creating a dish using some of the amazing fresh fish that comes into the fishing ports of Northern Ireland. When you visit a fishing harbour, such as Ardglass, you can speak directly with the fishermen and often grab yourself some fantastic fish at a fraction of the retail price. The coast of Northern Ireland is great for scallops, which are particularly good in winter and spring. The fishmongers in Belfast's Victorian St George's Market offer a huge selection of fish and seafood (Friday is the best day to get your fresh fish there). I've used scallops as my main ingredient for this recipe, served with Irish black pudding, crispy bacon and a sweet red onion marmalade to bring the dish together and get that feel of eating fresh local scallops in one of Derry's harbourside restaurants.

Gluten-free
Preparation time: 30 minutes
Cooking time: 35 minutes

Serves 4

INGREDIENTS

Red onion marmalade
1 tbsp vegetable oil
2 large red onions, halved and thinly sliced
2 garlic cloves, finely chopped
75ml red wine
75ml red wine vinegar
2 tbsp light brown soft sugar
Sea salt and freshly ground black pepper

For the scallops, bacon and black pudding
12 large scallops
2 tbsp olive oil
4 rashers rindless smoked streaky bacon
20g butter
8 slices of best quality black pudding (I used Clonakilty), thinly sliced
½ lemon
Sea salt and freshly ground black pepper

To serve
Mixed salad leaves
Extra virgin olive oil

Derry: Local hero

Miles Ryan

Miles Ryan was born in 1826 in Londonderry, where he initially trained as a blacksmith. On 29 September 1848 he enlisted with the Honourable East India Company at Banbridge in County Down and sailed for India on the troopship *Ellenborough*, arriving in India on 14 October 1849. While in India he served in the Anglo-Burmese War of 1852–53, receiving the Indian General Service Medal and clasp for serving in Pegu, and served throughout the Indian Mutiny, earning an Indian Mutiny Medal with two clasps for Delhi and Lucknow.

It was during the Indian Mutiny that Miles would also earn the Victoria Cross. On 14 September 1857, Miles Ryan was a drummer with the 1st Bengal Fusiliers during the assault on Delhi. During the battle, as assault troops waited at the Kabul Gate in Delhi, ammunition was being carried up onto the ramparts to be put into a small magazine. Three boxes exploded and two were set on fire by enemy shot. Without hesitation, Drummer Ryan – along with his comrade Sergeant James McGuire, from Enniskillen – seized the initiative and rushed into the flames, throwing the burning boxes over the parapet into a water-filled ditch below.

"The confusion consequent on the explosion was very great," reads the VC citation, "and the crowd of soldiers and native followers, who did not know where the danger lay, were rushing into certain destruction." However, as a result of Drummer Ryan and Sergeant McGuire's coolness and personal daring, the lives of many people were saved, at great personal risk. As a result of their heroism and bravery, both Ryan and McGuire were awarded the Victoria Cross for their actions. Unfortunately, in 1862, three years after he had been discharged from the Army, Sergeant James McGuire was found guilty of stealing a cow, and his Victoria Cross was forfeited.

Like McGuire, Drummer Ryan was discharged from the Army on 16 May 1859. It is believed he led a quieter life, settling in India where he passed away in January 1887 in Bengal, aged 60. There are few records of his death, and no formal grave to recognise this brave individual. His medals are not publicly held and there are no records to identify their location. But, in this book, Miles Ryan's legacy will live on.

Written by Claire Teague

METHOD

• Pre heat the oven to 100°C.

To make the red onion marmalade
• Heat the oil in a saucepan over a low-medium heat and sauté the onions and garlic, stirring frequently, for 3–4 minutes; season well, add the wine, vinegar and sugar and bring to a simmer.
• Simmer, stirring occasionally, for 15–20 minutes or until the onions are very soft and the liquid has reduced to a thickened, slightly sticky consistency; take the pan off the heat, cover with a lid and keep warm.

To cook the scallops, bacon and black pudding
• Dry your scallops with absorbent kitchen paper and put on a plate ready to be cooked.
• Heat a tablespoon of the oil in a large frying pan over a medium heat and fry the bacon rashers, turning several times and draining off any water released by the bacon, until crispy; transfer the bacon to an ovenproof tray and keep warm in the oven.
• Return the frying pan to the heat, add half of the butter and, when foaming, fry the black pudding slices on both sides until crispy then transfer to the tray with the bacon and keep warm in the oven.
• Give the frying pan a wipe and heat a tablespoon of olive oil over a medium-high heat. Season the scallops with sea salt and freshly ground black pepper, sear for about 1 minute, add the remaining 10g of butter, turn the scallops over and cook, basting with the foaming butter, for another minute then squeeze over the lemon juice and transfer the scallops to the warm tray with the bacon and black pudding; keep the cooking juices in the frying pan warm over a low heat.

To serve
• Dress the salad leaves with a little extra virgin olive oil and season with salt and freshly ground black pepper.
• Spoon the warmed red onion marmalade onto four warmed plates and arrange three scallops, two slices of black pudding and a rasher of crispy bacon on each plate; spoon over the cooking juices from the frying pan and serve with a small pile of the dressed salad leaves.

Patagonian toothfish pâté

Arlette Betts, award-winning Falklands guest house owner

The Patagonian toothfish (also known as Chilean sea bass) is a very expensive fish caught in South Georgia waters, but loved here in the Falkland Islands by a lot of people. My pâté recipe comes out on a regular basis when I'm entertaining; people love it.

**Preparation time: 30 minutes
 plus 1 hour chilling time**

Serves 4

INGREDIENTS

For the pâté
200g sea bass fillets (about 2 fillets), skinned
300ml milk
6 black peppercorns
1 bay leaf
60g butter, diced, at room temperature
2 spring onions, thinly sliced
50g cream cheese
½ lemon, juice only
1 tbsp chives, finely chopped
Salt and freshly ground black pepper

To serve
Crusty bread, thinly sliced and toasted

METHOD

To make the pâté
- Place the sea bass fillets in a small pan, pour over enough milk to cover the fish and add the peppercorns and bay leaf.
- Place the pan over a medium heat, bring to a gentle simmer for 2 minutes then remove from the heat and allow the fish to finish cooking in the residual heat; set aside until cool.
- Meanwhile heat 10g of the butter in a small pan and, when foaming, add the spring onions and cook for a couple of minutes until softened; set aside to cool.
- Once cool, flake the sea bass into a food processor with the cream cheese, remaining 50g of softened butter and lemon juice and blend to a coarse-textured pâté.
- Scrape the mixture into a bowl, mix in the chives and cooked spring onions and season with salt and pepper; cover with cling film and chill in the fridge for at least an hour until firm.

To serve
- Once chilled and firm serve the pâté in a small bowl with thin slices of toasted crusty bread.

Falkland Islands: Local hero

The Falkland Islanders of 1982

The Falkland Islands have been associated with the UK from as far back as 1592 when English navigator John Davis first sighted the uninhabited islands aboard the ship *Desire* – a moment that is encapsulated both on the flag of the Falkland Islands and in its motto, "Desire the Right". By 1833, Britain had established a garrison on the Falklands, and it has remained a British sovereign territory ever since. It became home to many from the British Isles, including a settlement of 30 military pensioners and their families in 1849.

The Falkland Islands' traditions and culture became a super-distillate of British stoicism, courage, pride and stubbornness, traits that would come to the fore in April 1982 when Argentine forces invaded. There were indications that an invasion had been planned for some days but, with insufficient notice, the British government were unable to reinforce the islands from a distance of 8,000 miles. This left the Falklands to be defended by a permanently stationed detachment of 68 Royal Marines, along with 11 naval personnel from HMS *Endurance* and 25 members of the Falkland Island Defence Force (FIDF), bolstered by an additional 15 ex-FIDF personnel and, of course, 1,800 local residents who weren't going to give in without a fight.

The FIDF were drawn from islanders across all members of society whose aims were to assist the Royal Marines by providing detailed local knowledge of both the terrain and the environment. Their determined spirit of fair-mindedness and intractable stubbornness, especially in the face of foul play, was what lay in wait for the Argentine invaders.

Trudi McPhee was a sixth-generation islander whose reaction to the Argentine invasion wasn't fear, but fury. When the local chief of police asked her to assist the British soldiers, she – along with other farmers – didn't hesitate. The local terrain was rough and there were no roads, so local knowledge of the boggy ground conditions proved invaluable in moving supplies, ammunition, troops and medics across the island. During the battle for Mount Longdon, Trudi led a convoy of vehicles at night in pitch darkness over the rough ground close to the frontline, only visible by the large white gloves she wore.

Patrick Watts was working as a broadcaster on the Falklands' only radio station. The governor, Rex Hunt, had told islanders that he expected to declare a state of emergency before dawn and that the station would stay on air throughout the night. Patrick took phone calls from residents reporting what they were seeing from their houses, and playing songs like "Stranger On The Shore" until Argentine soldiers stormed the building, put a gun in his back and told him to stop his transmission. "I will never forget that night," said Patrick. "But it wasn't heroic – I was just doing the job Rex Hunt asked me to do."

Today the islanders are as fiercely proud of their Britishness as ever, as demonstrated by the referendum of 2014. A parade is held in Stanley each year on 14 June, Liberation Day, followed by an Act of Remembrance at the Liberation Memorial. The memorial has the names of every service person lost in the conflict along with the three local islanders who also lost their life. In 2014, Prime Minister David Cameron announced that the Falkland Islanders were to receive the "South Atlantic medal" in recognition of "a direct and grave threat to their sovereignty", a tribute to the islanders' quiet courage and resolution in 1982.

Written by Squadron Leader Jon Pullen, RAF (retired), and Captain Christopher Locke MNM, Royal Navy

Kokoda

Sergeant Adi Nayacatabu, Army

Fijian cuisine is traditionally healthy. It is based on a lean diet and is famous for its seafood. Kokoda is a traditional Fijian dish made from marinated white fish left to cure in lime juice for several hours, which, in essence, cooks the fish – in that sense it is very similar in preparation to a ceviche. It is generally made with mahi-mahi or snapper but any white fish works well. Coconut milk, which is a commonly used ingredient in Fijian cooking, is mixed into the cured fish and the dish is traditionally served in a halved coconut shell. Kokoda would be customarily served as a starter followed by a heavier meal with rice or roti as a main course. As they say in Fiji, mai kana, or come and eat.

Gluten-free, dairy-free
Preparation time: 15 minutes
Cooking time: 4 hours marinating time

Serves 4

INGREDIENTS

6 large white fish, snapper traditionally
  but any white fish works fine
4 limes, juiced
2 red chillies, finely diced
250ml coconut cream
5 large tomatoes, deseeded and
  finely chopped
1 large handful of coriander,
  coarsely chopped
6 spring onions, shredded
1 green and 1 red pepper, finely diced
1 red onion, finely diced
Rock salt and cracked black pepper
Coconut shells to serve (optional)

METHOD

- Remove any skin or blood from the fish and cut it into small dice, around 1cm dice is ideal.
- In a glass bowl mix the diced fish with the lime juice and chillies and marinate for 4 hours; ensure the fish is opaque, which indicates that it's thoroughly cured.
- Drain the marinated fish, transfer to a clean bowl and mix with the coconut cream, diced tomatoes, coriander, spring onions, peppers and red onion.
- Mix thoroughly and season well with cracked black pepper and rock salt.
- Serve alongside a fresh citrus salad in a coconut shell with a wedge of lime.

Fiji: Local hero

Sergeant Talaiasi Labalaba BEM

Sergeant Talaiasi Labalaba was born 13 July 1942 in Fiji. He joined the British Army in 1961, aged 19, via the Royal Ulster rifles, before quickly making his way into the SAS. Known to his colleagues as a "gentle giant", he was part of a team of nine SAS soldiers based outside Mirbat, Oman, on a secret military operation (named Operation Jaguar) to protect the Sultan of Oman from 400 guerrillas.

On 19 July 1972, a day before they were due to go home, the team were attacked by the Popular Front for the Liberation of the Occupied Arabian Gulf. Knowing that they were severely outnumbered, and with the advancing enemy beyond the range of conventional weapons, Sergeant Labalaba ran several hundred metres in order to man a 25-pounder artillery gun, usually operated by a team of four to six men. Eventually another SAS member, Trooper Tommy Tobin, made it to Labalaba's position and they held out for two and a half hours against the 400 guerrillas, repelling wave after wave of attacks, until Omani air support arrived. By that time, however, it was too late for both Labalaba and Tobin, who were both killed by gunfire. It is estimated that the guerrillas lost over half of their men that day, mainly due to the actions of Labalaba.

For his actions, Sergeant Labalaba was mentioned in dispatches and awarded the British Empire Medal (BEM). There have been calls for him to be posthumously awarded the Victoria Cross but, as the mission was classed as secret, this has yet to be done. Andy McNab described the battle of Mirbat as the "stuff of regimental legends" and "the Rorke's Drift of the SAS". Fellow Fijian Sekonaia Takavesi served with Labalaba in Oman and described him as an SAS legend.

In 2009, a statue of Labalaba was erected outside SAS headquarters in Hereford, near Labalaba's burial site. In 2012, he was honoured by the BBC as one of the 60 "New Elizabethans", those whose actions during the reign of Queen Elizabeth II have had a significant impact. In 2018, another statue of him was unveiled outside Nadi International Airport in Fiji, unveiled by the Duke and Duchess of Sussex. The 25-pound gun that Labalaba used to hold back the guerrillas is now housed in the Royal Artillery Museum in Woolwich.

Written by Corporal Josua Taubale Vosakiwaiwai, Adjutant General's Corps, Army

> *"In 2012, Labalaba was honoured by the BBC as one of the 60 'New Elizabethans', whose actions during the reign of Queen Elizabeth II have had a significant impact"*

Cullen skink

Sophie Thompson, award-winning actress and Celebrity MasterChef winner

Glasgow

The legendary Cullen skink comes from the small fishing port of Cullen on the east coast of Scotland. The word "skink" means a soup or an essence. The local fishermen would smoke the smaller fish of their catch and these, with some locally grown potatoes, formed their staple diet. This is a recipe that I learned from my Scottish grandmother, Granny Megsie. The aroma of Cullen skink takes me right back to her kitchen and the vision of an array of socks drying on the bar of her old coal-fuelled Aga.

Gluten-free
Preparation time: 15 minutes
Cooking time: 1 hour

Serves 4

INGREDIENTS

350g (approximately) smoked haddock fillet
2 bay leaves
1 large onion, chopped
900ml water
500g potatoes, peeled and quartered
575ml full-cream milk
1 vegetable stock cube
40g butter
Salt and cracked black pepper
Chopped chives to garnish

METHOD

• Put the haddock, bay leaves, chopped onions and water into a pan and bring to bubbling then reduce the heat, gently poaching your fish for about 10 minutes.
• Peel and chop your potatoes in readiness.
• Lift your haddock fillets from the pan with a fish slice and remove the skin; return the skin to the broth (skink!) and simmer uncovered for 25 minutes.
• Flake the poached haddock and leave to cool.
• Strain the fish stock (I leave the bay leaves in) and return to the pan, adding the peeled and chopped potatoes; cook these until properly tender.
• Remove the potatoes from the liquid letting them steam in a sieve while you add the milk and vegetable stock cube to the pan.
• Bring this liquor up to a gently rolling simmer.
• Roughly mash the tatties with your generous knob of butter; then whisk the buttery rough mash into the pan until the soup is thick and creamy. The potatoes can be left unmashed for a chunkier soup.
• Add your flaked haddock and a good quantity of cracked black pepper.
• Garnish with chives – I tumble my chives in a drizzle of olive oil to make them shine.
• Serve with freshly torn hunks of bread.

Private James Stokes VC

James Stokes was born on 6 February 1915 in the Gorbals, Glasgow, one of four children. After the early death of his parents, James was sent to Ireland to work on a relative's farm, returning to Glasgow to marry and start a family

James enlisted with the Royal Artillery in 1943. In June 1944, he took part in the Normandy landings with the 2nd Battalion of the King's Shropshire Light Infantry. Like many of the forces that landed on the beaches, the 3rd Division – of which the King's Shropshire's was a part – suffered heavy casualties before pushing east as part of the Allied front. Later in 1944, during a period of leave in Glasgow, James took offence to an insult to his wife and the ensuing fight left another man seriously injured. The judge noted that the 5ft 2in Stokes was a man who seemed to enjoy a fight and that he had the choice between prison or joining the infantry where "Mr Stokes would be better taking his aggression out on the Nazis".

On 1 March 1945, James was part of a platoon that had reached the town of Kervenheim on the Dutch–German border. That morning the platoon faced a barrage of gunfire from a set of German-occupied buildings. Private Stokes took it upon himself to charge the first building, with no order to do so, and ended up returning with 12 German prisoners! He continued this assault on the second building, rousing his comrades to do the same, and returned with five more prisoners. When charging the third and final building Private Stokes was felled by enemy gunfire and would not get back up. He was found to have numerous injuries in the upper part of his body. His allies, inspired by his actions, captured the building and the town. Private Stokes's self-sacrifice and courage saved his platoon many serious casualties and he was posthumously awarded the Victoria Cross for the gallantry he demonstrated in the face of adversity.

James Stokes is memorialised throughout Glasgow. As an avid Celtic supporter there is a Celtic supporters club named after him and there is a memorial garden in the Gorbals dedicated to him. He even appeared multiple times on the front cover of the boys' comic *Victor*, in 1965, 1975 and 1986, immortalised as "The soldier who would not give up".

Written by Lieutenant Aren Tingle, Royal Navy

> ## "He appeared multiple times on the cover of the boys' comic Victor, immortalised as the soldier who would not give up"

The power to succeed

As well as sponsoring the Scottish champions Rangers, EightyOne Powerdrink has been working with military veterans on a range of sporting and professional initiatives

eighty-one-uk.com

Energy drinks have the potential to make people feel great but they don't always taste as good as they could. When Swiss entrepreneur Pit Heeb founded EightyOne it was partly based on the desire to create a drink that tasted clean and refreshing while remaining invigorating and energising. The result is a drink that has a cleaner taste than leading brands while offering the same effects. The Swiss company is making an impact in the rest of Europe, particularly in Scotland as the official partner of the Scottish Premiership champions, Rangers.

"We are building our profile and are already widely available in Scotland as we are sponsors of Glasgow Rangers, who share our values by doing a huge amount for military veterans," says Peter Knoflach, who went into partnership with Pit Heeb to introduce EightyOne to the UK. "This is an energy drink that tastes a lot better than the competitors. We have the normal drink, and coming soon is a low-sugar version and protein drinks which are currently in development. Later we will be launching a mineral water. We have also signed the Armed Forces Covenant and veterans are involved in our marketing, sales and promotions – they are very helpful as their skills are completely transferable."

Another strand of EightyOne Powerdrink's offering to veterans was created when Peter was in the Swiss resort of Klosters, working with a charity that goes skiing with military personnel who have experienced life-changing injuries. He was hugely impressed by the way these ex-service personnel operated as a team and decided to create a similar enterprise for motorsport. Peter is a former international motorsport driver and he used his connections within the automotive industry to create Racing Heroes, a racing team that utilises the unique skills and experiences of disabled and non-disabled veterans working alongside disabled and non-disabled civilians. "Much of the team consists of wounded and disabled military veterans, who we train as race engineers, mechanics and drivers," he says. "This gives them a whole new career after what they have been through. Our unprecedented goal is to field an all-inclusive race team at Le Mans."

EightyOne Racing Heroes has a flexible approach to training and employment so the company can accommodate the requirements of injured veterans, who work in tandem with able-bodied civilian staff. Their transferable skills have been put to good use within the race team but they also work directly for EightyOne Powerdrink in areas such as marketing, sales and promotion. This gets to the heart of the EightyOne Powerdrink ethos, which promotes inclusivity and is targeted at anybody who takes pride and passion in what they do. The company has developed several partnerships in sports and supports athletes from grass-roots level to established professionals to encourage an atmosphere of excellence and achievement, celebrating fair play and positive role models. The culture is one of family, community and teamwork – taking your personal energy and using it for the benefit of all. This is an attitude that aligns with that of military veterans.

"We started EightyOne Racing Heroes as a veterans racing team but we have since opened out to become a very inclusive team that has veterans, men, women, disabled and able-bodied personnel all working together to support veterans and each other," explains Peter. "Motorsport is very much a lifestyle – it's not a job, it's not 9-to-5. Like in the military, you are completely immersed and your personal and professional lives are completely intertwined. We have created a very passionate and empathic team."

Ital soup

Catering Services Kevin Cordice, Royal Navy

Ital soup is a vegetarian meal intended to improve your health and energy. Ital, meaning natural and clean, is a Rastafari belief that advocates vegetarianism. The use of simple and delicate flavours from plant-based foods is popular in Jamaican cuisine; this dish will give you a taste of the Caribbean you won't forget.

Vegetarian, vegan, gluten-free
Preparation time: 20 minutes
Cooking time: 45–60 minutes

Serves 4

INGREDIENTS

400ml coconut milk
400ml water
1 onion, cut into 2cm dice
2 plum tomatoes, cut into 2cm dice
3 cloves of garlic, finely chopped
1 scotch bonnet chilli, finely chopped
1 tbsp fresh thyme leaves
1 tsp turmeric
1 tsp cracked black pepper
1 tsp ground allspice
1 large carrot, cut into 2cm dice
1 medium sweet potato, cut into
 2cm dice
1 medium cassava or potato,
 cut into 2cm dice
½ butternut squash, cut into 2cm dice
1 bay leaf
50g jackfruit, cut into 2cm dice
 (use canned if fresh is unavailable)
1 plantain, cut into 2cm dice
6 okra, cut into 2cm slices
10g coriander, coarsely chopped

METHOD

• Pour the coconut milk and water into a large saucepan and bring to the boil.
• Reduce the heat to a simmer and add the onions, tomatoes, garlic, chilli, thyme leaves, turmeric, black pepper and allspice.
• Simmer for 3 minutes then add the carrot, sweet potato, cassava and butternut squash and bay leaf; continue to simmer for 20 minutes.
• Stir in the jackfruit, plantain and okra and simmer for a further 15–20 minutes.
• If you prefer a thicker soup simmer for a further 10–15 minutes.
• Remove the bay leaf and add the chopped coriander to serve.

Jamaica: Local hero

John Perkins

John Perkins was born a slave in the middle of the 18th century in Kingston, Jamaica. However, by the time he passed away in 1812 he had established a legacy as the first mixed-race officer in the Royal Navy, and as an important spy. Little is known about his childhood and early life, but it is believed that his entry into the Royal Navy was due to him being the illegitimate son of a prominent white man who provided an education to prepare him for an administrative or clerical role.

His name first appeared in records in 1775 when he was appointed to the 50-gun HMS *Antelope* as a pilot. Three years later, Perkins was placed in command of the schooner HMS *Punch*, from which his nickname "Jack Punch" is believed to have originated. Over the next two years, Perkins claimed the capture of 315 ships, an average of three per week! He also conducted clandestine intelligence gathering on the enemy ports of Cap-Français in Haiti and Havana in Cuba.

In 1782, Perkins captured a larger vessel containing several important French officers and was subsequently awarded his lieutenant commission and appointed master and commander of *Endeavour*. For several years between 1783 and 1790, following Britain's peace treaty with the French, Perkins disappeared from Royal Navy records; it is suspected that he turned to piracy in the Caribbean waters he knew so well.

Following the Spanish Armament or "Nootka Crisis" of 1790, Perkins was re-employed by the Royal Navy as a spy, gathering intelligence in Hispaniola and Cuba. He was imprisoned and threatened with execution on the island of Saint-Domingue by the French, supposedly for supplying arms to rebellious black natives. This may have been revenge for his role against the French in the previous conflict. Perkins was freed once the 32-gun frigate HMS *Diana* and

> *"He annoyed the enemy more than any other officer, by his repeated feats of gallantry, and the number of prizes he took"*

the 12-gun sloop-of-war HMS *Ferret* threatened to blow up one of the local French forts.

After the French Revolutionary War broke out in 1793, Perkins was given command of the schooner HMS *Spitfire*. Four years' later he was promoted to commander on HMS *Drake* and was involved in the destruction of eight enemy ships near Port-de-Paix in Haiti. On 6 September 1800 he was promoted to captain on the 32-gun frigate HMS *Meleager*, and then in 1801 the 22-gun frigate HMS *Arab*.

From 1801, Perkins participated in the Battle of West Key (against the Danes) and the capture of the Sint Eustatius and Saba Islands (from the French). His final mission, in January 1804, was as a British observer to the slave revolt in Haiti. He retired for health reasons and died on 27 January 1812; his obituary in the *Naval Chronicle* described his actions while he was in command of the schooner *Punch*. "He annoyed the enemy more than any other officer, by his repeated feats of gallantry, and the number of prizes he took."

Written by Lieutenant Aren Tingle, Royal Navy

The beat of a different rum

Launched by ex-service personnel, Pull The Pin Rum is creating a range of spectacular infused spirits that celebrate the best things in life

www.pullthepinrum.com

When former Army Commando Tom Foster had to leave the Armed Forces after a career-ending injury, he and physiotherapist Kerry Francis decided to move in an entirely new direction when they formed Pull The Pin Rum. Little did they know that they would have to change their business model almost immediately. "We launched in September 2019 and received considerable interest and sales for the next five months," says Kerry. "Then lockdown hit, and Tom and I had to immediately rewrite our business plan and switch our focus online. It was like Tom's battlefield training suddenly kicked in!"

Tom's parents are both chefs and he grew up with a fascination for flavour, which he wanted to develop in rum. The Royal British Legion supported him through a distillery course and in getting finance to set up the company. Tom and Kerry's aim is to produce the most exciting infused spirits on the market, and their current range includes a flagship Spiced Rum, a light Silver Rum flavoured with passionfruit and pineapple, and a fruity Pink Rum flavoured with strawberry and raspberry. Each comes with a variety of serving suggestions and cocktail ideas.

"The name is a metaphor for life," says Tom. "Follow what's good and pull the pin on what's not." It reflects Tom's experience after his injury: finding a new purpose in life after ten years in the forces was essential, as Kerry affirms. "If you can't find the job that you want, then create it," she says. "Live life to the full and celebrate what is great. This is

the foundation of the company and is remembered every time a bottle is created."

Lockdown became an opportunity, rather than a challenge. Pull The Pin Rum focused on developing new products, such as gifts, as well as sponsorship partnerships. "This has been a chance to really establish the integrity of our brand, its quality and range," says Kerry. "The lifestyle message has resonated with so many people. We all feel that now is the time to appreciate the small things and pull the pin on those that don't matter. The play on words appeals to our customers: celebrate what's good in life. That's never been truer than right now."

Malaysian noodle soup

Melissa Hemsley, chef and bestselling cookbook author

Two of my vegetarian friends made something similar for me about 10 years ago when we were all in a Devon house together in the depths of winter and the boiler wasn't working properly. This warmed us up instantly and I remember thinking it was one of the most delicious things I had ever eaten. Double or triple the amount of spice paste you make and store in the freezer. It can be used to brighten up any soup or as the base for a fish or chicken curry. You could swap the noodles for chopped squash, or use cooked lentils, quinoa or beans.

Malaysia

Dairy free
Preparation time: 15 minutes
Cooking time: 20 minutes

Serves 4

INGREDIENTS

330g buckwheat noodles
1 tbsp extra virgin olive oil
2 large carrots
1 x 400ml tin of coconut milk
200ml stock/bone broth or water
350g spinach
1 tbsp fish sauce

Spice paste

1 large red onion, roughly chopped
2 lemongrass stalks, tough outer leaves
  removed, roughly chopped
1 fresh red chilli, deseeded (or to taste)
3 garlic cloves, peeled
3cm piece of ginger, roughly chopped
Stalks from a large handful of fresh
  coriander (leaves saved to garnish)
2 tbsp curry powder
Juice of 1 lime
1½ tbsp coconut oil
A big pinch of sea salt

To serve

2 tbsp cashew nuts
1 lime, cut into four wedges
Chilli flakes

METHOD

• Scatter the cashew nuts (to serve) in a large, dry frying pan and toast over a medium heat for a minute or so, tossing occasionally to make sure they don't burn, then set aside.

• In the same pan, cook the noodles according to the packet instructions until al dente (about 5 minutes instead of the usual 6–8). Rinse with cold water to stop them cooking further and toss in the olive oil to prevent them from sticking.

• Meanwhile, blend all the spice paste ingredients together in a food processor or high-powered blender. Using the same pan as before, wiped clean with kitchen paper, fry the paste on a medium heat for about 5 minutes, stirring occasionally, until the raw ingredients no longer smell as pungent.

• Meanwhile, make carrot "noodles" using a spiralizer or julienne/standard vegetable peeler.

• Add the coconut milk and stock to the pan and stir well. Bring to a medium simmer to cook for 5 minutes, lid on, then stir in the spinach and the carrot noodles and cook for another minute.

• Return the cooked buckwheat noodles to the pan, add the fish sauce and cook for 1 minute to warm through, then remove from the heat and taste for seasoning. Serve each bowl topped with the reserved coriander leaves, toasted nuts and lime wedges.

Recipe taken from *Eat Happy* by Melissa Hemsley, published by Ebury Press

Sybil Kathigasu

Sybil Medan Kathigasu was born on 3 September 1899 in Medan, Sumatra. She was the fifth child and only girl of parents who were both of mixed European and Malay heritage; her elder brother Michael was killed at Gallipoli in 1915 while serving with the British Army. Sybil was a nurse and midwife who, along with her husband Dr Abdon Clement Kathigasu, provided medical treatment to anti-Japanese forces as well as members of Special Operations Executive (SOE) Force 136 (Malaya) during World War Two.

From 1926 they lived in Ipoh, Malaysia, where they operated a clinic, before escaping to Papan days before the Japanese invaded. The couple provided medical treatment, much needed medicines and information gleaned from BBC radio broadcasts to the Malayan People's Anti-Japanese Army soldiers operating in the Kledang jungles and to members of Force 136. They were eventually arrested in 1943 by the Kempeitai (the feared Japanese military police) and charged with treachery.

Despite three years of brutal interrogation and torture at the Batu Gajah prison, and being forced to watch the torture of her husband, Sybil revealed little to no information. She was left with broken bones, no fingernails and was unable to walk. After the end of the Japanese occupation on 30 August 1945, she was rescued by British troops and flown to Britain for treatment. Sybil was awarded the George Medal for gallantry just months before she succumbed to her wounds on 12 June 1948, aged only 48. Her worst injury was a Japanese boot to the jaw, with the resulting septicemia from the wound causing complications that ended her life. She was buried initially in Lanark, Scotland, but in 1949 her body was

> *"Sybil is remembered as 'Malaysia's Florence Nightingale', has a road named after her, and a TV mini-series was created about her life"*

returned to Ipoh and buried near her wartime address in St Michael's Church Cemetery. She is the only Malayan woman known to have received the George Medal.

Sybil is remembered as "Malaysia's Florence Nightingale" and has a road named after her in Fair Park, Ipoh. A TV mini-series, *Apa Dosaku*, was created about her life, where she was played by Malaysian actress Elaine Daly – Sybil's grand-niece. Her memoir *No Dram Of Mercy* was completed in 1948 and published in 1954 in the UK and 2006 in Malaysia. In 2016, to commemorate her 117th birthday, Google released a GoogleDoodle depicting Sybil in her Papan residence.

Written by Lieutenant Commander Andy "Tank" Murray AFC, Royal Navy

Cinnamon chicken with cranberry and rum sauce

Leading Aircraftsman Josh Billingham, RAF

This is my own recipe, which I have created using the various taste combinations and colours of the Caribbean island of Montserrat. I have chosen to make a starter that blends lovely flavours and produce that you wouldn't always think of putting together and is true to Montserrat's rich culinary heritage.

Gluten-free, dairy-free
Preparation time: 30 minutes
Cooking time: 20 minutes

Serves 4

INGREDIENTS

For the cranberry and rum sauce
400g cranberries
200ml dark rum

For the chicken skewers
400g chicken thigh, cut into 1½cm dice
10g ground cinnamon
200g cherry tomatoes
200g onions, cut into wedges
200g plantain (or banana), cut into 1½cm
  pieces and tossed with 2 tbsp lemon juice
Salt and freshly ground black pepper

METHOD

• If using wooden skewers soak them in cold water for
  an hour before using them.

To make the sauce
• Place the cranberries into a saucepan, pour over the rum,
  place over a medium heat and bring to a simmer; cook for
  10–15 minutes, stirring occasionally, so that the cranberries
  start to break down and thicken the sauce.
• Taste the sauce and add more rum if needed, you are
  looking for a punch of flavour. If slightly bitter, add some
  dark brown sugar, which will balance out the taste and
  complement the cinnamon.

To prepare the chicken
• Preheat the grill to medium-high.
• Season the chicken with salt and pepper and toss with
  the ground cinnamon to thoroughly coat.
• To build the skewers, alternate chicken, onion, cherry
  tomato and plantain or banana until you have eight skewers.
• Place the skewers on a baking tray and cook under the grill
  for 15–20 minutes until the chicken is cooked through to
  the middle, alternatively they can be cooked in the oven.
• Once cooked place the skewers onto a serving plate,
  drizzle over the cranberry and rum sauce and serve with
  fried black beans.

Flight Lieutenant Osmund Kelsick DFC

In December 1940, as the Nazis advanced across Europe and Britain looked to its Empire for assistance, the small Caribbean island of Montserrat sent four young men to England to join the RAF. Kinsley Howes would become a bomber navigator and prisoner of war; Eugene Vanier was a fighter pilot who would die in combat; Charles Weekes would survive the war as a bomber rear gunner; and Osmund Kelsick would train to become a pilot and return home with a Distinguished Flying Cross.

Osmund was born in Montserrat on 22 July 1922 to Thomas Henry Kelsick and Christiana Kelsick, née Bladen. He attended Montserrat Grammar School, distinguishing himself as an athlete, before leaving to join the RAF aged 18. He qualified as a Hurricane pilot, initially specialising as a night-fighter pilot before transitioning to a day-bomber specialist with 175 Squadron, who were responsible for providing close air support during the Dieppe raid as well as convoy patrols and fighter sweeps across Northern France.

A close call came on 1 July 1943 after a bombing raid on Poix aerodrome in France, when Kelsick bailed out of his damaged aircraft at only 800ft into the English Channel. He was pulled out 16 hours later suffering both cold and shock. Nevertheless, he returned to duty and, between May 1943 and February 1944, was engaged in bombing attacks on aerodromes and on North Sea shipping. Kelsick and 175 Squadron were heavily involved in the Normandy landings in June 1944, concentrating their attacks on German forward positions, tanks, trucks and flak guns. This was a highly risky endeavour that almost resulted in him being shot down by American ground positions while he was providing them close support from under 2,000 ft. It was during this period that Kelsick was awarded Command of B Flight as a full Flight Commander and the DFC for his accumulated service.

Kelsick would return to his home in 1946 as Private Secretary to the Governor of the Leeward Islands before embarking on a very successful career as the first West Indian hotelier in Antigua before passing in 1992. He is remembered not only by his family as a gentle, caring, generous but no-nonsense father and uncle, but also by both the Montserrat and Antiguan communities for his uniqueness, his fearlessness, his leadership qualities and his integrity.

Written by Squadron Leader Malcolm Craig, RAF

Security with pride

WH Management specialises in high-end security that is firm but courteous, using the specialist skills of ex-military personnel

www.whmg.co.uk

Douglas Hinckley had a distinguished career briefly as a police officer and later as a commissioned officer in the Royal Dragoon Guards, but his interest in event security goes back to his teens. "Before I went to Sandhurst, I was brought up on a showground," he says. "I helped out for pocket money as many young kids do and, as I got older, I realised the quality of event security back in the 1990s and early 2000s just wasn't quite up to scratch."

After leaving the regular Army, the thought returned to Douglas as he saw an opportunity to employ ex-soldiers. Many of them needed work but had little idea of what civilian life entailed. WH Management was born. "The gap in the market for us was security at equestrian events," he explains. "We wanted to smarten it up and make it more approachable, and at the same time deliver a high-end protective service wherever needed."

Out went the black T-shirts and aggressive attitudes of stereotypical security guards. Instead, Douglas's security teams wear chinos and a blazer to events. If they need to decline someone entry, they do so politely, while recognising when someone has genuinely lost their pass or invitation. As its guidelines for dealing with incidents, the company uses the Joint Emergency Services Interoperability Principles (JESIP), which serve as multi-agency principles of incident command.

The approach has been a success for nearly 15 years, with clients including Burghley, Wimbledon, the Henley Royal Regatta and the Royal Windsor Horse Show. Douglas continued in his Army role for the first few years as WH Management built up its client base. He went full-time in 2009, but continued to work as an Army reserve officer until 2020.

The company now employs up to 600 people at times, and WH Management is a Gold Award holder in the Armed Forces Covenant Scheme. The scheme supports those who are serving or have served in the Armed Forces, including helping them get started in a new career afterwards. Douglas has a simple but effective recruitment strategy. "If someone is reliable, hard-working and honest, the rest will come from their foundation military or emergency services training," he says.

WH Management now includes event management and logistics services, as well as providing close protection and residential security teams. "We regularly have a number of opportunities for both employed or self-employed staff, and it ranges from that fairly high-level close protection, through the different grades of security, fire and medical," says Douglas. "Planning, reconnaissance and intelligence is 95 per cent of our job. And if you get that right, then the day, the week, the month will be a lot smoother both for the client and for the team on the ground. We need people who recognise that, but who can up the ante very quickly if it does go wrong."

Tasks can sometimes be unexpected and WH Management staff always remain flexible to even the most surprising of requests. These extend well beyond security: from helping party planners with finishing touches at high-profile weddings to removing dogs from hot cars at sporting events. At various challenging national events, the skills learned by some ex-Forces employees to rescue bogged-in vehicles have also come in handy. "It is all about having a multitude of skills," says Douglas, "which we use with a can-do attitude."

Pork momo and Nepali chutney

Corporal Purja Gurung, Army

Momos are steamed dumplings commonly eaten across Asia and India; Nepalese momos are similar to Chinese and Japanese dumplings but are slightly lighter in texture and the flavour is unique to Nepalese cooking. Although traditionally filled with ground meat, vegetarian and vegan momos have become a lot more popular. This dish for me, being Nepalese, brings back so many memories of growing up and reminds me of that feeling I get when I fly home to see family and friends. If you've ever been to Nepal and visited one of the large cities, such as Pokhara or Kathmandu, you will have seen the dozens of stalls preparing and selling momos to tourists and locals on their lunch breaks. Enjoy this recipe and bring the flavours of Nepal into your home.

Sergeant Lachhiman Gurung VC

Lachhiman Gurung was born 30 December 1917 in the Tanhu district of Nepal, the Gurkhas' homeland. He joined the 8th Gurkha Rifles in the British Indian Army at the end of 1940, although, at 4ft 11in, he was an inch short of the brigade's minimum height standard.

On the night of 12 May 1945, rifleman Gurung was manning the forward post of his platoon on the west bank of the Irrawaddy River, 100 yards ahead of the main company. Just after 1am, more than 200 Japanese attacked the position, with the brunt of the assault falling on Gurung's post. For four hours, Gurung remained alone at his post, calmly waiting for each new onslaught, firing into his attackers at point blank range, determined not to yield an inch of ground. His comrades could hear him shouting: "Come and fight a Gurkha!" Of the 87 enemy dead counted in the immediate vicinity, 31 lay in front of this rifleman's section. Had the enemy succeeded in over-running and occupying Gurung's trench, the whole of the reverse slope position would have been turned. He was awarded the Victoria Cross for his remarkable bravery. After his heroic stand, Lachhiman lost his right hand and was left blind in his right eye. He remained on active service until 1947, when India became independent and he transferred to the Indian Army, retiring later that year with the rank of havildar (or sergeant).

I had the pleasure of meeting Gurung in the British Gurkhas Kathmandu mess in 2004. He struck me as a proud family man with a heroic aura about him. He had a welcoming smile but also curtly reprimanded the children running around him too fast. He also said how much he liked the dal bhat created by the Gurkha chefs.

In 2008, Gurung, wearing his row of medals, became a familiar sight in the British media, as the actress Joanna Lumley, the daughter of a British Gurkha officer, led a successful campaign to allow Gurkha veterans to settle in Britain on retirement. Gurung also persuaded the Home Office to rescind a deportation order against his granddaughter, who was looking after him in Hounslow. He died aged 93 on 12 December 2010. He is survived by his second wife, Manmaya, their two sons, and two sons and a daughter by his first wife.

Written by Major Matthew Pittaway, Royal Logistics Corps, Army

"His comrades could hear him shouting: 'Come and fight a Gurkha!'"

Preparation time: 40 minutes
Cooking time: 20 minutes

Serves 4

INGREDIENTS

For the dough
400g plain flour
Salt
A dash of olive oil
200ml water

For the spicy tomato chutney
8 large tomatoes, cores removed
  and halved
1 tbsp vegetable oil
4 large garlic cloves, whole
2 red chillies, finely chopped
1 tsp chilli powder
½ lemon, juiced
2½cm piece of ginger, peeled
  and very finely chopped
Salt and pepper

For the momo filling
1 onion, finely diced
1 spring onion, finely chopped
2 garlic cloves, crushed
1 red chilli, finely chopped
1 small piece of ginger, grated
40g fresh coriander, finely chopped
350g pork, minced
25ml soy sauce
Salt and pepper

METHOD

• Preheat the oven to 220°C.

To make the dough
• Sift the flour, add a pinch of salt, the oil and enough of the water to form
  a firm dough; transfer to a lightly oiled mixing bowl, cover the surface of
  the dough with a piece of clingfilm and set aside to rest for 30 minutes.

To make the chutney
• Place the tomatoes in a baking dish, add the vegetable oil and toss to coat;
  place in the preheated oven and roast for 15 minutes, add the garlic cloves,
  mix to coat in the oil and continue to roast for another 15 minutes.
• Remove from the oven and allow to cool.
• Transfer the roasted tomatoes and garlic to a food processor, add the
  chillies, chilli powder, lemon juice and ginger; pulse until the larger pieces
  are broken up then blend until smooth and season with salt and pepper
  to taste.
• Place the chutney to one side in a covered serving bowl ready to dip
  your momos.

To make the momo filling
• Place the onions, spring onions, garlic, chillies, ginger and coriander into
  a mixing bowl; add the pork mince and soy sauce, mix thoroughly and
  season with salt and pepper. Cover and store in the fridge until you're
  ready to fill the momos.

To fill the momos
• Divide the dough into 24–28 equal-sized pieces (6 or 7 momos per person),
  roll into neat balls, lightly dust the worktop with flour and roll out the
  dough balls as thinly as possible; keep the dough wrappers covered with
  a damp tea towel to prevent them from drying out.
• When filling the momos it is important to work as quickly as possible
  and, ideally, with a partner. Hold the rolled-out dough in one hand, place
  a spoonful of the filling mix in the centre and pinch together the edges to
  form a semi-circle and place back under the tea towel to keep your momos
  fresh and to prevent a skin forming on the dough.

To cook the momos
• Heat up the steamer; electric is fine but traditionally we use bamboo
  steamers back home.
• Once all the momos are ready, oil the steamer tray and arrange the
  dumplings in the steamer (allow enough space around each one to prevent
  them from sticking to each other) and steam for 20 minutes until
  thoroughly cooked through to the centre.
• Remove the momos from the steamer and serve alongside the chutney.

The Welsh trio (lamb, leek and cake)

Sergeant Karla Wickham, RAF

Wales is rightly famous for its lamb, which was given PGI (Protected Geographical Indication) status by the European Union in 2003. The leek is widely recognised as the national emblem of Wales. In Shakespeare's Henry V, Fluellen says to King Henry: "Your majesty says very true: if your majesties is remembered of it, the Welshmen did good service in a garden where leeks did grow, wearing leeks in their Monmouth caps; which, your majesty know, to this hour is an honourable badge of the service; and I do believe your majesty takes no scorn to wear the leek upon Saint Tavy's day." To which King Henry replies: "I wear it for a memorable honour; For I am Welsh, you know, good countryman." The Welshcake has been popular since the 19th century as an afternoon tea treat. My Welsh trio is the combination of all these traditional Welsh ingredients, to make a savoury starter.

Preparation time: 30 minutes
Cooking time: 5 hours

Serves 4

INGREDIENTS

For the slow cooked lamb
1 small leg of lamb
2 medium onions, thickly sliced
1 garlic clove, coarsely chopped
2 large sprigs of rosemary
250ml lamb or beef stock
50g flour
4 small sprigs of rosemary to garnish
Salt and freshly ground black pepper

For the Welshcakes
10g butter
50g leeks, halved lengthways
  and finely sliced
230g self-raising flour
Pinch of salt
115g margarine
1 medium egg, beaten
Splash of milk

For the buttered leeks
25g butter
1 small leek, cut in half lengthways
  and cut into 1cm slices
Salt and freshly ground black pepper

METHOD

To slow-cook the lamb

• Preheat the oven to 160°C and season the lamb leg with salt and pepper.
• Place the onion, garlic and rosemary into a roasting tray, place the lamb leg, skin side up, on top and pour the stock into the tray.
• Place a square of baking parchment on top of the lamb (to prevent tinfoil from sticking), cover tightly with foil and cook in the preheated oven for 4–5 hours, checking occasionally, until the lamb is falling from the bone.
• Remove the lamb from the oven, set aside to cool slightly before pulling into shreds with a couple of forks; set aside.
• Place the tray with the roasting juices over a medium heat, bring to a simmer and gradually whisk in enough of the flour to make thickened, lump-free gravy; strain the gravy into a saucepan, season and set aside.

To make the Welshcakes

• Heat the butter in a saucepan over a medium heat, add the leeks when the butter is foaming and cook, stirring frequently, for about 5 minutes until the leeks have softened; season with salt and pepper and set aside to cool.
• Sift the flour with a pinch of salt, rub the margarine into the flour with your fingertips till it resembles breadcrumbs then mix in the cooled leeks.
• Mix in the beaten egg and knead to form a smooth dough, adding a splash of milk if the dough is too dry; take care not to overwork the dough as you want the cakes to be a little crumbly.
• Roll out the dough on a lightly floured surface to about 1cm thick.
• Cut out eight rounds of the dough using a 6cm cutter, then cut a hole in the middle of each one with a 4cm round cutter, reusing the cut-out dough.
• Lightly oil a frying pan, place over a low-medium heat and cook evenly on both sides until golden brown and cooked through to the middle.

To cook the buttered leeks

• Heat the butter in a saucepan over a medium heat, add the leeks when the butter is foaming and cook, stirring frequently, for about 5 minutes until the leeks have softened; season with salt and pepper and keep warm.

To serve

• Reheat the gravy over a medium heat, stir in the pulled lamb, check the seasoning and simmer until thoroughly heated through.
• Place two of the Welshcake rings on each of four small plates, pile the pulled lamb into the centre, top with the buttered leeks and garnish each with a small sprig of rosemary.

Newport: Local hero

Company Sergeant Major John Henry Williams VC DCM MM & Bar

Born in Nantyglo, Monmouthshire on 29 September 1886, John "Jack" Henry Williams became the most highly decorated Welsh soldier during the Great War, receiving the Victoria Cross, the Distinguished Conduct Medal and the Military Medal and Bar.

Having left school at the age of 12 to work as a blacksmith in Cwm Colliery, he enlisted in the South Wales Borderers in 1906 before discharging to return to the colliery. In November 1914 he re-enlisted, alongside hundreds of his work colleagues, eventually joining the 10th Battalion, South Wales Borderers.

Williams was awarded a DCM for his "continued and sustained coolness and gallantry" during the First Battle of the Somme in July 1916. A year later he was awarded the Military Medal for bravery at the Battle for the Passchendaele Heights. He then went on to receive a Bar to the Military Medal after a raid on German lines at the Battle of Armentieres, where he rescued a wounded comrade and guided him to safety under gunfire. In the last full month of the war, during the attack on Villers Outreaux, he observed that his company was suffering heavy casualties from an enemy machine gun. Under heavy fire he rushed the enemy post and single handedly captured 15 German soldiers. His conspicuous bravery and initiative resulted in him being awarded the Victoria Cross.

After suffering severe shrapnel wounds, he was discharged from the Army on 17 October 1918. Three months later he was awarded the French equivalent of the VC, the Medaille Militaire. On 22 February 1919, King George V awarded Williams his VC at Buckingham Palace; Williams had not yet fully recovered from his wounds and required medical attention before he could leave the Palace. Williams returned to Ebbw Vale, serving as the commissionaire at the local steelworks – a position he held until his death – and President of the Ebbw Vale British Legion. For his service, the steelworks gave him a house and granted him a lifetime supply of coal and electricity. During the Second World War, Williams served as a captain in the Home Guard. He passed away on 6 March 1953. There is a commemorative plaque in his honour at the former site of the steelworks.

Written by Squadron Leader Andy Mortimer, RAF

A very social security

Lead Element Security uses military veterans
to provide specialised security services of all kinds

LeadElementSecurity.co.uk

"In two years we have made incredibly fast progress and that's down to the quality of the girls and guys we've got on the books," says Mo Alin, Operational Manager and co-founder of Lead Element Security. "We get recommended because of that. Clients look to us for security, which to us is a natural because we've been doing it in theatres like Northern Ireland and Afghanistan. They look to us and listen to us."

There are some 2,000 security companies currently operating in London alone, whose standard Lead Element co-founder Tony Norton politely describes as "variable". Lead Element has an edge over its competitors in that the company is founded, run and operated by military veterans from all branches, from top to bottom. Mo and Tony themselves have been brothers in arms for over 20 years, serving in Iraq and Afghanistan.

Lead Element's mission is not only to provide a platform for those who have left the military and face an uncertain future but also to provide a higher quality of service by drawing on the vast pool of experience from all the veterans nationwide.

"It's silly not to tap into it," says Tony. "We can provide work for them where they feel at home, feel valued. We can provide ex-military personnel who have a minimum of three years' service across any of the three forces."

Lead Element's personnel are as adept at defusing situations as they are at enforcement. The firm's range of services can include close protection, residential security or dealing with anti-social behaviour. One project was a scheme in Holloway Road in north London to house the homeless during the COVID-19 crisis. "We turned that around in 24 hours and handled the day-to-day running," says Tony. "We saw the benefit, at first hand, of helping people with alcohol and substance abuse issues to come off the street. And they connected with us, confided in us, talked to us. There was a human connection." Thanks to Lead Element's efforts, some of those people have gone on to find secure accommodation, even work.

Ultimately, the core values of Lead Element are courage, discipline, respect for others, integrity, loyalty and selfless commitment," says Mo. "They're the values of the Army itself."

Yellow split pea and bacon soup with stotties

Corporal Andy McClurg, RAF

Northumberland

Stotties, or stottie cakes, are a traditional North-East bread and are a regular addition to most working families' butty boxes. Traditionally, at the end of the working day, any leftover dough from bread making was flattened, placed in the bottom of the oven and cooked in the residual heat as the oven cooled. In my recipe I am serving the stottie with yellow split pea and bacon soup as a nod to the North-East classic, ham and pease pudding stottie.

Preparation time: 90 minutes
Cooking time: 2 hours

Serves 4

INGREDIENTS

For the stottie cake
300g strong white flour
7g (1 sachet) fast-action dry yeast
Pinch of sugar
Pinch of salt
Pinch of white pepper
50ml milk mixed with 100ml water,
  warmed until tepid

For the soup
1 tbsp vegetable oil
250g thick bacon lardons
100g onion, peeled, halved and diced
200g carrots, peeled and diced
150g celery, diced
300g yellow split peas (soaked overnight)
1.8 litres chicken stock
Salt and black pepper
2 tbsp flat-leaf parsley, chopped

METHOD

For the stottie
- Sieve the flour and mix with the yeast, sugar, salt and white pepper in a large mixing bowl.
- Make a well in the centre and pour in the water and milk; mix well and knead on a lightly floured work surface until a smooth ball has formed.
- Cover and leave to rest in a warm place for 1 hour or until doubled in size.
- Preheat the oven to 180°C.
- Knock back the dough, form into a ball and roll into in to a disk approximately 25cm across; cover and leave for 10 minutes.
- Prick with a fork several times and push a deep indent into the middle with your finger.
- Bake in the preheated oven for 20 minutes or until the crust is crisp and starting to brown; tap the bottom of the stottie, it should sound hollow.
- Cool on a wire rack then cut or tear into four or six pieces, depending on how hungry you are.

For the soup
- Heat half of the oil in a large saucepan over a medium-high heat.
- Add the bacon and fry until browned; remove with a slotted spoon and set aside.
- Add the remaining oil and, when hot, add the diced onion, carrots and celery; fry, stirring occasionally, for about 5 minutes until they are starting to soften.
- Drain and rinse the split peas and add to the pan along with the stock; bring to a boil, reduce the heat, cover and simmer, stirring occasionally, for about 50 minutes.
- Stir in the cooked bacon and continue to simmer for a further 10 minutes or until the peas have softened and the soup has thickened.
- Taste and season with salt and black pepper as necessary then ladle into bowls and garnish with a little freshly chopped parsley.

VEGETARIAN/VEGAN ALTERNATIVE
- For a vegetarian version, replace the chicken stock with vegetable stock and omit the bacon.
- For a vegan version make the soup as above and substitute the milk in the stottie with a vegan milk alternative.

Private Daniel Laidlaw VC

On 26 July 1875, Daniel Logan Laidlaw was born in the village of Little Swinton, Berwick-upon-Tweed. He originally apprenticed as a miller in Northumberland, before enlisting on the 11th April 1896, joining the 2nd Durham Light Infantry. He was initially posted to India where he, alongside the other members of the 2nd Durham, was tasked with assisting the local government in Bombay with fighting an outbreak of the bubonic plague. In 1898, he transferred to the Kings Own Scottish Borders as a Piper until he left to join the reserves in 1911. As a civilian, Laidlaw was a canteen manager at Alnwick Co-operative Stores, worked for a firm of horse-breeders in Donnington and served as an assistant scoutmaster at Alnwick.

With the outbreak of the Great War, Laidlaw re-enlisted in the 7th battalion, King's Own Scottish Borderers in September 1914 and, by February 1915, was deployed to join the fight in France. At the Battle of Loos on 25 September 1915, during the worst attack of the battle and with his company suffering with the effects of gas, Laidlaw demonstrated his bravery and courage. Disregarding all risks from the incoming attack, he marched up and down the parapet playing his company out of the trenches with his beloved bagpipes, to the tune of the regimental march "Blue Bonnets Over The Border".

This conspicuous display of bravery lifted his company, who immediately rushed out from the trenches and attacked the enemy. Despite being injured by shrapnel to the ankle, Laidlaw continued to play his pipes and inspire his comrades until the position was won. Laidlaw was later evacuated back to Lord Derby Hospital in Warrington for treatment. For his actions that day he was promoted to Corporal and forever known as "the Piper of Loos". On 18 November 1915, he was awarded the Victoria Cross, which he received from King George V at Buckingham Palace on 3 February 1916.

Laidlaw also received an address from the citizens of Alnwick, a gold-mounted walking stick, a cheque for £5 and war stock to the value of £60 from a fund raised by the *Berwick Journal* and the *Berwickshire News*. He also received a gold watch from the Worshipful Company of Musicians at Mansion House on 28 February 1916, and played the pipes at various wartime concerts. He was a member of the VC Guard for the Unknown Soldier, playing the bagpipes for the funeral procession.

Laidlaw left the regular army in April 1919 and transferred over to the Class Z reserve. Struggling to find work after the war, he endured long periods of unemployment before eventually seeking assistance from the King's Own Scottish Borderers Association, receiving support from a public fund to educate his youngest son. He had a brief film career, playing the pipes in the silent movie *The Guns of Loos* (1929) and appearing in the documentary film *Forgotten Men* (1933). He accompanied a troupe of highland dancers on a tour of Norway in 1934, and piped for the Scottish Country Dancing Club in London. Just before the Second World War, he became the sub-postmaster of Shoresdean in Northumberland and then head warden of the Air Raid Precautions (ARP) in the Norham and Islandshires district.

Laidlaw died at Shoresdean, near Berwick-upon-Tweed, on 2 June 1950, and was buried in St Cuthbert's churchyard in Norham, Northumberland, where a memorial headstone, organised by the King's Own Scottish Borderers Museum and members of the Laidlaw family, was placed over his grave on 2 June 2002. As well as the VC, Laidlaw was awarded the 1914–15 Star, British War Medal in 1914–20, George VI Coronation Medal in 1937, Defence Medal 1939–45 and, on 1 May 1917, the Croix de Guerre with Bronze Palm by France. He is only one of two pipers to have been awarded the VC during the First World War.

Written by Corporal Rebecca Croker, RAF, and Corporal Matthew Lockwood, RAF

Supreme confidence

With decades of experience supplying the NHS, Attends creates products that give confidence, independence and comfort to its users

www.attends.co.uk

It's estimated that 8 million people in the UK at any one time experience some form of incontinence, making this a more common condition than hay fever. However, there is still a stigma about discussing incontinence, or admitting that you have issues with your bladder or bowel. That's something that Attends is hoping to change by producing solutions and offering a variety of containment products such as pads and pants that allow people to continue living proudly independent lives despite their condition.

"There is a lot of stigma around incontinence that needs to be challenged. It is important to understand that incontinence can be treated and, in many cases, cured," explains Jane Smith, Product Specialist and Registered Nurse. "Attends have a lot of experience manufacturing and supplying these products and we understand the needs of people suffering with incontinence. As a company we strongly believe that we add the personal touch to help individuals select the best product to meet their needs."

Attends has more than four decades experience in the healthcare sector, providing a variety of products for the NHS as well as other healthcare providers. The company also supplies products to leading high-street and local pharmacies. "To ensure that Attends products are used correctly," says Jane, "our highly trained Attends team provide training and support to nurses, healthcare professionals, pharmacists and people in their own homes. This ensure that the product they are choosing offers security and discretion while maintaining dignity. It helps that Attends products, offer a combination of comfort, discretion, and odour protection, which allow you

to go about your daily business without fear of embarrassment and have confidence in the Attends brand."

It's this level of trust and strong customer support that differentiates Attends from other companies. To enhance the Attends service, healthcare professionals and the public can speak to Attends' friendly trained customer advisors via the customer helpline. The team members are happy to help, provide support, recommend products, and resolve any queries that customers may have as quickly as possible. Attends also encourages people to seek medical advice to help with symptom control.

"We care," says Jane. "We understand that incontinence can be a difficult subject to discuss as it is personal to each individual. Attends is empathetic to your needs. We want to reduce stigma by making the public more aware of how common incontinence is, and that it can affect people at all ages and for so many different reasons. The traditional British stiff upper lip can be a problem for people who suffer with incontinence as it is still a taboo subject, but it can be treated. As you undergo treatment, Attends can offer products so that you can live your life as normal by staying dry, comfortable and confident."

Although the products are disposable, Attends is taking every measure to promote sustainability and reduce carbon footprint. "We are working hard to reduce our carbon footprint through our manufacturing, logistics, product and packaging," says Jodie Moore, UK Marketing Associate. "We endeavour to operate more efficiently and are constantly reviewing our ways of working, however the most important aspect of our business is that we care about the individual."

Shropshire Gold wings with Wrekin blue sauce

Senior Aircraftsman Yu-Ting Yau, RAF

Shropshire is a county with amazing produce. For this recipe we will be using the finest Shropshire Gold beer and Wrekin blue cheese, produced only 11 miles from where I grew up (Wrekin is the hill that I used to run up and down when I was in college). I have used these ingredients to make an amazing platter of beer-marinated chicken wings and a deep and rich cheese sauce with the Wrekin blue. It's perfect for gathering friends together to have a good old catch-up.

Preparation time: 3 hours,
  including marinating time
Cooking time: 20 minutes

Serves 4

INGREDIENTS

To marinate the chicken wings
16 free-range chicken wings
1 pint (568ml) Shropshire Gold ale
1 clove garlic, finely chopped or crushed
1 tsp English mustard

For the Wrekin blue sauce
100g butter
100g plain flour
1 pint (568ml) Shropshire Gold ale
200g Wrekin blue or Shropshire
  blue cheese
1 tbsp Worcestershire sauce
2 tsp English mustard

To cook the chicken wings
Vegetable oil for deep frying
200g plain flour
30g paprika
Salt and pepper
4 medium eggs

To garnish
20g chives, chopped

METHOD

To marinate the chicken wings
• Cut the wings into drumettes and winglets (the tips are optional, for me they are delicious when they're crispy), give them a wash under cold water and pat them dry on absorbent kitchen paper.
• Mix the ale with the garlic and mustard in a plastic container, add the chicken wings, ensuring that they are fully submerged, cover with a lid and leave to marinate in the fridge for 2–3 hours; even better, overnight.
• Discard the marinade, pat the wings dry, lay them out on a tray and keep them covered at room temperature.

To make the Wrekin blue sauce
• Melt the butter in a saucepan over a medium heat, stir in the flour and cook, stirring frequently, for 4–5 minutes until lightly coloured.
• Add the ale, a little at a time to avoid lumps, and keep stirring until you get a smooth and thick sauce; bring to a simmer and continue to cook, stirring often, for a couple of minutes.
• Take the sauce off the heat and crumble in the Wrekin blue cheese, stirring it into the sauce until melted.
• Once the cheese has melted, stir in the mustard and Worcestershire sauce (these will cut through the richness of the blue cheese), season with salt and pepper and keep warm.

To coat and cook the chicken wings

- Preheat the oven to 120°C and in a deep, suitable pan heat enough of the vegetable oil to deep-fry the wings at 190°C.
- Season the flour with the paprika, salt and pepper, then crack the eggs into a separate bowl and whisk them up.
- Toss the wings in the seasoned flour, a few at a time; ensure that they are fully coated then shake off any excess flour before dipping them in to the whisked eggs then back into the seasoned flour to coat again; repeat this process until all the wings are coated.
- Gently lower the coated chicken wings into the hot oil and cook, stirring occasionally, for 10 minutes until they are golden and crispy; I recommend that you cook them in two or three batches depending on the size of your pan, this will ensure that the wings cook evenly.
- Once the first batch of wings are cooked, place them in a single layer on a baking tray and keep hot in the oven while you cook the next batch.
- Always make sure you allow the oil to get back to 190°C between batches to ensure consistent results and skim off any bits that have risen to the surface.

To serve

- Once all your wings are cooked, lay them out on kitchen paper to absorb any excess oil.
- Pile the crispy wings in a large serving bowl or platter and serve with bowls of the blue cheese sauce garnished with a sprinkle of chopped chives.

Shropshire: Local hero

Corporal Ricky Furgusson MC

Born in Telford, Ricky Furgusson joined the British Army straight from school at the age of 16. By the time his regiment, the Royal Green Jackets, were rebadged as "The Rifles" in 2007, Ricky was already an established Junior Leader in the 4th Battalion, having completed 18 months in Northern Ireland and a further six months in Iraq in 2007, prior to deploying to Afghanistan in October 2009.

On his first patrol in Helmand, his squad struck a large IED (improvised explosive device). With no regard for his own safety, Ricky rushed to evacuate a colleague, saving his life. A month later, he aided comrades twice in one day alone, saving a second man's life in the process. Before the end of 2009, he aided yet another comrade who had been caught in an explosion. "As section commander you look after those in your section," said Ricky. "Unfortunately, some of those attached to our section got hit by IEDs. I was always one of the first to get there to give them the best first-aid possible."

On 13 January 2010, Ricky himself was seriously injured by an IED, and his life would change forever. He was evacuated from Afghanistan to Headley Court, a unit for injured service personnel. He lost both his legs, his left eye and five fingers, and suffered deep facial scarring. Following six months' treatment and after 10 and a half years of service, Ricky was discharged from the Army as a result of his injuries.

For his actions, Corporal Ricky Furgusson was awarded the Military Cross. His citation states: "Furgusson's bravery, personally ignoring the ever-present IED threat when dashing to the aid of wounded men, and his outstanding leadership, time and again rallying his soldiers in the disorientating aftermath of IED strikes, saved men's lives." When meeting the Queen at Buckingham Palace in December 2010, he had just received his first pair of prosthetic legs. Determined not to receive his award in a wheelchair, Ricky walked to meet the Queen and receive his medal with the help of two walking sticks.

He was honoured to carry the Olympic Torch in Broseley in May 2012. He also received the Millie Award for Life Saving, was made Freeman of the Borough of Telford and Wrekin, and carried the Premier League Trophy for Manchester United onto the pitch at Old Trafford. Ricky even competed in the 2014 Invictus Games, running the 100 metres IT2 (for athletes with above-knee amputation).

Written by Squadron Leader Malcolm Craig, RAF

Bak kut teh (pork bone tea)

Corporal Rob Donnelly, RAF

Bak kut teh is a wonderful pork broth from Singapore that's full of amazing herbal and umami flavours. It is usually made with a lot of Chinese soured spices; I have recreated it with ingredients that can be found in your local supermarket. Bak kut teh is traditionally served as a lunchtime dish.

Singapore

Gluten-free (if gluten-free tofu is used), dairy-free
Preparation time: 15 minutes
Cooking time: 1 hour 45 minutes

Serves 4

INGREDIENTS

300g pork short rib
450g belly pork

Dry ingredients
15g black peppercorns
3 star anise
10g Szechwan peppercorns
1 cinnamon stick
5 cloves
10g fennel seeds

Broth ingredients
110g shiitake mushrooms
35g ginger
1 garlic bulb, cloves separated but
  not peeled
2 spring onions
1 shallot, peeled
200g chestnut mushrooms
60g tofu puff (optional)
4 tbsp dark soy sauce
2 tbsp caster sugar
2 tbsp white wine vinegar
1 small bunch of coriander, leaves picked

METHOD

• Place the whole pork ribs and belly into a large pan, cover with cold water, place over a high heat and boil for 15 minutes; remove the meat and run under cold water to remove any of the scum and set aside; discard the water.
• Place all the dry ingredients into a porous cloth (ideally muslin), gather up the sides and tie the top with string to create a fragrant tea bag. Place the bag into a large pan along with the shiitake mushrooms, ginger, garlic cloves and 4 litres of water; bring to a boil then simmer for 45 minutes.
• Add the pork to the broth and simmer for a further 40 minutes, removing any scum that comes to the surface, you want a nice clear brown liquid (note the pork for Bak Kut Teh should be firm, you are not trying to make pulled pork).
• While the broth simmers, finely chop the spring onion, finely slice the shallot into rings, quarter the chestnut mushrooms and cut the tofu puffs in half.
• Remove all the pork from the broth and set aside to cool slightly. Cut the pork rib into individual ribs and the belly into 1cm slices.
• Using tongs, remove the tea bag from the broth, squeezing all the liquid out, and strain the broth through a fine sieve into a clean saucepan.
• Add the chestnut mushrooms, soy sauce, sugar and vinegar to the broth and simmer for 5 minutes.
• Portion the pork ribs, pork belly, tofu and shallot rings into your serving bowls, pour over the hot broth and scatter over the spring onion and picked coriander leaves.

Lieutenant Adnan Saidi

The heroic Adnan Saidi has become part of Malayan military folklore and even features on a Singapore bank note. Born in 1915, the eldest of six siblings, Saidi left school with the intention of becoming a teacher but eventually joined the newly formed Malay Regiment in 1933, aged 18. He graduated as Best Recruit in 1934, was promoted to Sergeant in 1936 and, following his representation on parade in London a year later for the accession of King George VI, was promoted to Company Sergeant Major. Selected for a commission, the now Second Lieutenant Saidi joined "C" Coy as 7 Platoon Commander and was posted to Singapore in late 1941. He sent his family back to Kajang as the Japanese prepared for invasion.

On 13 February 1942, the Japanese were intent on taking Pasir Panjang Ridge to the south of Singapore, which would allow them access to the Alexandra area where the British main ammunition and supply depots and military hospital were located. Despite intense aerial and artillery bombardment, the ridge was successfully held thanks to stiff resistance from "C" Coy.

At midnight, "C" Coy received orders to establish a defensive position at a location known as Opium Hill. Deploying his men, Saidi strengthened his position by means of a wall of sandbags. Soon troops dressed as British-Indian Sikhs appeared on the hill, but Lieutenant Saidi – with typical attention to detail – noticed that they were marching in rows of four, in the style of the Japanese army, rather than the British rows of three. Twenty enemy soldiers were killed in the ensuing skirmish. Two hours later, the Japanese launched an all-out assault, overwhelming "C" Coy, who, out of ammunition, resorted to hand-to-hand combat. Refusing to surrender and honouring their vow of "*Taat Setia*" (faithfulness and loyalty) and their company motto "*Biar lutih tulang, jangan putih mata*" (better to die in battle than live with tears of regret), they courageously fought on. Saidi was eventually captured, hung by his legs from a cherry tree and repeatedly bayoneted before his body was burnt. What later became known as the Battle of Opium Ridge was immortalised in the 2000 Malay film *Leftenan Adnan*.

Survived by his wife Sophia, who died in 1949, and two sons, Saidi is commemorated by a memorial plaque in Kent Ridge Park and on the Kranji War Memorial, both in Singapore. His legacy continues in the Malayan Defence Forces, with the Malaysian infantry fighting vehicle (MIFV) being called the ACV-300 Adnan, and he features on the Singaporean $20 bill alongside six other individuals that contributed to the nation of Singapore.

Written by Warrant Officer Kevin Morley, RAF

> *"Saidi refused to surrender, honouring his company's motto: better to die in battle than live with tears of regret"*

The feast from the east

With nearly half a century of experience, SeeWoo Foods is now expanding its client base, bringing authentic East Asian ingredients and kitchenware to a wider British audience

www.seewoo.com

When the three Tse brothers started SeeWoo Foods in 1975, their aim was simple: they wanted to serve the community of first-generation Chinese who had emigrated from Hong Kong to the UK. SeeWoo Foods was born as an importer and distributor of ingredients for the restaurants and takeaways this generation had set up across the country.

In those days, it was a humble shop in Chinatown, central London. Now the company has become a household name among its retail and wholesale customers and has many fans among the wider British audience. SeeWoo Foods has a headquarters in Biggleswade and two cash-and-carry stores in Greenwich and Glasgow which are open to the public.

One thing that has not changed is that SeeWoo Foods is a family business. Managing Director Emily Tse represents the second generation to run the company, which now imports foods from all over Asia. "My father Tony Tse (pictured, opposite, top left) dedicated his whole life to the business, and that's why it's so successful," she says. "Over the years, SeeWoo Foods has become a one-stop-shop for catering – so we do the woks, the chopsticks and the steamers, as well as food ingredients. At the time, this was quite revolutionary, as my father and his brothers saw a niche in the market."

Throughout the past 45 years, much has changed for SeeWoo Foods and in the market generally, and the new, modern headquarters opened last year to reflect this. "Before COVID-19 happened, we were already in transition," Emily explains. SeeWoo Foods had the same head office for more than 15 years before 2020, but was now a company of about 250 staff in several separate sites. The market for its goods had also changed, and they needed to adapt. The new 60,000 square foot site is a central distribution centre which consolidates thousands of different stock lines from major ports all over the world on a daily basis.

The demographic has also changed. While ethnic Chinese moving to the UK from Hong Kong were the main customers to begin with, many now migrate here from mainland China – bringing their own customs and cuisine with them. "We are looking to cater for these people as well now," says Emily. "We are also looking to do more for the younger market."

Another area of expansion is vegan ingredients, which are becoming increasingly popular. "There are also a lot of British westerners who are interested in foodie culture and veganism," says Emily. "This crowd is interested in trying unusual and authentic Asian dishes with genuine ingredients."

As the market has changed, so have the companies for which SeeWoo supplies ingredients. A recent addition was Little Moons, a British company making Japanese-style ice-cream mochi, which launched in 2010. "We're always evolving and looking at new things we can offer," says Emily.

Glasgow is home to over 12,000 Chinese, and the megastore at the heart of the city serves their requirements for pan-Asian ingredients, allowing them to purchase products from home. This was one of the reasons that led the late Tony Tse to start SeeWoo Foods in Scotland. Both the London and Glasgow cash and carry stores have a live seafood counter and fresh meat deli.

"Since we've moved to this brand-new, state-of-the-art distribution warehouse, staff are really excited for the future," says Emily. While the company adapted to COVID-19 and thrived, she is looking forward to the end of lockdown and a chance to implement SeeWoo Food's five-year transformation plan. "We just want to get back on track after the pandemic," she says, "but we have an exciting time ahead."

Crab tortellini with chilli, ginger and coconut

Senior Aircraftsman Jody Huteson, RAF

This is a vibrant, light starter for a lovely winter's day using fresh local ingredients native to the Solomon Islands. Over the years, these Pacific islanders have taken a lot of influence from Thailand and this is reflected in many of the islands' recipes and commonly used ingredients. When creating this recipe, I also wanted to pay homage to my recent time doing work experience at Newquay's Porth Beach Hotel with chef Andrew Durham, where I learnt to make tortellini.

Dairy-free
Preparation time: 45 minutes,
  plus overnight resting for the pasta
Cooking time: 40 minutes

Serves 4

INGREDIENTS

For the pasta
4 medium eggs
1 tsp saffron powder
500g tipo "00" pasta flour

For the tortellini filling
500g white crab meat
100g brown crab meat
1 red chilli, finely diced
8g fresh ginger, finely diced
2 garlic cloves, finely diced
2 kaffir lime leaves, finely diced
30g Thai basil, shredded
Salt and pepper

For the basil oil
100ml rapeseed oil
50g basil

For the sauce
2 tbsp coconut oil
2 shallots, finely diced
2 garlic cloves, finely diced
3 tbsp ginger, finely diced
200ml fish stock
2 kaffir lime leaves, whole
1 stem of lemon grass, bruised
1 carrot, unpeeled and cut into large pieces
400ml (1 can) coconut milk

For the garnish
100g fresh coconut shavings
Micro Thai basil (optional)

METHOD

To make the pasta
- Blend the eggs and saffron in a food processor until smooth, sieve the flour into a mixer bowl, make a well in the centre, then pass the egg and saffron mix through a sieve into the well.
- Mix on a medium speed for 8 minutes, stopping halfway through to scrape down the sides of the bowl; turn out and gently knead until smooth then wrap in clingfilm and store in the fridge overnight.

To make the tortellini filling
- Place the crab meat, chilli, ginger, garlic, lime leaves and Thai basil into a bowl, mix until thoroughly combined, season with salt and pepper and set aside.

To make the tortellini
- Pass the pasta through a pasta machine, gradually reducing the thickness, until you get a thin sheet; lay out the pasta sheet on a lightly floured surface and cut out discs with an 8cm round cutter.
- Have a small bowl of cold water ready. Place a teaspoon of the filling into the centre of each pasta disc, dip you finger into the bowl of water and moisten one side of the disc and fold in half, making sure there is no air trapped inside the pasta; with your fingers, tease out the rim where the two halves join so it's the same thickness as the rest of the pasta.
- Wrap the tortellini around your index finger on the filling side, make a crease and pinch the two corners together to firmly seal, making sure there is a lip of pasta around the outside to form the traditional bonnet-like shape.

To make the basil oil
- Place basil and oil into a food processor, blend until smooth, strain the oil through a fine sieve and discard the basil.

To make the sauce
- Heat the coconut oil in a saucepan over a medium heat, add the shallots, garlic and ginger and cook, stirring frequently, for a couple of minutes.
- Add the fish stock, lime leaves, lemongrass and chopped carrot then simmer for about 20 minutes, until reduced by half.
- Strain the broth through a sieve into a clean saucepan, discard the vegetables and herbs and return the saucepan to the heat; add the coconut milk, bring to a simmer and reduce to a thin sauce consistency then season with salt and pepper to taste and turn the heat to its lowest setting to keep the sauce warm.

To cook the tortellini
- Bring a large saucepan of salted water to a rapid boil, add the tortellini and cook for 3–4 minutes until the pasta is al dente and the filling is cooked through to the middle.

To serve
- Drain the tortellini, place into a mixing bowl and fold in the sauce.
- Portion the tortellini into pasta bowls, drizzle over the basil oil and garnish with the coconut shavings and micro Thai basil (if using).

VEGETARIAN/VEGAN ALTERNATIVE
- Replace the crab with a mixture of chopped tofu, seaweed and mashed chickpeas for the tortellini filling, make the sauce with vegetable stock and, for vegan pasta, use the recipe below.

For vegan pasta
240g semolina flour
120g plain flour
250ml hot water

- Place the semolina and flour into a food processor then blend in the water until you get a firm dough; wrap in clingfilm and refrigerate overnight.

Solomon Islands: Local hero

Sir Jacob Charles Vouza KBE GM

Jacob Vouza was born in 1892 on Guadalcanal, one of the Solomon Islands, and was educated at the South Seas Evangelical Mission School. He joined the Solomon Islands Protectorate Armed Constabulary in 1916, rising through the ranks to Sergeant Major, before retiring after 25 years' service in 1941.

After the Japanese invasion of Guadalcanal in June 1942, Vouza returned to active duty with the British Forces, volunteering as a native scout and coastwatcher for the intelligence-gathering network that the Allies used to observe enemy movements in the Pacific islands.

Following the arrival of United States 1st Marine Division on Guadalcanal on 7 August 1942, Vouza rescued a downed US pilot from Japanese-held territory, guiding him safely to US lines. Using his knowledge of the jungles, Vouza volunteered to scout behind enemy lines in August 1942, but was captured by Japanese forces, who found a small US flag in his possession. Vouza was brutally interrogated but refused to give any information to the enemy. Frustrated Japanese troops tied him to a tree and bayoneted him in the arms, throat, shoulder, face and stomach and left him for dead. However, with an almost superhuman determination, Vouza did not die that day. Using his teeth to untie himself, he crawled through miles of jungle to the US lines where he received urgent medical aid and warned the US forces of an impending attack. His information allowed the 2nd Battalion 1st Marines located at the Ilu River just enough time – 10 minutes – to prepare their defences for the upcoming attack. In the subsequent Battle of the Tenaru, the Japanese suffered heavy losses. For his astonishing courage and bravery, Vouza was awarded the George Medal by the British, while the US military awarded him the Silver Star and the Legion of Merit.

After the war, Vouza continued serving his country, as President of the Guadalcanal Council and the Solomon Islands Advisory Council. He was awarded the MBE in 1957, and was knighted by Her Majesty The Queen in 1979. Sir Jacob Vouza died on 15 March 1984 and was buried in his Marine Corps tunic. A monument in his honour stands in front of the police headquarters in Honiara, the capital of the Solomon Islands.

Written by Flight Lieutenant RAJ Wells, RAF

"Using his teeth to untie himself, he crawled through miles of jungle to the US lines where he received urgent medical aid and warned the US forces of an impending attack"

A taste of Italy

The Little Pasta Company's home-cooking kits allow you to recreate the fresh, intimate and authentic experience of an Italian restaurant in the comfort of your own home

www.thelittlepastacompany.co.uk

Authentic experiences and lasting memories are at the heart of everything The Little Pasta Company does. "Food is such an emotive thing," says the company's founder Daniel Webber-Quick. "My wife always jokes: 'You can't remember what I told you to do last week, but you can tell me what you ate when you were six in a restaurant in Italy'."

A childhood spent exploring and tasting the delights of the Italian landscape sparked Daniel's lasting love of food, leading to the launch of this fresh pasta and high-quality meal delivery business in the summer of 2020. Helped by his wife and his sister-in-law, this family business has spent decades in the making. "The first thing I learned to cook was a carbonara," says Daniel. "It was my brother's favourite dish and a real staple in our house. That's really where my love of food started."

The aim of The Little Pasta Company is to create all-natural cook-at-home cuisine as authentic as the most intimate Italian restaurant. "I get up around 3am and make all the sauces and pasta fresh to order," says Daniel. "I'm not producing a product that's got loads of stabilisers or preservatives, it's fresh, it's dispatched the day it's made."

Italian is the language of love so it's no surprise that the date-night meal kits are the most popular products, including the best-selling slow-cooked beef and red wine ragu, which comes with truffle-butter tagliatelle and side dishes including cured meats and vegetarian antipasti. "It's about creating those special moments at home," says Daniel. "A lot of people buy them as gifts for someone – it's more than giving something physical, it's about saying I'm thinking of you in that moment."

In little under a year, this family business has grown big enough to warrant a move into commercial premises, bolstered by support from pop stars, actors and publications such as *Vanity Fair* and *Hello!* magazine. Plans for the future include a wedding service and food truck, not to mention festivals and markets. "It's the feedback that makes it so worthwhile," says Daniel. "When I hear from the recipient saying how much they love it, it puts a smile on my face."

Cawl

Lance Corporal Ben Stewart, Army

Dating back to the 14th century, cawl is the national dish of Wales. In modern Welsh, the word cawl is used to describe any soup, stew or broth; however, in English, it refers to the traditional Welsh stew "cawl Cymreig". If you're looking for a great dish to cook on a cold evening or a tasty winter's lunch, look no further than a bowl of cawl. This version is inspired by traditional recipes and I've used an array of vegetables to modernise and enhance what was once a super-simple meal. I've also added a little flour to thicken the broth; traditionally the unthickened broth would be served as a starter and the meat, vegetables and potatoes served as the main course alongside bread to fill out the meal. I suggest serving it as a main course alongside some really fresh crusty bread. Although lamb neck fillets make a great-tasting cawl, my preference is to use lamb leg steak as I think it gives a better flavour.

Preparation time: 30 minutes
Cooking time: 2 hours

Serves 6

INGREDIENTS

3 tbsp plain flour
400g lamb leg steaks or neck fillets,
  cut into 2cm dice
2 tbsp olive oil
1 large white onion, peeled and cut
  into large dice
2 large potatoes, peeled and cut into
  large chunks
2 carrots, peeled and cut into
  large chunks
½ swede, peeled and cut into
  large chunks
1 medium turnip, peeled and cut into
  large chunks
2 parsnips, peeled and cut into
  large chunks
1 small bunch of thyme
2 leeks, finely shredded
Handful of parsley, coarsely chopped
Sea salt and cracked black pepper

METHOD

• Place the flour in a large mixing bowl, season generously and mix well.
• Toss the lamb in the seasoned flour to thoroughly coat and shake off the excess.
• Heat the olive oil in a casserole or large pan over a medium-high heat, add the lamb and cook, stirring frequently, for about 5 minutes until the meat is well browned (do this in a couple of batches to avoid overcrowding the pan); transfer the lamb to a large plate or bowl with a slotted spoon and set aside.
• Add the chopped onions to the hot oil and fry, stirring frequently, until they are well caramelised (this will bring a sweet hint to your dish); once your onions are caramelised return the lamb to the casserole (including any juices that have collected on the plate), turn the heat to low, add 1.8 litres of water and bring to a simmer.
• Once the water has begun to simmer add the potatoes, carrots, swede, turnips, parsnips and thyme, season generously, cover with a lid and simmer, stirring occasionally, for 1 hour 40 minutes, ensuring the liquid simmers very gently to ensure the vegetables don't overcook.
• Check the lamb (it should be moist and tender), add the leeks, give it a good stir before replacing the lid and simmering for a further 20 minutes.
• Remove the casserole from the heat, check the seasoning, remove the thyme stalk and stir in the chopped parsley.
• Serve in large bowls with some crusty bread; fresh tiger bread is a great accompaniment to this classic meal.

Group Captain Lionel Wilmot Brabazon Rees
VC OBE MC AFC

Lionel Wilmot Brabazon Rees was born in Caernarfon on 31 July 1884. He was educated at Eastbourne College before following in his father's footsteps and entering the Royal Military Academy at Woolwich as a gentleman cadet, joining the Royal Garrison Artillery at the age of 19.

Obsessed by planes, Rees learned to fly at his own expense, and was seconded to the newly formed Royal Flying Corps in 1914, initially as an instructor. He first saw action flying the Vickers Gunbus with No. 11 Squadron RFC in 1915, earning a reputation as an aggressive pilot. In July 1915, Rees managed to shoot down an enemy biplane despite having his main and rear spar damaged. In August that same year he was engaged in an aerial dogfight for over 45 minutes, having to return to the base for more ammunition before going back to destroy the enemy aircraft. On 21 September, he attacked a faster, more manoeuvrable German biplane by divebombing it. For his conspicuous gallantry and skill, Rees was awarded the Military Cross on 29 October 1915.

On 1 July 1916, during the Somme offensive, Rees was attacked by a German patrol. Against the odds, he forced away the first German attacker and seriously damaged two more German planes. He chased two others and was wounded in the thigh, but recovered enough to use up all his ammunition while firing at close range. He returned home safely but spent several weeks in hospital, ending up with a permanent limp. For his valour and courage, Rees was awarded the Victoria Cross by King George V on 14 December 1916.

For the rest of the war, Rees commanded the Air Fighting School in Ayr. In 1918, he was awarded the Air Force Cross, and in 1919 the OBE. In 1920, he was made a freeman of Caernarfon. Rees retired from the RAF in 1931 and in 1933 he single-handedly crossed the Atlantic, travelling in a ketch from Wales to the Bahamas, where he later lived. During the Second World War, Rees rejoined the RAF as a Wing Commander and commanded an aerodrome in the Middle East. He retired in December 1942 as a Group Captain and returned to his new home in the Bahamas where he passed away in September 1955. A plaque in the medieval tower at Porth yr Aur commemorates him, and in 2019 a RAF BAe 146 jet from 32 Squadron was named in his honour.

Written by Emma Adams, widow of Major Gareth Rhys-Evans, Intelligence Corps, Army

A hit of home

One of Britain's most celebrated brands for nearly a
century, Branston Pickle's unique, tangy taste and crunch
still provides an emotional connection with customers

bringoutthebranston.co.uk

Generations of Britons have grown up knowing the special tang of Branston Pickle, so when Branston launched a new advertising campaign in 2020 it was easy to remind viewers that the taste and emotional connection for consumers with Branston was like "a hit of home". Just like the long-running "Bring Out The Branston" campaign, the advert proved to be a smash hit, demonstrating that Branston – as it approaches its centenary in 2022 – continues to hold a special place in the affections of the British public. "It's all about the comforting feeling people get when they taste Branston or even see that familiar packaging," says Angharad Wilson Dyer Gough, the Senior Brand Manager for Branston Pickle. "It instantly connects them to home. That is such a powerful feeling."

Branston Pickle has had a place on the British dining table since 1922. Thought of as mysteriously exotic and unmistakably delicious, it was named after the village of Branston in Staffordshire where it was made, and swiftly became the country's best loved and most popular brand of sweet pickle, the first choice of millions when they wanted to jazz up a cheese sandwich or shepherd's pie. Production moved to Bermondsey in south London in 1926, where the smell of pickle became indelibly linked to the area. The Bermondsey factory closed in 1969 and the company has been located in Bury St Edmunds since 2004, by which time Branston Pickle was firmly established as one of the country's most cherished condiments, having been voted one of the UK's top 50 brands of the 20th century in 1999.

In 2013, Branston was acquired by Japanese firm Mizkan, which has proudly maintained the Branston heritage while introducing new products into the market. "For a long time we relied on the heritage and very recognisable adverts like 'Bring out the Branston'," says Angharad. "Since 2013 we've introduced new products to ensure Branston's legacy for years to come." Additions include the chutney and relish ranges, including Mediterranean Tomato Chutney, Caramelised Onion Chutney, Orchard Fruity Chutney, Dorset Ale & Apple Chutney, Tomato & Red Pepper Relish and Branston Rich & Fruity Sauce.

Unchanged since 1922 is the iconic Branston Original pickle itself – a combination of root vegetable, sugar, vinegar and spices, cooked to a secret recipe. "For millions of customers around the world, Branston Pickle is the taste that creates the ultimate sandwich," says Angharad. And, with the small chunk and smooth variants available, consumers are able to also choose their perfect level of crunch, without taking away the tangy taste they know and love. Looking to the future Branston is exploring new packaging options to improve its packaging recyclability and the amount of recycled plastic used in its squeezy bottles.

Throughout all these developments, Branston Pickle is still made to its traditional recipe using tried-and-trusted methods in the company's factory in Bury St Edmunds. And it continues to be a hugely popular condiment, passed down through the generations, a treasured national heirloom in a distinctive jar. "The hardest thing for any brand leader to do is maintain your place without diminishing quality," says Angharad. "But we are fortunate in that our customers are very loyal. Part of the reason we have been around for so long is that Branston is trusted to deliver on flavour and crunch – when they open a jar, people know exactly what they are getting every time."

Chutney Camembert catherine wheels

Ready in 40 minutes
Serves 4

INGREDIENTS

1 x sheet of ready rolled puff pastry
2–3 tbsp of Branston Mediterranean
  Tomato Chutney
200g grated Cheddar
1 egg
1 wheel of Camembert

METHOD

• Preheat oven to 180°C.
• Spread a sheet of puff pastry with Branston's Tomato Chutney and sprinkle Cheddar cheese over the top.
• Roll the sheet of puff pastry from the bottom, upwards so that you are left with a long sausage. Slice this into swirls, roughly 2cm wide.
• Lay the swirls out around the wheel of Camembert, on a baking tray.
• Brush the edges of the pastry with egg wash and bake for 30 minutes, until puffed out and golden. Impress friends and family by adding these delicious swirls and baked Camembert to your next cheese board.

Vegan sausage roll

Made with Branston Small Chunk Pickle

Ready in 45 minutes
Serves 4

INGREDIENTS

1 tbsp olive oil
½ an onion, finely diced
1 clove of garlic, finely diced
6 sprigs of sage, finely chopped
800g chestnut mushrooms, finely diced
50g roasted walnuts, finely chopped
50g roasted hazelnuts, finely chopped
50g roasted cashew nuts, finely chopped
200g vegan cheese, grated
1 roll of shop-bought puff pastry
3–4 tbsp Branston's Small Chunk Pickle
Vegan butter to glaze

METHOD

• Preheat the oven to 200°C.
• Soften the onion, garlic, sage and mushrooms with the oil in a large pan for 10–15 minutes, then turn off the heat and stir in the roasted nuts and grated vegan cheese.
• Cut a sheet of puff pastry in half, widthways; spread Branston's Small Chunk Pickle down the centre of each half and top with the mushroom mixture.
• Fold each sheet of pastry over the filling and crimp around the edges with a fork to seal.
• Gently score each roll and brush with vegan butter.
• Place your vegan sausage rolls on a lined baking tray and bake in the oven for 25 minutes until golden and puffed out.

Safe and sound

Staffordshire-based firm EBB has become a one-stop
shop for all health-and-safety requirements, from
fire safety to occupational safety

www.ebblimited.co.uk

Health and safety is an area which is constantly in the spotlight, with awareness growing as to how vital it is to get it right at every level. Eric Barbour (pictured, above), owner of EBB Ltd, has 30 years' experience in this field, yet he would say that he never stops learning. "I had 23 years' service in the Royal Marines focused on weapon safety," he says. "When I left the services I moved into a group health and safety role at Lloyds Banking Group where I continued in the same line of work for 20 years and, in 2015, I decided to use that combined knowledge and expertise to set up EBB Ltd in Staffordshire. The aim was to build a business which offered clients cost effective and quality health and safety practices, as well as providing ongoing support on any issues causing them concern."

This network of support inspired such confidence in clients that the business continued to evolve. "A client asked me to do their fire extinguishers check, a service I didn't offer then," says Eric. "I gave them contact details for another firm and they very quickly came back and said they preferred my working methods, so I decided to train for my

BAFE (British Approvals for Fire Equipment) qualifications and make that service part of what I offered. I also qualified in health-and-safety training, as that was a further service my clients needed and I'm now looking for apprentices to take the business forward."

As an authorised stockist and supplier of fire extinguisher and fire safety products, and also fire door inspections, EBB Ltd has grown into a one-stop point of contact and services for local businesses, becoming a finalist at Newcastle-under-Lyme Business Boost Awards in 2019. Eric is also an approved Institution of Occupational Safety and Health (IOSH) and National Examination Board in Occupational Safety and Health (NEBOSH), and holds PETALS (Preparing to Teach in The Life Long Learning Sector) qualifications allowing the delivery of a variety of courses onsite and in-house.

"Diversifying has made this business," says Eric. "Once customers work with me, they want to keep me and I want to keep them, so if I'm asked for something new, that's the next qualification and service I aim for."

Staffordshire oatcakes with yeomanry sauce

Warrant Officer 1 Catering Services Jason Deane, Royal Navy

Staffordshire

The oatcake is synonymous with Staffordshire, so much so that Stoke City FC's fanzine is called The Oatcake. The Staffordshire oatcake is different to those found in other areas of the UK. Rather than being a cake or biscuit, it is more akin to a pancake, often eaten with savoury toppings and fillings or as an accompaniment to a breakfast fry-up. As with many parts of the UK, Staffordshire has more than one associated regional dish, and an almost forgotten dish from the county is the yeomanry pudding, which is, in fact, a pie filled with an almond custard. I have chosen this custard as a sauce to accompany my oatcakes.

Vegetarian
Preparation time: 1 hour
Cooking time: 20 minutes

Makes about 10 oatcakes

INGREDIENTS

For the oatcakes
225g fine oatmeal (you can grind
  porridge oats in a food processor)
225g whole-wheat or plain flour
  (or half of each)
1 tsp salt
1 tsp caster sugar
7g (1 sachet) fast-acting dried yeast
420ml warm milk
420ml warm water
Butter to cook

For the yeomanry sauce
225ml single cream
340ml whole milk
115g granulated sugar
½ tsp vanilla essence
6 egg yolks
1½ tsp almond essence

To serve
Strawberry or raspberry jam

METHOD

For the oatcake batter
• Place the oatmeal, flour, salt and sugar in a bowl, add the yeast
  to one side, keeping it apart from the salt.
• Mix the warm milk and water together and gradually add to the dry
  ingredients, mixing it with your fingers or a wooden spoon as you scrape
  the mixture down from the sides of the bowl; add all of the liquid until
  you have a smooth batter the consistency of thick double cream.
• Cover the bowl with a clean damp tea towel and place in a warm dry
  place for an hour.

For the sauce
• Heat the milk, cream, 55g of the sugar and vanilla essence in a heavy-based
  saucepan over a low heat, bring to a gentle simmer (do not allow to boil)
  and set aside.
• Whisk together the egg yolks, remaining sugar and almond essence in a bowl.
• Whisk a ladleful of the warm liquid into the egg mixture and, once fully
  incorporated, whisk in another ladle of the liquid; continue this process
  until the egg mixture is warm to the touch.
• Pour the egg mix into the remaining milk and cream in the saucepan and
  return to a gentle heat, stirring continuously, ensuring that you scrape the
  thickening mixture away from the edge of the pan, until the custard is thick
  enough to coat the back of the spoon.

To cook the oatcakes
• Heat a large frying pan or griddle over a medium heat, add a knob of
  butter and, once melted, ladle in enough batter to make an oatcake
  of about 15cm across and 4mm thick.
• Once bubbles appear on the surface, turn the oatcake over and cook
  until golden brown on both sides.

To serve
• Spread the oatcakes with jam, fold in half and serve two per portion with
  the yeomanry sauce.

Sergeant Ernest Albert Egerton VC

Ernest Egerton was born in Longton, near Stoke-on-Trent on 10 November 1897. After being educated at Queen Street, Crook Street and Blurton Church Schools in Longton, he took a job as a haulage hand by the Florence Coal and Iron Company. Following the outbreak of war in Europe, Ernest enlisted in the 3rd North Staffordshire Regiment on 27 November 1915, transferring to the 1st North Staffordshire in Boulogne and then on to the 16th Sherwood Foresters in November 1916, eventually being promoted to Lance Corporal and Corporal in 1917.

On 20 September 1917, Ernest and his regiment were south-east of Ypres, Belgium, during the Battle of Passchendaele. Following incessant bombardment of enemy positions, the regiment charged through the smoke and fog to assault the German lines. Due to the poor visibility, the two leading waves of the attack passed over hostile enemy dugouts without clearing them; allowing enemy gunfire from these dugouts to cause severe casualties. Ernest immediately responded to a call for duty for volunteers to help in clearing up the situation and he dashed for the dugouts under heavy fire at short range. He was the first to arrive at the enemy position and by the time the support had arrived, Ernest had shot a rifleman, a bomber and a gunner, and 29 of the enemy had surrendered.

Ernest was granted leave from 1–5 December 1917; this was extended to 19 December to allow Ernest to be presented with the Victoria Cross at Buckingham Palace. He then returned to France, where he was promoted to Sergeant in May 1918. In August 1918, he returned to the UK to

"By the time the support had arrived, Ernest had shot a rifleman, a bomber and a gunner, and 29 of the enemy had surrendered"

commence officer training, but decided against taking a commission and became an instructor in Sunderland.

After surviving a gas attack during the war, Ernest was troubled with tuberculosis and as a result was discharged in April 1919. He went on to serve with the Home Guard during the Second World War, as well as becoming a lodge man for the Staffordshire Potteries, Meir Heath for 14 years. He died in February 1966. There is a plaque on the wall of his house in Uttoxeter Road, Blythe Bridge in remembrance, and his VC is on display at the Sherwood Foresters Museum in Nottingham Castle.

Written by Warrant Officer Guy Davies, Army (retired)

Sussex bacon, apple and blue cheese tart

Catering Services Lasarusa Tuimanu, Royal Navy

My tart is based on the traditional Sussex churdle, which dates back to the 17th century. A churdle is essentially a type of pie filled with liver, bacon and herbs; the filling is piled into the centre of a square or disc of pastry and the sides are pulled up and over the filling before baking. It is supposed that the churdle derived its name from this method of filling the pie – "churd" is an old English word meaning to churn or turn over. As with many early variations of pies and pasties, churdles were probably made for Sussex farm workers to take out to work, where they would sustain them throughout a day of hard labour. My alternative version of this dish replaces the liver with blue cheese, something for which Sussex is well known, and, rather than form the churdle into a pie, I have kept it open as a tart.

Preparation time: 20 minutes
Cooking time: 30–40 minutes

Serves 4

INGREDIENTS

200g puff pastry
10g lightly salted butter
½ small red onion, thinly sliced
1 apple, peeled and cut into 1cm dice
2 tbsp honey
4 rashers smoked back bacon, cut
   into 1cm dice
1 tbsp water
50g Sussex blue cheese, crumbled
10g hazelnuts, grated
1 tbsp fresh thyme leaves
1 egg, beaten
Salt and freshly ground black pepper
25g rocket
4 tbsp balsamic vinegar

METHOD

• Preheat the oven to 180°C.
• Lightly dust your worktop with flour, roll out your puff pastry to about 2mm thickness (if you're not using ready-rolled puff pastry) and cut into four equal squares.
• With a sharp knife, score a 1cm border around each square, ensuring you do not cut through the pastry.
• Place the squares of pastry onto a baking tray lined with baking parchment, cover with clingfilm and place in the fridge until the filling is ready.
• Melt the butter in a saucepan over a medium heat and, when foaming, add the sliced red onion; cook, stirring frequently, for 8–10 minutes until lightly caramelised.
• Add the diced apple, honey, bacon and water to the onions and simmer for between 8–10 minutes until the bacon is cooked and the apples are tender; season with salt and pepper to taste.
• Neatly spread equal amounts of the filling within the scored border of each pastry square and brush the border with the beaten egg.
• Bake the tarts for 7 minutes in the preheated oven, then scatter over the crumbled blue cheese and grated hazelnut and sprinkle over the fresh thyme.
• Return to the oven and continue to bake for a further 8–10 minutes, or until the pastry is golden brown and puffed-up around the edges.
• Serve warm with rocket drizzled with balsamic vinegar.

VEGETARIAN/VEGAN ALTERNATIVE
• For a vegetarian alternative, replace the bacon with sliced chestnut mushrooms.

Wing Commander John Bell MBE DFC LoH

John Bell was born in Wandsworth on 25 March 1923 and raised around London and Surrey. In June 1941, aged 18, he fulfilled his boyhood dream by enlisting in the Royal Air Force. Between May and December 1942 he was taken to Oudtshoorn, South Africa with the 45th Air School to conduct flight training. He was considered too tall to be a pilot, so he trained as an observer, which included navigation, bombing and air gunnery. On his return to the UK, Bell was selected as a bomb-aimer and posted to No. 619 Squadron at RAF Woodhall Spa. It was there that he first flew in the Lancaster bombers, completing numerous raids on Berlin and the Ruhr Valley.

As Bell and some of his crew had not reached the significant achievement of completing their 30 operations, they came to a joint decision to carry on as a "crew" and volunteered to fly with No. 617 "Dambusters" Squadron. Still operating as an observer and bomb-aimer on the Lancaster bomber, Bell continued with raids on northern France.

Bell and his crew were involved in one of the many counter-intelligence operations surrounding the D-Day landings – Operation Taxable. On the evening of 5 June 1944, eight Lancasters flew towards the French coast, two miles apart at 3,000ft while flying at 180mph. When they neared the French coast these crews dropped bundles of aluminium foil in order to jam the German radars – a "smoke screen" to hide the largest amphibious invasion in history.

In total, Bell completed 50 operations through the war and was awarded the Distinguished Flying Cross for "acts of valour, courage or devotion to duty whilst flying in active operations against the enemy". He was also awarded an MBE, and a Legion d'Honneur from the French president.

After the war, Bell returned to his previous employment as an accountant but this time for the RAF, stationed in Berlin. On his return to the UK in 1951, he transferred to become a photographic interpreter – examining aerial reconnaissance images for the RAF – which remained his career for the next 25 years. He was heavily involved with the RAF Bomber Command Memorial in Green Park, London – the "bomb aimer" figure is modelled on him. He is still active with his local RBL branch in Storrington, West Sussex.

Written by Chief Petty Officer Ryan "Barney" Barnett, Royal Navy

> *"When they neared the French coast these crews dropped bundles of aluminium foil in order to jam the German radars, hiding the largest amphibious invasion in history"*

Taking care with your food

Avery Healthcare's care homes make sure that its award-winning chefs give residents the finest and most nutritious food – and that includes easy-to-eat cutlery-free meals

www.averyhealthcare.co.uk

Food is important for people of all ages, vital as much for its social value as its nutritional content. That's why Avery Healthcare has always placed food at the centre of its offering to the residents of the 59 premium care homes it operates in England. All kitchens are of a professional standard and staffed by award-winning chefs who ensure that mealtime is a social highlight for residents. This core offering will be enhanced still further in 2021, with the arrival of an exciting new concept in care-home dining – cutlery-free food that has been carefully designed for the many residents who have conditions that impact on their motor skills but who still want to be able to feed themselves while sitting at a table with their friends.

"There are many reasons why a person may have difficulty using cutlery to eat a meal or a snack," explains Jo Crossland, Avery's Head of Dementia Care. "Conditions such as Parkinson's disease, arthritis or a stroke can all affect how an individual can manipulate cutlery. Cognitive illnesses, including dementia, can cause a person to have difficulty processing their environment or cause problems with sequencing and coordinating actions."

Up to 70 per cent of residents have some form of memory loss, and as dementia progresses it can often lead to a loss of motor skills. These residents often don't want to be fed by carers, so to help such residents remain independent and involved during one of the most sociable and positive times of the day, Jo, along with Simon Lawrence, Avery's Head of Culinary and Hospitality, created a comprehensive solution in the form of cutlery-free dining. This would need to be more than just finger food, which would not satisfy

dietary requirements. So the challenge was to create delicious and nutritious food that could be eaten by hand without falling apart while still delivering essential nutritional value. The result has been an expansive menu that includes such delights as an entire roast meal, carefully designed, cooked and proportioned to be eaten by hand.

"As chefs working in the care sector, it is of fundamental importance that we continue to develop and innovate through our culinary teams," says Simon. "Finger foods have often been a misunderstood concept. A chef new to the sector may visualise buffet items, but that is an inaccurate perception. We have worked hard to develop strong guidance and comprehensive training that ensures that all our chefs can adapt everyday menu choices into cutlery-free meals. With guidance and encouragement, we are limited only by our imagination."

Every day within its care homes, Avery chefs cook for residents, including many military veterans, who enjoy the culinary delights. The company has developed a training programme for chefs and staff to ensure the new menu is available at all care homes. "We have a collective responsibility to ensure that every resident living in a care home environment can enjoy nutritious, appetising meals and snacks every day," says Jo. "At Avery, we work tirelessly to ensure that residents are treated with dignity and respect in every aspect of their lives, and mealtimes are no exception. In the development and implementation of our comprehensive approach to cutlery-free dining we will ensure that our residents receive the very best nutritional support we can offer every day."

Mupotohayi (cornmeal cake)

Catering Services Carlos Kalowekmo, Royal Navy

Maize is probably the most common staple food consumed throughout Africa and, depending on the dish being prepared, it is cooked in various ways – boiled, steamed or roasted. Mupotohayi (also called chimodho) is a form of cornmeal bread common in the part of southern Africa formerly known as Southern Rhodesia and now known as Zimbabwe, and was hugely popular in the 1980s and 1990s. It is best served buttered and/or with jam or marmalade but can also be eaten plain. African cornmeal cake has many different names and different recipes depending on which country it comes from. This is my take on the popular Zimbabwean version.

Vegetarian
Preparation time: 15 minutes
Cooking time: 45 minutes

Serves 4

INGREDIENTS

120ml buttermilk
1 tbsp vegetable oil
1 medium egg
60g cornmeal
15g ground almonds
60g plain flour
1 tsp baking powder
½ tsp bicarbonate of soda
A pinch of salt
30g caster sugar
1 tsp lemon zest

METHOD

• Preheat the oven to 180°C, brush the inside of a 450g loaf tin with oil and dust with a little flour.
• In a jug, mix the buttermilk, vegetable oil and egg together and set aside.
• Sieve the cornmeal, ground almonds, flour, baking powder, bicarbonate of soda and salt into a large bowl then mix in the caster sugar.
• Make a well in the middle of the dry ingredients, pour in the buttermilk mix and slowly bring it all together into the centre with a fork.
• Once all of the liquid has been added ensure it is thoroughly mixed and well combined, creating a thick batter then fold in the lemon zest.
• Pour the batter into the loaf tin and bake for 45 minutes or until a cocktail stick pierced into the centre comes out clean.
• Leave the cake to rest in the tin for 10 minutes then transfer to a wire rack to cool before cutting into thick slices.

Zimbabwe: Local hero

Squadron Leader Ioannis Agorastos "John" Plagis DSO, DFC & Bar

Ioannis Agorastos Plagis, known to all as "John", was born one of six siblings on 10 March 1919 in Gadzema, in what was then Southern Rhodesia, and showed an early love for flying. Following the outbreak of the Second World War, he volunteered for the Southern Rhodesian Air Force but was turned down as his Greek ancestry made him a foreign national. In 1940, after Greece joined the war on the side of the Allies, Plagis was accepted into the RAF, passing out of training at the rank of Flight Sergeant.

He started with the No. 266 (Rhodesia) Squadron flying Spitfires, where he painted a letter "K" on the side of his aircraft, after his adored sister Kay. As a Flying Officer he helped to protect the island of Malta, which was being besieged by the Germans and Italians. After his best friend was shot down, Plagis pledged to "shoot down ten for Doug". He shot down five enemy aircraft in the next two weeks, earning him the Distinguished Flying Cross (DFC) and the title of "Spitfire Ace". Within three months he had completed his pledge of downing ten enemy aircraft, earning himself a Bar to the DFC. At one point, Plagis led a flight of four Spitfires against 180 German bombers and 80 fighters, taking four of them down in the process.

As commanding officer of 64 Squadron and 126 Squadron, he and his crews provided cover for the invasion of Normandy. He was shot down over France during Operation Market Garden at Arnhem but escaped with minor injuries. Plagis survived the war as a Squadron Leader with a full tally of 16 kills and many damages. Along with his DFC & Bar he also received the Distinguished Service Order and the Airman's Cross from the Netherlands. He was described as "a brave and resourceful leader whose example has proved a rare source of inspiration".

Plagis was promoted to Wing Commander before retiring to Rhodesia in 1948 as the country's most distinguished flying ace. A road in the capital Salisbury (now Harare) was named John Plagis Avenue in his honour. He opened a bottle store bearing his name, was a director of several companies (including Central African Airways) and unsuccessfully contested one of the capital's constituencies in 1962. He married in 1954 and had three sons and a daughter before his death in 1974.

Written by Lieutenant Seb Sheppard, Royal Navy (retired)

"At one point Plagis led a flight of four Spitfires against 180 German bombers and 80 fighters, taking four of them down in the process"

Ale and hearty

Home to the tallest chimney in Swindon, Arkell's Brewery has been producing some of the country's finest handcrafted stouts, lagers, bitters and pale ales for nearly two centuries

www.arkells.com

At its distinguished Knightsbridge location in London, members of the Special Forces Club meet to swap stories and remember old friends while drinking excellent beer, provided by Arkell's Brewery in Wiltshire. It's an apt choice of ale. Arkell's was founded in 1843 and has had a strong connection to the military for 150 years. Current chairman James Arkell, who was in the Territorial Army and commanded the Royal Yeomanry Regiment, reels off a list of the family's military connections all the way from his great-great-great-grandfather, who joined the Second Wiltshire Rifle Corps in 1888, to his son who served in Afghanistan. "We have beer and military service running through the family veins," says James, whose father served in the Special Operations Executive during the Second World War and was awarded an OBE while chairman of Arkell's.

You can hardly miss the Arkell's brewery in Swindon – it's the building with the tallest chimney in town. While Arkell's beer can be found in regional supermarkets and online, the company proudly maintains a local focus, providing beer to the five surrounding counties in which it runs around 100 pubs and a number of small hotels. That allows Arkell's to have a bigger impact on the local community, building strong bonds with customers. As a brewer, Arkell's finds a balance between tradition and innovation but always grounded in quality. The company has a lager called Malthouse and has recently developed an American Pale Ale called Voyager, but the most popular beer on draught remains the "very quaffable" BBB, a best bitter that it has produced since 1910. They also produce one-offs and seasonal specialities, including a beer for the Duchess of Cornwall when she visited to help celebrate Arkell's 175th anniversary.

"We are still based in our Victorian brewery and still use open fermenters, but to get the flavours now you have to get all sorts of hops from around the world," explains James. "English hops have excellent flavour but they didn't have the strength and those citrus notes, so we have to look further afield. We have to adapt, while maintaining our core traditions. Running a brewery is much like being in the Army, and we keep soldiering along."

Chapter two

Main courses

Our main courses take you on a global culinary journey. As well as British classics like Yorkshire pudding, Cockney pie and mash, toad in the hole, fish and chips, Lancashire hotpot and Scouse, you'll find unique pies from Gibraltar, Gloucestershire, Northamptonshire, Leicestershire, Kent, Scotland and the Isle of Man; curries from London, Birmingham, India, South Africa and Nigeria; and delicious seafood dishes from Essex, Cornwall, Bermuda, Australia, Sussex, Mauritius, St Helena and Grenada.

Western Australian fish pie

Leading Chef David Bulpitt, Royal Navy (retired)

This classic, tasty and comforting pie was served in many Australian households as a way of getting some "brain food" into the kids, without breaking the bank. Cheaper cuts of fish could be used and, with "mousetrap" cheese in the sauce and mash on the top, it made a lovely winter warmer. Fish pie used to go down well on board the Navy ships, too, so now I've recreated it with some delicious additions from the shores of Western Australia; with fresh produce in abundance it is still a firm family favourite.

Australia

Preparation time: 40 minutes
Cooking time: 15–20 minutes

Serves 6

INGREDIENTS

For the mashed potato

1kg floury potatoes, peeled and
   coarsely chopped
85g butter
80ml single cream
Pinch of freshly grated nutmeg

For the pie filling

500ml milk
1 brown onion, peeled and quartered
2 dried bay leaves
2 sprigs fresh thyme
6 peppercorns
350g firm white fish fillets (such as
   snapper, dhufish or flathead)
45g butter
2 sticks celery, cut into 1cm dice
1 large carrot, cut into 1cm dice
Fronds from 1 fennel bulb or fresh dill
2 garlic cloves, crushed
50ml good Margaret River Chardonnay
   (you may have to use French!)
40g plain flour
300g of cleaned, de-veined green
   Exmouth prawns (or tiger prawns will do)
12 scallops (with or without roe)
1 tbsp chives, chopped
1 tbsp tarragon, chopped
1 tbsp lemon zest, finely grated
1 tbsp lemon juice
Salt and ground white pepper

METHOD

- Boil the potatoes in salted water until tender, strain through a colander and leave for a few minutes to drain and steam dry.
- Mash the potatoes until smooth, beat in the butter and cream and season with salt, white pepper and a pinch of nutmeg; set aside to cool slightly.
- Place the milk, onion, bay leaves, thyme and peppercorns into a frying pan over low-medium heat and bring to a gentle simmer.
- Add the fish fillets and poach for 3–4 minutes or until fish is just cooked through.
- Transfer the fish to a plate with a slotted spoon and strain the poaching liquid through a sieve into a jug and reserve.
- Preheat the oven to 180°C and flake the fish fillets onto large pieces.
- Heat 25g of the butter in a large saucepan over medium heat, add the celery, carrot, fennel fronds (or dill) and garlic and cook, stirring occasionally, for about 5 minutes until vegetables have started to soften.
- Add the wine and simmer rapidly for about 2 minutes or until almost completely evaporated.
- Reduce the heat to low-medium, add the flour and cook, stirring continuously, for a couple of minutes.
- Gradually stir in the reserved fish poaching milk, bring to a simmer and cook, stirring frequently, for 5 minutes or until the sauce is smooth and thickened; season with salt and ground white pepper.
- Remove from the heat and stir in the flaked fish, prawns, scallops, chives, tarragon, lemon zest and juice; pour the mixture into a 2-litre baking dish.
- Top with the creamy mash, dot the remaining butter over the top and bake in the preheated oven for 15–20 minutes or until bubbling around the edges and golden brown on top.

Captain William J Rowlinson DCM & Bar

William "Bill" Josiah Rowlinson was born in Balgowlah, New South Wales in 1919. He joined the Australian Army in 1941 but his regiment never saw service outside of Australia during the Second World War. After the war he served as a volunteer in tropical disease research with 113 Australian General Hospital before leaving the Australian Army in 1946.

On 25 June 1950, North Korean forces, supported by China and the Soviet Union, crossed the border into South Korea and initiated the Korean War. The UN Security Council denounced the invasion and authorised forces to aid South Korea, and Australia was one of the countries to answer the UN's call. At this point, Bill re-enlisted with 3rd Battalion, Royal Australian Regiment, as a corporal. It was during the Battle of Kapyang on 22–25 April 1951 that he earned his first medal for gallantry. He and a number of his section were wounded during enemy attacks, but Bill refused to abandon his position, ordering the remaining wounded to be evacuated while he led his section against continuous assault. Approximately 150 enemy personnel attacked his position but Bill's section repelled the assault, killing 25 enemy troops. For his bravery and leadership, he was awarded the Distinguished Conduct Medal (DCM).

Bill was promoted to sergeant and, while taking part in Operation Commando (3–12 October 1951), he again demonstrated his leadership under fire during an attack on Hill 317 with the Commonwealth Division (known as the First Battle of Maryang-San), launched to prevent Chinese forces from attacking UN supply lines near Seoul. On 5 October, the company commander was wounded near the start of the battle and Bill was put in charge of 12 Platoon. He swiftly led the charge under a fusillade of gun fire. Despite being wounded in the leg he continued to lead his troops without seeking medical help. By the end of the day, the platoon had completed its objectives, killing 32 enemy troops and capturing 14. It is widely accepted as the greatest Australian feat of the Korean War. For his leadership and bravery, Bill was awarded a Bar to his DCM.

In early 1952 he gained a commission as a lieutenant but, later that year, was involved in a training accident where an explosion led to the amputation of his right hand and forearm. He still remained in the Army until 1957, retiring as a captain. He died in 1998. A 1980 portrait of him by John Bloomfield is in the collection of the Australian War Museum.

Written by Joan Murray, wife of the late Sergeant George Murray of the 13/18 Royal Hussars

> ## "Approximately 150 enemy personnel attacked his position but Bill's section repelled the assault, killing 25 enemy troops"

Fried fish and fungi

Flight Sergeant Stu Harmer, RAF (retired)

Fungi (pronounced "foon-gee") is a traditional staple of the British Virgin Islands (BVI) diet. It is generally served with boiled fish and is essentially cornmeal boiled with okra. There are, however, many variations of sauces and preparation. In my recipe, rather than boil the fish, I have flavoured it with some typical BVI spices and sea salt, pan-fried it and served it on the fungi with the sauce ladled over the top. Unless you live in a metropolitan area, cornmeal can sometimes be quite hard to get hold of – if you can't find it you can substitute it for polenta, which is basically coarse ground cornmeal, but your fungi won't be as smooth as when using fine yellow cornmeal.

Preparation time: 30 minutes
Cooking time: 35 minutes

Serves 4

INGREDIENTS

For the sauce
2 tbsp vegetable oil
1 medium onion, finely diced
1 stick of celery, finely diced
1 red pepper, cut into 5mm dice
2 garlic cloves, finely chopped or crushed
1cm piece of ginger, grated
1 red chilli, halved lengthways
 and shredded
½ cinnamon stick (or ¼ tsp ground)
1 tsp dried thyme
1 tsp ground allspice
¼ tsp chilli flakes
1 tsp tomato purée
400ml passata
2 tsp white wine vinegar
2 ripe tomatoes, seeds removed
 and cut into 5mm dice
2 tbsp parsley, coarsely chopped
1 lime, juiced
Salt and freshly ground black pepper

For the fungi
500ml water
¼ tsp salt
150g okra, cut into 1cm slices
125g fine yellow cornmeal
25g butter
Freshly ground black pepper

For the fish
4 fish fillets (such as snapper, red mullet,
 bream or sea bass)
1 lime
1 tsp sea salt
¼ tsp cracked black pepper
¼ tsp dried thyme
Pinch of ground nutmeg
Pinch of ground cloves
1 tbsp vegetable oil

METHOD

To make the sauce

- Heat the oil in a sauté pan or saucepan over a medium heat, add the onions and celery and cook, stirring frequently, for 5 minutes until the vegetables have softened.
- Stir in the red pepper, garlic, ginger, red chilli, cinnamon stick, thyme, allspice and chilli flakes and continue to cook for a further couple of minutes.
- Add the tomato purée, passata, vinegar and tomatoes then stir in 200ml of boiling water, season with salt and pepper, bring to a simmer and cook, stirring occasionally, for 10 minutes.
- Finally, stir in the parsley, squeeze in the lime juice, check the seasoning and turn the heat to its lowest setting to keep the sauce warm.

For the fungi

- Bring the water to a boil over a medium-high heat, season with the salt and boil the okra for 3 or 4 minutes until tender.
- Gradually stir in the cornmeal until thoroughly combined, reduce the heat to medium and cook, stirring frequently, for about 5 minutes, adding a little boiling water if the fungi becomes too thick; stir in the butter and season with black pepper and a little more salt if necessary.

For the fish

- Score the skin of each fish fillet on an angle two or three times with a sharp knife.
- Cut the lime in half; keep one half to squeeze over the cooked fish and cut the other half into four wedges and set aside to serve with the fish.
- To make the fish seasoning mix together the sea salt, cracked black pepper, dried thyme, nutmeg and ground cloves in a small bowl.
- Rub the fish fillets all over with the seasoning.
- Heat the oil in a large non-stick frying pan over a medium-high heat and, when hot, fry the seasoned fish fillets, skin side down, for about 4–5 minutes (depending on the thickness of your fillets) until the skin is well browned; flip the fillets over, turn off the heat and allow the fish to finish cooking in the residual heat for a couple of minutes then squeeze over the lime juice.

To serve

- Spoon the fungi onto four warmed plates, place the fish fillets on top and ladle over the sauce; sprinkle with a little of the fish seasoning and serve with the lime wedges.

British Virgin Islands: Local hero

Lance Corporal Samuel Hodge VC

Samuel Hodge was born in Tortola on the British Virgin Islands in 1840 and joined the West India Regiment as a pioneer in the 4th Battalion. His unit was based in the Gambian capital Bathurst (now Banjul): many parts of Africa were garrisoned by West Indian regiments as it was believed that they coped better in tropical conditions than indigenous British soldiers, who suffered terribly from malaria, dysentery and blackwater fever. In June 1866, Hodge's regiment of approximately 270, led by Lieutenant Colonel George D'Arcy, marched against a rebellious Marabout tribe leader named Amar Faal who had fortified a nearby town, Tubabecolong, with a stockade of upright wooden posts and stakes, ready for battle. The British were later joined by 500 irregular African warriors from the allied Soninke tribe.

The attack started on 30 June but the British forces only had light weaponry and were unable to break through the stockade. Colonel D'Arcy called for volunteers to help him breach the walls. Hodge was one of 17 men to volunteer, each grabbing an axe and following D'Arcy into battle. The assault team came under intense fire and only three arrived at the walls unscathed – D'Arcy, Hodge and another private called Boswell. Boswell was killed as they started to hack a gap through the wooden posts of the fortress, and D'Arcy led Hodge through the gap. Hodge then used his axe to hack at the fastenings on two gates opening the way for a full assault and victory at bayonet point, but he was hit by gunfire and severely injured.

Six months after the battle, the *London Gazette* announced that Hodge was to be awarded the Victoria Cross for his efforts and he was promoted to Lance Corporal. On 24 June 1867, still suffering from his wounds, he was presented with the VC in Newtown Barracks, British Honduras (now Belize). Hodge was only the second black man (after the Canadian sailor William Hall) to receive this honour.

Sadly, he never recovered from his battlefield wounds. Less than a year after receiving the VC, he caught a fever and died on 28 January 1868, aged 28. Despite public recognition of his outstanding bravery, Hodge was buried in an unmarked grave in a Belize City Military Cemetery that was destroyed during a road-widening scheme. His final resting place and the location of his medal remain unknown.

Written by Lieutenant Matt Le Feuvre, Royal Navy

Poppy and coconut beef kebabs with roasted chilli salsa

Ainsley Harriott MBE, chef and TV presenter

When I wrote my Caribbean Cookbook, I wanted to show people that Caribbean cooking is so much more than jerk chicken – it's fresh, vibrant, nutritious and tasty. This recipe encompasses all of those things for me. As I mention in my book, the islands are a melting pot of cultures: from the original inhabitants – the Native American Caribs and Arawaks – on to the colonists and migrators from Western Europe, Africa and Asia. All of this is reflected in the local cuisine. These kebabs are lovely to cook on the barbecue, but are just as good made on a chargrill pan if the weather isn't ideal. The toasted coconut adds a nutty sweetness to this spicy dish. Go on, have a go at Caribbean cooking and open up a whole world of flavours in your kitchen.

Barbados

Gluten-free, dairy-free
Preparation time: 25 minutes
  plus 1 hour marinating time
Cooking time: 20 minutes

Serves 4

INGREDIENTS

1kg beef sirloin, cut into 2½cm dice
3 tbsp olive oil
2 tbsp minced garlic
2 tbsp minced ginger
1 tsp dried red chilli flakes
3 tbsp poppy seeds
3 tbsp white sesame seeds
1 tbsp cumin seeds
4 tbsp desiccated coconut

For the roasted chilli salsa
3 long green chillies, tops trimmed
6–8 tbsp extra-virgin olive oil, plus an extra
  drizzle for oiling the chillies
1 garlic clove, peeled
a large handful of flat-leaf parsley
a handful of mint
juice of 1 lemon
sea salt and freshly ground black pepper

METHOD

• Preheat a barbecue (if using).
• Place the diced beef in a large bowl. In a separate small bowl, mix together the olive oil, garlic and ginger and pour over the beef. Mix with your hands to ensure the beef is well coated. Cover the bowl with clingfilm and marinate in the fridge for 1 hour.
• Next, make the salsa. Unless using a barbecue, preheat the grill to its highest setting.
• Place the green chillies on a small baking tray and lightly drizzle with oil. Place the tray under the hot grill for 5–10 minutes, until the chillies are charred and blistered – they should be nice and soft. Alternatively, this can be done directly on the barbecue.
• Put the garlic, parsley, mint, lemon juice and charred chillies into a food processor and pulse for 4–5 seconds. Add the oil and pulse again, until the mixture is well combined but still quite coarse. Season with salt and pepper and set aside.
• Heat a small dry frying pan over a low heat, add the chilli flakes, poppy seeds, sesame seeds, cumin seeds and desiccated coconut and lightly toast. As soon as the coconut turns golden, remove from the heat and tip into a pestle and mortar. Grind to a coarse texture.
• Remove the marinated beef from the fridge, add the spice mixture and massage the spices into the beef. Thread the pieces of beef onto skewers.
• Place the beef skewers on the barbecue (or on a pre-heated chargrill pan) and grill, turning frequently, for about 6 minutes, depending on how you like your beef cooked. Once cooked, remove from the heat and let rest for 5 minutes before serving.
• To serve, place the beef kebabs on a board and spoon over the salsa.

Recipe taken from *Ainsley's Caribbean Kitchen*, published by Ebury Press

Flying Officer Errol Walton Barrow

Born in Barbados in 1920, Errol Walton Barrow was a bright and naturally gifted young man who was brought up in a prosperous religious family. In 1940, aged 20, he travelled to Britain to volunteer for the RAF, alongside 11 of his countrymen – they were later known as "the second Barbadian contingent".

Barrow initially enrolled as an aircraftman as part of light bomber crews before training as a wireless operator. His intellect and airmanship was apparent from the outset as he was quickly selected as an air navigator and then promoted to Sergeant on 25 November 1943. After a further four months of training in Canada, Barrow and his crew returned to England and joined 88 Squadron, flying Douglass Boston (DB-7) light bombers. Barrow flew over 50 operational bombing missions across Europe, including supporting ground forces during the Battle of the Bulge.

After VE Day, Flying Officer Barrow was appointed as the personal navigator to the then Commander in Chief of the British Zone of occupied Germany, Air Chief Marshall Sir William Douglas. Douglas, who later became chairman of British European Airways, remained a close friend, making Barrow godfather to his only child. Barrow's final RAF posting saw him oversee the education and vocational training initiatives for ex-servicemen from the colonial territories in the Colonial Office.

In 1950, after completing two concurrent degrees in London, in law and economics, Barrow returned to Barbados where he was elected to parliament. Over the next 10 years he established the Democratic Labour Party (DLP) and in 1959 became chairman. In 1961, the DLP won the general election and Barrow served as the Premier of Barbados, pushing for independence. Following the Barbados Independence Act 1966, he became the new nation's first Prime Minister. He introduced measures to reduce poverty and improve the life of ordinary Barbadians as well as developing industry, tourism and commerce.

He served 10 years in office before his party's defeat in the 1976 election. After a further 10 years in opposition he was re-elected in 1987, but a year later died at the age of 67. As "the father of independence and social transformation", Barrow was one of the ten National Heroes of Barbados. A local park in the capital Bridgetown is named in his honour, as is the Errol Barrow Centre for Creative Imagination at the University of the West Indies. His birthday, 21 January, is a national holiday, and there is a statue of him in Bridgetown's Independence Square. "A bloody good navigator – first class," said his RAF Squadron Leader, Alfred Barnes. "Get you there, get you back. Never saw Barrow get in a flap. A good man to have along."

Written by Lieutenant Commander Alex Kelley, Royal Navy

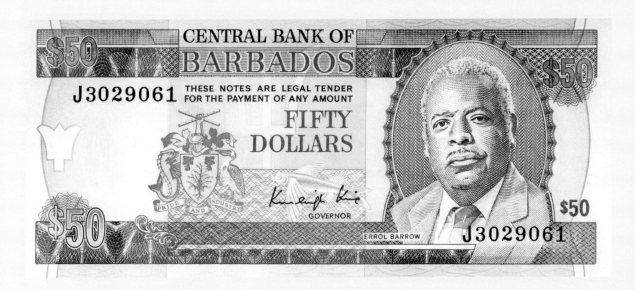

Van of action

Volkswagen's California Camper Van and Transporter have been iconic symbols of freedom and versatility for more than 70 years – and they're still adapting to suit every need and taste

www.volkswagen-vans.co.uk

The Volkswagen Camper Van is one of the most iconic vehicles of all time, and Volkswagen Commercial Vehicles continues to produce an updated California range alongside other vans that can be used for holidays, business or leisure – or simply to help families go about their daily lives. "We have helped a huge number of individuals to drive their businesses and go on holiday," says Kate Thompson, Head of Marketing, Press and Public Relations. "Whether you need a van for your business, large or small, or a camper van to explore the world or simply need to take the kids and dog to the park, we provide the products that match people's lifestyles. Looking ahead that means responding to the demand for electric vehicles and alternative fuel solutions."

The Transporter – also known as Bulli, Kombi, VW bus or microbus – recently celebrated its 70th birthday. This model first rolled off the Wolfsburg production line in March 1950, and since then 13 million have been sold. During the Covid pandemic, enterprising users were able to maintain and even grow their businesses thanks to the adaptability of the Volkswagen fleet and the maintenance and support network provided by the company. This meant that customers were able to deliver essential goods and services around the country at this crucial time.

"We have several customers who added a pillar to their business, such as a personal trainer who could no longer operate from a gym so went to visit customers in parks, and the gin distillery that switched production to hand sanitiser," says Kate. "We also worked with FareShare, the food-waste charity." This relationship between Volkswagen Commercial Vehicles and its customers is what makes the company different.

As well as the Transporter, Volkswagen Commercial Vehicles' full line-up includes the Crafter, the Caravelle, the Caddy, the California and the Grand California. There are also a number of variations and conversions available for these vans. Volkswagen Commercial Vehicles believes it is essential that its customers have the right vehicle for their needs, and that includes supporting customers when they make the move to electric. "The change to electric vehicles is coming," says Kate. "We already have the ABT e-Transporter. It is very important we have these products available for customers and that we support them as they make the change from diesel vans, which they will have run for years."

The ABT eTransporter has an all-electric range of 82 miles with cargo space of 6.7 cubic metres. It can be 80 per cent charged in just 45 minutes. New products are in the pipeline too, including the ID Buzz, a retro-styled all-electric minivan, designed for passengers or goods, and inspired by the classic Type 2 Microbus from the 1950s. "It fits so well to what the brand stands for," says Volkswagen design boss Oliver Stefani. "It's emotional, it has functionality and it makes your life easier."

That commitment to supporting customers extends to after-care. The company runs a dedicated network of Van Centres and authorised repairers, ensuring van customers receive specialist attention and are treated as carefully as car owners. "These extend across the country so somebody is no further than 40 minutes from one of our technical experts," says Kate. "We put as much effort into dealing with vans as we do cars. These dedicated sites are staffed by specially trained personnel with specialist equipment, so they can provide the best service and technical expertise."

Salt codfish and coconut dumplings

Leading Catering Services Kenron Mercury, Royal Navy

The practice of preserving cod by drying and salting was started in the 18th century by Bermudian slaves; the technique was born out of necessity by the poor as it was plentiful and cheap. A popular choice for a late breakfast or brunch on a Sunday, these saltfish dumplings are generally served with potato, egg, avocado and banana. My take on this popular dish, with sweet potato, plantain and green bananas steamed in their skins, can be served as a hearty main course for the winter months.

Bermuda

Dairy-free
Preparation time: 30 minutes, plus
  overnight soaking for the cod
Cooking time: 40–45 minutes

Serves 4

INGREDIENTS

4 skinless, boneless salt cod fillets

For the steamed sweet potato and fruit
1 tsp salt
1 large sweet potato, unpeeled
1 large firm ripe plantain, unpeeled
8 young green bananas, unpeeled

For the coconut dumplings
200g plain flour
100g grated coconut
1 tsp salt
1 tsp sugar
125ml water

To cook the salt codfish
2 tbsp olive oil
1 medium onion, cut into 1cm dice
6 garlic cloves, finely chopped
1 large tomato, cut into 1cm dice
1 medium red pepper, halved and sliced
1 sprig of fresh thyme
2 chives, chopped
Salt and freshly ground pepper

To serve
1 small cucumber, sliced

METHOD

• Soak the salt cod overnight, rinse twice then shred, removing any bones.

For the steamed sweet potato and fruit
• Wash the sweet potato, plantain and bananas and bring a large pot of water to a boil.
• Add the salt, sweet potato, plantain and green bananas and boil for 15 minutes or until tender; drain, cool then peel and slice ready to serve.

For the coconut dumplings
• Bring a pan of water to a boil over a medium-high heat.
• Mix the flour, grated coconut, salt and sugar together in a bowl and mix in enough of the water to make a firm dough.
• Knead the dough until smooth, divide into four even round balls and flatten to 5cm thick.
• Drop the dumplings into the boiling water and cook for 10 minutes; drain, cool then cut the dumplings into slices.

To cook the salt codfish
• Heat the olive oil in a large frying pan or skillet over a low heat, add the onion, garlic, tomato, red pepper, thyme and chives and cook, stirring occasionally, for 5 minutes.
• Add the shredded cod and cook, stirring frequently, for 10 minutes then season with salt and freshly ground black pepper to taste.

To serve
• Spoon the salt codfish mix onto four plates, divide the sliced cucumber between the plates and serve with the sliced sweet potato, plantain and bananas.

Flying Officer Herman Francis Grant Ede DFC

Flying Officer Herman Francis Grant Ede, an RAF Gladiator pilot, was the first Bermudian killed in the Second World War when HMS *Glorious* was sunk during the evacuation from Norway. Born in 1917, Ede was raised in the Pembroke Parish of Bermuda by his mother Winifred Louise Ede after his father, Royal Navy Lieutenant Commander Ernest Grant Ede, had been killed during the battle of Jutland during the Great War.

In 1937, at the age of just 20, Herman joined the Royal Air Force and, on completion of his training at the RAF College Cranwell, joined 111 Squadron. Shortly after he was posted to 263 Squadron and was swiftly despatched to Norway to join HMS *Furious* to engage in the ill-fated defence of the country.

A skilled and talented pilot, 33307 Flying Officer Herman Francis Grant Ede was credited with two biplane victories. In May 1940, he engaged a German Messerschmidt Bf110 twin-engine fighter and, although he was up against a faster aircraft with greater fire power, Ede was able to out-manoeuvre the enemy to gain a firing solution, causing one German to crash. On the same day, Ede, along with two other RAF Gloster Gladiators, attacked a lone Heinkel He111 bomber. He also shot down a Focke-Wulf 200 and damaged a Junkers Ju 90 the following day. Unbeknown to Ede, these would be his last airborne missions.

Although 263 Squadron conducted useful work strafing German ground units, the Allied defenders could not prevent Germany's victory in Norway. The squadron was ordered to evacuate in HMS *Glorious* and return to Britain. During its transit, on 8 June 1940, the ship was attacked by the German battlecruisers *Scharnhorst*, *Gneisnau* and *Hipper* and was sunk about 360 miles west of Narvik in northern Norway. Only 40 of the 900 or so men on the *Glorious* survived, rescued by Norwegian ships: the rest of the RAF and Fleet Air Arm aircrew onboard perished, including Ede, who was only 23 at the time. On 7 August 1940, Ede was posthumously awarded the Distinguished Flying Cross for his airborne contribution to the campaign. His memory is immortalised on the Runnymede Memorial in Surrey.

Written by Lieutenant Commander Alex Kelley, Royal Navy

> *"Although he was up against a faster aircraft with greater fire power, Ede was able to out-manoeuvre the enemy to gain a firing solution, causing one German to crash"*

Guardian angel

Taking Care provides a wide range of personal alarms and monitored devices that quickly connect customers to emergency-response operators

www.taking.care

Independence is everything. It's good for mental and physical health and it is particularly valuable for older people, with reports showing that those who maintain their independence in later life have an increased sense of purpose and greater levels of happiness and satisfaction. That's why Taking Care's products are so valuable. The company's personal alarms allow customers to instantly contact emergency-response teams in the event of an accident or emergency, meaning that users can remain in their own homes for even longer.

"Personal alarms and telecare can help reduce anxiety for those who live alone or those who have health conditions that mean they need a bit of extra support," explains Steve Gates, the Managing Director of Taking Care, the UK's largest provider of personal alarms. "They enable people to stay safe and secure in their own homes and provide a lifeline to the outside world in the event of a fall or other emergency. Having a reliable personal alarm service also gives families the reassurance and peace of mind that help is always on hand should they need it."

Each year, Taking Care handles more than 25,000 emergency alarm calls from older and vulnerable people. The company's Age Co personal alarm and fall detector are the only alarms approved by Age UK, the UK's leading charity dedicated to helping people make the most of later life, and Taking Care is also the first *Which?*-approved personal alarm provider in the UK. "We have committed to the *Which?* code of conduct," says Steve. "We are regularly assessed to ensure we continue to meet the high standards of the Which? Consumer Association."

Taking Care's customers have enjoyed rich and rewarding lives, and many remain active thanks to their personal alarms. They include numerous members of the military, such as a 97-year-old Bomber Command pilot who still instructs visitors on how to use the Spitfire simulator at the Spitfire and Hurricane Memorial Museum in Ramsgate, or the MBE-winning squadron leader who joined the Hackney Home Guard in 1940 at the age of 18 before spending 30 years at the RAF.

One such customer explains the difference that Taking Care's services have made to her life. "I am 86 years old and can live independently in my own family home," explains Mrs Sheehy. "This is mainly down to me having the reassurance of wearing my Taking Care pendant/alarm which not only gives me peace of mind but also gives my family that bit of comfort to know that if I need help it's always going to be at the end of the phone, and the pendant is around my neck and easy to press if needed. I have used my pendant many times as I have falls due to hearing loss and balance issues. I simply press the pendant and it calls the 24-hour service team who call me straight away asking if I need assistance and then call either my named neighbours or a family member or an ambulance. Once I woke in the middle of the night with severe chest pains and I pressed my pendant and within five minutes my neighbour and an ambulance were taking care of me. It was a minor heart attack and my pendant saved my life. That's why we call it our guardian angel."

Pan-fried Aylesbury duck

Senior Aircraftsman Sam Shepheard, RAF

This dish will always remind me of my basic chef training at RAF Halton in Buckinghamshire. My parents stayed in nearby Wendover before travelling back home and they told me that they had just eaten a superbly presented Aylesbury duck dish at a local pub. I made sure that it was the first thing I cooked for them when I returned home. It was a roaring success and has been a family favourite ever since.

Preparation time: 35–40 minutes
Cooking time: 50–60 minutes

Serves 2

INGREDIENTS

For the fig jam
250g ripe figs, halved
¼ orange, zested
100g granulated sugar
¼ lemon, juiced

For the butternut squash purée
1 medium butternut squash
Salt and pepper

For the garlic and chive mash
450g potatoes, peeled and diced
100ml milk
1 tbsp butter
50g sour cream
1 garlic clove, finely chopped or crushed
1 tbsp chives, chopped plus extra
  for garnish
Salt and ground white pepper

For the duck
2 Aylesbury duck breasts
60ml freshly squeezed orange juice
1 tsp orange zest, finely grated
Pinch of salt

For the buttered Savoy cabbage
15g butter
½ medium onion, halved and thinly sliced
Few sprigs of thyme, leaves stripped
1 small Savoy cabbage, trimmed and
  thinly shredded
Salt and pepper

METHOD

For the fig jam
- Place the fig halves in a saucepan with 35ml of water, bring to a simmer and gently bubble for 5 minutes, until the figs have softened and released their juices.
- Add the orange zest, sugar and lemon juice, bring to a simmer and cook for further 5 minutes or until thick.
- Skim any of the foam that rises to the surface, remove from the heat and set aside.

For the butternut squash purée
- Preheat the oven to 180°C and line a baking tray with a piece of baking parchment.
- Slice the squash in half lengthways, scoop out the seeds and strings, place both halves, cut side down onto the lined baking tray.
- Roast uncovered for 45–50 minutes or until tender; remove from oven and allow to cool enough to handle.
- When cool, scrape the flesh from the skin, blend to a purée in a food processor or blender until smooth; season with salt and pepper, transfer to a clean pan and keep warm.

To salt the duck
- Score each duck breast on the skin in criss-cross pattern, this will help the fat render as it cooks.
- Lightly salt both sides of each breast and leave to stand at room temperature for 15–20 minutes.

For the garlic and chive mash
- Once the squash is halfway through its roasting time, prepare the mash: place the potatoes in a saucepan and boil for 15–20 minutes in salted water over a medium-high heat until tender.

- Drain the potatoes through a colander, leave for a few minutes until dry then return to the saucepan and mash until smooth, add the milk, butter, sour cream, garlic and chives; mix well, season with salt and white pepper, cover with a lid and keep warm.

To cook the duck
- While the potatoes are cooking, place the duck breasts skin side down in a cold non-stick frying pan, place over a medium heat and gradually heat; as the fat is released, tilt the pan towards you and spoon off the fat; cook for about 4–6 minutes then turn the breasts over.
- Add the orange juice and zest and continue to cook for another 3–4 minutes: remove the duck from the heat and rest, covered with a piece of foil, on a board for 10 minutes. Set aside the pan with the orange juice and duck cooking juices.

For the buttered Savoy cabbage
- Cook the cabbage while the duck breasts are resting: melt the butter in a saucepan over a medium heat, add the onion and thyme and cook, stirring occasionally, for around 5–6 minutes until the onions are soft.
- Add the cabbage and a tiny splash of water, stir well, cover the pan with a lid and steam for a few minutes, until the cabbage has wilted and season to taste.

To serve
- Reheat the fig jam and duck cooking juices (add a little boiling water if the pan is too dry).
- Carve the duck breasts into thin slices and serve on warmed plates with the fig jam, garlic and chive mash, butternut squash purée and buttered cabbage then spoon over the duck cooking juices.

Buckinghamshire: Local hero

Able Seaman Arnold Hargreaves

Arnold Hargreaves had a tough start to life. Born in 1917 in Hull he was orphaned at the age of 7 and taken in by Barnardo's children's charity, who helped him find a job with a printer in Bedford when he was 16. At the outbreak of the Second World War he received his call-up papers and chose to join the Royal Navy. He was sent to Portsmouth for training and assigned as an Able Seaman to the destroyer HMS *Bulldog*. Hargreaves crossed the Atlantic several times on convoy protection duties before playing a significant part in the single most important intelligence capture of the war.

On the morning of 9 May 1941, HMS *Bulldog* intercepted a German U-boat, *U-110*. Its captain, Fritz Julius Lemp, had already sunk 100,000 tonnes of vital Allied shipping, but his luck had run out and this time his submarine was hit and forced to the surface. Two Allied ships lined up to ram the stricken *U-110*, but Bulldog's captain, Joe Baker-Cresswell, realised that there was a possibility of capturing the U-boat intact. Hargreaves was detailed to hastily join a boarding party to round up prisoners. While collecting any materials with an intelligence value, his team scooped up a Kurzsignale code book and an odd-looking typewriter, not knowing that they were in possession of an Enigma Machine. Both were sent to Bletchley Park, where they were used to crack German code.

"I was just part of the gang," Hargreaves would later recall. "It was another job, like going down to get the milk. We were told not to say anything about it, but then I was mentioned in dispatches and my mother-in-law found out." So important was the prize that the Admiralty ordered the *U-110* to be scuttled and the surviving German crew interned on Iceland for fear that news of the Enigma's capture be reported back to Germany.

Hargreaves was discharged from the Royal Navy in 1946, returning to his wife and his job as a printer. He died on 15 October 2017, aged 100, the last of the *Bulldog*'s boarding party. In 1945, King George VI described the discovery of the Enigma Machine as "perhaps the single most important event of the war".

Written by Flight Lieutenant Katie Leonard, RAF

Sovereign technology

TriCIS is a UK sovereign company that uses world-class industry expertise to advise the military and government on IT security

tricis.co.uk

As the third generation of her family to enter the military, Ann-Marie Warner-Read carries the ethos to serve through her bones. But when she started working in the defence industry, she recognised that security was struggling to keep up with evolving technological capability. "I wanted to bring the right people together to ensure protection, to make a real difference to those still on the ground," she says.

Ann-Marie has found this same focus as the Defence Advisor of TriCIS, a modern company whose technical expertise offers both new solutions and the modification of existing computing, networking and portable devices to meet the highest IT security requirements. As a UK sovereign company, TriCIS works across the defence community, everywhere from central government to military stations much further afield, for UK and NATO customers as well as commercial clients.

"We listen to our customers and understand the challenges they face," says Ann-Marie. "We work with them to engineer solutions that will protect them and their assets at all times. Whether it's protecting a person situated in an overseas embassy, or helping a soldier on the ground make mission-critical decisions, our customer is at the heart of everything we do."

During the company's rapid growth it has met a number of challenges. "While we've been busy protecting our clients' technical infrastructure," says Ann-Marie, "we've remained focused on protecting ourselves commercially, developing good governance and best practice to match our technical abilities."

As well as working with CEO Antony Summerfield to implement the company's core values, one of Ann-Marie's proudest achievements is supporting military personnel and charities to

improve their goals. "We are proud to support the causes close to our hearts, and give what we can, where it makes a difference," she says. "A quarter of our staff are ex-Forces, we've signed the Armed Forces Covenant, and we're looking to create a veterans' employment scheme. We truly believe in what we're trying to achieve."

As military strategy continues to evolve, so will TriCIS. "We want to help in all the areas we can," says Ann-Marie. "The technical digital revolution is only going to continue, and we'll keep supporting our government and defence customers through all of those changes."

Roast leg of Welsh lamb

Lance Corporal Ben Smith, Army

Welsh lamb is justifiably famous and is served in some of the best restaurants and venues around the world. To be classified as Welsh lamb it must meet certain criteria, not least of which is that the lamb must have been raised on grass pasture in the Welsh countryside. Welsh lamb has a very different flavour from New Zealand lamb: it is brighter in colour and has a sweeter flavour. It is said that Welsh lamb is so good due to the many years of traditional farming techniques passed down through the generations, which have created a wonderful and consistent meat.

Preparation time: 30 minutes
Cooking time: about 2 hours,
  depending on the size of your lamb leg

Serves 4–6

INGREDIENTS

For the lamb
1–1.2kg lamb
4 tbsp white wine vinegar
1 tbsp brown sugar
Olive oil
2 large handfuls of fresh mint
Salt and pepper
900g new potatoes, whole
2 springs of rosemary

For the lamb gravy
Roasting juices from the lamb
1 tbsp flour
1 medium glass of red wine
500ml beef stock

For the mint sauce
2 large handfuls of fresh mint, stalks
  discarded and leaves roughly chopped
200ml boiling water
2 tbsp malt vinegar
2 tbsp sugar
Pinch of salt

To serve
Seasonal vegetables of your choice,
  my favourite is tenderstem broccoli

METHOD

- First you will need to weigh your lamb. My recommendation is to roast the lamb for 25 minutes per 450g plus 25 minutes; if you like your lamb slightly rarer adjust the cooking time accordingly.

To marinate the lamb
- Mix the vinegar, sugar, a good splash of oil, the mint and some salt and pepper together in a bowl.
- Make several slits in the lamb with a sharp knife to allow the flavours to get into the flesh and place on a tray; pour over the marinade, rub it into the lamb, cover and place in the fridge to marinate for 2 hours, turning every half hour.

To roast the lamb and potatoes
- Preheat the oven to 180°C.
- Place the marinated lamb into a large roasting tray, pour over the marinade and roast on the middle shelf of the preheated oven, basting every 20 minutes, until the lamb is cooked to your preference.
- 1 hour before the lamb is cooked, add the new potatoes and the rosemary to the roasting tray and coat with the lamb juices.

To make the mint sauce
- Place the chopped mint in a bowl, pour over the boiling water, leave for 1 minute to blanch, drain in a sieve and rinse under cold water.
- Transfer the mint to a serving bowl and mix well with the vinegar, sugar and salt; set aside for at least 30 minutes to let the flavours infuse.

To rest the lamb and make the gravy
- Transfer the lamb to a large plate or platter, cover with foil and set aside to rest for 20 minutes. Place the roast new potatoes on a clean roasting tray and keep warm in the residual heat of the oven.
- Tilt the roasting tray and, with a large spoon, scoop off and discard the fat from the surface of the liquid; leave a tablespoon or two to keep some extra lamb flavour and take care not to spoon off the darker juices as these are the gems of the gravy.
- Place the roasting tray over a low-medium heat directly on the stove and, as the juices simmer, scrape the corners and bottom of the tray to loosen any of the sediment.
- Once the juices begin to simmer add the flour and stir until well mixed and thick.
- Gradually add the red wine and beef stock while constantly whisking to prevent your gravy becoming lumpy.
- Once all the wine and stock have been added, reduce the gravy to a coating consistency, add any juices that have collected on the plate while the lamb was resting and strain into a gravy boat or jug.

To serve
- Carve lamb into three generous slices per portion, fan on warmed plates and serve with the roast new potatoes, seasonal vegetables, lamb gravy and a bowl of the fresh mint sauce to pass around the table. That's Sunday lunch sorted. Enjoy.

Cardiff: Local hero

The Young Family

Hundreds of thousands of families around the Commonwealth had to face the tragedy of losing a family member throughout the Second World War. The Young family from Cardiff had to endure the almost unbearable burden of losing three.

Born in 1901 in St Maria, Jamaica, Wilmot George Young moved to Cardiff in the 1920s, following the Welsh coal, steel and slate boom. He met and married Beatrice Silva, a second-generation Welsh-Portuguese woman, and they settled in Pomeroy Street, Tiger Bay. Together with their seven children, the Young family embedded themselves in the bustling multi-racial community that surrounded Cardiff's docks.

The eldest son, Jocelyn, following his father's footsteps, worked as a merchant seaman on a Japanese cargo ship trading at Cardiff docks. Tragically, shortly after the bombing of Pearl Harbour in December 1941, communications from the Ministry of War Transport with Jocelyn's vessel were lost, and he was declared missing at sea along with his fellow crew members. Just months later, the family suffered another devastating loss as the father, Able Seaman Wilmot George Young, was one of 11 crew killed when his ship *Ocean Vanguard* was torpedoed on 13 September 1942 by U-515 and sank 45 miles east of Galera Point, Trinidad. Proportionally, the Merchant Navy suffered the heaviest losses of Britain's Armed Forces as Germany's unrestricted submarine warfare accounted for 30,248 fatalities from an estimated 185,000 seamen active throughout the Second World War.

The final blow to the Young family came with the death of RAF Sergeant Arthur Wilmot Young (pictured, right), a wireless operator and gunner. Born 26 September 1923, Arthur was a talented trumpet player with a love of jazz, who joined the RAF at the age of 17. He trained in Morse code and wireless telegraphy and then attended the No. 10 Air Gunnery school at Walney Island in Cumbria. In March 1944, he married Florence May Silver in his hometown of Cardiff and quickly returned to prepare for Operation Bluecoat.

On 30 July 1944, Arthur's Lancaster bomber from 106 Squadron took off from RAF Metheringham at 6am carrying a 9,000lb payload. Joining 378 other aircraft, Operation Bluecoat would target German strongholds across Normandy. After four hours circling over the target, Young's Lancaster was instructed to abort due to poor

weather. On its return to base the Lancaster crashed into Salford's Littleton Road playing fields, having suffered aircraft damage over Normandy. All seven crew members were killed. The Young's story was repeated through families across the globe during this time, as people sacrificed everything in the pursuit of an Allied victory.

The youngest of Wilmot George Young's seven children was Patricia Maude Young, later Patti Flynn. A contemporary of Shirley Bassey, Patti was a talented jazz singer, author, presenter and actress who spearheaded a 26-year campaign to honour and recognise the sacrifices of all servicemen and women of colour from around the Commonwealth. In 2019, a year before Patti's death from cancer, she witnessed success as a Welsh National War Memorial was proudly unveiled in Cardiff's Alexandra Gardens in conjunction with the Royal British Legion.

Written by Warrant Officer Stephen Mark Perham, RAF

The online defence force

Cyber-security specialist Pervade Software uses a battlefield skillset when dealing with the threats posed by hackers, online criminals and cyber terrorists

pervade-software.com

When John Davies served in the Armed Forces in the 1980s he was trained to instinctively follow tried and tested processes, to learn to think like his enemy and to identify risks and neutralise them as swiftly as possible. These are skills that have served the signals specialist well in his post-military career in cyber security. He co-founded Pervade Software in 2009 and continues to support the military by employing ex-forces personnel when possible, as their skillset is so aligned with the global battle against cybercrime.

"Almost everything cyberists do can be traced to the military," he says. "They perform core processes like equipment checks, kill-chain analysis and incident management that are straight out of military manuals. This means that I can shortcut the education of an individual by bringing them into the industry from the military because they know so much already – often without even knowing they know it! Many military people don't appreciate the value of this capability because for them it's been a way of life and they don't relate it to civvy street – but if they don't know they have these skills and aptitudes then they can't tell employers."

Based in Cardiff, Pervade Software provides a range of innovative cyber-security solutions for clients including UK law-enforcement agencies, the NHS and private businesses. These include a cyber-security monitoring system that is used by the UK police to help private businesses so police forces can locate the origins of cyberattacks, and a dark web intelligence-gathering platform also used by private firms such as car manufacturers to trace stolen or counterfeited parts.

Pervade Software also works in compliance, helping companies obtain the certification required to show they are cyber-secure. The Pervade team includes reservists, veterans and military spouses – the whole military family.

"We are working in a fast-moving, fluid, combative situation where malicious people are developing new techniques and different forms of attacks all the time," says John. "Military training allows you to spot threats before they unfold and it comes naturally to ex-forces folks. It's an understanding that is directly transferable and means, with a bit of content training, the whole team can get into the mind of the hacker."

Hip hops

Grey Trees is an independent craft brewery that draws from local Welsh heroes and puts a modern twist on age-old beer traditions to create a range of award-winning ales

www.greytreesbrewery.com

During the Anglo-Afghan Wars of the 1800s, the British Army was kept lubricated by a new type of beer – India Pale Ale. In a nod to this match of brewing and military history, Grey Trees, a small, focused microbrewery in the Welsh valleys, has developed the multi-award-winning Afghan Pale Ale. "We never compromise on the quality of the beer," says co-owner Tracey Kerslake-Davies. "We use the very best hops and we still can't make enough to satisfy demand. We have built up a strong reputation and have won loads of CAMRA, SIBA and Great Taste awards. We never have any ullage returns, and pouring beer away is unheard of for us."

As the name of the Afghan Pale Ale suggests, the military connection is of particular importance to Tracey and her husband Ray, who is the Head Brewer. Ray served in the Parachute Regiment and then moved on to the SAS reserves, while Tracey's grandfather was a secretary of the Royal British Legion in her local area. "Growing up we had so much to do with the Legion," she says. "Every Saturday night from July onwards we all sat at home making poppies for Grampy, putting them together for Armistice Day, which is still a major event in the family."

After leaving the Army, Ray ran a pub, with the support of Tracey, and started a small brewery in the pub car park. This proved so successful that the couple decided to open a brewery in the Welsh town of Aberdare. Naming themselves Grey Trees after the literal English translation of the name of the Welsh village (Llwydcoed) where the brewing started, they sold their first barrel in September 2013. The brewery now produces around 10,000 bottles a month and 20,000 litres in cask. Alongside its Afghan Pale Ale (a double CAMRA Gold Champion Beer of Britain), there is Digger's Gold, a golden ale that has been a CAMRA champion of Wales for several years in a row, and the Drummer Boy best bitter, named in honour of Stuart Cable, a family friend and the drummer in Welsh band Stereophonics who lived in Aberdare until his death. Caradog's Bitter is named after composer Griffith Rhys Jones Caradog, who has a statue in Aberdare, while the JPR Pale Ale is named after Welsh rugby legend JPR Williams. "I saw him in the pub one day and said I was going to name a beer after him," says Ray. "JPR said that was great as long we shared it with him. He opened our brewery and does occasional events with us."

There are also seasonal stouts, porters, wheat beers and single-hop beers, which are usually named after the dominant hop. Occasional specials and one-offs are trialled in their nearby craft pub, the National Tap, which draws a knowledgeable crowd. Brewery tours allow visitors to get an idea of the recipes and processes used by this special brewery. "We keep the hand-crafted element and have never considered getting a machine to save on labour which could reduce quality," says Tracey. "We produce everything on-site to maintain the quality and dedication each brew deserves. All of our bottle products are produced by hand, providing a natural carbonation. By using the right quantities of yeast and sugar, it's very similar to the process used for making champagne, with the sediment at the bottom of the bottle, retaining the flavour of the quality ingredients. Our beer is the champagne of the Welsh valleys!"

Pie, mash and liquor

Lance Corporal Christina Davies, Army

Pie and mash is a traditional working-class dish dating back to the 19th century. From the cobbled streets of Georgian London (where pie and mash was served from carts or braziers) to the modern-style Victorian food shop, it was part of the staple diet for Londoners from all walks of life. Traditionally, pies are filled with cheap minced meat but I have gone with a lean mince for my recipe (which I think is even better) served alongside mashed potato and a liquor sauce. Note that "liquor sauce" doesn't contain alcohol – it's a stock-based parsley sauce (originally made with eel stock)and is the perfect accompaniment to pie and mash. Whether eaten on the backstreets of London or in a traditional pie-and-mash shop, with white tiled walls and marble floors, this dish never fails to satisfy.

City of London

Preparation time: 30 minutes
Cooking time: 1 hour

Serves 4

INGREDIENTS

For the pie filling
1 tbsp vegetable oil
1 onion, finely chopped
3 cloves garlic, finely chopped
450g minced beef steak or beef mince
2–3 tbsp plain flour
2 tsp English mustard
170ml good brown ale (try The Cranborne
  Poacher by Badger Beer)
2 tbsp tomato purée
100ml of good-quality beef stock
Salt and freshly ground black pepper

For the suet pastry
365g self-raising flour, plus extra for dusting
240g beef suet
Dried mixed herbs, just a small sprinkle to
  give the pastry a deep flavour throughout
Cold water to bind (about 5 tbsp)

For the pie crust
500g ready-made shortcrust pastry
1 large egg, beaten to egg-wash the pastry
  lid to give it a lovely colour on top

For the mashed potatoes
4 large potatoes
120ml warmed milk
A large knob of butter

For the parsley liquor
70g butter
¼ white onion, super-finely diced
2 garlic cloves, crushed or very finely chopped
50g cornflour
500ml chicken stock
Handful of parsley, finely chopped

METHOD

To make the pie filling
• Fry the onions and garlic in the oil over a medium heat until they are soft; seal the beef in the same pan, tossing the onions and garlic through the mince to get a good base flavour.
• Stir in the flour, cook for a couple of minutes then add the remaining pie ingredients, bring to a simmer and remove from the heat; season at this point to ensure you have a good balanced flavour and set aside to cool.

To make the pastry
• Place the flour, suet and mixed herbs into a large mixing bowl, mix well and add enough cold water to bind the mixture into a firm dough. Cover the dough and set aside for 10 minutes to rest.
• Roll out the dough on a floured surface to about 2mm thick (about the thickness of a £1 coin) and cover until needed.
• Next roll out the ready-made shortcrust pastry to the same thickness as the suet pastry and cover until needed.

To make and cook the pies
• Pre heat the oven to 185°C.
• Grease four individual pie dishes and line with the suet pastry, ensuring that the dough is pressed into all the corners of the dishes; add your pie filling and top with the shortcrust pastry; crimp well to seal the pie and egg-wash the lid.
• Place the pie dishes in a deep roasting tray and pour in enough boiling water to cover halfway up the pies.
• Place in the preheated oven and bake for 40 minutes – this will be enough time for the suet pastry to steam and the shortcrust to cook properly, which will give you a pie with a unique flavour and texture.

To make the mash
• Boil the potatoes for 18–20 minutes until tender, while the potatoes are cooking bring the milk to a simmer, remove from heat and cover with a lid.
• Strain the potatoes through a colander, allow them to drain for a few minutes, return to the pan and mash with the butter and milk.
• Season well, cover with a lid and place to one side.

To make the liquor
• For the parsley sauce (liquor) fry the onions and garlic in the butter over a medium heat until soft, stir in the cornflour until you have a roux-like mix. Add the stock, bring to a boil, reduce the heat to low and simmer, stirring frequently, for 2–3 minutes until smooth and thickened.
• Stir in the chopped parsley and check the seasoning, adding salt and pepper to taste.

To serve
• Place a generous serving of mash on the plate, top with a pie and finish with some liquor to add a great flavour.

Flight Lieutenant Billy Strachan

Born on 16 April 1921 in Kingston, Jamaica, an 18-year-old William Arthur Watkin Strachan arrived in England in March 1940, one of the first Jamaicans to volunteer in the war. He sold many of his possessions – including his beloved saxophone and bicycle – to fund his journey. Billy applied to the RAF and, following 12 weeks of basic training, was employed as a wireless operator on bombers, making his first flight in 1941. He ascended rapidly through the ranks and graduated to a sergeant and an air gunner, while his bomber squadron was tasked with conducting nightly raids against German industrial targets.

His 30 raids over hostile territory would have made him eligible for a ground-based role. Instead he applied to train as a pilot and was able to fly solo after only seven hours of training. He loved to play tricks, paying unauthorised visits to friends in airstrips across England. Promoted from Sergeant to Flying Officer and then Flight Lieutenant, his last promotion brought with it his own "batman", or personal servant. Describing him as a "real smooth Jeeves type", Billy instinctively called him "Sir", only to be told: "No, Sir, it is I who call you 'Sir'!"

When pursued by enemy fighters, Billy's trick was to wait until the German aircraft was on his tail, before cutting the engine and entering a steep dive, letting the fighter sail by. He severely damaged his hip in a crash during training and was shot in the leg during an operational sortie, both of which caused him complications for life. After a near miss with the spire of Lincoln Cathedral, Billy realised that his luck could only last so long and retired from flying.

After the war, Billy was introduced to communism in 1947, which strongly resounded with his anti-racist ethos. He became secretary of the London branch of the Caribbean Labour Congress and was instrumental in setting up its journal, *Caribbean News*. He welcomed the *Empire Windrush* passengers to a meeting in London within days of their arrival in 1948.

Studying alone, he achieved a degree in law in 1967 and subsequently became a senior clerk to magistrates in courts all over London. He wrote several legal guides on subjects ranging from drink driving to adoption. He was also an avid horse rider and one of the founding members of the Disabled Riders Association. A key figure in black British history, Flight Lieutenant Strachan pioneered the fight against racism in Britain until his death in April 1998, aged 77.

Written by Lieutenant Aren Tingle, Royal Navy Air Squadron

> *"When pursued by enemy fighters, Billy's trick was to wait until the German aircraft was on his tail, before cutting the engine and entering a steep dive, letting the fighter sail by"*

Underwriting veterans

One of the world's oldest and most venerable companies, located in the heart of the City of London, Lloyd's has long had a commitment to military veterans and their families

www.lloyds.com

With a history stretching back an astonishing 330 years, Lloyd's is one of the oldest and most respected companies in the world. It is also the founder of the world's oldest military charity of its kind, the Lloyd's Patriotic Fund (LPF), which was founded in 1803 and continues to support veterans by aiding the transition to civilian life for veterans and their families. Since 2010, LPF has donated more than £3.5 million to support serving and ex-service personnel and their families.

Lloyd's itself is the world's specialist insurance market, collating the expertise of nearly 45,000 insurance professionals around the world to help clients manage their risks. By allowing clients to syndicate risk – sharing it across multiple insurers – Lloyd's enables innovation and helps to create a braver world. "Innovation remains an essential element of our philosophy," says Chief Marketing and Communications Officer Jo Scott. "Key initiatives include a Future at Lloyd's strategy which is developing a move towards a digital-first marketplace to deliver the best possible outcomes for market professionals and their clients."

In February 2021, Lloyd's launched Futureset, designed to help customers manage and protect against the risks of the future – both known and unknown. This provides a global platform and community for insurance and risk professionals to create and share insight, expertise and solutions to our most

challenging problems. "We are also determined to build a more sustainable market and a more sustainable world," says Jo, "focusing on climate action and environmental challenges in the insurance sector, and promoting a more diverse and inclusive culture where all voices are heard. This focus on community includes our charitable work, which includes supporting several other charities alongside the Lloyd's Patriotic Fund."

Lloyd's initiatives include partnerships with the veterans' mental-health charity Combat Stress and with RFEA The Forces Employment Charity, which both help address the mental health and employment needs of veterans and their families through two projects. With Combat Stress, Lloyd's is funding pioneering research into the use of sensory modulation, which aims to help improve the way veterans can manage complex mental health needs through using their senses. In 2021, a Research Lead was recruited for the role, and research started with focus groups working with veterans using the treatment. New sensory modulation and resilience workshops have been created and delivered with veterans. The aim is to use this research to embed this therapy strategy into mental-health treatments for veterans and their partners.

Working with RFEA, Lloyd's is funding Families Employment Advisors to support spouses and partners of serving and ex-serving personnel into employment. The programme aims to help build confidence, develop their strength and help apply for jobs in a tough market. In January 2020, two new Employment Advisors registered individuals for support in employment and training.

"Our military connections run deep," says Jo. "Many of our staff are ex-military, as has been the case throughout our long history. The market recognises the particular skills and talents of former members of the military, and for ex-military staff there may well be a natural alignment between protecting the UK as a member of the Armed Forces, and continuing those efforts by helping to protect against risks that could cause significant negative impacts to UK businesses and society as a whole."

Cornish moules

Rick Stein, celebrity chef and restaurateur

This is my Cornish take on a classic French mussel dish, moules marinière, but instead I'm using Cornish cider and spring onions. I cooked this on a beach near Mevagissey in September 2020 as part of a new series I'm doing called Rick Stein's Cornwall. All the crew thought it was really quite special.

Preparation time: 10 minutes
Cooking time: 10 minutes

Serves 4

INGREDIENTS

1.75kg mussels
1 garlic clove, finely chopped
4–6 spring onions, chopped
15g butter
A bouquet garni of parsley,
 thyme and bay leaves
100ml dry cider
120ml double cream
Handful wild sorrel leaves,
 coarsely chopped or 200g
 baby spinach leaves, washed
Freshly ground black pepper
Crusty bread, to serve

METHOD

• Wash the mussels under plenty of cold, running water. Discard any open ones that won't close when lightly squeezed.
• Pull out the tough, fibrous beards protruding from between the tightly closed shells and then knock off any barnacles with a large knife. Give the mussels another quick rinse to remove any little pieces of shell.
• Soften the garlic and spring onions in the butter with the bouquet garni, in a large pan big enough to take all the mussels – it should only be half full.
• Add the mussels and cider, turn up the heat, then cover and steam them open in their own juices for 3 or 4 minutes. Give the pan a good shake every now and then.
• Remove the bouquet garni, add the cream and chopped sorrel or baby spinach and remove from the heat, season with freshly ground black pepper.
• Spoon into large, warmed bowls and serve with lots of crusty bread.

Commodore Muriel Hocking RD RNR

Born Muriel Cutts in 1945, Commodore Muriel Hocking joined the Women's Royal Naval Service in 1963 as a radar plotter. She was commissioned in 1967 at the Royal Naval College Greenwich and went on to qualify as a photographic interpreter. In those days, Wrens did not have the opportunity to go to sea and were very restricted in their career options. After marrying naval dental surgeon Malcolm Hocking in 1969, she transferred to Royal Naval Reserve (RNR) before serving around the world at Maritime Headquarters Pitreavie in Rosyth, Hong Kong, HMS *Vivid* Plymouth, HMS *Calpe* Gibraltar and HMS *Dalriada* Greenock.

Hocking was eventually selected as the first female to command an operational reserve unit, taking on the role of Commanding Officer of *Dalriada* and then *Vivid*. She was presented with her Reserve Decoration (RD) in 1980 while in Gibraltar and its clasp in 1991. In 1995, Hocking was promoted to the senior staff of the RNR as Director of Training and also became one of three Aides-de Camp to the Queen. She was reappointed as an Aide-De-Camp in 1997 when she became the first female naval one star (regular or reserve) and took over as the first female Head of the Reserves at a ceremony on board HMS *Victory*. Hocking made a significant improvement to the management of the RNR and was a very popular and respected senior officer. She flew her blue swallow-tailed broad pennant from HMS *Vivid* and thereon was affectionately known as "Mega-ma'am". Her promotion to Commodore RNR was based on professional merit and was a natural culmination of her regular and reserve naval service.

Such was the exemplary and groundbreaking nature of her performance and achievement that it took a further 23 years before another female was appointed Head of the RNR. Commodore Hocking always retained her sense of humour and her interest and concern for those who served under her. She was an inspiring figure who broke a glass ceiling and paved the way for other women to follow her into the regulars and, in time, into full equality with their male counterparts. After retirement from the Navy, her service to the Royal British Legion in Cornwall was equally impressive. Hocking was president of the Tideford & St Germans Branch from 2001 until she passed away in February 2020, receiving her Legion Gold Badge in 2019.

Written by Petty Officer Aircraft Engineering Technician (Mechanical) Hollie Hill, Royal Navy

"Commodore Hocking was an inspiring figure who broke a glass ceiling and paved the way for other women to follow her into the regulars and, in time, into full equality with their male counterparts"

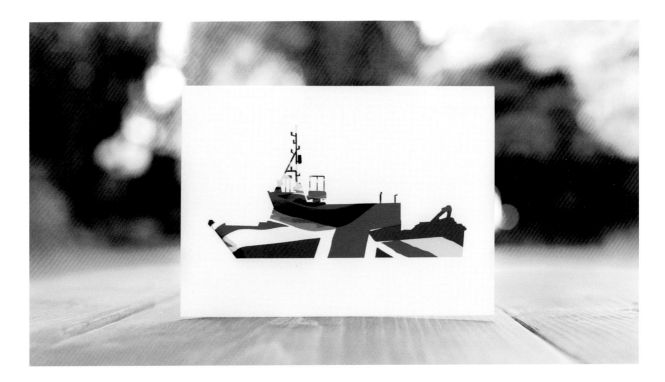

The art of war

From a studio in Portsmouth, Gillian Jones Designs
creates greeting cards, merchandise and quirky artworks
inspired by military aircraft, vehicles and warships

www.gillianjonesdesigns.com

When artist Gillian Jones and her husband left university and entered the world of work they quickly got restless. Deciding they needed more of an adventure, they joined the Royal Navy. "We trained at Dartmouth together and initially we were assigned to the same division," she says. "I was then doing art as a hobby. I've always been interested in military art – I used to do watercolours of uniforms as a teenager as well as painting models. Then my obsession with military designs quickly developed into this career."

Combining her talent for art with a love of the military, Gillian creates striking eye-catching prints with a strong military theme. After experimenting with a style that replicated 1920s travel posters, she settled on a design that uses the Union Flag to form the silhouette of Navy ships, iconic RAF aircraft such as the Spitfire, Hurricane and Harrier, and British Army vehicles such as the Challenger 2 tank. Gillian wanted to provide a dramatic and contemporary alternative to traditional paintings of "grey ships on grey seas with grey skies" and her solution has proved

hugely popular among former and serving military personnel. These are often bought as leaving presents when personnel rotate to new deployments, as gifts by family and friends or by veterans in memory of their own military careers.

Gillian obtains the silhouettes of ships from old copies of *Jane's Fighting Ships*, an annual publication featuring ships from navies all over the world. She and her team make bespoke commissions – including for international ships and submarines with the relevant flags – and can personalise any print to feature the name of the recipient and other relevant information. She can even make prints for retirees showing every craft they have served on – one of these featured an impressive 30 different ships, which kept her busy for weeks. Prints, as well as keyrings, mugs and T-shirts, are available via her online shop but they can also be found in local art shops around her home in Portsmouth and via the stall of the Royal Navy and Royal Marine charity. "Doing this means I still get to work every day with people in the military," she says. "They are like my second family."

The element of surprise

Distilled and bottled in the heart of Cornwall, The Cornish Gin
Distillery makes Elemental Cornish Gin – a small-batch, classic
dry gin – and a variety of fruity flavours

www.elementalgin.co.uk

Nicki and Joe Woolley (pictured, above) did not set out with
the intention of becoming owners of a craft gin distillery in
Cornwall, but as soon as they saw – and tasted – Elemental
Cornish Gin, they were hooked. Now their plan is to take
this local secret from a distillery in the bottom of their
garden out to the rest of the UK.

"I was looking at business acquisition and we
stumbled across this gin business that was for sale," says
Joe. "Almost as a joke I said to Nicki, 'Shall we buy a gin
distillery in Cornwall?' Nicki loves gin and it didn't take
much for her to say yes. It was a package deal for the house,
business and distillery and we came down to visit almost
hoping we wouldn't fall in love with it, but going home
after seeing the business for the first time it felt as if we
were driving in the wrong direction. It was a really small
business with a really good product that needed some
energy and drive to take it to the next level."

Elemental Cornish Gin had started in 2013 at the
onset of the gin revolution. It was one of the first gins
to be exclusively distilled and bottled in Cornwall for
over 300 years and had already established an excellent
local reputation when the Woolleys came on the scene.

The founders wanted new owners who shared their love
of Cornwall and obsession with finely crafted gin, and
Nicki and Joe fitted the bill perfectly. After taking over
the company in February 2020, the Woolleys retained the
previous distillery manager – the founders' son – to help
them navigate this new territory and, by the end of their
first year, Elemental Cornish Gin had a new look and was
winning "gold" at the prestigious Taste Of The West awards.

For Christmas 2020, Nicki and Joe felt confident enough
to launch the first of what might become regular seasonal
experimental variations, a non-traditional take on sloe gin,
using blackberries rather than sugar for sweetness. "We did one
full batch of 91 bottles which went down extremely well," says
Nicki. "We might do more seasonal experimental editions but
we are still learning and want to make sure we get things right."

The company currently makes three products – a Cornish
gin, an apple gin and a raspberry gin – each of which is labelled
and bottled by hand, with a capacity of around 180 bottles
per distillation. "It's small-batch handmade gin made with
quality ingredients and organic grain alcohol using four 40-litre
copper stills," explains Nicki. "It's done in the traditional
one-shot method and is proudly made in Cornwall, using spring
water from Bodmin Moor and working with local suppliers,
designers and packagers."

Sustainability is another important factor, with the
couple harbouring hopes to open a carbon-negative eco-distillery
visitor centre. They are already pursuing other changes in this
direction, introducing a biodegradable cellulose seal and using
non-plastic print on bottles. The company's ambitions are not
just limited to gin – Joe is a whisky lover and would love to
explore other spirits, but for now, the focus is gin. "For years,
this gin has been a local secret," says Joe. "It only really left
Cornwall when tourists discovered it and brought it home.
We now want to become a nationally known brand but retain
those authentic qualities. That is the balance we need to strike
as we look ahead."

Smart vision

From its base in County Durham, Britain's only television manufacturer Cello Electronics specialises in internet-compatible sets that are made to the highest standards

celloelectronics.com

Amid all the technological turmoil of recent decades, the television set remains the great British unifier. Families gather round the set to watch major events, play games or – in the case of the Covid pandemic – take part in inter-generational indoor PE lessons. If they want to do that on a TV made in Britain, there is only one brand they can turn to – Cello Electronics.

"There is nobody else making TVs in the UK," says CEO Brian Palmer. "There has always been an element of consumers who want to buy British and I get emails from people all the time who want to buy British products. In 2020, we signed a partnership deal with Google that means our TV is as good as any on the market and it is made right here in the UK at our factory in Bishop Auckland."

Brian (pictured, above) has always worked around TVs. His first job was on the assembly line in a factory making TV screens. As he progressed into senior positions, he moved into wholesale and then manufacture, predicting the boom in the market that would take place in the switch from analogue to digital. He chose to

manufacture in the UK so he could maintain strict quality control. The company remains innovative: Cello was the first UK company to make TVs that could stream from the internet and it produces solar-powered TVs for the African market. As well as producing smart TVs in all sizes up to 86 inch, it operates in several niche markets, such as TVs with built-in DVD, and travel TVs that run off 12-volt batteries and can be used for boats, lorries and campervans. Brian also supports the Armed Forces community where possible, donating TVs free of charge to the Royal Navy for use on its ships.

"We have a factory of about 45,000 square feet and we do everything in one place," he says. "We have our offices, a showroom, distribution, stocks, parts and a call centre as well as two assembly lines. We have the potential to make 250,000 TVs a year and we currently sell around 200,000. We have always invested to keep up with the major brands and with our deal with Google we now get access to their technology free of charge, which is great news for the customer."

Panacalty

Leading Aircraftman Chris Simpson, RAF

County Durham

A traditional dish throughout the North-East, particularly County Durham, panacalty (or "panackelty") and its ingredients will vary from town to town. In working-class communities and during times of austerity this was a great way to use up any leftover vegetables and meat. Originally it was cooked in a pan over a low heat on the stove-top, hence its name; it's a proper "home cooking" dish and, with layers of corned beef, potatoes and vegetables braised in beef stock, it's obvious why it's a regional favourite. This is a childhood favourite of mine and is a cross between the Junior Ranks Mess classics, corned beef hash and Lancashire hotpot.

Preparation time: 20 minutes
Cooking time: 1 hour

Serves 6

INGREDIENTS

4 large potatoes, peeled and thinly sliced
1 large onion, peeled, halved and
 thinly sliced
3 carrots, halved lengthways and
 thinly sliced
680g (2 x 340g tins) corned beef, sliced
550ml beef stock
50g butter, melted
100g smoked bacon lardons
6 medium eggs
1 tbsp vegetable oil
1 tbsp flat-leaf parsley, chopped
Salt and cracked black pepper
Crusty bread and butter to serve

METHOD

- Preheat the oven to 180°C.
- Layer a quarter of the sliced potatoes in a lightly buttered oven-proof dish, overlapping slightly, to cover the bottom and season with salt and black pepper.
- Add a third of the onions, carrots and corned beef ensuring an even layer.
- Repeat twice more, creating three layers in total not forgetting to season each layer.
- Add a final layer of potatoes, again overlapping slightly, season, pour over the beef stock and brush the top with the melted butter.
- Lay a sheet of baking parchment or greaseproof paper on the potatoes and cover with tin foil; place in the preheated oven and cook for about 50 minutes.
- Once the vegetables have started to soften uncover and cook until golden and the stock has reduced.
- In a frying pan cook the smoked bacon over a medium-high heat for around 4–6 minutes or until crispy; remove and keep warm.
- Use the same pan to fry your eggs and cook to your preference (add a little more oil if necessary).
- Serve the panacalty with a fried egg, crispy bacon and chopped parsley on top, and crusty bread and butter on the side.

VEGETARIAN/VEGAN ALTERNATIVE

- To make a vegetarian panacalty, omit the corned beef (you can also substitute this with some thinly sliced root vegetables) and replace the beef stock with vegetable stock.
- For vegans, make the vegetarian version, as above, but use a vegan butter substitute.

Sergeant William McNally VC, MM & Bar

William McNally was born in County Durham on 3 May 1894, where he attended Murton Colliery School. Aged 14 he joined his father at Murton Colliery, working six shifts a week as a pit pony boy. In September 1914, along with thousands of Durham miners, William responded to Lord Kitchener's call to arms, joining the 8th (Service) Battalion, Yorkshire Regiment, better known as the Green Howards. After a year of training, he experienced the horrors of trench warfare at the Battle of Loos, France, where he received the first of three leg wounds during the Great War.

Following his recovery, William was sent back to France to join 69th Brigade (23rd Division) where he would earn his first Military Medal (MM) for attending to a wounded officer and dragging him to safety during the Battle of the Somme. In early November 1917, he was awarded a bar for his MM for his actions near Passchendaele when he rescued several of his company who were under heavy shell fire.

Transferring to the Southern Front in October 1918, the now Sergeant McNally and his company were under severe machine-gun fire from an enemy position at Piave River, Italy. William rushed the enemy post and single-handedly killed the enemy team and captured their gun. Two days later, at Vazzola, he crept up to the rear of an enemy post, and attacked and killed several of the enemy before capturing their machine-gun. Later that day he came under siege while holding a captured ditch. He effectively controlled his team's fire, inflicting severe casualties upon his enemies and secured the safety of his company. For his conspicuous bravery, skilful leadership and innumerable acts of bravery he was awarded the Victoria Cross.

William returned home to a hero's welcome; the local pit was even shut for the day to recognise his achievements. On 11 November 1920, he was included in the VC Guard of Honour for the interment of The Unknown Warrior in Westminster Abbey. William joined his local defence volunteers during the Second World War. He worked at the pit until he turned 50, when he moved to an office job at the local timber yard before retiring in 1958. He also raised six children with his wife, Elizabeth. William McNally died in January 1976 and received a funeral with full military honours. On 27 October 2018, he was honoured with the laying of a commemorative paving stone in Murton Village Green.

Written by Corporal Matt Lockwood, Army

"*William returned home to a hero's welcome; the local pit was even shut for the day to recognise his achievements*"

Toad in the hole

Paul Ainsworth, patron of the Michelin-starred
Number 6 in Padstow, Cornwall

*This is our take on the classic toad in the hole with
Cumberland sausage. Best simply served with mashed
potato, proper onion gravy and apple compote.*

Preparation time: 30 minutes
Cooking time: 40–45 minutes

Serves 4

INGREDIENTS

1 tbsp vegetable oil
1 six-inch Cumberland sausage ring
  (ask your butcher to skewer with toothpicks)
5 large Spanish onions, halved and
  thinly sliced
200g stale bread (ideally sourdough)
50g unsalted butter
½ bunch thyme
1 clove of garlic, finely grated
1 bunch of sage
2 tbsp sherry vinegar
1 tablespoon Colman's English mustard
1 tablespoon of wholegrain mustard
2 packets of all-butter puff pastry
3 egg yolks mixed with 1 tsp of
  Colman's English mustard
Fine salt

METHOD

For the Cumberland sausage

- Heat a large frying pan over a high heat, add a tablespoon of vegetable oil, gently place the sausage ring in the pan, then roast quickly for one minute until lightly caramelised, then turn and repeat; take out of the pan and place onto a wire rack to cool.

For the stuffing

- To make the stuffing that's going to top your sausage, place the sliced onions into a large pan on a medium-low heat (no need for oil or butter) with some fine salt and cook until dark brown, stirring at all times.
- For the breadcrumbs, gently pulse the stale bread in a food processor, but not too finely.
- Heat the butter in a frying pan over a medium heat and, once the butter has started to foam, add the breadcrumbs, some fine salt, some thyme and the finely grated garlic; cook until nice and crispy, then pour out onto a large tray.
- Pre-heat oven 180°C, full fan.
- Now finely chop the sage.
- In a mixing bowl, place the sage, breadcrumbs, cooked onions, sherry vinegar, Colman's mustard and wholegrain mustard; mix together, taste and season.

To build the toad in the hole

- Cut three disks out of the pastry; firstly, cut a 21cm disk out of the pastry.
- Then cut a 17cm disk out of the pastry, in this one cut out a 1cm round hole in the dead centre.
- Lastly cut one disk 2cm wide and with a little toothpick put a small hole in the middle.

- Cut a long strip of pastry and place in the fridge.
- Cut a sheet of baking parchment big enough to place the toad in the hole onto and place on a baking sheet.
- Place the 17cm disk on the greaseproof paper and brush liberally with the egg yolk mixture.
- Place the sausage on top, then add the breadcrumb mix on top.
- With the other large disk, fold over the sausage mix to form a pithivier.
- As you join all pastry together, gently flour your hands and work it round to make sure it's all joined together.
- Crimp with a fork to seal any holes and brush all over with the egg yolk mixture.
- With the strip of pastry on a floured surface gently pull apart without breaking it. Now cut a 17cm disk out of that and lay it on top of the puff pastry; cut a hole out of the top to line up with the hole in the first disk.
- Now egg wash all of the lattice and egg wash your last 2cm disk and put that on top to cover the hole, poke a little hole out the middle to help the filling leak out so it doesn't explode while cooking.

To cook

- Now place onto an oven rack and bake in the preheated oven for 30 minutes, turning after 15 minutes to ensure even cooking.
- Take off the baking parchment, return to the tray and bake for a further 10–15 minutes until the pastry is golden all over and the bottom is nice and crispy.
- Enjoy!

Reverend Theodore Hardy DSO MC VC

Born in Exeter in 1863, Theodore Bayley Hardy was the third of seven children. Before joining the Army he was ordained as a Deacon, became a schoolteacher and a curate in Nottinghamshire, and was made Headmaster at Bentham Grammar School. In 1913, he relocated to Hutton Roof in Cumbria as a parish priest. Tragically, his wife passed away the following year.

By this time Hardy was over 50, but still felt the need to volunteer at the outbreak of war. Front-line duty was refused as the authorities felt the front was no place for an older clergyman. However, after the slaughter of the Somme during the summer of 1916, Reverend Hardy was sent as chaplain to Etaples, a safe post on the French coast. He was determined to minister the fighting men in the mud and gore of the trenches and, in December 1916, he persuaded the Army to allow him to join the 8th Battalion Lincolnshire Regiment, at Vieille Chapelle.

Reverend Hardy ministered to the troops during the build up to Passchendaele, dodging the snipers, handing out sweets and cigarettes, writing letters for the troops, and calming many a lost and frightened soul, resulting in the award of a Distinguished Service Order. He continued to work at the front and was later awarded a Military Cross "for repeatedly going out under heavy fire to help the stretcher bearers during an attack".

In the spring of 1918, his regiment was moved to the Somme. In April that year, Hardy demonstrated his courage and devotion, tending to a wounded officer some 10 yards from a German machine gun; rescuing – under heavy fire – a soldier buried by a shell; and saving the life of an officer in no-man's land. On 9 August 1918, King George V presented Hardy with the Victoria Cross at Frohen-le-Grand, and appointed him Chaplain to His Majesty, hoping to remove him from the front. Reverend Hardy, however, returned to his battalion.

On 10 October 1918, Hardy was hit by machine-gun fire as his regiment crossed the river Selle by night. Eight days later he was dead. He was buried in the Commonwealth Cemetery, near Rouen. His medals are held by the Museum of Army Chaplaincy, Amport House, Hampshire. There are memorials to him at Carlisle Cathedral, the Harrow Arts Centre, City of London School and in his old church at Hutton Roof in Cumbria.

Written by Warrant Officer Ricky Kavanagh, Army (retired)

"Hardy demonstrated his courage and devotion, tending to a wounded officer some 10 yards from a German machine gun; rescuing – under heavy fire – a soldier buried by a shell; and saving the life of an officer in no-man's land"

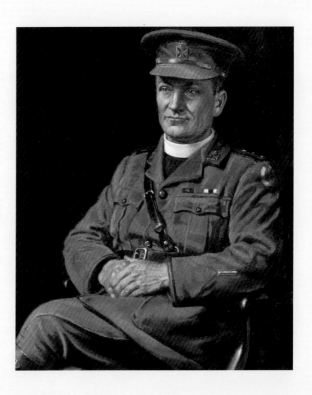

Pushing the boat out

Based in Cumbria, Boatwork Ltd repairs, restores and maintains boats and yachts for professional sailors and enthusiastic amateurs alike

www.boatwork.co.uk

"Our desire is to surpass people's expectations," says Mark Bestford who, with his wife Julie, owns and operates the yacht repair, restoration and maintenance business Boatwork Ltd. Undertaking a wide range of projects, from new builds to complete restorations of modern and traditional yachts, their aim is to reduce the pressure for owners, with a reliable service which produces craftsmanship results at competitive prices. Also material offcuts from projects are handcrafted into bespoke pieces of art reflecting timeless aspects of the sea.

Mark and Julie are Royal Navy veterans with decades of experience of the marine industry. Keen sailors, they've always retained an attachment to the sea and understand, as sailors, how hard it can sometimes be to find reliable service providers. Although their base in Whitehaven, Cumbria serves as a "one stop" facility, benefiting from sharing a yard with specialists in marine electronics and marine engineering, they pride themselves on being able and willing to travel to any part of the country to work with clients, bringing the boat yard with them, so to speak.

One such example is Pip Hare, who in November 2020 participated in the Vendée Globe, the single-handed, non-stop, round-the-world race in which yachts with seven-figure budgets and prestigious backers are pitted against competitors such as Pip, who subsist as much on passion and enthusiasm as sponsorship. Pip herself has written appreciatively of the 800-mile round trip that Mark, Julie and their dog Oaken made to Poole to work on her 20-year-old, 60-foot craft *Medallia* (pictured, below). "We're proud of helping Pip in her dream simply to reach the starting line of the race," says Mark.

Boatwork's clients also include young families looking for a pastime they can all enjoy, to those contemplating retirement looking for a craft on which they can explore the UK's waters and beyond. "In France, sailing is a mainstream sport for all ages," says Mark. "The UK is surrounded by water but people haven't had the opportunity to fully access this. That's changing and dream creators like us are helping enable that change."

A taste of the Lakes

Initially a specialist in Cumbrian jams and chutneys, Lakeland Artisan now sells beers, liqueurs, syrups and luxury treats infused with the spirit of the Lake District

www.lakelandartisan.co.uk

Cumbria is famous for the lakes and mountains that have influenced artists and poets and offered memorable holidays for millions. The county is also getting a reputation as a foodie hub. Two of these foodies are Geoff and Mary Monkman, whose company Lakeland Artisan has become a champion for locally produced food and drink.

The business started in 2006, making preserves and relishes using fructose. "But there are only so many different jams and chutneys you can make, hence the need to diversify," says Geoff. "So I launched a range that celebrated everything Cumbrian – including Westmorland damson chutney, rum butter and sticky toffee sauce. I was selling at the Christmas markets in Manchester and, over the years, I became very good friends with Nigel Mawson, the third-generation owner of Mawson's Traditional Drinks. When the opportunity came to buy the business off Nigel I thought it would be great to sell Mawson's drinks alongside my fruit preserves."

Geoff's first experiment was mixing Westmorland damson syrup with prosecco at his wedding in 2017. "It went down so well that we decided to bottle it and sell it alongside our other products," he says. Geoff and his wife Mary then launched Lakeland Liqueurs which now produces more than 20 different varieties, using gin, rum, vodka and whisky. They also invested in a gin still and launched Herdwick Distillery in 2021.

The pair currently have five shops in Cumbria selling their vast range of produce alongside other amazing local produce, including Kendal Mint cake, luxury truffles and handmade gingerbread, all of which are sold online through Lakeland Hampers. "We want to promote other local business alongside our own," says Geoff. "They have been around for years and we want to support each other. People buy us as a reminder of their happy holiday in the Lake District, or they are sent by locals to friends and family to remind them of the Lakes." Lakeland Artisan also stocks beers from over a dozen local breweries under the newly created website Lakeland Ales. "Having won over 60 Great Taste Awards in the last few years, we're obviously doing something right!" says Geoff, with a grin.

Chicken kebabs, tzatziki, flatbreads and village salad

Sergeant Andy Epps, RAF

I was fortunate enough to live in Cyprus for three years and taste the simple but delicious local food. British Forces have been in Cyprus from the late 1800s to the present day, and many British people who have spent any amount of time there have their own interpretation of different Cypriot dishes. My recipes are my own take, which use simple Cypriot ingredients to produce lovely food.

**Preparation time: 45 minutes, plus
  2–3 hours to marinate
Cooking time: 10–15 minutes**

Serves 4

INGREDIENTS

For the chicken kebab
12 boneless chicken thighs (3 per portion)
4 garlic cloves, crushed
2 tsp paprika
1 red chilli, deseeded and finely sliced
Juice of 1 lemon (half for the marinade
  and half to squeeze over the chicken
  before serving)
3 tbsp natural yoghurt
2 tbsp coriander, coarsely chopped
2 tbsp parsley, coarsely chopped
2 tbsp dried oregano
Salt and pepper to taste

For the tzatziki
½ cucumber, grated
500g goats milk yoghurt from St Helen's
  Farm (or natural yoghurt)
3 tsp mint sauce
1 tsp paprika
Salt and pepper to taste
Mint leaves to garnish

For the village salad
½ cucumber, halved lengthways and
  finely sliced
2 salad tomatoes, quartered, de-seeded
  and finely sliced
½ red onion, quartered and finely sliced
1 green pepper, deseeded and cut into
  large pieces
20 kalamata olives
100g feta cheese, cut into 1cm dice

For the salad dressing
3 tbsp olive oil
1 tbsp lemon juice
1 tbsp red wine vinegar
2 garlic cloves, crushed
1 tsp dried oregano
Salt and pepper to taste

For the flatbread
300g plain flour (plus extra for dusting)
185ml milk
3½ tbsp vegetable oil

Cyprus: Local hero

Ömer Faik Müftüzade OBE QGM

Ömer Faik Müftüzade was born in Larnaca in November 1915 and started his career as a teacher at the Lefkoşa Türk Lisesi. In 1940, he joined the newly formed Cyprus Regiment, a unit of the British Army comprising 30,000 Greek and Turkish Cypriot volunteers. During the Second World War, he predominantly served in the Gulf of Aqaba before being promoted through the ranks to major and, from 1946–49, commanding the regiment.

In 1950, Faik relinquished his commission before undertaking a number of roles in the island's civil service, including in the police and the prison service. He was a keen footballer, referee and football manager: his son relates a story about his father refereeing a match in 1950s Larnaca when a spectator threw a bottle onto the pitch. As Commissioner of Larnaca, Faik had the man arrested before blowing the whistle and re-starting the match.

On 20 July 1974, Faik was the area officer for the British military bases on Limassol when the Turkish army invaded and heavy fighting broke out between Greek and Turkish Cypriot forces. Faik was given the role of negotiating a ceasefire to allow the safe evacuation of British personnel. Accompanied by a British officer and three soldiers, he drove into Limassol, through Greek Cypriot National Guard checkpoints where the party was disarmed before heading to the Turkish commander. His vehicle was hit and damaged by gunfire, and negotiations took place among sporadic small arms and mortar fire. At the National Guard roadblock they recovered their weapons before changing vehicles and drove on to the National Guard commander to confirm the acceptance of the ceasefire.

The actions of Faik and the four servicemen enabled the safe evacuation of 11,000 British service personnel and their families to safety. Faik (pictured above, right, with his wife, centre, and Governor of Cyprus Sir Hugh Foot, left) was awarded the Queen's Commendation for Bravery, which cited his outstanding courage and devotion to duty. He went on to be the first London representative for the Turkish Federated State of Cyprus before returning to Cyprus in 1991. He died on 9 July 2002 aged 87 and is buried in Nicosia.

As a seven-year-old boy, I can remember that convoy of vehicles coming on to RAF Akrotiri and the agitated British military families congregating on football pitches opposite the Astra Cinema. Our safety was assured through the courage of Ömer Faik Müftüzade.

Written by Squadron Leader Jon Pullen, RAF (retired)

METHOD

For the chicken kebab

- Score three or four incisions in each of the chicken thighs with a sharp knife.
- Mix the garlic, paprika, chilli, juice of half a lemon, yoghurt and herbs together in a bowl and season with salt and pepper.
- Add the chicken, mix to thoroughly coat, cover and leave to marinate in the fridge for 2–3 hours.
- Once marinated thread the chicken onto skewers and cook on the barbecue, or under a hot grill, for about 2 or 3 minutes on each side until the chicken is thoroughly cooked through to the middle.

To make the tzatziki

- Combine all the ingredients and garnish with fresh mint leaves, chill in the fridge until required.

For the village salad and dressing

- Combine the cucumber, tomatoes, red onion, peppers and olives together in a bowl, mix the dressing ingredients together and dress the salad just before serving until well coated then top with the feta.

For the flatbread

- Place all of the ingredients in a mixer and combine to a smooth dough. If the dough seems a little sticky add a little more flour.
- Wrap the dough in clingfilm and rest at room temperature for 30 minutes.
- Cut the dough into four equal portions and roll into balls; dust the worktop with a little flour and roll out the balls into 2mm thick discs.
- Heat a little oil in a frying pan over a medium heat and cook the flatbreads for about 2 minutes on each side or until golden brown.
- Once all the flatbreads are cooked cover with a clean tea towel until ready to serve.

To serve

- Remove the skewers from the chicken and squeeze over the juice of half a lemon; serve with the warm flatbreads, tzatziki and dressed village salad.

VEGETARIAN/VEGAN ALTERNATIVE

- Replace the chicken with a selection of vegetables such as peppers, courgette, mushrooms, red onion and aubergine.
- For a vegan option substitute the natural yoghurt in the kebab marinade for olive oil and use vegan yoghurt to make the tzatziki, or substitute the tzatziki for houmous.

Way to goat

St Helen's Farm in Yorkshire is Britain's favourite supplier of goat milk – and an enthusiastic supporter of philanthropic causes

www.sthelensfarm.co.uk

When St Helen's Farm started producing goat milk back in 1986, there were very few other producers on the market. Over time, it has grown to become the UK's favourite supplier of goat milk, all of it coming from its dairy in the Vale of York, where the milk is produced along with other goat products such as butter and yoghurt as well as goat cheese produced with Singletons in Lancashire. And, as St Helen's Farm is owned by a charitable trust, 100 per cent of profits go to support a range of good causes in the UK and abroad. More than £63 million has been donated by the Kavli Trust since its conception, when it was set up to carry on the philanthropic work of the Kavli Group's founders, Olaf and Knut Kavli.

"What is unique about the business is, because of our history and the fact we are owned by a charitable trust, we really care about the community and that runs through everything we do," says Gareth Watson, the Brand Manager. "When we began supplying goat milk, we knew that there was a better way – a better milk. People struggled to find goat milk in supermarkets, and we fulfilled the needs of customers who enjoyed its gentle wonders. That community has really backed us ever since."

Goat milk is versatile, delicious and nutritious. "It's just great milk," says Gareth. It also has additional health benefits. It is four times higher in prebiotics than cow milk, which helps it to maintain the digestive tract and gut. It has slightly lower lactose levels, which may explain why some people who experience sensitivity

to lactose can enjoy goat milk more than cow milk. And, as you'd expect from any great milk, it's bursting with many essential vitamins and minerals that the body needs to function and stay healthy.

The dairy at St Helen's Farm now produces millions of litres of its gentle milk each year as well as its traditionally crafted yoghurt and butter. "There is still a real family feel at St Helen's Farm, and a lot of Yorkshire pride in the team," says Gareth. "Everyone is personally invested in our common goal – creating great-tasting products to support good causes."

Kilkeel mussels in Guinness with soda bread

Corporal Karla Wickham, RAF

Northern Ireland is famous for its seafood; Ardglass, Kilkeel and Portagovie are the three main fishing ports that make County Down shellfish central. Kilkeel is situated in the heart of the ancient kingdom of the Mournes and it is renowned for its thriving fishing industry and its famous mussels.

Down

Preparation time: 20 minutes
Cooking time: 45 minutes

Serves 2

INGREDIENTS

For the soda bread
250g plain flour
1 tsp salt
1 tsp bicarbonate of soda
190ml buttermilk
½ egg, beaten
50ml Guinness
50g black treacle (plus a bit extra
  for brushing the top of the soda bread)
45g mixed seeds (such as pumpkin,
  sunflower, golden linseeds)
Butter for serving

For the mussels
1kg mussels
10g butter
2 shallots, finely diced
1 clove garlic, crushed or finely chopped
½ leek finely sliced
50ml white wine
150ml Guinness
100ml double cream
1 spring onion, finely sliced
Salt and freshly ground black pepper

METHOD

To make the soda bread
• Preheat the oven to 170°C and grease a 500g loaf tin.
• Mix the flour, salt and bicarbonate of soda together in a mixing bowl.
• In a separate bowl, mix together the buttermilk, egg, Guinness and treacle; add to the dry ingredients and quickly mix, as soon as the dough is combined stop, do not overwork it.
• Shape the dough into an oblong and place in the prepared loaf tin, place in middle of the preheated oven and bake for 35–40 minutes until golden brown; tap the bottom of the loaf, it should sound hollow.
• Remove from the oven, turn out onto a cooling rack, brush with treacle and sprinkle with the mixed seeds.

To cook the mussels
• Once the soda bread is in the oven, start cooking the mussels.
• Clean and "debeard" all of the mussels. If any are open give them a tap and, if they do not close, discard.
• Melt the butter in a large pan, add the shallots, garlic and leeks and cook without colour.
• Add the white wine, reduce by half then pour in the Guinness.
• Add the mussels, cover the pan with a lid and cook for 3–4 minutes until the mussels have opened; you will need to shake the pan a couple of times while the mussels are cooking.
• Once the mussels have opened, remove them with a slotted spoon and place into a bowl, if any mussels are closed discard them.
• Return the pan with all of the cooking liquid to a medium-high heat, stir in the cream, bring to a simmer and reduce until it has slightly thickened, season with salt and pepper to your taste.
• Remove the pan from the heat, tip in the mussels, including any juice that has collected in the bowl, and stir to coat with the sauce.

To serve
• Portion the mussels into bowls, spoon over the sauce, garnish with the sliced spring onion and serve with the sliced warm soda bread and butter.

Rear Admiral The Honourable Edward Barry Stewart Bingham VC, OBE

Edward Barry Stewart Bingham was born on 26 July 1881 at Bangor Castle in County Down and was the third son of John, 5th Baron Clanmorris, JP, DL, aide-de-camp to the Lord Lieutenant of Ireland. He joined the Royal Navy in 1895 and trained on the Dartmouth-based training ship HMS *Britannia* before being commissioned as a midshipman in 1897. An excellent horseman, he was a member of the Royal Navy polo team, winning the Inter-Regimental and Ships Cup in Malta in 1903.

By the start of war in 1914 he had risen to the rank of Lieutenant-Commander and engaged in two early battles aboard HMS *Invincible*: the Battle of Heligoland Bight and the Battle of the Falklands, where he played a prominent role in the defeat of Vice-Admiral Graf von Spee's Pacific Squadron. He was promoted to Commander on 31 December 1914. In early 1915, while in command of HMS *Hornet*, he led the daring rescue of 500 crewmembers from HMS *Argyll* that had run aground off the coast of Dundee.

On 31 May 1916, during the Battle of Jutland, he commanded a division of destroyers from his ship HMS *Nestor*. He closed to within 2,750 metres to fire torpedoes on the enemy while under intense enemy fire but his ship eventually succumbed to German firepower. "It was clear that the doomed *Nestor* was sinking rapidly," he recalled in his memoirs. "At that moment I gave my last order as her commander, 'Abandon ship'." Amazingly, he managed to evacuate his entire crew into small boats and destroy all classified documents. The survivors were picked up by a German destroyer and Bingham was held as a prisoner for the rest of the war. He became the only member of the Royal Navy to be awarded the Victoria Cross while in captivity during the war, eventually receiving the medal on 13 December 1918 from King George V. He ended up serving as an aide-de-camp (or personal assistant) to the king, before retiring in 1932 as a Rear-Admiral, settling in Evershot, Dorset. He died in a London nursing home in 1939.

In 1941, Bangor Borough Council purchased his birthplace and converted it into the Town Hall. His medals were purchased in 1983 from a private collector for £18,000 by North Down Borough Council, and were subsequently displayed in the Heritage Centre.

Written by Sergeant Scott Turner, RAF

Nutritious knowledge

The Nutrition Society has been researching issues of nutrition, public health and food science for eight decades

www.nutritionsociety.org

On 23 July 1941, at the Royal Institution in London, 28 individuals from different disciplines in nutrition came together and formed the Nutrition Society. The aim was to enable workers studying different aspects of the same nutritional problem across agriculture, policy, science and medicine to meet and help each other with information, and constructive criticism.

"Initiatives to help people eat a balanced diet during times of shortage are surprisingly similar today," says Dr Carrie Ruxton, Trustee of the Nutrition Society. "People are urged to cook from scratch, reduce portion sizes, avoid waste, eat plant-based foods, and choose fruit and vegetables in season."

The rationing system used during the Second World War had already been worked out in 1939, following the establishment in 1935 of a government advisory committee on nutrition. As tensions in Europe mounted, the nutritional state of the nation was of immediate concern for a country at war. Full communication was essential between official bodies and scientists who could aid the programme of preparing schemes for rationing food, and for the proper utilisation of supplies that looked likely to decrease when war might cut off essential food imports from overseas.

In 1940, Dr Kon of the National Institute for Research in Dairying at Shinfield in Berkshire organised informal meetings of key nutrition specialists who met monthly to exchange ideas and information on the increasing problems of wartime nutrition and food supplies, just as rationing schemes came into force. These informal meetings soon led to the formation of the Nutrition Society which, by September 1941, had more than 250 members and had elected Sir John Boyd Orr, Director of the Rowett Research Institute, as its first President. Sir John was later ennobled as Baron Boyd Orr in 1949, the same year that he was awarded the Nobel Peace Prize for his hunger relief work with the United Nations.

The Nutrition Society's initial scientific meetings more than fulfilled the hopes of its founders, at a time when there were increasing pressures of wartime restrictions due to air raids, losses of sea convoys and extension of war in the Far East. Its members stepped up efforts to ensure good nutrition for the maximum war effort and the ultimate survival of the UK. "One of the Nutrition Society's important modern-day functions is to present strong evidence to government and policy makers on the importance and longevity of nutritional science," says Carrie. "Some of the journal articles published in the 1940s are still being cited today."

The Nutrition Society is now celebrating its 80th anniversary and has nearly 3,000 members based in 85 countries around the world. Members of the Nutrition Society are today still working to improve the nutritional state of their nations, facing many complex global nutritional and public health issues such as those relating to obesity, malnutrition, diabetes and cardiovascular disease.

"As in times of food rationing, plant-based meals are in," says Penny Hunking, Trustee of the Nutrition Society. "Dishes of meat and fish can be 'extended' with beans, pulses, lentils and vegetables to make everyday meals such as salads, soups, stews and curries. Most parts of animals can be eaten and perhaps we can consider adding pigs' trotters, kidneys, heart, sweetbreads and tripe to our menus? At least today we have the advantage of owning freezers, fridges and microwaves so our food can be stored and cooked safely and inventively to minimise any waste."

Sussex smokie

Leading Catering Services Bunama Bojang, Royal Navy

Traditional Sussex smokie is said to date back to the early 19th century and, with a fantastic selection of fresh fish available along its coast, this classic Sussex dish is still very popular. There are many variants, but it's essentially a baked dish of smoked haddock and leeks in a cheese sauce topped with breadcrumbs. My take on this dish turns it into a fine-dining delight, using all the traditional ingredients.

**Preparation time: 45–60 minutes,
 plus 12 hours chilling time
Cooking time: 1½–2 hours**

Serves 4

INGREDIENTS

For the potatoes
300ml double cream
200ml milk
2 garlic cloves, finely chopped
Pinch of nutmeg
500g Maris Piper potatoes, peeled
 and thinly sliced
100g cheddar cheese, grated

For the white wine sauce
10g butter
1 shallot, finely diced
1 tsp fresh thyme leaves
100ml white wine
100ml double cream
2 tbsp lemon juice
1 tbsp parsley, coarsely chopped

For the haddock
100g plain flour
2 eggs
100g fresh breadcrumbs
4 smoked haddock fillets
Salt and freshly ground black pepper

For the vegetables
4 baby leeks
12 asparagus spears
5g butter
Salt and freshly ground black pepper

METHOD

To prepare the potatoes

- Preheat the oven 160°C.
- Pour the cream and milk into a saucepan, add the chopped garlic and a pinch of nutmeg, place over a medium heat, bring to a simmer then set aside to infuse.
- Layer the potatoes in a lightly buttered baking dish, sprinkling a little cheese, salt and pepper in between each layer then scatter the remaining cheese on top.
- Pour the hot milk and cream mix over the potatoes, allowing it to settle between the layers, and bake in the preheated oven for 45–60 minutes or until golden brown on top and the potatoes are tender through to the middle.
- Remove the dish from the oven, allow to cool at room temperature then chill in the fridge overnight, ideally with a suitably sized weight on top to press the potatoes.

For the white wine sauce

- Melt the butter in a pan over a low-medium heat and gently fry the shallots and thyme for about 10 minutes until the shallots are soft and translucent.
- Increase the heat to medium-high, pour in the wine, bring to a boil and reduce by half.
- Whisk in the cream, bring to a simmer, remove from the heat, stir in the lemon juice and parsley and season with salt and black pepper; set aside ready to reheat.

To cook the potatoes

- Preheat the oven to 180°C.
- Once set, turn out the potatoes, cut into four neat squares, oblongs or rounds; place on a baking tray lined with a piece of baking parchment and reheat in the oven for about 20 minutes until heated through to the middle.

For the haddock

- Prepare the coating for the haddock. Place the flour in a shallow container and season generously with salt and pepper, beat the eggs in a second container and tip the breadcrumbs into a third.
- Coat the haddock fillets in the flour, shake off the excess, dip in the beaten egg until completely covered then evenly coat with breadcrumbs; place on a baking sheet.
- Bake in the oven with the potatoes for about 10 minutes or until thoroughly cooked.

For the leeks & asparagus

- While the potatoes and fish are baking in the oven, blanch the baby leeks and asparagus in salted boiling water until just tender; drain and dry on absorbent kitchen paper.
- Heat the butter in a frying pan or griddle and sear the vegetables until heated through and lightly coloured.

To serve

- Reheat the sauce, plate the haddock, potatoes and vegetables and serve with a small jug of the sauce.

East Sussex: Local hero

Warrant Officer Albert "Bert" Avann LoH

Born on 1 April 1925 in Robertsbridge, East Sussex, Albert "Bert" Avann always dreamed of joining the Royal Air Force, serving as a cadet of his local Air Training Corps. In October 1943, not long after his 18th birthday, he enlisted at the Air Crew Receiving Centre in St Johns Wood, London, assigned the service number 3030746.

On completion of his initial training, Bert was sent to No. 4 Air Gunnery School at RAF Morpeth, Northumberland, to undertake his training as an air gunner before being assigned to No. 218 (Gold Coast) Squadron (named after the Governor of the Gold Coast, modern-day Ghana). He carried out the dangerous role of a rear gunner on the Lancaster bomber.

Up to 27 December 1944, Bert successfully completed 30 operations, rising to the rank of Warrant Officer. In the run up to the D-Day landings, Bert and his squadron were heavily involved in Operation Glimmer, a series of diversionary bombing raids designed to fool German forces into thinking that the landings were taking place outside of Normandy. These proved critical to the success of Operation Overlord and the overall success of the D-Day landings.

Bert is the proud holder of the Bomber Command Clasp along with his 1939–45 star. In May 2017, the French president awarded him the rank of "Chevalier" in the Ordre national de la Légion d'honneur. This is the highest decoration bestowed in France and can be awarded to foreign recipients for military and civil merits. Bert was awarded this for his steadfast involvement in the liberation of France during the Second World War.

When I had the privilege of meeting Bert in October 2020, he told me of his stories during the war and what he had done after the war back home. He shared with me his love of cricket and talked about his job with Gray-Nicolls in Robertsbridge in East Sussex, who make some of the world's best cricket bats. He also talked about his love of his mother's rabbit pie, which was always a treat when he would come home on leave. Bert is still very active with his local Royal British Legion branch in East Sussex. He has been married to Jean for 66 years now and they have two children, three grandchildren and two great grandchildren.

Written by Chief Petty Officer Ryan Barnett, Royal Navy

Yorkshire puddings with onion gravy

James Martin, chef, restaurateur and TV presenter

This recipe is an old favourite of my family's and, if I am honest, the batter is my grandmother's old recipe. She used to live in York, so did her sister, and we used to enjoy this every Sunday. I still make it to this day and always will.

Preparation time: 10 minutes,
  plus overnight resting
Cooking time: 30–40 minutes for the
  puddings and 20 minutes for the sauce

Makes 10–12

INGREDIENTS

For the Yorkshire puddings
225g plain flour
8 medium eggs
570ml milk, full fat
8 tsp dripping
Pinch of salt

For the onion gravy
50g butter
3 onions, peeled and sliced
100ml madeira
25ml sherry
500ml veal jus
50ml red wine

METHOD

For the Yorkshire puddings
• Preheat the oven to 200°C.
• Whisk all the ingredients for the Yorkshire puddings together in a bowl. Allow to rest in the fridge overnight.
• Put the dripping into pudding moulds and put in the oven until smoking hot, ladle the mix in or pour from a jug and cook for 30–40 minutes.

To make the onion gravy
• Cook out the onions in half the butter until deeply coloured add the madeira wine, sherry, jus and red wine to a saucepan, bring to the boil and reduce by half. Season and finish with the rest of the butter.

John "Jack" Harrison VC MC

John Harrison, known to all as "Jack", was born on 12 November 1890 to John and Charlotte Harrison in East Hull. He was educated at Craven Street School, excelling at rugby and swimming, before continuing his studies at St John Training College. As well as securing a teaching position with Lime Street School, he played professional rugby league, initially for York RLC and then for Hull FC. During the 1914/15 season he scored 52 tries for Hull – a record that still stands today – and he went on to score a total of 106 tries in 116 matches. On 6 June 1915, just before the birth of his son Jackie, he witnessed the first Zeppelin raid over Hull, which inflicted huge destruction on his town. On Boxing Day 1915, Jack played his last game for Hull FC, before training as a cadet in the Officer Training Corps.

Jack was commissioned as Temporary 2nd Lieutenant and assigned to the 11th Battalion East Yorkshire Regiment (Hull Tradesmen) 6 Platoon on 4 August 1916. On 25 February 1917, during a battle near Hebuterne, he led a patrol into no-man's land and, after bringing back a prisoner and handling his platoon with courage and skill, he was awarded the Military Cross.

On 3 May 1917, during the battle of Aras, his platoon was pinned down by enemy machine-gun fire. In the darkness and the smoke, Jack led his company against the enemy trench under fire. He single-handedly made a dash at the machine-gun, to knock out the gun and save the lives of many of his company. His self-sacrifice and absolute disregard of danger earned him a Victoria Cross, but his body was never found.

His wife, Lilian Harrison, was presented with Jack's VC at Buckingham Palace by King George V in March 1918. Their son Jackie went on to serve during the Second World War and was tragically killed at Dunkirk. When Lillian died on 5 December 1977, she bequeathed Harrison's medals to the East Yorkshire regimental museum. In 2003, a memorial plinth was erected at the KC Stadium, home of Hull FC, and a memorial fund established in his name. Each year, Army and Navy teams compete for the Jack Harrison VC Memorial Trophy.

Written by Sergeant Richard Street, Army, and Kimberly Thornton Medical Support Officer, Army

> *"During the 1914/15 season he scored 52 tries for Hull – a record that still stands today – and went on to score a total of 106 tries in 116 matches"*

Safety first

Bespoke Guardians uses military expertise to address the complex needs of some of the country's most troubled children

www.bespokeguardians.co.uk

When two terrified parents employed Rob Firmin to protect them from their adopted teenage son, the former soldier was forced to rely on all his training learnt during a decade in the Army. "The lad had a knife he wasn't going to put down," he remembers. "He had all sorts of childhood trauma and it took me months to build his trust. But we slowly got there."

This challenging encounter would set Rob Firmin on a path to creating Bespoke Guardians, an organisation dedicated to providing intense support for young people with complex needs, and guiding them towards healthy, safe and fulfilling futures. From its head office in Wiltshire, Rob's team of more than 30 support workers now operate across the UK, bringing their expertise to help some of society's most troubled children.

"Most of the children we meet have already had over 200 rejections from homes," he says. "They're severely traumatised, with almost all of them having suffered sexual, physical, emotional abuse or neglect in their past."

At the request of local authorities, the staff will do everything required to provide a safe environment, from painting a child's bedroom to taking them to the zoo. "We're trying to keep them in the community, giving them the most normal life they can have," explains Rob.

As well as being the first in the UK to provide this level of support, Bespoke Guardians is uniquely equipped to deal with the personal risk presented by these disturbed children. Rob provides bespoke training for his staff, most of whom share his military background.

"Everyone in my team remains calm in very complex, often threatening situations, reassuring the child and everyone around them," he says. "They're extremely robust in challenging circumstances, and I'm very proud of them."

Rob has huge hopes for the growth of Bespoke Guardians, to include homes across the country ready to welcome the children the rest of society can't handle. "One boy told me he'd never flown a kite in case he tied it around his neck, so we flew a kite," he remembers. "For me, it's all about the kids. Their lives have been taken from them, often by an adult when they were too young to defend themselves. We're just trying to give them back."

Tickle on the tongue

Puckett's Pickles are created in York using fresh British ingredients and traditional recipes that come handed down from Sarah Puckett's ancestors

www.puckettspickles.co.uk

Sarah Puckett started embracing all things pickled in 2013 when she started Puckett's Pickles from her kitchen armed with nothing more than some fresh vegetables, spices, a couple of wooden spoons, and her grandparents' recipe books. From these, she started to craft delicious chutneys and pickles such as her legendary piccalilli – the "Puckalilli" – based on an old family recipe. "My grandfathers were seafarers who would bring home spices from all over the world, which my grandmothers would make into chutney and pickles," says Sarah. "The Puckalilli is our best seller. It's made to my grandma Betty's recipe. Her brother was on the HMS *Rawalpindi*, which sank in 1939."

The Puckalilli is so good it can convert any sceptic. Sarah (pictured, opposite) uses only the freshest vegetables, locally sourced where possible, ensuring they are pickled as soon after picking as possible. To these she adds the finest quality vinegars and spices, creating high-impact, wholesome, healthy pickles free of preservatives and food miles. "It's lovely when you are doing a food show and people try our piccalilli, with the lovely cumin and coriander and fresh vegetables from Lincolnshire and Yorkshire, and are converted on the spot as it isn't the gloop they are used to," she says. "We take care over the flavour and texture and the origin of the ingredients."

Before she started Puckett's Pickles, Sarah worked for Pret A Manger. After 15 successful years that included opening the first Pret in New York City, she grew tired of coffee and sandwiches, and decided to turn her love of pickling into a viable business. As well as her grandmothers' recipes, she used her father's recipe for pickled onions and her own instinct

for flavour and freshness. Since those early days, Puckett's Pickles has gone from strength to strength. The company distributes to customers the length of the country – from the Scilly Isles to the Orkneys – and grew by an astonishing 600 per cent during lockdown as the British public looked for taste experiences that were different but nostalgic, authentic and packed with memorable flavour.

As well as the acclaimed Puckalilli, Puckett's Pickles produces chilli chutney, a carrot & cardamom chutney, a pea and mint ketchup, picked onions, a spice tomato chutney, a pear & apricot chutney, a red onion chutney, a redcurrant jelly with port, an apple sauce with cider and a chilli ketchup, a horseradish sauce with gin with other sauces, pickles and chutneys added to the portfolio depending on the season. Collectively, it's a celebration of the very finest British food and produce and Puckett's has been acclaimed by Michelin-starred British chefs, who appreciate the superior quality and flavours.

"We celebrate British produce and we keep it simple," says Sarah. "If a product is picked and pickled really quickly, it tastes amazing. So we get the best tomato and add some lovely spices and sugar and vinegar and you have something special. We have simple and straightforward packaging so the food does the talking, with small labels that allow the food to be the focus. We want to keep things simple and honest. My favourite supper as a child was the fridge-cleaner – the leftovers with the pickles from my dad's pickle cupboard. I want my customers to get that same warm feeling when they see a jar of Puckett's on the table."

Steak and oatmeal pie

Senior Aircraftman Connor Mackie, RAF

This dish is based on a recipe handed down to me from my great grandad, George Barnett, who was an RAF chef during the Second World War. I have received a few recipes that he used during his time in the RAF and have adapted them to take advantage of modern cooking techniques and ingredients. My grandad was very well known in East Fife as he owned several bakeries in the area, called GH Barnett's – the bakeries are still running to this day, under the stewardship of his son Stuart Barnett.

**Preparation time: 30 minutes, plus
  30 minutes pastry resting time
Cooking time: 1 hour 45 minutes**

Serves 4

INGREDIENTS

For the filling
2 tbsp vegetable oil
500g beef silverside, diced
1 onion, coarsely diced
50g tomato purée
180ml beef stock
2 garlic cloves, finely chopped
  or crushed
1tsp thyme, coarsely chopped
50ml vinegar
50g sugar
100g oats
Salt and pepper to taste

For the pastry
250g plain flour
50g cornflour
1 tsp salt
1 tsp white pepper
125g salted butter
1 egg, beaten
Cold water as required

For the sauce
60ml red wine
1 litre beef stock
20g butter (or 10g liquid glucose)

METHOD

To make the filling

- Heat the oil in a skillet or large frying pan over a high heat, add the beef and sear until well browned all over (do this in a couple of batches to avoid overcrowding the pan) and transfer to a casserole or heavy-based saucepan.
- Add the onions to the skillet, cook, stirring frequently, until well caramelised and add to the beef in the casserole; set the skillet to one side, without cleaning, to use for the sauce.
- Place the casserole with the beef and onions over a high heat, pour in enough water to cover and bring to a simmer; reduce the heat and simmer for 30–45 minutes until the liquid has reduced by half.
- Add the tomato purée, beef stock, garlic and thyme and bring back to a simmer.
- Meanwhile simmer the vinegar and sugar in a small saucepan over a medium heat until reduced by half, pour into the casserole and simmer until the liquid has reduced to a coating consistency sauce; season with salt and pepper, stir in the oats and set aside to cool at room temperature.

To make the pastry

- Mix the flour, cornflour, salt and pepper together in a bowl and rub in the butter with your fingertips until it resembles fine breadcrumbs.
- Make a well in the centre, add the egg and enough cold water to make a smooth firm dough; wrap in clingfilm and rest in the fridge for 30 minutes.

To make and cook the pie

- Preheat the oven to 180°C and lightly butter a pie dish.
- Spoon the pie filling into the pie dish, roll out the pastry slightly larger than the pie dish, brush the rim of the dish with the beaten egg, drape the pastry over the pie and press to seal the edges.
- Crimp the pastry to give a classic look to your pie by pinching the edge of the pastry lid between your index finger and thumb on one hand, while gently pressing in between with your other index finger at the same time; brush the top with the beaten egg, pierce a small hole in the centre of the pie and bake in the preheated oven for 35–40 minutes.

To make the sauce

- Place the skillet used to seal the beef over a high heat, add the red wine, reduce by half then pour in the beef stock and simmer until reduced by three-quarters (you should have about 250ml of sauce); season, strain into a clean saucepan and whisk in the butter (or glucose) when you're ready to serve.

To serve

- Cut the pie into four equal wedges, portion onto plates and pour over the sauce; I recommend serving the pie with honey-roasted root vegetables (carrots, parsnips and turnips) and Dauphin potatoes (deep fried balls of mashed potato mixed with choux paste).

Edinburgh: Local hero

Corporal Mark William Wright GC

Mark William Wright was born in Edinburgh on 22 April 1979 to Robert and Jemma Wright. He attended Prestonfield Primary and then St Serfs at Westercoats, Edinburgh, but was keen to leave school early and fulfil his dream of joining the Parachute Regiment.

Wright joined the Army in January 1999 and successfully completed training before his first posting to the 3rd Battalion Parachute Regiment in October. By 2003 he had completed three tours of Northern Ireland and was working as a Number One in a mortar detachment, in charge of commanding and aiming the mortar. In May 2003, he deployed with the 3rd Battalion to Iraq where he served with distinction and by 2006 he was promoted to corporal, employed as a mortar fire controller.

He was deployed to Afghanistan in May 2006. On 6 September, on patrol in Helmand, one of Wright's patrol, Lance Corporal Hale, stepped on a land mine, which blew his leg off. Seeing the incident from a distance, Wright rushed to enter the minefield, ordering two soldiers to manage Hale's treatment and ordering other non-essential soldiers out of the minefield. Realising Hale was likely to bleed to death, Wright ordered a helicopter and directed a route to be cleared to the landing site. This was done by Corporal Stuart Pearson, who unfortunately stepped on a mine which blew his left leg off. Wright administered initial first aid to Pearson until a medic could take over. When the Chinook arrived, Wright stood up to move to it but set off another mine causing serious injuries. By now there were seven injuries, three with lost limbs. Throughout the chaos and bloodshed, Wright maintained the morale of all soldiers under his command. Sadly Corporal Wright later died of his injuries.

On 14 December 2006, he was posthumously awarded the George Cross for an act of "the greatest gallantry and complete disregard for his own safety in striving to save others". He was cremated at Mortonhall Crematorium, Edinburgh. His life story and the events of 6 September 2006 have been immortalised in the 2014 film *Kajaki* and his medals are on loan to the National War Museum of Scotland. On 17 August 2009, the first purpose-built Army Recovery Centre was officially opened and named Mark Wright House in his honour.

Written by Corporal John Drummond, Army (retired)

Making the connection

Pimento Connection is an executive recruitment firm specialising in working with high-calibre candidates to help clients who are looking to grow their business

www.pimentoconnection.com

After 34 years of military service, Cliff Allum MBE was well aware of the difficulties that former service personnel faced in civilian life. Nowadays, of course, there is an effective resettlement service, but in 2007 this was not the case. During a discussion with fellow soldiers at a military club in London he conceived the idea of Pimento Connection, naming it honour of his friend and hero Tony Brooks (see page 196). Tony was an agent for the Special Operations Executive in the Second World War, leading a resistance circuit in France called Pimento.

Fast forward to 2021 and Pimento Connection is an established executive recruitment firm with strong military ties. "We specialise in the placement of former service men and women, and similarly qualified civilians," says Cliff. "Quality people come from a variety of backgrounds and they may or may not have served in the Armed Forces. The essential qualities in candidates we look for are commitment, loyalty, tenacity, enthusiasm and attention to detail. These are the qualities of the warrior but they are not confined to those who have served."

Pimento Connection is a signatory of the Armed Forces Covenant and has won a number of successful contracts with major national and international customers specialising in – but by no means confined to – defence, defence IT, engineering and construction. It supplies high-quality, permanent, contractor and consultancy personnel in both the UK and across the globe. Pimento also provides a consultancy service internationally.

The most recent addition to Pimento Connection is the development of Veteran Connection. "We created Veteran Connection to enable veterans to access successful business opportunities in the UK and internationally,"

says Pimento's CEO Caroline Bentley. "Businesses are often keen to specifically employ former service men and women. Here veterans can create a profile to showcase their wins and successes throughout their career, which will be very attractive to our customers. We also provide accessible information for mental health and wellbeing, CV writing and interview techniques plus overseas opportunities. Veteran Connection is constantly evolving to meet the needs of our candidates and our customers. Our aim is for Veteran Connection to enable service personnel to recognise their intrinsic value to the business world."

Pimento's ethos has always been "right people, right place, right time". It focuses on providing a professional service to its customers and – equally important – the same quality and attention to detail is given to its candidates. Pimento enjoys working with service personnel and civilians in equal measures.

Cliff joined the Army in 1970 as a soldier and was later commission into the Royal Tank Regiment, serving across the world in a variety of operational and training roles, and ultimately receiving an MBE. He made his own transition into civvy street after he was headhunted by a private business, which recognised the skills and talents he had honed while serving in the military.

So what were those particular qualities that he gained from his decades of military experience? "I learnt tenacity, adaptability and flexibility, but most importantly I developed a sense of humour," he says. "I had some understanding of technology from the military skills but the people skills are the key thing. We operate globally, we provide an exceptional personal service to candidates and customers, and we enjoy every moment."

Leigh-on-sea sole, cooked in a smoky seafood broth

Jamie Oliver MBE, restaurateur, best-selling author and TV presenter

This is a great dish I made near my family's historical stomping ground on the Essex coast: Leigh-on-Sea. I used Dover sole, but any sustainable or MSC-approved flatfish like plaice, dab or lemon sole would also be fantastic. Dover sole can be a bit on the pricey side, but they are so tasty that they are a wonderful treat every now and then. You want them skinned, with the heads left on, so ask your fishmonger to do this for you. I've used fresh cockles and peeled brown shrimps, which are deliciously sweet, but way underrated. This dish is best made for two so you can cook everything together quickly in one large pan. There's something about the way these ingredients work together that makes it such a luxurious dinner. Hope you love it.

Total time: 25 minutes

Serves 2

INGREDIENTS

125g fresh cockles or small clams
 (or mussels), from sustainable sources
2 rashers of higher-welfare smoked
 streaky bacon
Olive oil
2 sprigs of fresh rosemary
A small knob of unsalted butter
2 x 450g Dover sole, skinned,
 from sustainable sources
50g peeled brown shrimps or small
 prawns, from sustainable sources
A small bunch of fresh chives
2 lemons

METHOD

• Sort through the cockles or clams and tap them. If any stay open, throw them away. Give them a wash and slush about in a bowl of cold water. Put a large frying pan on a medium heat and slice the bacon into matchsticks, then add to the pan along with a drizzle of olive oil and fry until lightly golden. Strip the leaves from the sprigs of rosemary and add to the pan. Fry for a few more minutes, then remove everything to a plate with a slotted spoon. Add a small knob of butter to the bacon fat, give it a little shake and carefully lay both fish in the hot pan, head to tail. You're going to cook them at a medium-high heat, so it won't take long, but the cooking shouldn't run away from you. Cook the fish for about 4 minutes, then carefully and confidently turn each one over with a large fish slice. Quickly return the rosemary and bacon to the pan and add the shrimps and the cockles or clams. Using a tea towel to protect your hands, cover the pan immediately with a lid or tinfoil, making it as airtight as you can. Cook for another 4 minutes, or until the cockles have all opened.
• Finely slice the chives, then remove the foil when the time is up. Squeeze in the juice of a lemon, scatter over the chives, add a good pinch of salt and pepper, then chivvy the pan around with a sense of urgency and remove the fish to a warm platter or two plates, pouring over all the juices and seafood from the pan. Nice served with wedges of lemon on the side and a simple pea and spinach salad, some buttered asparagus or new potatoes.

Tips

Okay, here's a quick pep talk for you: every house needs an extra-large non-stick frying pan, so if you don't have one, go and get one, otherwise you won't be able to cook two fish at the same time. You will also need a large fish slice. Cooking flatfish like this is very simple, but you mustn't overcook it. How do you know when it's cooked perfectly? Simple: gently try to pull the meat away from the thickest part next to the head. If it moves, it's cooked. If it doesn't, it's not.

Tony Brooks DSO MC

Anthony Morris Brooks was born in Orsett, Essex on 4 April 1922. After his parents separated, he lived in Switzerland and France, learning perfect French. He was educated at a "British" school in Switzerland until, following the death of his mother, his father's family sent him to Felsted boarding school in Essex.

Brooks was living with his uncle in France when war broke out. He attempted to enlist in the British Armed Forces but, aged 17, he was too young and was still staying with his family in France when the Germans invaded. In 1940, Brooks encountered, by chance, a British soldier and tried to help him escape to Spain. Brooks then discovered that his own aunt was helping other British personnel on the run in France. He joined her in working for an escape network that helped servicemen to evade capture and reach neutral Spain.

By May 1941, Brooks was under suspicion from the Vichy regime and escaped to Spain, where he was caught and imprisoned. After six weeks at Miranda de Ebro concentration camp, the British embassy arranged for him to be released back to England via Gibraltar. His services were declined by MI9 (the escape and evasion organisation) and the Secret Intelligence Service (MI6), but the Special Operations Executive (SOE) took him on and he was commissioned in 1942 as their youngest agent, aged just 20.

After extensive training, Brooks was parachuted near Limoges in July 1942, surviving a difficult landing with the assistance of a French family. Over the next two years, under the codename "Alphonse", Brooks created a large and effective resistance network, known as Pimento. He organised scores of parachute supply drops and carried out many sabotage operations. Brooks's network was one of the most effective during the D-Day landings, delaying the progress of the 2nd SS Panzer Division to Normandy. As his war was reaching its conclusion, Brooks was arrested in Lyon but his cover story

> *"He was arrested by the Nazis but his cover story was so convincing, and his French so good, that they released him"*

was so convincing, and his French so good, that they released him. He was awarded the Distinguished Service Order and the Military Cross, ending the war as a 23-year-old major.

After the war, he continued his career with the Secret Intelligence Service in Sofia, Suez and Cyprus, and served as British Consul General in Geneva. Before retiring in 1977 he was seconded to MI5 for Cold War counter-espionage work. He is on the Special Forces roll of honour and the SOE official historian named him "one of the best half dozen SOE agents". Brooks was the subject of an acclaimed 2018 biography *Saboteur*, written by Mark Seaman. "In an age when we so often take our heroes from the worlds of 'celebrity'," reads the foreword, "it is perhaps salutary to be reminded of a young man who ended the war in command of a disparate force of some 10,000 armed resistance fighters, and decorated with two of this country's highest awards for gallantry. He was just 23 years old."

Written by Corporal Chris Swift, Parachute Regiment, Army (retired)

The golden years

Inspired Villages creates supported retirement communities in picturesque parts of England that give residents the freedom to enjoy the best years of their lives

www.inspiredvillages.co.uk

At any one of the six retirement communities run by Inspired Villages, there is always time for a cup of tea. That's a fundamental principle of the company founder Jamie Bunce, who came into the field determined to offer support for residents' holistic wellbeing rather than simply provide them with bricks and mortar. "You'll never get told off if you stop to have a cup of tea with a resident," he says. "That's the centrepiece of what we do: making time for people."

Each village supports around 200 residents who live in a range of stylish, comfortable homes, which can be rented or bought outright. At the heart of each community is a vibrant village centre containing a restaurant, café, bar, gym, pool, studio and spa. Residents can participate as much or as little as they choose in the numerous communal activities organised, but there's an overall commitment to fostering connection and providing emotional support as well as offering independence within a secure environment. Each village held huge parties to celebrate the VE Day anniversary in 2020, and

Jamie has signed the Armed Forces Covenant to recruit former service personnel, including those who have been injured in combat who he feels will benefit from an environment that has been designed to support people of all mobilities.

With the support of leading investor Legal & General, Jamie is currently building three more villages and then intends to expand at the rate of eight a year. He has also started a befriending service called Inspired Friendships to tackle the epidemic of loneliness across the UK.

"I felt that, if we were truly vocational, we should spend half an hour a week having cup of tea – virtual or actual – to do what we can," he says. "We are at the private fee-paying end of the market but at our core is holistic wellbeing and being there for the moments that matter in anybody's life. We offer this to anybody who needs it – it doesn't need to be a resident – and I do it myself and find it very rewarding. It's one of the elements that show our desire to do the right thing."

Domoda (Gambian stew)

Private Richard Darboe, Army

Domoda is a Gambian peanut stew or sauce originating from Mali; peanut-based stews are a staple food across the whole of West Africa. The Mandinkan word for this stew is "domodah" but it's also known as "tigadegena" – which literally translates as peanut (tige) paste (dege) sauce (na) in the Bamanankan language of Mali and beyond. Its unique flavour and texture comes from the peanuts. Traditionally, it would be served with whatever vegetables were available at the time, but typically pumpkin and sweet potato are used to give it a sweet flavour alongside the peanut.

Gluten-free, dairy-free
Preparation time: 10 minutes
Cooking time: 1 hour

Serves 4

INGREDIENTS

For the domoda
2 tbsp vegetable oil
2 onions, finely diced
4 garlic gloves, finely chopped or crushed
600g chicken breast, cut into 2cm pieces
4 tomatoes, coarsely diced
2 red chillies, finely diced
120g smooth peanut butter
3 tbsp tomato purée
750ml water
2 large sweet potatoes, peeled
 and cut into 2cm pieces
2 carrots, cut into 2cm pieces
Pinch of cayenne pepper
Salt and freshly ground black pepper

To serve
Boiled rice

METHOD

To make the domoda
• Heat the oil in a casserole or large pan over a medium heat and fry the onions, stirring frequently, until they become soft; add the garlic and chicken and continue to cook until the chicken is well sealed.
• Add the tomatoes and cook, stirring continuously, for another minute then stir in the chillies, peanut butter, tomato purée and water; bring to a boil, lightly season, reduce the heat and simmer for 20 minutes.
• Add the sweet potatoes and carrots and continue to simmer for a further 15 minutes until the sweet potatoes and carrots are just cooked.

To serve
• Add a small pinch of cayenne to the domoda, check the seasoning, ladle into bowls and serve with boiled rice.

VEGAN ALTERNATIVE
• Omit the chicken and add two 400g tins of drained chickpeas to the domoda with the sweet potatoes and carrots.

The Gambia: Local hero

Company Sergeant Major Ebrima Jalu DCM

The Gambia, a thin coastal nation surrounded by the former French colony of Senegal, was Britain's most northern and smallest colony in West Africa. Before the Great War, Gambia's military contribution to the West African Frontier Force was an infantry company titled the Gambia Regiment, consisting of five Europeans (a captain, two lieutenants and two NCOs) and 130 Gambian soldiers, holding ranks from private to company sergeant major. Little is known about the early lives of these Gambian soldiers, but they still sacrificed everything in defence of the British Empire.

During the Allied invasion of German Kamerun (what is now Cameroon), the Gambia Regiment was deployed in stages. The signallers were first absorbed into Allied Force headquarters, then half the company followed on 15 January 1915 before finally the remaining half of the company embarked on 19 September 1915. It was during the Cameroon Campaign that the Gambia Regiment had its finest hour.

On 3 May 1915, during an attack on a number of heavily entrenched German positions at Wumbiagas, one of the British officers of the Gambia Regiment was killed and Company Sergeant Major Ebrima Jalu immediately stepped up and took command of the unit, leading them effectively to victory. He was awarded the Distinguished Conduct Medal (DCM) for his leadership and gallantry.

His citation read: "At the action at Mbila River, Jaunde Road, on 3 May 1915, CSM Ebrima Jalu was in command of one of the hottest parts of the firing line after Lieutenant Markham-Rose was killed. Although deprived of the moral support of any European for several hours, he displayed the greatest coolness and showed a fine example by the way in which he controlled his men and directed their fire throughout the day."

Two more Gambian soldiers – Private Saljen Sidibi and Sergeant Sambah Bah – were also awarded the DCM.

Sadly, Sergeant Sambah Bah didn't survive the war, and nor did Ebrima Jalu – both were killed in later stages of the Cameroon campaign.

On the Gambia Memorial in Banjul are the names of nine men of the Gambia Company who died in this battle, all of whom are buried in the Cameroon bush. The Gambia Company was never strong enough to be deployed on its own operations but, in Cameroon, they earned a proud reputation for their courage and contribution towards the wider war effort.

Written by Corporal John Drummond, Army (retired)

Fighting for us all

The Commonwealth Legion fights for the rights of Armed Forces service veterans from around the Commonwealth – and their communities – who have served Britain

www.thecommonwealthlegion.org

The Commonwealth Legion is a young but very ambitious organisation founded in June 2020, with the aim of becoming a fully-fledged charity. It was started by a group of Ghanaian Veterans and service personnel, all of whom volunteer their services to advise, support, assist and promote the interests of the Commonwealth Armed Forces communities in the UK and abroad as well as the wider community of those who served and continue to serve.

"We wanted to form an organisation to project ourselves nationally and internationally," says Samuel Asante-Nnuro, a veteran of the Royal Logistics Corps who is also Chair of The Commonwealth Legion. "Commonwealth service personnel have contributed enormously to British society both in peace and war times, yet they are often the forgotten heroes and many veterans fall through the net after leaving the services."

Irrespective of length of service, all immigration applicants face exorbitant fees of £2,389 per person in applying to regularise their stay in the UK after service, which can reach prohibitive levels for families. "At present Commonwealth service personnel are reviewing this and we wholeheartedly support a reduction in immigration fees in light of the service these veterans have given to this country," says Samuel. "There are other challenges we offer support with, including access to safe and secure housing, job security, discharge, resettlement and other challenges facing members of the Armed Forces. It can be hard to adjust to civilian life, especially with added pressures such as culture shock and racism."

The Commonwealth Legion is the only organisation in the UK dedicated to helping veterans and service personnel of Commonwealth descent in the Armed Forces. "We believe that with the right support and information, we can help veterans and service personnel survive and also thrive," says Samuel. "We want to reach out to everyone who could help source the right support and resources to develop our organisation in order to afford us the opportunity to help those who will need to access our services. At present we are all dedicated and passionate volunteers helping those who served and continue to serve and our aim is to become a charity and employ the right people to carry on this work. There's no doubt that the services we offer are very much needed and can make a vital difference in the lives of our heroes and the communities in which they live."

Gibraltar pie

Catering Services Mourika O'Garro, Royal Navy

Gibraltarian cuisine is the result of three centuries of British rule combined with the arrival of immigrants from a variety of Mediterranean countries. This resulted in a peculiar cuisine where some dishes are made as in the country of origin, whereas others have been adapted for various reasons. Some dishes were modified because the ingredients were difficult to obtain during the many sieges the Rock has suffered, whereas others were adapted simply because the cooks were from a different country and were used to different ways of cooking. In Gibraltar, this pie is traditionally eaten on Good Friday – this stems from the tradition of not eating meat on main festive days and, since it does not contain meat, it is often prepared during Lent. However, it is great to enjoy all year round.

Gibraltar

Vegetarian
Preparation time: 2½–3 hours
 (including resting time for the
 puff pastry)
Cooking time: 35–50 minutes

Serves 4

INGREDIENTS

For the pastry
200g strong flour
1 pinch of salt
200g baking margarine
100ml cold water
¼ lemon, juiced

For the filling
100g Swiss chard (use extra spinach
 if unavailable)
400g fresh spinach (or 350g frozen)
30ml olive oil
30g onions, finely chopped
1 or 2 red chillies, finely chopped
2 garlic cloves, finely chopped
200g Edam cheese, grated
20g dry breadcrumbs
Salt and black or white pepper
2 large eggs, beaten
1 egg, beaten, to seal and brush
 the pie top

METHOD

To make the puff pastry

- Sieve the flour and salt into a mixing bowl and rub in 40g of the margarine with your fingertips until it has a sandy texture.
- Make a well in the flour, add the water and lemon juice and mix to a smooth dough.
- Knead until the dough is smooth, cover and rest for 20 minutes.
- Roll the remaining 160g of margarine between two sheets of greaseproof paper into a 4mm thick rectangle, roughly A4 size.
- Roll the dough a third longer, and slightly wider, than the margarine and cover two thirds of the dough with the margarine sheet, leaving a small space around the edge.
- Fold the third of the dough without the fat, over half of the dough with the fat layer then fold in half (so you have 2 layers of fat and 3 layers of dough); pinch the edges together to seal.
- Roll out to a rectangle 5mm thick and repeat the step above; this is one half turn.
- Roll out and fold the pastry a further four times to make five half turns in all, leaving to rest covered in the fridge for a minimum of 15 minutes between each turn; you will have 729 pastry layers in your puff pastry once complete.

To make the filling

- Wash the Swiss chard and spinach, remove the stems from the leaves and finely chop; if using frozen spinach, defrost and finely chop.
- Heat the olive oil in a saucepan, add the onions and sweat until softened and translucent; transfer the cooked onions to a mixing bowl and set aside to cool.
- Mix the chard, spinach, chilli, garlic, grated cheese and breadcrumbs with the onions, gradually add the beaten eggs and season with salt and pepper.

To make the pie

- Preheat the oven to 180°C. Lightly grease a 23cm round pie dish or similar.
- Divide the pastry into two pieces, one slightly larger than the other.
- Roll out the larger piece to line your dish with a little excess over the edge, prick the base several times with a fork and add the filling.
- Roll out the smaller piece of pastry slightly larger than the pie top.
- Brush the overhang of the pastry base with the beaten egg, place on the pastry top, trim off the excess, pinch the edges together to seal then crimp around the edge.
- Poke a hole in the centre of the pie lid to allow the steam to escape during cooking and brush the top with the beaten egg.
- Bake in the preheated oven for 30–45 minutes or until golden brown and thoroughly heated through to the middle.
- Allow to cool to room temperature before serving.

VEGAN ALTERNATIVE

- Substitute the eggs with silken tofu (1 egg is equivalent to 75g blended tofu).
- Replace the Edam with grated vegan hard cheese.

Sergeant Alfred Holmes BEM

For any tourist who comes to Gibraltar, a "must do" during every visit is a walk halfway up the Rock to Queen's Gate to see the troop of macaque monkeys at the Ape's Den. These monkeys are Gibraltar's most famous tourist attraction. From 1913 to 1991, the British Army was charged with the safety and welfare of all the macaques on the Rock. The hero of this story is Sergeant Alfred Holmes BEM. Born in Gibraltar in 1931, Alfred enlisted in the Gibraltar Regiment in the 1950s and later ascended to the rank of sergeant. Early in his career he was appointed to the position of Officer-in-Charge of the Apes, a role he would proudly hold for the next 38 years.

Legend has it that as long as the Barbary macaques exist on Gibraltar, the territory will remain under British rule. So strong is this belief that, during the Second World War, when the monkey population dwindled to just seven macaques, Prime Minister Winston Churchill ordered their numbers to be bolstered and reinforcements were quickly brought in from the tiny areas of forest in Algeria and Morocco.

For over three decades Sergeant Holmes fed, nurtured, protected and guarded the monkeys, and the troops of macaques flourished. On several occasions he would take sick or injured monkeys to Gibraltar Royal Hospital, where he expected them to be treated with the same care that would be given to an enlisted soldier. Able to identify individual monkeys, Alfred knew them all so well that he named them, often after high-ranking officers, governors and other high-profile residents of Gibraltar.

Affectionately known as "El de los monos" – Spanish for "He of the monkeys" – Alfred was also a keen sportsman and played as goalkeeper for the Gibraltar Regiment at both football and hockey. Alfred was a hard man – he was even known to "head" oncoming hockey balls off his goal line! – and his supreme fitness allowed him to scramble up and down the slopes of the Upper Rock to shepherd his charges. He was a true local hero.

Alfred succumbed to cancer in 1994. For the past 30 years the macaques have been managed by the Gibraltar Ornithological and Natural History Society, who have kept up his good work.

Written by Lieutenant Commander Richard Lewis QVR, Royal Naval Reserve

"Alfred often named his monkeys after high-ranking officers, governors and other high-profile residents of Gibraltar"

Gloucester squab pie

Corporal Rajesh Babooram, Army

Squab pie is a traditional dish from south-west England that has been popular in the region for well over 100 years, especially in Gloucestershire, where it is still served in pubs and bistros across the county. Generally made with mutton or lamb and apples, the original recipe may have contained squab (young pigeon); however there is also a story that the word "squab" is short for "squabble" after an argument over whether to have mutton or apple pie. One would assume that the "squabblers" settled on a compromise. In my recipe I have used a combination of lamb, sweet potatoes, apples, spices, red wine and herbs with a pastry lid, which works really well together. This is a very comforting, flavourful and delicious dish; a perfect meal for winter suppers especially when served with creamy mashed cauliflower and steamed green vegetables. Squab pie is listed among the "at risk" British regional classic dishes.

Preparation time: 30 minutes
Cooking time: 1 hour, 30 minutes

Serves 4

INGREDIENTS

25g plain flour
½ tsp mixed spice
2 tsp sea salt
1 tsp ground black pepper
1 tsp light brown soft sugar
500g lamb neck fillet, cut into 2½cm dice
2 tbsp of olive oil
30g unsalted butter
250g shallots, sliced
250g Bramley apples, peeled, cored
 and thinly sliced
1 star anise
1 tsp thyme leaves
1 tsp rosemary, finely chopped
150ml red wine
400ml lamb stock
250g sweet potatoes, peeled and
 cut into 4cm dice
500g ready-made shortcrust pastry
1 medium egg, beaten

METHOD

• Mix the flour, mixed spice, salt, pepper and brown sugar together in a bowl.
• Add the diced lamb and toss to thoroughly coat in the flour mixture.
• Heat a saucepan or casserole over a medium-high heat with the olive oil and butter and brown the lamb pieces all over.
• Add the shallots and apples, cook for further 2–3 minutes then add the star anise, thyme and rosemary.
• Pour in the red wine, simmer until reduced by half then pour in the lamb stock.
• Continue to simmer for 15 minutes then add the sweet potatoes; reduce the heat to low, cover with a lid and simmer gently for 30–40 minutes until the meat is tender.
• As the lamb is cooking add a little water if necessary, you want a thick gravy.
• Once the lamb is tender remove the pan from the heat, season with salt and pepper and pour into a pie dish (or individual pie dishes); cover and set aside at room temperature to cool for 30 minutes.
• Preheat the oven to 170°C.
• On a lightly floured surface, roll out the pastry to 3mm thick, cut out a lid large enough to cover the pie dish (or dishes).
• Brush the edge of the pie dish with a little beaten egg, lay the pastry lid on top, crimp the edges and, with the point of a small knife, make a small hole in the middle of the pie to allow the steam to escape during cooking.
• Cut out small leaves with any leftover pastry to decorate the top.
• Brush the pie with the beaten egg and bake in the preheated oven for 30–40 minutes until the pastry is well browned and the filling is thoroughly heated through to the middle.
• Remove the pie from the oven and leave it to sit at room temperature for 5 minutes before serving.

Colonel James Power Carne VC DSO

James "Fred" Power Carne was born on 11 April 1906. His family were brewers and wine merchants, but he chose a military career. After training at the Imperial Service College in Windsor and at Sandhurst, he was commissioned as a second lieutenant in the Gloucestershire Regiment on 3 September 1925. He moved through the ranks throughout the Second World War and, by 7 February 1949, had been promoted to Lieutenant Colonel.

On the outbreak of the Korean War in 1950, Carne was given command of the 1st Battalion, The Gloucestershire Regiment. In April 1951 he led 700 men against more than 10,000 Chinese in the Battle of Imjin River. His battalion were pinned and outnumbered but, despite incessant mortar and machine-gun fire, Carne moved among the whole battalion and inspired his troops to resist the Chinese. He even personally led successful assault parties that drove back the enemy. His courage, coolness and leadership resulted in Carne being awarded the Distinguished Service Order (DSO) on 13 July 1951.

Despite their valliance the Glosters were eventually overrun and captured by Chinese forces. Most were kept by their communist captors for "re-education", but Carne was kept in solitary confinement. He later described how, for 19 months, he was plied with brainwashing drugs to "make his brain like a sponge". When eventually released, he had lost three stone in weight and had deteriorated eyesight. On his arrival at the Commonwealth Centre in Japan, his troops seated him in an armchair and carried him to the Officers' Mess for a stiff drink.

As a result of his ordeal, Carne was awarded the Victoria Cross, which he received on 27 October 1953. When asked by the Queen about prison conditions, he said: "They were not too bad, ma'am. The worst part was the boredom." That month he and the Gloucestershire Regiment were given permission to wear the Distinguished Unit Citation by the US President for gallant and distinguished services during United Nations operations.

Carne was promoted to colonel in April 1954 and retired in 1957. He was appointed Deputy Lieutenant of Gloucestershire in 1960 and retired to the small village of Cranham. For 18 years, he attended the village church where he was churchwarden. He passed away on 19 April 1986. In 2015, the South Koreans honoured Carne by featuring him on a postage stamp.

"Colonel Carne is one of the legendary figures of the regiment," says Chris Chatterton, General Manager of the Soldiers of Gloucestershire Museum. "The fact that he's recognised for the phenomenal sacrifice and bravery that he showed at the battle of the Imjin River is testament to not just him, but all the Glosters on that battlefield."

Written by Warrant Officer Alun Evans, Army

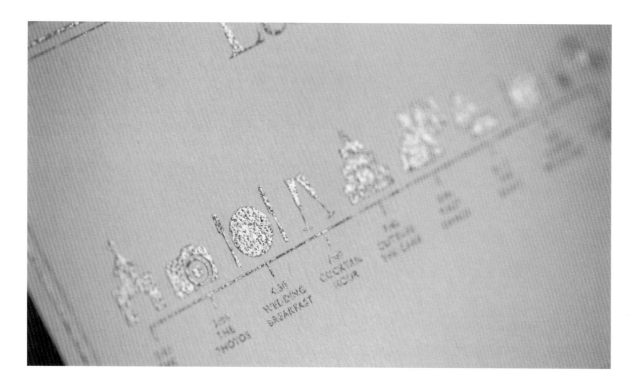

Prints charming

Barnard & Westwood is a 100-year-old printer and bookbinder that specialises in high-quality bespoke stationery, hand-bound books, invitations and much, much more

www.barnardandwestwood.com

At London's historic printer and bookbinder Barnard & Westwood, the traditional and contemporary work together in constant synergy. The company was founded 100 years ago in 1921 and holds two Royal Warrants. Clients include luxury car brands, champagne houses and fashion designers – as well as national institutions such as Westminster Abbey and The Royal Academy of Arts. Barnard & Westwood offers a range of services including digital and lithographic printing, foil blocking, letterpress, die-stamping, gilding, box making and bespoke bookbinding. "These can be one-off items such as a single copy of a presentation book or a complicated medal box," explains Director Alasdair Abrines. "We can produce a very simple leaflet or an intricate gold die-stamped gilded invitation but all with the same attention to detail and personal service. We have a diverse range of skills and processes in-house, so if people come to us with a vision we have the tools and experience to make it happen."

Many organisations have used Barnard & Westwood's services for decades, but it also works with an array of smaller businesses and private individuals who come to its workshop looking for a unique mix of creative ideas and design inspiration.

"We can create very modern-looking items using traditional techniques," says Alasdair. "So we might print an invitation for a fashion show using vibrant neon inks but incorporate texture that comes from a traditional process such as die-stamping. There's something quite exciting about using a press made in the 1920s to print an invitation for an event in the 2020s."

Despite a clear link to its historic roots, Barnard & Westwood keeps ahead of advancements in technology so it can offer the latest processes across its products and reduce its environment impact. "There are always new materials and combinations of colour and texture to play with," says Alasdair. "Working with companies that have very intricate crests and logos demands exceptional skill, precision and exacting standards. That is something that is apparent across the business from start to finish, whatever the job."

Phil's Cockney oxtail curry

Phil Daniels, actor and Celebrity MasterChef contestant

Greater London

This is my very own Cockney oxtail curry. I've always liked home-made curries and I love oxtail, so I experimented a bit and came up with this.

Gluten-free
Preparation time: 30 minutes
Cooking time: 3 hours

Serves 4

INGREDIENTS

6–8 pieces of oxtail
1 thumb-sized piece of ginger, peeled
5 garlic cloves, peeled
2 large onions, halved and thinly sliced
3 birds-eye chillies (less or more –
  it's up to you), finely chopped
2 tbsp vegetable oil
2 tbsp (heaped) curry powder
4 tbsp (heaped) natural yoghurt
2 large potatoes, cubed
425ml chicken stock
Salt and pepper

METHOD

• Season the pieces of oxtail with salt and pepper.
• Finely chop the ginger and garlic or blitz in a blender with a little water to make a paste.
• Heat the vegetable oil in a casserole over a medium-high heat and brown the oxtail pieces all over; do this in a couple batches to avoid overcrowding the pan.
• Once browned, remove from the casserole and set aside on a plate.
• Turn the heat up to medium, add the onions to the casserole and fry, stirring frequently, for 7–10 minutes, adding a little more oil if needed.
• Add the ginger, garlic and chillies and, using a wooden spoon, stir around for 2 minutes; add the curry powder and stir until you have a dry paste mixture.
• Pour in the chicken stock, bring to a simmer then add the yoghurt; stir well then return the oxtail to the casserole with a bit more salt.
• Bring to a boil, turn the heat to low, cover with a lid and simmer for about 3 hours or until the oxtail is tender; if necessary add a little boiling water to make sure that the oxtail pieces stay covered with the sauce during cooking.
• Stir in the potatoes 20 minutes before the end of the cooking time and continue to simmer until cooked through.
• Check the seasoning and serve with rice.

Nurse Elizabeth Webber Harris

There are many accounts of the bravery of personnel serving in the Armed Forces. This story, however, highlights the selfless work of a soldier's partner. Elizabeth Webber Harris was born Elizabeth Matthews in 1834, the second child of James Matthews and Mary Ann Bailey. In February 1859 she married then Captain Webber Desborough Harris (born 1823) of the 2nd Bengal Fusiliers (later renamed the 104th).

In 1868, Webber Harris was promoted to Lieutenant Colonel and assumed command of the 104th Foot Bengal Fusiliers. He was stationed at Peshawar, where his wife Elizabeth accompanied him. In 1869 there was a cholera outbreak (in one week ten children lost their lives) and, for their safety, a large portion of the regiment was sent to a camp seven miles outside the district. Elizabeth Webber Harris was the only female to accompany them, having recently recovered from the disease herself.

For three months, the regiment formed a pattern whereby every night they would stop, bury their dead in the morning and carry on. Dozens of soldiers succumbed to cholera but Elizabeth saved many more by treating them using her own clothing and mustard plasters. She also kept up the spirits of the survivors, organising sing-songs and other entertainment.

Life on the edge of the North-West Frontier, outside Peshawar, was very dangerous. On one occasion, Elizabeth was attacked late at night by two tribesmen who seized her horse in what she later described as "an alarming incident". The regiment finally made camp at Cherat where they remained until the disease finished its course. They arrived back in Peshawar on 12 December 1869.

After Elizabeth's months of selfless devotion, the regiment's officers felt that she had lived up to the traditions of the Victoria Cross. They obtained "special permission" from Queen Victoria to make their own gold replica VC to reflect Elizabeth's "indomitable pluck during the cholera epidemic of 1869", presented by General Sir Samuel Browne. When Elizabeth Harris died in 1917, aged 83, it sparked a petition to allow the VC to be officially presented to women, something confirmed by a 1920 Royal Warrant. However, Elizabeth Harris remains the only woman to have received a VC, with the medal on display at London's Imperial War Museum.

Written by Captain Stephen Blanks, Army

"Dozens of soldiers succumbed to cholera but Elizabeth saved many more by treating them using her own clothing and mustard plasters"

Enriching lives and landscapes

London-based real-estate consultancy Knight Frank
is celebrating its 125th year by looking forward and
supporting a range of progressive initiatives

www.knightfrank.com

As Knight Frank celebrates its 125th anniversary, the leading real-estate consultancy has developed a near unrivalled menu for success. For starters, it begins with its foundation as a partnership. This creates a culture that allows the firm to commit to growing its global business while remaining independent and united by a common purpose – working responsibly while enhancing people's lives and environments.

These values have enabled the firm to oversee high-profile work around the world on landmark buildings such as the purchase of Stonehenge in 1915 and advising on the sale of world-class properties at Chelsea Barracks. The partnership is now one of the most respected real-estate advisers in the world, with an unparalleled record of success. "It is an honour to be supporting the Royal British Legion in celebrating its 100th year," says Alistair Elliott, Senior Partner and Group Chairman. "At Knight Frank we celebrate 125 years by looking forward. Fairness, social inclusion, environmental impact and charitable giving are key ingredients which are gathering great momentum and – as we go forward – will be embraced even further."

Since it was founded in 1896, Knight Frank has grown to 20,000 people in 57 territories. These people share core values – they value individuals, encourage collaboration and endeavour to make a difference by acting with integrity and building trust. As a partnership, employees are encouraged to work with a long-term view. This benefits clients and helps foster enduring, mutually supportive relationships. "Property is where we live, work and play," says Alistair. "By understanding each client's unique personal and business situations, Knight Frank can offer the right property solutions across any market."

Beyond this, the firm has a long-term duty of care to the communities and environment in which it operates.

It supports LandAid, which has a goal to end youth homelessness, while core initiatives cover paperless and plastic-free commitments. Every two years, Knight Frank staff take part in a Day of Giving, most recently raising more than £250,000 for charities including the Alzheimer's Society and Contact the Elderly. "As we look to the future, I feel passionately that, as an industry, we need to rise to the occasion," says Tim Hyatt, Head of Residential. "We need to be operating safely, driving balance, committing to lower carbon emissions and investing in our people for the years to come."

All great meals end with a dessert. For Knight Frank, this provides the opportunity to reflect on its successful history while identifying opportunities for the future. Knight Frank will continue to invest in and champion its people, nurturing talent from diverse backgrounds through a broad range of initiatives. Technology and an ESG focus are essential, while Knight Frank will remain at the cutting edge of sustainable, intelligent and healthy buildings. Knight Frank's market-leading research teams are at the forefront of predicting the future of the residential, commercial and international sectors, and the firm are leading the charge in fast expanding sectors such as healthcare, automotive, student housing, senior living and data centres.

"While our heritage is to be cherished, our sights are set on the opportunities in our next 125 years, be it providing clients with market-leading industry insight, addressing environmental, social and governance challenges, or creating bespoke people-focused initiatives to champion those that are leading the firm into its future," says Stephen Clifton, Head of Commercial. "Our partnership ethos places innovation and collaboration at the heart of all that we do, internally and with our clients."

Grenada

Oil Down

Private Simbai Akomba, Army

If there is one dish that really represents Grenadian cuisine, it is definitely Oil Down. It has many variations made with all types of meat and fish: I have used cod in my recipe as the firm flesh works well and it's the most common way of eating it in Grenada. The name of the dish describes how it is traditionally cooked until only the coconut oil remains at the bottom of the dish. The preparation of the ingredients is key: it is traditionally cooked over an open fire in a large pot on the beaches where families spend the summer days into the cooler evenings. It makes a great meal to have with friends and family at the end of the day watching the sunset. I have adapted the recipe to allow for ease of finding ingredients in supermarkets.

Preparation time: 20 minutes
Cooking time: 1 hour

Serves 4–6

INGREDIENTS

2 tbsp olive oil
2 large white onions, peeled and
  coarsely diced
2 hot chillies, finely shredded (Scotch
  bonnets are often used to give the
  dish its fiery flavour)
3 garlic cloves, finely chopped
1 tbsp ginger, peeled and grated
Small handful of parsley, roughly chopped
2 large potatoes, peeled and cut into
  2cm dice
3 large carrots, peeled and cut into
  2cm pieces
2 sprigs of thyme
2 large handfuls of spinach
1 tsp turmeric
500ml coconut milk
250ml water
125ml double cream
1kg fresh cod, cut into large pieces
Sea salt and cracked black pepper

METHOD

• Heat the oil in a casserole or large saucepan over
  a medium heat, add the onions and cook, stirring
  frequently, until they are soft and translucent.
• Add the chillies, garlic, ginger and parsley and cook,
  stirring frequently, for a further minute.
• Add the potatoes, carrots, thyme and spinach, and
  continue to cook for 3 minutes.
• Mix in the turmeric then stir in the coconut milk,
  water and cream; season lightly and bring to a simmer.
• Season the cod pieces with salt and pepper and place
  on top of the vegetables.
• Simmer gently over a low-medium heat for 40–45 minutes
  until the sauce has reduced and thickened; the fish will
  gently cook in the steam as it rises through the vegetables.
• Serve simply over some freshly steamed rice finished
  with a little cracked black pepper and sea salt over
  the top; best enjoyed on the beach but equally good
  at home.

Grenada: Local hero

Staff Sergeant Johnson Beharry VC

Johnson Gideon Beharry was born in Grenada on 26 July 1979, one of eight siblings. In 1999, aged 19, he left Grenada for the UK, hoping to make a better life for himself. He settled in Hounslow with his aunt, working as a painter and decorator and on building sites. After the shame of getting involved in a gang and dealing in drugs, Beharry decided to join the Army, enrolling in the Princess of Wales's Royal Regiment in August 2001.

After initial training, he became a tank driver in C Company, 1st Battalion. His first tour was in Kosovo, before completing three months in Northern Ireland. On 1 May 2004 in Iraq, Beharry was driving a Warrior armoured vehicle that was called to assist a foot patrol caught in a series of ambushes. It was hit by multiple rocket-propelled grenades, causing damage and loss of radio communications. A number of soldiers in the vehicle were injured and, due to a damaged periscope, Private Beharry was forced to open his hatch to steer his vehicle, exposing him to small-arms fire. He drove through the ambush, leading his crew and five other Warriors to safety. Still under fire he then extracted the wounded soldiers from the vehicle to safety. He was cited on this occasion for "valour of the highest order".

On 11 June 2004, Beharry returned to duty driving the lead Warrior of his platoon through Al-Amarah when his vehicle was ambushed. A rocket-propelled grenade hit the vehicle six inches from Beharry's head, and he received serious shrapnel injuries to his face and brain. Other rockets hit the vehicle, incapacitating his commander and injuring several of the crew. Despite his life-threatening injuries, Beharry retained control and drove the vehicle out of the ambush area before losing consciousness. He required brain surgery for his injuries, and was still recovering in March 2005 when he was awarded the Victoria Cross. Describing his injury, which cost him 40 per cent of his brain, Johnson said: "some days you are the bug, some days you're the windshield".

Beharry is a regular at Remembrance Day events and has appeared on TV shows such as *Dancing On Ice* and *The Great British Menu*. He carried the torch for the 2012 London Olympics through the National Memorial Arboretum. In 2006, he wrote his autobiography *The Barefoot Soldier*, and in 2014 he set up the JBVC foundation to keep those aged 15–25 off the streets and out of gangs. In 2017, he was invested as a Commander of the Order of Grenada. "Maybe I was brave," he said after receiving his VC. "I just didn't know. At the time I was just doing the job. I didn't have time for other thoughts."

Written by Warrant Officer Class 2 James Hawker, Army (retired)

"Despite his life-threatening injuries, Beharry retained control of his vehicle and drove it out of the ambush area before losing consciousness"

Prevent and protect

Zidac Laboratories is one of the UK's leading manufacturers of infection control and hygiene products, helping to keep us clean and safe under lockdown and beyond

www.zidac.co.uk

When Covid-19 hit the UK in March 2020, sanitiser quickly became an essential part of society's everyday life. Zidac Laboratories, with extensive experience in manufacturing oral and personal care products from its purpose-built factory in Portsmouth, responded by producing its own-brand hand sanitiser which emphasised skin care as well as disinfection.

"We understand the market and its needs," says Managing Director Luigi Weissbarth. "People suffered from dry hands and irritation, so we added glycerine and aloe vera to protect the skin. We distributed around 18 million bottles of sanitiser under our brand and received only positive feedback. NHS workers praised it for its soothing qualities. With constant usage, it is vital to use quality sanitiser which does not dry out your hands."

In addition to its range of sanitisers (including both hospital-grade and surgical versions), Zidac's own branded products include disinfectants, oral care and personal care products. However, Zidac's key focus is to create custom-made solutions for its customers and has already developed a few thousand unique formulations across a wide range of products. Zidac develops products and delivers solutions according to its customers' needs and problems. Corporate social responsibility is also an integral part of the company. To date, Zidac has donated over £700,000 worth of products to the NHS and to charities and will continue to give.

Always addressing the changing needs of customers, Zidac remains innovative. An example of this is when a major healthcare organisation were looking for a solution to irritated skin from daily mask wearing. In response, Zidac developed Mask Relief Spray which reduces skin discomfort and chafing by providing a hydrating barrier between skin and mask. "People who truly care about quality and understand its importance, are interested in our products because they know what they will get," says Luigi. "Our repeat customers, who could find a cheaper alternative, choose to stay with us because we offer unique tailor-made solutions backed by thorough market knowledge and product expertise. After all, your health is our priority."

Cholay channa daal do pyazza

Cyrus Todiwala OBE, TV chef and proprietor
of Café Spice Namasté

*This is not a commonly found recipe and one that not many
would make either, I suppose. But the combination of both split
yellow peas and whole white chickpeas works well. It is very
simple and easy to make and will delight most palates. You can
use either canned chickpeas or soak raw dried chickpeas and boil
or pressure-cook them for best results. This is not a recipe with
limited spices but instead veers more towards the classical, so
I have added all that would normally be included in this dish;
feel free to cook it without the whole spices if you prefer.*

India

Vegetarian
Preparation time: 15 minutes plus soaking time for the peas
Cooking time: 50 minutes

Serves 4

INGREDIENTS

150g chickpeas, uncooked
150g split yellow peas, uncooked
1 piece of cinnamon or cassia bark,
   approximately 5–7cm
4 or 5 whole cloves
2 bay leaves
5 or 6 cracked black peppercorns
1 tbsp (heaped) cumin seeds
1 piece of ginger, approximately 5–7cm
4 or 5 cloves of garlic, finely chopped
2 or 3 finger type chillies, cut into
   four lengthways
2 small onions, very finely chopped
½ tsp ground turmeric
1 tbsp ground coriander
1 tsp chilli powder
2 medium tomatoes, chopped
½ tsp garam masala powder
2 tbsp (heaped) fresh coriander, chopped
2 tbsp vegetable oil
2 tbsp butter
Salt

METHOD

- Soak the chickpeas in warm water for approximately 2–3 hours at least or overnight, which is better. Once soaked, boil well until soft with a little salt. If in a hurry, add some bicarbonate of soda and the chickpeas will cook faster.
- Soak the split yellow peas separately for a few hours but don't cook them just yet. Once the chickpeas have cooked, drain the water over the split yellow peas and then boil them. Split yellow peas will cook much faster but you don't want them to be overcooked, just until they are soft enough. Drain once cooked, but keep the water to finish the dish.
- Heat the oil in a deep casserole, roughly 23cm in diameter, until it forms a haze and add the whole spices (the cinnamon or cassia bark, cloves, bay leaves and cracked pepper corns) and after 10–15 seconds add the cumin seeds and turn the heat down a little.
- As soon as the cumin changes colour add the chopped ginger, garlic, sliced green chillies and the butter; sauté until the garlic colours slightly, then add the chopped onions.
- Once the onions are in, stir well and continue to sauté over a medium heat.
- Meanwhile, put the turmeric, chilli and coriander powders in a cup or glass and add enough water to make a thin paste. Let this rest until the onions become a pale brown, then add the paste and stir well.
- Cook this until the liquid dries up and you see tiny beads of oil emerging at the bottom of the pan. This shows that the powders have now cooked.
- Add the two peas with the water you have reserved and the chopped tomato then simmer until the sauce is thick and the cooked peas are well coated.
- Add the garam masala powder, stir in well and finally stir in the fresh coriander; taste to ensure that you are happy with the salt content and turn off.
- Serve with hot flatbreads as an accompaniment to a meal, or with steamed rice and some fresh red onion and mint salad.

Risaldar Badlu Singh VC

During the First World War, Badlu Singh was one of six men from India who were awarded the Victoria Cross. He was born on 13 January 1876 in the village of Dhakla in Haryana, and on 10 September 1895, aged 19, Badlu Singh joined the British Army, enrolling into the 14th Murray's Jat Lancers, a cavalry regiment largely drawn from the Hindu Jat community. He reached the rank of Lance Dafadar (Lance Corporal) by 1908, was commissioned as a Jemadar (Junior Officer) in 1915 and was promoted to Risaldar (Major) in 1917.

As the Great War spread, Badlu and the Lancers were called to serve on the North-West Frontier in 1915, taking part in the Mohmand war, as well as the charge at Hafiz Kor (the battle that resulted in the award of a VC to Charles Hull, a shoesmith for the 21st Lancers). In May 1916, the Lancers were sent to France to reinforce the 6th Cavalry Division where they remained until March 1918 when they were transferred to Palestine.

On 23 September 1918, his squadron charged a strong enemy position between the village of Samariyeh and the west bank of the River Jordan. As they drew closer to the enemy position, Badlu Singh realised the squadron was suffering heavy casualties from a small hill on the left front armed with heavy machine guns and 200 infantry soldiers. He did not hesitate and corralled six other ranks, who – with total disregard for danger – sprinted towards the enemy position to capture it, saving the lives of many Allied troops. Badlu was mortally wounded on the top of the hill when single-handedly capturing a machine-gun post, but before he died all guns and infantry had surrendered to him. As a result of the valour and initiative he demonstrated, he was awarded the Victoria Cross.

In accordance with his Hindu beliefs, Badlu Singh was cremated on the site where he fell, with his son Chotan Singh receiving his posthumous VC. His name is inscribed on the Heliopolis Memorial in Cairo and his Victoria Cross is displayed in London's Imperial War Museum as part of the Lord Ashcroft collection. On 1 September 2019, Badlu Singh's statue was unveiled in his native village. Six sandstone memorial marker stones were also installed and unveiled at the "India and the Great War" reception on 30 October the same year.

Written by Warrant Officer Class 2 Chris Campbell, Army (retired)

"With total disregard for danger, Badlu Singh sprinted towards the enemy position to capture it, saving the lives of many Allied troops"

Doing the right thing

G3 Systems Ltd is a UK company that supports the Armed Forces around the world in the most challenging and dangerous locations

www.g3-systems.co.uk

As a company that works in support of the British Armed Forces and other militaries all over the world, G3 Systems shares many of those institutions' innate qualities of adaptability, resilience and organisation. The company was founded in 2001 to support the British Army by producing deployable systems and facilities – integrating facilities like offices, headquarters, workshops and communication centres into shipping containers for rapid deployment around the world. Over time the company has adapted to clients' requirements and pivoted to producing fixed infrastructure for the vast US and UK military camps in Iraq and Afghanistan, as well as providing facilities and services for NATO, the Foreign Office and other large organisations operating in challenging locations and circumstances.

"It's about remaining agile and entrepreneurial so we can move into adjacent spaces," explains Mike Puckett, G3 Systems' Managing Director. "The heart of the company is our engineering design and technical expertise, which we build from. So, we supply the infrastructure and systems, but we also provide the supporting services. We are constantly looking for more clients and market sectors in the UK and abroad, building on the skills we have already developed."

In explaining their remarkable versatility, Mike cites as an example a hospital that G3 Systems built for NATO in Kandahar in Afghanistan. Once the building was completed, while the medical staff were supplied by NATO, the facility management was undertaken by G3 employees. NATO was so impressed by their professionalism that G3 Systems won a contract with them to provide Emergency Response Services on the airfields. This led

to the company helping other clients develop their emergency and critical incident responses, underpinned by the expertise that comes from operating in remote locations, and often in austere and challenging environments.

With up to 80 per cent of its workforce deployed overseas with its clients, G3 Systems strives to create a welcoming environment for all employees. The company is signed up to the Armed Forces Covenant and around 35 per cent of its workforce are veterans, finding themselves at home in a company that takes their service and security seriously. "We employ 20 different nationalities and treat everyone equally," says Mike. "Some of our people have spent ten years in Afghanistan. We have a good reputation as an employer because we see them as a family. We are a commercial enterprise but we won't take risks when it comes to our people. That's why we are delighted to support the RBL's 100th anniversary. It does so much for veterans and their families and it is a great cause to support."

The company also remains focused on its clients' needs. This is reflected in its history to date, developing from one line of business to several, covering fixed and deployable infrastructure and logistic and emergency services. "Rather than say – 'this is what we do, how many do you want?', we'll ask our clients what they want to achieve," says Mike. "We then use our engineering skills and expertise to develop the solution and work closely with them. We won't walk away from a problem. Contracts can get difficult but we persevere even when things get sticky. We pride ourselves on delivering good quality products and services, and as a result we get a lot of referrals and repeat business. We strongly believe in doing the right thing, just as the RBL has always done."

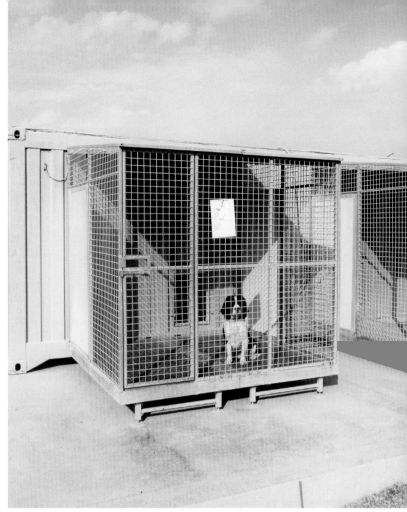

Smoked fish and potato pie

Catering Services Alyon Adams, Royal Navy

This recipe is based on fatherless pie, a traditional Isle of Man recipe made with layers of shortcrust pastry and potatoes covered with diluted milk and baked; this simple pie is traditionally eaten with boiled fish on Good Friday. From the mid-1800s onwards, kippers (smoked herrings) were ever-present on Victorian and Edwardian tables, not to mention the Savoy's breakfast menu, and the Isle of Man curer families have always been famous for producing them. I have created a dish that incorporates these two elements of the Isle of Man's culinary history, including both kippers and the fatherless pie, to ensure you get a true taste of the island.

Preparation time: 15 minutes
Cooking time: 35–45 minutes

Serves 4

INGREDIENTS

1kg Maris Piper potatoes, peeled
  and thinly sliced
200g lightly salted butter, chilled
  and diced
2 kipper fillets, skinned and cut
  into 2cm dice
2 smoked mackerel fillets, skinned
  and flaked
1 smoked haddock fillet, skinned
  and cut into 2cm dice
80g Isle of Man cheddar, grated
100g garden peas
6 spring onions, sliced
10g chives, finely chopped
250ml milk
250ml water
Salt and pepper
Shortcrust pastry
1 egg, beaten

METHOD

• Preheat the oven to 180°C and lightly butter a suitable pie dish.
• Separate the potatoes into five equal amounts and put one even layer onto the bottom of the pie dish.
• Separate the butter, fish, cheese, peas, spring onions and chives into four even amounts.
• Scatter a layer of the filling over the potatoes in the dish, top with another layer of potatoes, season with salt and pepper and repeat three more times.
• Once the final layer of potatoes is on top, mix the milk and water together in a jug and carefully pour over the layered dish, allowing it to settle and not overflow.
• Roll out the pasty and lay on top of the filling, trim so there's a slight overhang and crimp the edges.
• Brush with the beaten egg and pierce a small hole in the top to allow the steam to escape during cooking.
• Cook in the preheated oven for 35–40 minutes or until the pastry is golden brown and the potatoes are cooked through.

Major Robert Henry Cain VC

Robert Henry Cain was born on 2 January 1909 in Shanghai, China to Manx parents. They returned to the Isle of Man when Cain was young and he attended King Williams College. After leaving school, Cain worked for the Shell Oil Company in Siam and Malaya, also serving as a reservist in the Territorial Army. He was placed on a supplementary reserves list in 1931 and in 1940 got an emergency commission into the Army as a Second Lieutenant in the Royal Northumberland Fusiliers, later transferring to the South Staffordshire Regiment.

In 1944, Cain was commanding a rifle company during the Battle of Arnhem, part of Operation Market Garden. The objective was to seize a string of bridges through the Netherlands that would give the Allies a foothold as they moved towards Berlin. Unfortunately for them, the 9th SS and 10th SS Panzer Divisions were in Arnhem for rest and refit. After a failed initial assault on 18 September 1944, Cain's company were separated from the battalion, alongside the 1st Para Brigade, for almost a week. During this time they came under heavy German fire, and Cain made it his personal objective to destroy as many German tanks as possible, using a specialist anti-tank weapon called a PIAT (projector infantry anti-tank). His fearless nature saw him often acting alone with no concern for his personal safety, and he was seriously injured by shrapnel on one occasion. By the end of the battle, it is estimated that Cain was responsible for the destruction or disabling of six German tanks, as well as numerous enemy guns. Of all the survivors of Arnhem, Cain was the only one to be awarded the Victoria Cross for his gallantry and leadership. In May 1945, he took part in Operation Doomsday, overseeing the German surrender in Norway.

After the war he returned to work for Shell before retiring to the Isle of Man. He died from cancer in 1974 and his ashes are in the family grave at Braddan Old Kirk Cemetery on the island. He is remembered in the Staffordshire Regiment Museum, where his smock and maroon beret are kept, alongside a series of commemorative coins that were unveiled by his daughter, who wasn't aware of his VC until after his death (as "he'd never thought to mention it"). He featured in a BBC documentary on the Victoria Cross in which his son-in-law, the TV presenter Jeremy Clarkson, detailed his heroic actions.

Written by Petty Officer Aircraft Engineering Technician (Mechanical) Hollie Hill, Royal Navy

> "*Cain made it his personal objective to destroy as many German tanks as possible*"

Called to the bar

For anyone wanting to refit the tap room of their pub, restaurant, office or home bar, Love Beer Bars Ltd can provide stylish solutions and ongoing maintenance

love-beer.co.uk

Over the past five years, Love Beer Bars Ltd have become the go-to guys for countless beer shops, restaurants, offices and home brewers up and down the country who need to install and maintain a bar. The Kent-based business was founded by Charles Richer, a marketing and events veteran who spent more than a decade setting up temporary bars for huge festivals, including Glastonbury and Latitude. "It started as a fun-filled hobby," says Charles, "and it's become a passion."

Love Beer Bars Ltd has installed many high-end office bars in central London for the likes of Facebook, Crabtree & Evelyn, Hello Fresh and The7Stars media agency. Under lockdown, this market might have temporarily disappeared, but Charles has still been kept busy with doorstep deliveries and household bars. "Under lockdown, the home market instantly kicked in," he says. "People who are into specialist beers are really drawn to us. You'll be surprised at how many people keep beer on tap in their homes, or possibly in their shed, or 'man cave', and we're constantly making onsite visits to service and maintain these home bars. We're specialists in what we do and pop-up bars in the home have become very popular over the past year."

Charles has even turned his Land Rover into a bar. "It's my current pride and joy," he says. "It's a 45-year-old Land Rover which was once used by the Ministry of Defence on a nuclear de-commissioning site. We've restored it under lockdown to its original military colours and we can now drive anywhere in it and dispense festival levels of beer out of the back. It's the perfect size for large events and looks great – easily spotted through a crowd."

Charles is already seeing a massive bounce back as restrictions ease. "People are looking forward to being together again for all sorts of celebratory events like 21st birthdays, graduations, weddings, and parties just for the sake of it," he says. "And I'm really looking forward to that. It feels like there's a whole generation of people waiting to start partying again, whether at home or with others. It's going to be the Roaring Twenties all over again and we'll be at the heart of it!"

Scads and taties

Chief Petty Officer Catering Services Russell Keitch, Royal Navy

Isles of Scilly

A diverse array of visitors from all walks of life and nationalities stop over on the stunning Isles of Scilly every year. The inspiration for this recipe comes from a cookbook sent to me by the Isles of Scilly Museum. Titled Holy Mackerel by Jinny Stevens and friends from St Martin's Church, it was compiled from traditional island recipes and published to raise money for the church restoration. In the recipe for Conger pie it states that in the late 1800s scads (a local name for mackerel) were used in pasties to replace the costly meat; the prose at the top of the page reads: "Scads and Taties all the week long and Conger Pie for Sunday". I have taken this intriguing idea and created my own version of scads and taties.

Gluten-free
Preparation time: 20–30 minutes
Cooking time: 1 hour to 1 hour 20 minutes

Makes 4

INGREDIENTS

10g unsalted butter
1 medium red onion, halved
 and sliced
700g (4 large) Maris Piper or
 Desirée potatoes, peeled
 and thinly sliced
200g spinach
4 fillets (about 300g) smoked
 mackerel, skinned and flaked
50g frozen peas
1 tbsp fresh thyme leaves
 (or 1 tsp dried)
1 tbsp parsley, coarsely chopped
600ml double cream
2 garlic cloves, crushed
1 lemon, zest and juice
1 tbsp creamed horseradish
1 slice of wholemeal
 bread, crumbed
75g medium cheddar, grated
Salt and freshly ground
 black pepper

METHOD

• Preheat the oven to 150°C.
• Melt the butter in a frying pan or saucepan over a medium heat, add the onions and cook, stirring frequently for about 5 minutes until soft and translucent.
• Lightly butter an ovenproof baking dish and spread a thin layer of the sliced potatoes on the bottom and season lightly with salt and black pepper.
• Heat the spinach in a dry frying pan over a medium heat for 1½–2 minutes, stirring continuously, until wilted; set aside to cool slightly, squeeze out any excess liquid, season with salt and black pepper and layer the spinach on top of the potatoes.
• Mix the cooked onions, flaked smoked mackerel, peas, thyme, parsley and remaining potatoes together in a bowl season generously with salt and freshly ground black pepper.
• Bring the cream to a simmer in a saucepan over a medium heat, remove from the heat and stir in the garlic, lemon zest, juice and creamed horseradish; set aside to infuse for 5 minutes.
• Meanwhile mix the breadcrumbs and grated cheese together.
• Mix the infused cream with the potato and mackerel mix, check the seasoning and spread in an even layer over of the spinach, top with the cheese and breadcrumb mix, grind over a couple of twists of black pepper and bake in the preheated oven for between 1 hour and 1 hour 20 minutes or until the potatoes are soft and cooked through and the crumb is brown and crunchy.

Lieutenant Daniel Lomenech

Hiding 28 miles to the west of Cornwall, the five Scilly Islands are a little-known semi-tropical gem that were the unlikely sanctuary for a flotilla of small boats conducting special operations in 1940. Our hero is a 21-year-old Frenchman, Daniel Lomenech, who had escaped from France to join the Royal Navy Volunteer Reserve (RNVR) working for the Secret Intelligence Service (SIS). In 1941, one of his operations was to visit his home town of Pont-Aven to set up a resistance group known as "Réseau Johnny", a network to which his family soon belonged.

Well versed in the habits of the Breton fishing fleets, Lomenech pioneered the use of converted fishing boats to run clandestine intelligence missions between the Scillies and occupied France. The boats had their hulls ingeniously reconfigured and were equipped with powerful engines hidden below the waterline while the structure above the waterline was cloaked to resemble a French fishing vessel. Lomenech personally oversaw the conversion work to ensure that they appeared authentic.

These stealthy "spy boats" could cross the Channel under the cover of darkness at 20 knots, mingle with the large fleets of Breton fishing boats and meet pre-arranged contact vessels for the transfer of agents, weapons, intelligence or returning downed air crew. During one of Lomenech's missions the Allies recovered a top French agent and his family, codenamed Remy, whose secret papers contained detailed plans of Hitler's coastal defences– it had been smuggled out of German HQ by a painter and decorator who concealed it in a roll of wallpaper. This document would later shape the D-Day landings.

In 1943, after 13 successful missions, Lomenech was transferred – much to the disappointment of his fans among the Scilly Islands land girls – to work on Royal Navy submarines where he remained until the end of the war. Tragically he learned that his mother and father had been killed in concentration camps having been identified as active members of the Resistance, while his sister died shortly after from the effects of her incarceration. For his acts of courage working for the SIS, Lieutenant Lomenech was awarded the DSC and Bar and the Croix de Guerre with Palms. He passed away in Pont-Aven in October 1996, aged 75. In July 2000, the Holdsworth Special Forces Trust placed a small plaque overlooking Tresco in the Scilly Isles, commemorating Lomenech and the brave men of the secret naval flotilla.

Written by Lieutenant Commander Richard Lewis QVRM, Royal Naval Reserves

"Well versed in the habits of the Breton fishing fleets, Lomenech pioneered the use of converted fishing boats to run clandestine intelligence missions between the Scillies and occupied France"

Oyster, beef and stout pie

Leading Chef Ashley Gilham, Royal Navy

Whitstable is a seaside town on the north coast of Kent well known for its native oysters. Oyster farming in Whitstable is said to date back over 2,000 years and oyster shells excavated from modern Rome have been traced back to the town. In the 1850s, when oyster farming was at its peak, it is said that 80 million oysters were sent to Billingsgate fish market in London each year and it became a plentiful food of the poor. Today, the native oyster is world renowned and in 1997 the sea beds around Whitstable were granted Protected Geographical Indication status by the European Union.

Squadron Leader Mohinder Singh Pujji DFC, PCS, BA, LLB

Born in 1918 in the mountainous area of Simla, Himachal Pradesh, Mohinder Singh Pujji was the son of a senior government official, the only Indian working alongside white British officers. Still in his teens, Pujji learned to fly as a hobby pilot with the Delhi Flying Club and later worked for Himalayan Airways. Keen to help after hearing news of German air attacks on Britain, Pujji volunteered for the Royal Indian Air Force in 1940. He was one of first batch of 24 trailblazing Indian pilots selected to receive a commission from the RAF, and one of the few who made it home despite having fought in all three major theatres – Europe, North Africa and the Far East – in the Second World War.

Awarded the King's Commission on 1 August 1940, he trained on the Hurricane and was thrust into active service with the "Fighting Cocks" of 43 Squadron, before moving to 258 Squadron where he provided daylight bomber escort over occupied France. He was also shot down in the West African desert but was fortunately rescued by British desert troops. Pujji insisted on always wearing his dastar – or turban fortress – even having special straps manufactured so he could wear an oxygen mask over it.

He was based in Asia from 1942 onwards and was promoted to squadron commander of No. 6 Squadron after his commanding officer failed to return from a sortie. Pujji tried to raise morale by posting his name first on the daily flight rotas and recording record flying hours every month. In September 1944, he heard of 300 US troops who were lost in the Burmese jungle. After the US Air Force and the RAF had launched multiple unsuccessful missions to spot them, Pujji went it alone, flying at an extremely low level directly over enemy soldiers before finding the beleaguered American troops, who had exhausted all food and ammunition and were close to capture. For his courageous efforts, Pujji was awarded the RAF's highest gallantry medal, the Distinguished Flying Cross.

Pujji's military career was brought to an abrupt end in 1946 after he survived a long battle with acute tuberculosis. He became the airfield manager at New Delhi Airport and then aerodrome officer for Bombay International. Pujji and his wife eventually moved to England, where he worked, variously, as an air traffic controller at Heathrow Airport, a driving instructor and a manager at the Strand Hotel.

In his later years he also became the chairman of the Undivided Indian Ex-Services Association and in 2000 was given the freedom of the London Borough of Newham. In 2007, he was recognised by Kent Police and Kent County Council for his bravery and personal commitment to Britain throughout his life.

In 2005, Pujji confronted the British National Party for using the Spitfire in their campaign literature. "The BNP forget that people from different backgrounds helped in the Second World War," he said. "I am proof of this."

Squadron Leader Mohinder Singh Pujji died in September 2010. A statue of him by sculptor Douglas Jennings was unveiled in Gravesend in 2014, bearing the inscription: "To commemorate those from around the world who served alongside Britain in all conflicts 1914–2014."

Written by Wing Commander Manjeet Ghataora, RAF

Preparation time: 1 hour
Cooking time: 5 hours

Serves 4

INGREDIENTS

For the pie filling
700g diced chuck steak or ox cheek
25g plain flour, seasoned with
 salt and pepper
4 tbsp sunflower oil
2 medium onions, cut into 1cm dice
2 medium carrots, cut into 1cm dice
200g pancetta lardons
440ml (1 can) Guinness
2 bay leaves
4 sprigs thyme
400ml beef stock
1 tbsp red wine vinegar
Salt and pepper to taste
8 oysters, shucked

For the pastry
350g plain flour
Pinch of salt
125g unsalted butter, diced
125g shredded beef suet
Iced water
1 egg yolk, beaten

METHOD

To make the pie filling
• Preheat the oven to 160°C.
• Toss the beef in the seasoned flour until well coated and shake off the excess.
• Heat the oil in an ovenproof casserole over a high heat and brown the beef all over in about three separate batches, taking care not to overcrowd the pan; once browned remove the beef, dab with a sheet of kitchen paper to absorb any excess fat and set aside in a bowl.
• Add the onions, carrots and pancetta to the casserole, and cook for 2–3 minutes, stirring frequently, until the onions are translucent and lightly caramelised.
• Add half the can of Guinness and bring to a simmer, scraping the bottom of the casserole to deglaze and release the flavours.
• Return the beef, along with any juices that have collected in the bowl, to the casserole, add the bay leaves, thyme, stock, red wine vinegar and the remaining Guinness and bring to a simmer.
• Cover the casserole with a lid and cook in the preheated oven for 2–2½ hours; remove the lid and continue to cook, uncovered, for a further 1½ hours, stirring occasionally.

For the pastry
• While the pie filling is cooking make and rest the pastry. Place the flour, salt, butter and suet into a large mixing bowl and rub all the ingredients together between your fingertips to form a breadcrumb texture.
• Mix in enough of the iced water, a little at a time, to make a soft pliable dough; wrap the dough in clingfilm and place in the fridge to rest for 1 hour.
• Once the pie filling is cooked, turn the oven up to 180°C.
• Spoon the pie filling into a pie dish and arrange the shucked oysters on the filling in a cross shape so that each portion has two whole oysters.
• Lightly dust the worktop with flour and roll out the pastry to 1cm thick and large enough to cover the pie dish.
• Carefully lay the pastry over the pie filling (remember where you placed your oysters) and trim the edges; pinch around with your finger and thumb to crimp and seal the edges then lightly score the pasty with the tip of a sharp knife into four portions, each with two oysters.
• Brush the pie top with the beaten egg yolk and bake in the oven for 45 minutes or until golden brown.

To serve
• Remove the pie from the oven and let it sit at room temperature for 10 minutes before cutting through the scored lines into four portions.

Careers at sea and beyond

Since being founded in the 1890s, Fleetwood Nautical College in Lancashire has developed an international reputation for excellence in naval and offshore training

fleetwoodnautical.blackpool.ac.uk

Fleetwood Nautical College specialises in preparing students for a career at sea, yet it's not quite enough for this 130-year-old maritime establishment. "We deliberately take our offer one step further," says Captain Neil Atkinson, Head of Fleetwood Nautical Campus. "We offer training and relevant qualifications for a career at sea and beyond, whether that's piloting ships, teaching or as a harbour master. We have two departments, maritime and offshore, and in both those areas there comes a time when people want to work on shore, though still connected to the sea. The average time spent working at sea is eight years, so it makes sense for us to actively look at qualifications to take people into the second part of their careers."

Neil reached the role of ship's captain in the Merchant Navy before taking over his role at Fleetwood Nautical College nine years ago. Like many of the team, he'd been trained in Fleetwood and, as a Lancastrian, was aware of the college's reputation from a young age. "I was delighted to come back," he says. "The staff are fantastic and all the training is cutting edge, including virtual reality and simulation, so we have total confidence in the capabilities we're giving our students. We do everything from short refresher courses up to our new BSc in Maritime Operations Management, launching in September 2021. Short courses continued throughout lockdown as we're part of so many key industries."

The maritime courses have very traditional roots and also embrace all relevant new technology, while the offshore training for oil, gas and wind turbines reflects the growth of these industries. This highly regulated market demands equally high-quality training and safety standards across the world and Fleetwood Nautical Campus's reputation for excellent professional development is valued by students and employers alike. "This is a very important sector for the UK, probably now more than ever," says Neil. "We train people to the highest possible standards, helping them make a career at sea and far beyond, with personal and professional development a constant key part of that."

A modern take on the Lancashire hotpot

Corporal Mark Harrison, RAF

Historical documents date Lancashire hotpot as far back as the 1750s and the start of industrialisation. All ages of the families had to work long, strictly regulated hours in the cotton mills, which made it impossible to cook food that required extensive preparation or cooking time. The housewives would carry their hotpot to the baker's oven and leave it there to cook all day while working in the mills. It has been described as "the stuff of legends" and, in the long-standing soap opera Coronation Street, hotpot was the signature dish on the Rovers Return menu, known famously as "Betty's Hotpot". My take is to deconstruct the dish and add a restaurant flair to create a simple, stunning meal to be enjoyed by all.

Gluten Free
Preparation time: 45 minutes
Cooking time: 1 hour 15 minutes

Serves 4

INGREDIENTS

For the hotpot potatoes
800g potatoes, peeled
50g butter, melted
500ml lamb, beef or vegetable stock
Salt and pepper

For the gravy
2 tbsp vegetable oil
1 large carrot, roughly diced
1 celery stick, roughly diced
1 large onion, roughly diced
500ml lamb or beef stock
75g frozen or fresh pearl onions

75g carrots, diced
2 tbsp fresh mint, shredded
50g cornflour mixed with 3 tbsp
  cold water
Salt and pepper

For the lamb
4 x 175–210g lamb rumps
50g butter
Salt and pepper

For the crushed minted peas
500g frozen peas
150ml vegetable stock
2 tbsp mint, shredded
Salt and pepper

Lancashire

METHOD

For the potatoes

- Preheat the oven to 180°C and brush an ovenproof dish with a little of the melted butter.
- Finely slice the potatoes about 3mm thick (use a mandolin if you have one) and arrange them in layers in the prepared ovenproof dish, lightly seasoning each layer with salt and pepper.
- Pour over the stock to just cover the potatoes, cover with tin foil and cook in the oven for about 1 hour 15 minutes or until the potatoes are tender and all of the stock has been absorbed.
- Remove the foil, brush the top of the potatoes with the remaining melted butter and return to the oven for an additional 5–10 minutes or until the tops of the potatoes are nicely golden.

For the gravy

- Heat the vegetable oil in a saucepan over a medium heat and add the roughly diced carrot, celery and onion; cook, stirring frequently for about 10 minutes until lightly coloured then pour off any excess oil.
- Pour over the stock, and simmer until the vegetables are soft.
- Pass the stock and vegetables through a sieve into a clean saucepan, pressing the vegetables through the mesh with the base of a ladle; this will give your sauce body and infuse all the flavours.
- Bring the gravy to a simmer over a medium heat, add the pearl onions and 75g of diced carrots and simmer until just tender.
- Add enough of the diluted cornflour to thicken the gravy to a coating consistency, season with salt and pepper, stir in the shredded mint and simmer for a couple of minutes.

For the lamb rumps

- Heat the butter in a frying pan or skillet over a medium-high heat and sear the lamb rumps, basting occasionally with the butter; once seared all over, season with salt and pepper and finish in the oven with the potatoes for 10–15 minutes. Cover with foil and set aside to rest while the potatoes finish browning in the oven.

For the crushed peas

- Place the peas in a saucepan with the stock and simmer until the stock has reduced by half.
- Remove from the heat and crush the peas randomly with a fork ensuring there are some mashed and some whole peas; season with salt and pepper and stir in the chopped mint.

To serve

- Divide the potatoes into four portions and serve each with a lamb rump, gravy and crushed minted peas.

VEGETARIAN/VEGAN ALTERNATIVE

- Instead of using a lamb rump an alternative can be a cauliflower steak cooked the same way as the lamb ensuring you use vegetable stock in the potatoes and sauce.

Gunner Samuel John Wadsworth

Samuel John Wadsworth was born on 13 September 1896 in Darwen, Lancashire. His early life was defined by his love of football and he ended up playing left back for a number of professional teams including Blackburn Rovers, Huddersfield Town and Burnley.

With the outbreak of the Great War, Sam – then playing for Blackburn Rovers reserves – attempted to enlist, aged only 17. He lied to the recruiting sergeant that he was 18 and was told: "Come back next month and tell me you are 19." Shortly after, he was enlisted as Gunner 55813 in the Royal Garrison Artillery, joining his brother Charlie on the Western Front.

Wadsworth experienced the horrors of war in the trenches of Belgium and Northern France. He suffered both physically and mentally, receiving shrapnel wounds to his left ankle and experiencing blackouts and traumatic stress throughout his life. Sam Wadsworth survived the war, but his older brother Charlie wasn't so fortunate. "I had lost my only brother and my best friend and supporter," said Sam.

On his return from the trenches, Wadsworth rejoined Blackburn Rovers. "It had been all I had lived for over four years of life and death in the trenches," he said. He was heartbroken when released by the club but, after a spell with non-league Nelson, he moved to Huddersfield Town in 1921. He stayed with them during their most successful decade, winning the FA Cup, three league titles and two Charity Shields. He even represented England nine times, wearing the captain's armband for his final four caps. After 281 league appearances and four goals for Huddersfield he transferred to Burnley FC in 1929.

Following his retirement from football in 1930, Wadsworth moved to the Netherlands where he enjoyed a successful career as a football manager for several clubs, including winning the league title with PSV Eindhoven. He passed away on 1 September 1961, aged 64. Prior to his death, Wadsworth recorded several tapes where his humility and good nature shone through for all to hear, telling stories of team spirit and friendship, duty and fair play – all qualities required to get through the harsh times in the trenches. "I was taught not only how to live well," he said, "but how to lose well."

Written by Corporal Becky Croker, RAF

"*Sam won the FA Cup, three league titles and two Charity Shields. He even represented England nine times, four as captain*"

Pork and Stilton pie

Corporal Lee Coxon, RAF

The humble pork pie has been around since the late 18th century and Dickinson and Morris have been baking the nation's favourite Melton Mowbray pork pies since 1851. I have decided to pair the iconic pie with a Leicester Stilton; Leicestershire is one of three counties that can produce this classic English blue cheese and it has a distinct, sharp taste that works really well with the pork. Packed into a crisp, hot water crust pastry case, this pie is a filling meal or snack for all occasions.

Dairy free
Preparation time: 1 hour
Cooking time: 1 hour 10 minutes

Serves 4–6

INGREDIENTS

For the filling
350g pork shoulder or belly
  (skin removed)
1 red onion, finely diced
90g blue Stilton, crumbled
1 tsp dried sage
1 tsp salt
1 tsp ground black pepper

For the pastry
350g plain flour
1 tsp salt
110g lard
140ml water
1 egg, beaten

METHOD

For the filling

- Cut the pork into small dice ensuring all skin and sinew is removed.
- Transfer the diced pork to a mixing bowl and mix in the rest of the pie filling ingredients.

For the hot water crust pastry

- Sieve the flour and salt into a large mixing bowl.
- Place the lard and water into a saucepan and bring to a boil, ensuring the lard has fully melted.
- Pour the lard and water into the flour and beat with a wooden spoon until combined.
- The pastry should come together nicely and feel hot to the touch, once cooled slightly, this is the perfect time to start working with the pastry; place a third of the pastry to one side for the pie lids.

Making the pies

- Preheat the oven to 190°C. Grease a deep muffin tin with melted lard.
- Roll out the pastry on a lightly floured surface to approximately ¾cm thick and cut into discs large enough to line the bases of the muffin moulds (I used a large glass).
- Gently ease your pastry discs into the muffin moulds, pushing the pastry down to the base of the mould; any holes or tears can be patched up at this stage. Ensure the pastry is slightly above and over the lip of each individual mould as this will ensure a snug fit for the pastry lid.
- Fill each pie generously, creating a dome of the filling in the centre; don't worry about your pie looking messy at this stage.
- Roll out the reserved third of pastry and cut into discs slightly larger than the top of the pies.
- Brush the exposed pastry around the top of the pies before placing the lids on top; the lids can be either pressed together with the base overhang to create a seal or crimped for a more traditional and professional finish. Pierce a hole in the centre of each pie lid to allow the steam to escape during cooking.
- Brush the lids with the remaining beaten egg and bake in the preheated oven for 20 minutes then lower the heat to 160°C and continue to cook for a further 50 minutes.

- Once the pies are cooked, allow to cool slightly before removing from the moulds; allow to fully cool before refrigerating overnight – this allows the meat to set within the pie case resulting in a better end product.

Top tips

- Preheat the oven to between 40–60°C to keep the pastry warm while working; once the pastry begins to cool it will become harder to work with and brittle.
- The Stilton cheese can be substituted for your favourite hard or crumbly cheese.
- Use a muffin tin for best results, however the pastry can be moulded around the bottom of a glass or rolling pin for a free-standing pork pie; this will require some practice so maybe only try one for the first bake.
- Piccalilli or a chutney are the perfect accompaniment to pork pies.
- Utilise spare pastry to create leaves to decorate the lid of your pie.

VEGETARIAN/VEGAN ALTERNATIVE

Make a vegan pastry

- Replace the lard with vegan margarine; rub the flour and margarine together to form a sandy crumble texture, gradually mix in cold water to form the pastry; this will make more of a shortcrust pastry rather than a hot water crust pastry. Rest the pastry for 20 minutes in the fridge before rolling out (note the mix will probably not require all the water stated above and will not require the water to be hot when forming the pastry).

Prepare a vegetarian or vegan filling

- Peel 150g butternut squash and 100g potatoes and cut into 1cm dice; cut 100g broccoli into small florets – these can be kept slightly larger than the potato and butternut squash.
- Par-boil the diced potato and squash in salted boiling water for approximately 6–8 minutes and allow to cool before mixing with the diced onion, crumbled Stilton (omit if making vegan pies, or use a vegan cheese), dried sage and seasoning.
- Build and cook the pies as in the main recipe.

Flight Lieutenant Bertram Nicholls DFM

"I'm no war hero: I'm just one of the others who came back," said RAF Bomber Command veteran Flight Lieutenant Bertram "Nick" Nicholls, speaking to his local newspaper in Leicestershire, the *Harborough Mail*, during his 100th birthday celebrations in 2019. "I always thought that I had not just one but three guardian angels looking out for me." His story is a significant tale of survival against the odds. Taking part in 50 bombing raids over German cities, his crew's efforts, like all those of RAF Bomber Command, greatly contributed to the Allied victory.

Nicholls was born in Leicester in 1919, growing up in Barwell and Earl Shilton, and joined the RAF in 1939, aged 20. He was posted to 83 Squadron at RAF Scampton, Lincolnshire as a wireless operator and navigator on the Handley-Page Hampdens, where he carried out night raids in enemy airspace. Nicholls completed 30 missions with 83 Squadron before being transferred to the Royal Canadian Air Force's (RCAF) 428 Squadron based at RAF Dalton, Yorkshire and later RAF Middleton St George in County Durham (known today as Teesside International Airport). There he flew another 20 missions. "We suffered terrible casualties," said Nicholls. "When I went into the RCAF there were 18 crews. Mine was the only crew that lived." Even that seems miraculous: returning from a raid near Wilhelmshaven, his aircraft came under heavy enemy fire and the tailerons were damaged. Despite this, they still managed to limp home over the English Channel.

For his valiant service, Nicholls was awarded the Distinguished Flying Medal by King George VI. He flew his 50th mission in 1943 and spent the remainder of the war training air crew. After the war, Bertram worked in the hosiery trade, becoming factory manager and director at J Leeson's in Leicester. He and his wife, Barbara, had three daughters, six grandchildren and nine great-grandchildren.

"I never regretted joining Bomber Command," he said. "I made a lot of good mates. It's just so sad that so many never got home." During the Second World War, Bomber Command flew 364,514 sorties, 297,663 of them at night. For every 100 men who flew with them, 56 were killed in the air or died of wounds received during a sortie. In all, 55,573 were killed, the average age of the dead being 22. The memorial to Bomber Command was erected in 2012 at London's Green Park.

Written by Flight Sergeant Katrina Harries, RAF

"For every 100 men who flew with Bomber Command, 56 were killed in the air or died of wounds received during a sortie"

Thinking outside the box

Good food is a way of life for Kelly and Jon Barfoot, the husband-and-wife team behind Boxxfresh, one of Britain's rising stars in home-delivered groceries

www.boxxfresh.com

Anyone looking for the very best in fresh, seasonal produce need look no further than Boxxfresh, a dynamic family-run business that is changing the way people shop for fruit and vegetables. "Most people associate home-delivered veg boxes with restrictive subscription services and fixed ingredients which can lead to food waste," says Boxxfresh co-founder Kelly Barfoot. "We do things differently. You're free to shop as and when you like, choosing exactly what goes in your box."

As a small family business, Boxxfresh works with other small businesses and growers to deliver the freshest produce. "We love all shapes and sizes at Boxxfresh," says Kelly. "Wonky, weirdly wonderful, misshapen – we take it all! This means less waste for everyone, especially the farmer. Good food means good in every way: good for the environment and good for social impact, as well as making us feel good. What we eat has huge effect on the planet." Boxxfresh is also leading on important environmental sustainability through plastic-free packaging.

The company connects with its customers each week with seasonal ideas and enticing recipes which can be found on the Boxxfresh website. "It's real food for real life," says Kelly. "Quick, simple, batchable and comforting dishes that make you want to cook and eat more of the good stuff."

The pandemic affected the British public in so many different ways. Since the beginning of the first lockdown, in addition to looking after its own customers, Boxxfresh has also worked with the Feed A Family Organisation in Hampshire – providing vulnerable people a fresh fruit and vegetable delivery service during the worst of the pandemic, ensuring nothing ever went to waste.

"We want our customers to connect with the seasons, build their box and be confident in where food comes from," says Kelly, "appreciating what freshness and taste really means to meal preparation, With so many carefully sourced food options to choose from without plastic or food waste, it's got to be better for you, your family and the planet."

Coconut ramen

This Boxxfresh recipe is the ultimate reset ramen: a bowl of tasty energising goodness.
You can serve this punchy soup as it is or with cooked noodles or rice. Make it your own
by adding whichever veggies you fancy – shredded kale, leeks, watercress or cauliflower.

Serves 2–3

INGREDIENTS

1 tin of coconut milk
1 vegetable stock cube
1 shallot, peeled and finely diced
1 or 2 chillies, seeds removed and finely sliced
2 cloves of garlic, peeled and grated
1 big thumb sized piece of ginger,
  peeled and grated
2 big handful of mushrooms, finely sliced
  or 1 punnet of exotic mushrooms
1 courgette, cut in half and finely sliced
1 big handful of tenderstem broccoli,
  roughly chopped
1 bag of spinach
Tamari sauce
1 lime

METHOD

• Place a large saucepan over a medium to high heat.
• Pour in the tin of coconut milk, crumble in the stock cube and then add two tins worth of fresh water to the pot.
• Let the coconut milk melt and the liquid come to a gentle simmer, stirring now and then.
• Add the diced shallot, chilli, grated garlic and ginger. Let the broth carry on gently bubbling for 5 minutes to allow all the punchy ingredients to flavour the liquid.
• Pour in one tablespoon of Tamari sauce and scatter in mushrooms and courgettes then bring the liquid back to a gentle bubble for 2 or 3 minutes.
• Add the spinach and let it wilt into the ramen.
• Cut the lime in half, squeeze the juice over the ramen and serve in warm bowls.

Maltese rabbit stew

Corporal Peter Farrington, RAF

My father-in-law comes from Malta and, having tried his amazing rabbit stew, I decided to research it and see if I could make it as well as he could. Rabbit stew has been around the Maltese islands since the Knights of St John, which certainly qualifies it as a cultural delicacy that contributes to Malta's rich and varied heritage. This recipe is as traditional as they get, using ingredients typically found in most Maltese dishes with local homegrown vegetables and herbs. If you're not keen on trying rabbit you can substitute it for diced pork shoulder, which will also make a wholesome stew with a rich and deep flavour.

Preparation time: 25 minutes
Cooking time: 1 hour 15 minutes

Serves 4

INGREDIENTS

4 tbsp olive oil
1 rabbit, jointed (get your butcher to do this for you)
¼ tsp Cajun seasoning
1 large onion, coarsely chopped
3 cloves garlic, finely chopped or crushed
125ml good quality red wine
1 bay leaf
500ml beef stock
¼ tsp freshly grated or ground nutmeg
2 tbsp tomato purée
¼ tsp caster sugar
4 large potatoes, peeled and quartered
1 stick of celery, coarsely chopped
2 carrots, peeled and coarsely chopped
1 sprig of thyme
100g frozen garden peas
Salt and freshly ground black pepper

METHOD

• Heat the oil in a large heavy-based pan or casserole over medium heat; seal the rabbit with a little seasoning and the Cajun spice until evenly coloured all over; transfer the rabbit joints to a plate and set aside.
• Return the pan to the heat, add the onion and garlic and cook, stirring occasionally, until fragrant; stir in the wine, bay leaf, beef stock, nutmeg, tomato purée and sugar and season lightly with salt and pepper.
• Return the rabbit joints to the pan (with any juices that have collected on the plate), add the potatoes, celery, carrots and thyme; pour over enough water to ensure everything is covered.
• Bring the stew to a boil; reduce the heat to low, cover with a lid and allow to simmer gently for about 1 hour until the rabbit is tender and the potatoes are completely cooked through.
• Stir in the garden peas, continue to simmer for 5 minutes and check the seasoning.
• Serve in a nice deep bowl with fresh crusty bread.

VEGETARIAN/VEGAN ALTERNATIVE
• Instead of using rabbit you can use Quorn pieces.

The people of Malta

Britain's links to the Mediterranean island of Malta go back to 1800 when the British assisted the Maltese in expelling the French. The island remained under British control and, until the 1930s, was home to the British Mediterranean Fleet. During the Second World War, Malta was the sole British harbour between Gibraltar and Egypt. Its geographical position provided a crucial base for Allied forces who could use Malta as a base to disrupt Axis supply lines in Italy or North Africa. It's why the island became a prime target for German and Italian air attacks.

Throughout 1941 and 1942, Malta was subjected to approximately 3,000 air raids from Axis forces, making the island the most bombed place on earth. From January to July 1942, there was only one period of 24 hours where no bombs fell, according to the George Cross Island Association. Due to the devastating air attacks, the Maltese people were forced to seek refuge in underground tunnels. Shelter was at a premium and was becoming hugely overcrowded. Unhygienic conditions resulted in epidemics of dysentery and typhoid among an already undernourished population. Relief by sea was attempted many times, but these convoys seldom arrived due to the constant attacks en route; during 1942, less than five of the 24 ships heading to Malta unloaded their cargoes.

It is estimated that 7,000 Maltese civilians and service personnel were killed during the siege. According to Maurice Agius, a young officer at the time of the siege, due tribute was paid to the population of Malta for not breaking down in the face of continuous air attacks, death, homes in ruins, suffering, hunger and privations. The praise is truly deserved, and the courage shown by all will long be remembered.

The George Cross has only been awarded to collective recipients on two occasions: to the Royal Ulster Constabulary, for bravery, in 1999, and to the island of Malta in 1942. "To honour her brave people, I award the George Cross to the island fortress of Malta to bear witness to a heroism and a devotion that will long be famous in history," wrote King George VI to the island's governor, Sir William Dobbie. At the ceremony on 13 September 1942 (pictured, right), Dobbie's successor, Lord Gort (left) presented the award to Malta's Chief Justice Sir George Bort (right). The cross was subsequently woven into the upper-left corner of Malta's national flag. The original medal is now on display at the National War Museum in Fort Saint Elmo, Malta.

Written by Lieutenant Terry Griffin, Royal Navy

> "*It is estimated that 7,000 Maltese civilians and service personnel were killed during the siege*"

Tuna vindaye

Corporal Rajesh Babooram, Army

A mouth-watering, exotic and popular fish pickle from Mauritius, this is an easy recipe to prepare and can be eaten hot or cold, but is often made in advance and stored in the fridge. Vindaye is mainly flavoured with mustard seeds and turmeric, which give it a sharp, hot and pungent flavour. Different types of vindaye can also be prepared using various other produce, such as vindaye octopus, meat or Quorn, and is usually served with plain boiled rice or crusty baguette. I have served this in my home country to many locals and tourists alike.

Gluten-free, dairy-free
Preparation time: 15 minutes
Cooking time: 20 minutes

Serves 4

INGREDIENTS

500g fresh tuna, diced
1 tbsp lemon juice
1 tbsp turmeric powder
3 cloves garlic, chopped
150ml olive oil
3 medium onions, coarsely sliced
2 tbsp freshly ground mustard seeds
2 tbsp white vinegar
1 green chilli, sliced
2 tbsp fresh coriander, coarsely chopped
Salt and ground black pepper to taste

METHOD

• Season the fish with the lemon juice, one teaspoon of the turmeric powder, ½ tsp of the chopped garlic and a little salt and pepper; mix well and leave to marinate for 10 minutes.
• Heat the olive oil in a shallow frying pan over a medium-high heat and pan-fry the fish until golden on each side.
• Remove the fish from the pan and set aside in a bowl.
• Return the pan to the heat and add the onions, ground mustard seeds and the remaining chopped garlic and turmeric powder; sauté for 1 minute.
• Return the fish, including any juices that have collected in the bowl, to the pan and cook for a further 2–4 minutes until the fish is just cooked through; add a little water if it becomes too dry.
• Check the seasoning and add extra salt and pepper to taste.
• Remove from the heat and add the vinegar, sliced chillies and coriander; carefully mix everything together, coating the fish with all of the spices.
• Serve warm with plain basmati rice and green salad or chilled on a crusty baguette.

Mauritius: Local hero

Lise Marie Jeanette de Baissac MBE

A clandestine agent during the Second World War, Lise Marie Jeanette de Baissac's remarkable story provided the basis for the 2008 film *Female Agents*, in which she was played by Sophie Marceau. Lise was born on 11 May 1905 to a French family in Mauritius and moved to Paris in 1919, aged 14. Like most Mauritians she was fluent in French and English, a highly sought-after quality for British secret services.

After the occupation of Paris in 1940, Lise's eldest brother Jean joined the British Army, while Lise and her other brother Claude made a convoluted escape to England via Spain, Portugal, Gibraltar and Scotland. She found employment at the *Daily Sketch*, while her brother Claude was recruited into the Special Operations Executive (SOE), a secret organisation that conducted espionage, sabotage and reconnaissance in occupied Europe. As soon as the SOE opened recruitment for women, Lise applied and was selected to set up her own circuit to aid those in the Resistance. She trained in Beaulieu alongside Odette Sansom (see page 281) and was commissioned in the First Aid Nursing Yeomanry in July 1942.

On 24 September 1942, Lise and Andree Borrel parachuted into the village of Boisenard, the first SOE agents to be inserted in this manner, in order to form a new circuit to gain information and deliver arms to the French Resistance. Her cover story was that she was a poor widow escaping life in the capital. She befriended a Gestapo chief, claiming to be an amateur archaeologist, which allowed her to cycle around freely and recce parachute drop areas. After returning to the UK for her own safety a year later, where she trained new agents, Lise returned to France in a Westland Lysander for her second mission on 9 April 1944. Two French schoolgirls in Lise's network helped to cripple 82 tank carriers as part of an operation.

With D-Day looming, she joined her brother Claude in Normandy, looking for suitable areas for paratroopers to hold while they established themselves in the initial 48 hours after landing. She even rented a room in a house occupied by the local German commander to gain info. Germans who searched her room failed to notice that she had hidden a British Army uniform, as well as a parachute disguised as a sleeping bag.

Lise was awarded the Legion d'honneur and Croix de guerre in France and an MBE in September 1945. She later worked for the BBC as a programme assistant, announcer and

translator, marrying Gustave Villameur, and lived in Marseille and Saint-Tropez. She passed away on 24 March 2004, just seven weeks shy of her 100th birthday. "She was the inspiring force for the groups in the Orne," states her SOE dossier. "Through her initiatives she inflicted heavy losses on the Germans thanks to anti-tyre devices scattered on the roads near Saint-Aubin-du-Désert, Saint-Mars-du-Désert, and even as far as Laval, Le Mans and Rennes. She also took part in armed attacks on enemy columns."

Written by Gill Knox, Royal Military Police (retired)

Peace of mind for all the family

Doro Care offers its customers specialist
support that can be accessed simply
by pressing a button

www.doro.com/en-gb/care

The home is often where we experience some of our fondest moments and, for many of us, is where we feel most comfortable. Doro Care is committed to helping people live safely and independently at home for as long as possible. The company provides a service of 24-hour support through a simple device – a pendant worn around the neck or wrist – with a button that, if pressed, will instantly connect the user to Doro's specialist team.

"Our service gives you, or a loved one, the freedom to get on with daily life, knowing help is at hand," explains Wendy Darling, Doro UK Country Director. "In simple terms it is a method of connecting you to our trained team of professionals when you feel vulnerable, at risk or if you simply want reassurance."

The home unit works with a pendant, which can be worn on the wrist or around the neck. Once the button is pressed the team assesses the situation and contacts the emergency services or friends and family if needed. The pendant can be used from anywhere in the home. If the operator gets no response via the clear loudspeaker on the unit, they will still send out help.

It's a sad fact but unfortunately around 8,000 people fall every day and, as people get older, the likelihood of tripping or losing balance naturally increases. However, with an alarm you know that if your loved ones do fall, they can access help to get them back on their feet in no time. And, with a Doro Care alarm, you know that help is coming from an organisation that knows exactly what it is doing from years of experience.

"Having a service like this means you can get the help you need immediately," says Wendy. "It could avoid undue upset or a hospital admission – something that's more important than ever given recent events. With that in mind, and the fact we've all been having to get used to staying away from many members of family and friends, here's perhaps never been a better time to think about putting Doro Care's services in place."

The leading edge

Merseyside-based organisation Maximum Edge works with communities, companies and individuals in need to provide support and mentoring

www.maximumedge.org.uk

Whether you're an individual seeking professional development, a company looking to develop your staff, or a sports club aiming high, Maximum Edge might be able to help. Based near Liverpool, this community interest company works with communities to provide support, identifying common concerns and the best solutions to deal with them.

"It's about life management, mental health, getting the right support and helping people and organisations understand that there is a way out and that you can move on," says Dave Sheridan, Director of Maximum Edge. "We also work directly with individuals, sports clubs and organisations or businesses looking to motivate and develop staff, trustees or service users. We offer a tailored solution, including workshops, one-to-one coaching, remote support, podcasts and resources to help people make positive changes at work, in sport and in the community and schools."

"Everyone involved has extensive third-sector experience and we were all aware of a gap in services and support especially around poverty and hardship," says Dave. "We eventually said 'Let's do this ourselves'."

Empathy plays a major role in Maximum Edge's success, illustrated by staff members like Martin O'Looney. "I was brought in to help specialise more in recovery programmes," he says. "We have veterans coming to us with addiction issues and PTSD and that used to be me. In 2009 I was on the verge of losing my wife and family and had already lost my job. I've been where they are in my past, and my experience is a big part of our recovery programme. They look at me and know I've been through it. They also help strengthen my own recovery."

Motivation is in short supply at present, but Maximum Edge inspires that first, important step. "Many people are isolated and unhappy, struggling with grief and poverty," says Dave. "Sometimes we're all the family they've got, which makes our very personal service even more important."

Scouse

Leading Catering Services Chris Maxwell, Royal Navy

Merseyside

Scouse was traditionally made from leftovers and scraps with whatever was in season or cheap at the time. The origins of the name come from a northern European stew, commonly eaten by seamen sailing in and out of Liverpool, called "Lobscouse" and hence "scouse". Liverpudlians thus became known as "Scousers". Scouse was originally made with lamb, as it was the cheapest meat at the time, but it has been adapted and many households use beef. Just as the city of Liverpool and its families are divided by which football team they support, the same can be said for the great scouse recipe. Scouse even has its own international day – 28 February each year is global scouse day and is celebrated as far and wide as the USA and Australia.

Gluten-free, dairy-free
Preparation time: 30 minutes
Cooking time: 2½ hours

Serves 4

INGREDIENTS

3 tbsp vegetable oil
600g chuck steak or lamb neck fillet,
  cut into 2cm chunks
2 large onions, cut into 1½cm dice
3 medium carrots, cut into 1½cm dice
½ medium swede, cut into 1½cm dice
400ml bitter
500g floury potatoes, cut into 1½cm dice
1 litre beef stock
1 sprig of thyme
2 bay leaves
20g parsley, coarsely chopped (optional)
1 tsp Worcestershire sauce (optional)
Salt and freshly ground black pepper

METHOD

• Heat 2 tbsp of the oil in a casserole or heavy-based saucepan over a high heat, season the beef with salt and pepper and sear all over in the hot oil until well browned; transfer to a bowl with a slotted spoon.
• Return the pan to a low-medium heat with the remaining oil, add the onions and carrots and cook, stirring frequently for about 10 minutes, until the vegetables have started to soften and the onions have become translucent.
• Stir in the seared beef (plus any juices that have accumulated in the bowl), swede and bitter; turn up the heat and let it reduce by half, this should take about 10 minutes.
• Add half of the potatoes, the beef stock, thyme and bay leaves.
• Bring to a boil, reduce the heat to low, cover with a lid and simmer gently, stirring occasionally, for 1½ hours.
• Stir in the remaining potatoes, replace the lid and continue to simmer for about 45 minutes to 1 hour, adding a little boiling water if the stew becomes too thick, until the potatoes and meat are tender.
• Stir in the chopped parsley and Worcestershire sauce if using, check the seasoning, adding a little salt and pepper to taste, and serve in a nice bowl ideally with pickled red cabbage and hot crusty bread with butter.

Private Matthew Rooney

The city of Liverpool paid a heavy price for freedom during the First World War; 120,000 of its citizens went to fight and, of these, 14,000 – more than one in nine – never returned. Nearly every family in Liverpool will have lost a relative or a close friend. Much is made of the few who won high honours, but many were no more heroic than anyone else: they were just in the right or wrong place at the right or wrong time. Even the lowliest infantryman must have had incredible courage to go over the top into a barrage of machine gun fire and march towards the enemy trenches.

Matthew Rooney is just one example. He was born in 1899 to Thomas and Mary Rooney at 7 Molyneaux Street, Bootle. Like many patriotic young men, he lied about his age and signed up at the tender age of 17, joining the Accrington Pals, one of the many "pals" battalions. Sent to France, Rooney was involved in several major battles from 1916 onwards. He was moved to several different regiments (including the Royal Welch Fusiliers, the Cheshire Regiment, the Manchester Regiment and the Royal Lancashire Regiment) as the formations he fought with lost men, or after he returned to the war following injuries.

After the Battle of Amiens, during the Battle at the River Warnave, Rooney was critically wounded having traumatically lost a leg in an artillery bombardment sometime around the 4 or 5 September 1918. He was transferred to a field hospital at Lembersart but died just a few days later from his injuries. Rooney was only 19 at the time, and his death occurred just two months before the end of the war. He was eventually laid to rest in the Rue-Petillon Military Cemetery in Fleurbaix and is commemorated on the Bootle War Memorial in Liverpool.

Matthew Rooney is very similar to the Unknown Warrior buried in Westminster Abbey. He may have been stood next to him when he was lost; he may have served with him. We must never forget that there were thousands of Matthew Rooneys who fought and died for their country and, as we say every Remembrance Sunday: "At the going down of the sun, and in the morning, we will remember them."

Written by Lieutenant Commander Andrew Murray
AFC, Royal Navy

> *"Like many patriotic young men, Matthew Rooney lied about his age and signed up at the tender age of 17"*

African chicken curry

Patti Boulaye, actress, singer and Celebrity MasterChef contestant

When I first started in show business, friends would come to my flat for a quick meal during the break or often after the show, knowing it would be ready in no time. This was my go-to dish. It always went down well. Years later, it became a favourite with my wonderful but late father-in-law Denis Komlosy. It's still one of my favourite go-to quick meals.

Preparation time: 15 minutes
Cooking time: 45–50 minutes

Serves 3

INGREDIENTS

For the curry
6 skinless chicken thighs
½ tsp salt
⅓ tsp dried oregano
⅓ tsp dried mixed herbs
1 chicken stock cube
1 garlic clove, finely chopped
2.5cm piece of fresh ginger
2 tsp palm oil
1 medium onion, finely chopped
400g (1 tin) chopped tomatoes
30g butter
1 tbsp (heaped) hot curry powder
¼ tsp ground nutmeg
½ tsp lemon juice
2 tbsp desiccated coconut
2 tbsp honey or 1 tbsp sugar
1 tsp (full) cornflour, dissolved in
   125ml cold water

For the plantain
2 tbsp vegetable oil
1 ripe plantain, sliced on an angle

To serve
Boiled white or brown rice
Basil leaves to garnish

METHOD

For the curry
• Pour 125ml of water into a saucepan with a lid. Add the chicken thighs, salt, dried oregano, mixed herbs, crumbled chicken stock cube, garlic and ginger. Bring to a boil and simmer for 5 minutes before reducing the heat and cooking for another 12 minutes.
• Meanwhile, heat the palm oil in a saucepan over a medium heat, add the onions and cook, stirring frequently, for 3–4 minutes.
• Add the tomatoes, butter, curry powder, nutmeg, lemon juice, desiccated coconut and honey or sugar. Cook for 10 minutes on medium-high heat, stirring constantly, to avoid the sauce sticking to the pan.
• After 10 minutes add the cooked chicken with the leftover cooking liquid and stir.
• Turn down the heat to very low, add the diluted cornflour to thicken and simmer for 10 minutes.

For the plantain
• Heat the vegetable oil in a frying pan over a medium-high heat, add the plantain with a little salt and fry the plantain, turning occasionally, for 3–4 minutes until both sides are brown at the edges.

To serve
• Serve the curry with the fried plantain and boiled rice and garnish with basil leaves.

Nigeria: Local hero

Sergeant Major Belo Akure MM DCM

Belo Akure is an example of one of the thousands from across the Commonwealth and Empire who fought in the Great War. He was born in a part of British West Africa known today as Nigeria and joined the West Africa Frontier Force in around 1901 as a bugler, but details are sketchy. "Akure" may not even be his surname as troops recruited from West Africa were often given the names of their hometowns as their surname, and Akure is the largest city in Ondo State in south western Nigeria.

Belo Akure was listed for a Distinguished Conduct Medal in 1908/09 for "acts of bravery in the field" and by 4 November 1914 he had risen to be a Company Sergeant Major, fighting the Germans in Cameroon. He single-handedly held off a German attack on the Mungo River while his soldiers escaped in a canoe. Once they were safe on the other side and gave covering fire, he swam across. He was awarded a clasp to his DCM medal for this and was mentioned in dispatches for his cool conduct and sound judgement.

In March 1917, Sergeant Major Akure was on a night patrol with three privates. They saw about 50 native soldiers, led by two German officers, preparing for an attack. He told his men to hold fire until he shot, killing one of the officers before the team gave rapid-fire then retreated while Akure provided cover. A week later, Akure was with Lieutenant Travers of the 4th Battalion on a patrol to ambush a German detachment. The German officer was the main target, and this time Akure shot him in the leg – then ran out under fire to bring him back as a prisoner. For these two acts of bravery, Belo Akure was awarded the Military Medal (MM). In his 1919 book *With The Nigerians In German East Africa*, Captain Walter Douglas Downes, another 4th Battalion officer, said of

> *"I have several times seen this Sergeant Major in action and can honestly state that I have never seen a braver man"*

Akure: "I have several times seen this Sergeant Major in action and can honestly state that I have never seen a braver man."

In 1924, Sergeant Major Akure (accompanied by his wife) joined a six-month exhibition in Wembley to celebrate African involvement in the war. More than 17 million people attended, and many wanted their photo taken with him. It ensured this heroic man would be marked in history.

Written by Staff Sergeant Mark John, Queen's Royal Lancers, Army

A reassuring call

With their easy-to-read text and large buttons, Doro phones are designed for senior citizens who require mobility and independence

www.doro.com

For numerous people around Europe, owning a Doro phone has been a literal lifesaver. The Swedish company was founded in 1974 and initially made desk phones and answerphones, but from 2007 began to focus on making mobile phones for the senior market across Europe including the UK, where it has more than 95 per cent share of the market. These phones are designed for ease of use, with large buttons, simple menus and bigger fonts and they all come equipped with a button that sends an instant alert to relatives and carers.

"We have a product called Response Premium by Doro that combines the phone with our care service, Doro Care," says MD Peter Marsden. "If somebody presses the Response button on their phone and pre-selected relatives are not available then we can route that call to our 24/7 care centre. Somebody will be there to talk to about their needs and requirements."

Doro phones are aimed at seniors who remain relatively mobile and independent but who seek some reassurance in case of an emergency. Doro's range includes mid-to-high-level smartphones and easy-to-use feature phones. "It's all about the needs of the user," says Peter. "They are simple to use, with loud and clear sound, but from a technology angle they meet all the latest specifications, so they are essentially a smartphone in a more usable body."

The phones allow seniors to retain independence for as long as possible, to the benefit of society, the individual and their relatives. For more vulnerable seniors, owning a Doro phone means the user can live life with added reassurance, whether out visiting the shops or walking the dog. As well as the premium service, the free-to-use Response by Doro feature means that if the assistance button is pressed, a pre-set group of relatives will instantly and simultaneously receive an alert and a map showing the location. Relatives can monitor the phone remotely to keep an eye on the battery level or to adjust ring volume, screen brightness and font size. "Our phone gives everybody peace of mind," says Peter. "Seniors want to live long, fulfilling and independent lives and all the evidence shows that the longer they are living at home, the happier they will be. That is how we can help."

Old Norfolk pheasant casserole

Sergeant Fred Cooper, Army (retired)

Growing up in rural Norfolk, I used to see this dish – served with herb-roasted potatoes and winter vegetables – being prepared and served in many homes across the county. Pheasant can sometimes be quite a dry meat so it lends itself perfectly to braising in a casserole. If you can get hold of it locally, hen pheasant is best as it has a layer of fat over the meat, making it juicier than cock pheasant. I have updated this recipe but kept it super simple to prepare and cook, just as I remember it being made back home by my mum all those years ago.

Gluten-free
Preparation time: 20–30 minutes
Cooking time: 1 hour

Serves 4

INGREDIENTS

For the pheasant
2 whole pheasants cut into 8 pieces
  (you can ask your butcher to do this)
100g butter
850ml chicken stock
1 orange, zest and juice
40g plain flour
Salt and pepper

Herb roasted potatoes
500g new potatoes, quartered
2 tbsp olive oil
2 tbsp dried thyme
2 tbsp dried rosemary
2 garlic cloves, crushed
Salt and pepper

Roast winter vegetables
3 red onion, peeled and quartered
1 yellow onion, peeled and quartered
2 medium parsnips, cut into small dice
2 medium carrots, cut into small dice
½ medium swede, cut into small dice
2 tbsp olive oil
1 tbsp dried mixed herbs
Salt and pepper

METHOD

• Preheat the oven to 200°C.
• Heat half of the butter in a casserole over a medium-high heat and, once the butter is foaming, brown the pheasant pieces all over in batches and transfer to a plate.
• Once all the pheasant is browned, reduce the heat to medium, add the remaining butter, stir in the flour and cook, stirring constantly, for a minute or two until lightly browned.
• Add the stock, orange zest and juice, stir until the sauce is smooth and thickened; return the pheasant pieces to the casserole, along with any juices that have collected on the plate, and cover with a lid.
• Place the potatoes in a bowl, add the oil, thyme, rosemary, garlic and seasoning; toss to thoroughly coat the potatoes and transfer to a roasting tray lined with baking parchment.
• Place both the pheasant casserole and potatoes in the oven and cook for 20 minutes.
• Meanwhile place the onions, parsnips, carrots, swede, olive oil, herbs and seasoning in a roasting tray lined with baking parchment, toss to thoroughly coat the vegetables.
• Once the pheasant and potatoes have been in the oven for 20 minutes, give the potatoes and pheasant casserole a stir and return to the oven, along with the vegetables, and continue to cook, stirring everything after 20 minutes, for a further 40 minutes.

To serve
• Place a piece of pheasant breast and leg on each plate, spoon the sauce over (if the sauce is too thin, simmer for a few minutes to thicken) and serve with the roast potatoes and vegetables.

Edith Louisa Cavell

Edith Louisa Cavell was born on 4 December 1865 in Swardeston, a village near Norwich, where her father was the local reverend. She was educated at Norwich High School for Girls, then boarding schools in Clevedon, Somerset and Peterborough. After working as a governess, including for a family in Brussels, she returned home in 1895 to care for her seriously ill father. This experience led her to apply to become a nurse probationer at the London Hospital in April 1896. She worked in various hospitals in England and as a private travelling nurse, treating patients in their homes. In 1897, she was sent to assist with a typhoid outbreak in Maidstone, resulting in her being awarded the Maidstone medal.

In 1907, she was recruited to be matron of a newly established nursing school in Brussels. By 1910, Edith was publishing the nursing journal, *L'infirmière*, and was soon training nurses for three hospitals, 24 schools and 13 kindergartens in Belgium. After the outbreak of war in 1914, the Germans occupied Brussels, and her clinic and nursing school were taken over by the Red Cross.

Edith began sheltering Allied soldiers. Around 200 wounded British and French troops, as well as Belgian and French civilians of military age, were hidden and provided with false papers, guides and funds to reach the neutral Netherlands. On 5 August 1915, Edith was betrayed to the German authorities by Georges Gaston Quien (who was later convicted by a French court). She was charged with harbouring enemy soldiers, sent to St Gilles Prison in Brussels, and signed a statement admitting her guilt. On 7 October 1915, she was found guilty and sentenced to death.

"Standing as I do in view of God and eternity, I realise that patriotism is not enough," she said to a chaplain, the night before her execution. "I must have no hatred or bitterness towards anyone." Her execution led to outrage across the world, with British newspapers seeing her as a Joan of Arc-style martyr. After the war, her body was exhumed and she was given a state funeral in Westminster Abbey before being re-buried in Norwich Cathedral. There are many tributes to her, including a stained-glass window in St Mary's Church in Swardeston where a flower festival is held every 12 October in her honour. It is on this day as well that the Church of England commemorates Edith in its Calendar of Saints.

Written by Emma Wilding, Help for Heroes

"Standing as I do in view of God and eternity, I realise that patriotism is not enough. I must have no hatred or bitterness towards anyone"

Chop chop

From its Derbyshire workshop using traditional techniques and materials, Blok Knives creates high-quality kitchen utensils that are favoured by the world's top chefs

www.blok-knives.co.uk

Blok Knives is a cutting-edge British business founded on time-honoured production techniques – an independent knife-maker that now equips some of the world's most celebrated chefs. But it started out as a relaxing hobby for Ben Edmonds, a graphic designer who sought relief from his desk job by experimenting in his Derbyshire workshop.

In typically British fashion, it all began one night down at the pub. "I've always had a project on the go, from tinkering with motorbikes to building furniture, and I enjoy cooking so decided to make a kitchen knife," says Ben (pictured, opposite). "Not long after, a chef at a local pub asked to see what I'd made, and a fellow drinker asked if he could buy one, and I wondered if I could sell more. I put a website up and, lo and behold, things went mad."

This is an understatement. Within two years, Blok Knives was receiving full-page spreads in the *Guardian* and the *Financial Times*. It even featured on Tom Kerridge's *Food & Drink* television show on the BBC, where co-host Arabella Weir visited Ben's workshop to make a knife of her own. "It went out on a Friday night and, within ten minutes, I took enough work to last two and a half years," says Ben, with a laugh. "So I thought, okay, I'll quit my job then, shall I?"

While most entrepreneurs would expand the business and take on more staff, Ben took a different route. "That becomes more about managing people," he says, "and it takes my time away from doing what I love, which is making knives." Instead, Ben and his small team make a small number of items then put them up for sale on the website every Friday, where they sell out in seconds. This allows him to focus on projects that matter to him on a personal level, including an upcoming run of special-edition knives for the Royal British Legion, featuring bespoke artwork and unique handcrafted boxes.

It's a return to traditional ideals, where quality takes precedence over disposable mass-produced merchandise. "We literally just want to make the best knife we can," says Ben. "Each one is made by hand using high carbon steel. It's what most knives used to be made from but it requires more looking after. Each one comes with a lifetime guarantee, plus support over the phone on how to sharpen it. The idea is that you'll learn how to care for it and you'll have a knife for life."

This commitment to quality led to Blok Knives being commissioned to create the trophies for the highly respected *Observer Food Monthly* awards in 2014 and each subsequent year. Designed as fully functioning kitchen knives, mounted on a plinth, these trophies have been awarded to high-profile figures such as Nigella Lawson and Mary Berry. And the support from major names doesn't end there, with chefs such as Simon Rimmer, Adam Handling and Jamie Oliver all proud owners of Ben's knives.

As for the future, Ben's main focus is innovation and improving his skills. "I love making knives so I never want that to become stale," he says. "My plans are to keep pushing and evolving, to keep trying new materials and techniques. I'll always be pushing for the next knife to be better than the one I made before."

Ham hock pie

Senior Aircraftman Jack Capel, RAF

Northamptonshire is a farming county with a lot of heritage and great country produce. For this reason I have chosen to make this traditional Northampton pie known as "Hock and Dough" (or Hough-and-Dough), using local produce such as ham, eggs, milk and lard. Instead of potatoes I have opted for sweet potato, for a twist, and have also included cider from Wellingborough and honey to my recipe to add colour and flavour to the dish.

Preparation time: 2 hour 45 minutes
Cooking time: 40 minutes

Serves 8

INGREDIENTS

To cook the ham hock
500g ham hock
2 oranges, sliced
1 garlic clove
10 peppercorns

For the hot water crust pastry
200g lard
200ml water
575g flour

For the filling
100g butter
4 medium shallots, peeled and finely diced
200g sweet potatoes, peeled and cut
  into 1½cm dice
2 tsp Dijon mustard
2 tsp honey
1 tsp cracked black peppercorns
2 tsp sage, shredded
50g plain flour
200ml milk
100ml Saxby cider
1 egg, beaten

METHOD

To cook the ham hock
• Place the ham hock in a deep saucepan with the oranges, garlic clove and peppercorns and pour in enough cold water to cover the hock – bring to a simmer and cook for about 1½ hours until the hock is tender.
• Once the ham is fully cooked, remove from the stock and set aside to cool before shredding the meat into roughly even-sized pieces (you can reserve the stock to make soup).

To make the pastry
• Place the lard and water in a saucepan, gradually heat until melted and bring to a boil.
• Sift the flour into a large bowl, pour over the hot water and lard and mix until well combined; set aside until cool enough to handle.
• Once cooled, knead the pastry until it becomes smooth and lump-free; remove one-third of the dough, wrap it in clingfilm and set aside for the pie top.
• Flour the worktop and rolling pin and roll out the dough until it's big enough to line a lightly buttered and floured 23cm pie dish or loose-based cake tin and, using the rolling pin to lift the dough, line the dish and gently press against the sides ensuring there is enough overhang to attach the pie lid; set aside to cool completely.

For the filling

- Melt the butter in a saucepan over a medium heat, add the shallots and cook until they are lightly coloured before adding the sweet potato; cook stirring frequently for a further couple of minutes then stir in the mustard, honey, peppercorns and sage.
- Mix in the flour and cook, stirring continuously for a minute, before gradually adding the milk and cider; bring to a simmer, cook until the sauce has thickened, season then mix in the shredded ham hock – set aside to cool for 10 minutes.

To finish and cook the pie

- Preheat the oven to 170°C.
- Fill the pastry-lined pie dish with the filling and brush the edges of the pastry base with the beaten egg.
- Roll out the remaining pastry to fit the top of the pie, cover the filling and press the edges of the pastry base and top together to seal.
- Make a small incision in the middle of the pie top to allow steam to escape during cooking, brush with the beaten egg (or use an egg yolk for a darker glaze) and bake in the preheated oven for 30–40 minutes until the filling is thoroughly heated through to the middle and the crust is golden brown.
- Once cooked allow the pie to sit at room temperature for 5 minutes before cutting into portions and serving with your choice of vegetables.

Northamptonshire: Local hero

Lieutenant Colonel Edgar Mobbs DSO

Edgar Roberts Mobbs was born in Northampton on 29 June 1882 to Oliver and Elizabeth Mobbs. He attended Bedford Modern School, where one of the houses is now named after him, and excelled at all sports. After playing rugby for Olney, Weston Turks and Northampton Heathens he was scouted by Northampton Saints where he became captain in 1907 after two seasons, a post he held for six years, scoring 177 tries. Mobbs was called up to the England squad in 1908 against Australia, winning the first of seven caps, before eventually retiring from rugby in 1913 to join his father in the automotive industry.

At the onset of the First World War, Mobbs, aged 32, was told he was too old to join the Army. He refused to be defeated and, in an act that would be repeated throughout the country in what would become known as the "Pals Battalions", he formed his own company, "Mobbs' Own", made up of 250 sportsmen, many of them rugby players. The company became the backbone of the Northamptonshire Regiment.

Mobbs arrived in France in September 1915 and participated in the Battle of Loos. Despite receiving an injury, Mobbs still returned to the rugby pitch, taking part in an England v Scotland exhibition match before returning to his unit. The following March, Mobbs was promoted to Major, a month later taking command of the 7th Battalion, before eventually being promoted to Lieutenant Colonel. Mobbs was awarded a Distinguished Service Order in December 1916 for his leadership as a Battalion Commander.

Sadly, Mobbs was not destined to survive the war. On 31 July 1917, he was killed while leading an attack on a machine-gun post in Zillebeke, Belgium during the Third Battle of Ypres. His body was never recovered and today his name is remembered like so many on the Menin Gate Memorial. Of the 400 or more volunteers that served in Mobbs' Own, only 85 are known to have survived the war. In 1921, thousands attended the unveiling of the Mobbs' Memorial in Northampton's market square. That year, the first Mobbs Memorial Match between East Midlands and Barbarians was played, a tradition that has carried on to this day and is currently played between the Army Rugby Union and Bedford/Northampton Saints, raising money for youth rugby in the area.

Written by Corporal Becky Croker, RAF

Sherwood Forest venison with blackberries and Stilton dumplings

Graeme Watson, member of the Master Chefs of Great Britain since 1995, operations director of Wilson Vale catering company

This is my modern interpretation of an old British classic, venison stew and dumplings. Food-wise, Nottinghamshire is renowned firstly for the king of cheeses, Stilton, with my personal favourite being from Long Clawson. Sherwood Forest is heavily populated by deer and has been providing venison for nobles' tables for many centuries. Finally, anyone who, like me, enjoys a little orienteering can testify (painfully) that the region is awash with brambles, so including the blackberry felt like a fitting completion of the dish.

Preparation time: 30 minutes
Cooking time: 30 minutes

Serves 4

INGREDIENTS

For the mash
400g Maris Piper potatoes,
  peeled and cut into quarters
75g crème fraîche (you can use
  oat-milk-based crème fraîche
  if you wish)
75g butter (or butter alternative)
Freshly grated nutmeg

For the dumplings
100g self-raising flour
50g beef suet (or a vegetarian
  alternative if you prefer)
50g Stilton, crumbled (half for the
  mix and half to sprinkle on top
  of the dumplings)
4 tbsp cold water
Salt and pepper

For the venison
4 x 150–175g pieces of venison
  loin, trimmed
50ml red wine
500ml venison or beef stock
12 blackberries

Nottinghamshire: Local hero

Corporal Harry Beet VC

Harry Churchill Beet was born on 1 April 1873 near Bingham in Nottinghamshire, the son of a sculptor. In 1892, he joined the Derbyshire Regiment (later the Sherwood Foresters), a career path that many of Nottinghamshire's sons would follow. Beet was initially sent to India, where he served on the Punjab Frontier in 1897 and 1898, winning an India Medal with two clasps. In 1899, he was posted to the South African War, serving under the command of Captain P Leveson-Gower, and was later given a field promotion to sergeant by Lord Kitchener.

Shortly after the dawn of a new century, Beet would find himself in action against the Boers. On 22 April 1900, a mounted infantry company of the regiment, together with two squadrons of the Imperial Yeomanry, were forced to retreat from a position near a farm at Wakkerstroom, below a ridge held by the Boers. In doing so, Corporal Burnett of the Imperial Yeomanry fell, wounded. Beet, with no regard for his own safety, remained with his fellow soldier. He placed Burnett under cover, dressed Burnett's wounds and – by use of selective fire, while fully exposed to the enemy – he prevented the Boers from approaching. After dark, Beet was joined by Dr Wilson, an Imperial Yeomanry Medical Officer, and under constant heavy fire, they were able to withdraw Corporal Burnett to safety.

For his actions that day, Corporal Beet was awarded the Victoria Cross by the Duke of York, later King George V, in August 1901. Beet was himself wounded in action in December 1902. He would eventually be promoted to Captain and, after the end of the Boer War, emigrated to Canada with his wife Annie Elizabeth Brown.

Such was his sense of duty that upon the outbreak of the First World War, Beet re-enlisted with the 32nd Reserve Canadian Infantry Battalion, serving in France with the Canadian Expeditionary Force before returning to Canada after the war. He died, aged 72, on 10 January 1946 in Vancouver, where he was buried. Beet's medal group is on display at the Sherwood Foresters Museum within Nottingham Castle.

Written by Warrant Officer Kevin Morley, RAF

METHOD

For the mash
- Boil the potatoes until just cooked, drain and mash thoroughly.
- Add the crème fraîche, butter and nutmeg.
- Season and place in a piping bag.

For the dumplings
- Reserve half of the Stilton and mix all other ingredients together.
- Roll into eight balls and place into a shallow baking dish containing 100ml of the stock.
- Sprinkle with the remaining Stilton, cover with a lid and bake at 200°C for 20 minutes; for a crispier top take off the lid after 15 minutes.

For the venison
- Heat a frying pan over a medium heat and add a splash of oil.
- Season the venison loin and then shallow fry for around 4 minutes on either side, depending on how you prefer your red meat cooked. For added flavour you can add some thyme stalks and whole cloves of garlic if you wish.
- For additional flavour and richness add a knob of butter half way through cooking and baste the meat with the foaming butter, which will also keep the meat moist.
- Once cooked to your liking, remove from the pan and rest in a warm place.
- Drain off the excess fat, add the red wine and scrape the bottom of the pan, ensuring you capture all the little crispy flavoursome bits that will have gathered in the bottom.
- Add the stock and reduce by at least half to a nice sticky gravy consistency. Finally add the blackberries and season.

To serve
- Pipe the mash onto a plate and place the dumpling on top.
- Carve your venison into four or five pieces and arrange next to the mash.
- Drizzle with sauce and blackberries.
- I like to serve this with roasted carrots and celery, which would also have been ingredients in the original old English stew recipe.

Designing responsibly

Newark-based consultancy BE Design is a team of architects, engineers and sustainability experts that create sustainable, functional and beautiful buildings

www.bedesign.co.uk

In an era when sustainability and wellbeing have never been as important for architects and engineers, the consultancy firm BE Design has thrived thanks to its expertise and passion in these areas. The company was founded in Nottinghamshire in 2013 by three colleagues who decided it was time to set out for themselves after their previous company was acquired by a bigger firm. "We set off with a clear focus that has remained the mantra for BE Design," says Stephen Oakden, who started BE Design with fellow directors Anna Tsartsari and Simon Powell. "We want to focus on our clients, their projects and our employees, producing sustainable designs that are architecturally innovative and offered engineering excellence."

BE Design is an agile and responsive consultancy of architects, engineers and sustainability experts. Its core design principles include climate resilience, wellbeing, biophilic design, low-carbon design, cost effectiveness and value-added approaches. The company employs a tailored business management system (the BE Zone) and is committed to using virtual prototyping and BIM (building information modelling) to facilitate a holistic approach, supporting clients throughout the lifetime of a project. Successful projects include a sustainable housing development in East Sussex, which is future proofed for the transition to zero carbon, millions of square feet of logistics buildings in the UK and Europe, a state-of-the-art retail park in Northamptonshire, several hyperscale datacentres and a number of regeneration projects in London's Olympic Park.

The Newark-based company now employs 35 staff, with an auxiliary office in Spain for its growing European work and plans to expand into Germany and London. True to the founding ethos, the directors ensure their staff are well-supported and given plenty of opportunities for training and development. "We talk about BE Design as a family and we see staff and clients as being part of it," says Anna Tsartsari. "We treat our clients as people we want to have longstanding relations with, almost as a part of that family. It is beneficial that we can provide expertise on all aspects of putting a building together, and that has helped us become one of the most successful consultancies."

Inspired learning

REAL Education provides alternative provision and independent special school placements for students across the East Midlands, many with special educational needs and mental health challenges

real-education.org

While mainstream education works for the vast majority of British children, a growing number of pupils struggle within the mainstream school environment, often due to specific learning needs which require a more tailored approach. The alternative provision sector is catering for more and more young people each year as schools and local authorities seek to commission appropriate provision for students often marginalised by their needs.

REAL Education – "REAL" being an acronym for Rethinking Engagement & Approaches to Learning – was founded by Richard Smith and his father Brian Smith MBE in 2008. The Smiths entered the alternative provision sector with a vision to provide a quality of learning that would engage the hard-to-reach and help them to achieve their potential. This involved rethinking engagement and the approaches to an individual's learning journey. The company now provides alternative education and independent school placements for 500 pupils a week across the East Midlands, with ambitions to take its model nationwide.

"We want to provide a continuum of excellence that gives young people real potential to thrive and succeed," says Richard, who runs the company with Joint Managing Director Steve Quinn since Brian retired in 2020. "Many of our young people have a very good level of resilience given what life has thrown at them. For us it was about personalising educational pathways to harness their talents and reignite the spark in learning. Tailoring the whole learning journey around their strengths and interests is a key ingredient to success for these young people."

A key to REAL thinking is keeping provision relevant by gearing it to future demands. This can be as diverse as offering the latest digital arts tuition to upskilling the motor and engineering team to deliver the latest in hybrid and electric vehicle technologies. By working alongside industry partners and pioneering in-house commercial ventures, REAL seeks to entrench its learners in real-life working environments to better equip them for the world of work, including partnerships with Sony Music US and the Armed Forces.

"One thing we all believe is that these young people are very talented," says Richard. "They might have struggled in school but if you re-engage them in something in which they see purpose, they will excel. We are engaging with industry so that businesses can understand the backgrounds of our young people as well as support us to deliver learning that is meaningful for our young people and creates opportunities for them to flourish in society and the world of work."

The education is provided in a range of environments, with a focus on ensuring the students are comfortable and secure, without the negative connotations that might come from a traditional educational environment. Success stories include a young woman who was awarded a Princess Diana Courage Award in recognition of the circumstances she had overcome, and a young man whose anxiety meant he had to be taught from behind a bedroom door initially, but is now confident enough to have continued his education at The Hague University in the Netherlands.

"The key word is relationships," says Steve. "We need to listen, understand and remove the pressures associated with the historical view on schooling. Once you have built a relationship and established trust, only then can you explore an appropriate educational pathway. The approach is wholly dependent on the child's strengths, interests and needs, which we are in a unique position to focus upon."

Pan-fried wood pigeon with pickled carrots and hazelnuts

Leading Chef Aaron Lee, Royal Navy

Living in Pembrokeshire in south-west Wales at the start of my culinary journey, I developed an immense passion for cookery. It is there that I learnt to look at the ingredients I was using in my cooking and started to move towards both the seasonality of produce and the concept of "locavorism" – with "locavores" being those who eat locally sourced food. The more I learnt, the more I appreciated the wealth of ingredients I had available in my locality. While searching through some old regional cookery books I came across a recipe for pigeon breast cooked on coals with preserved vegetables; this is my take on that forgotten dish.

Gluten-free
Preparation time: 30 minutes
Cooking time: 1 hour

Serves 4

INGREDIENTS

For the pickled carrots
160ml white wine vinegar
80ml cold water
2 tbsp sugar
1 tbsp salt
8 baby carrots, washed

For the wood pigeon
4 wood pigeon breasts
30g butter
Salt and freshly ground black pepper

For the bok choy (pak choi)
4 bok choy

To cook and serve
2 tbsp vegetable oil
25g hazelnuts, toasted and
  coarsely chopped

METHOD

To pickle the carrots
• To make the brine, place the vinegar, water, sugar and salt in a saucepan, place over a medium heat, bring to a simmer and stir to fully dissolve the salt and sugar.
• Taste and adjust the flavour, adding more salt or sugar to taste.
• Place the carrots in a small container and pour over the brine, ensuring the carrots are fully submerged; if necessary, add a little more vinegar or water to cover.
• Leave the carrots to marinate for a minimum of 1 hour or up to a maximum of 24 hours.

To cook the wood pigeon
• Season both sides of the pigeon breasts with salt, place a frying pan over a medium-high heat and add the butter.
• Once the butter is foaming add the pigeon breasts, skin side down, and cook for 3–4 minutes on each side, basting regularly with the butter.
• Transfer the pigeon breasts to a plate to rest and cover with a piece of foil; reserve the cooking juices in the pan.

To prepare the bok choy (pak choi)
- Cut the bok choy in half lengthways and wash thoroughly.
- Blanch in salted boiling water for one minute and refresh in ice-cold water.

To finish cooking and serve
- Heat a little vegetable oil in a small frying pan and fry the pickled carrots over a low-medium heat for 10–15 minutes until cooked through.
- Sauté the bok choy in a hot pan until slightly golden and season lightly.
- Meanwhile, warm the pigeon pan juices, including any juice that has collected on the plate.
- Serve the pigeon breasts on warmed plates with the pickled carrots and bok choy, spoon over the pan juices and garnish with a sprinkling of chopped hazelnuts.

St Davids: Local hero

Lance Corporal Hubert William Lewis VC

Born in 1896 and brought up in Pembrokeshire, Hubert William Lewis – "Stokey" to his friends – left his job in Milford Haven's fish market to answer Lord Kitchener's call to arms in 1914, following the outbreak of the First World War. Along with 75 other brave young men from Milford Haven, Lewis joined the 11th Service Battalion of the Welsh Regiment, one of the famous "pals" units. Following a brief stint in the trenches of the Western Front, Lewis and his comrades were dispatched to Greece in October 1915; part of the British Salonika Army to counter a threat from Bulgaria, which had entered the war on Germany's side.

Lewis soon found himself on the Macedonian Front near Thessaloniki where, in September 1916, his battalion launched an offensive raid against the combined German and Bulgarian forces. Though he was injured, Lewis refused aid, joining his commander, Captain Guthrie Morgan, and other comrades in a charge through 120 yards of wire entanglements to attack the enemy trenches. Wounded for a second time, he again refused medical assistance. At this point, three of the enemy were observed to be approaching as part of a counterattack, and Lewis immediately attacked them single-handed, capturing all at the point of his bayonet.

Lewis then went to the assistance of a wounded man and, under heavy fire, brought him safely back to the Allied lines – whereupon he collapsed, exhausted. For his numerous actions, Lewis was awarded the Victoria Cross by King George V at Buckingham Palace in 1917. Aged 17, he was then the youngest ever Welsh recipient of the VC. Lewis would return to the Balkans only 10 days later. In June 1918, he rescued Captain Morgan during an assault near Salonika. "It is impossible for me to express how grateful I am to you for saving my life," Morgan later wrote.

After the war, Lewis returned home and continued to work in the Milford Haven fish market for a further 43 years, where he became known as "VC Lewis". When he died in 1977, aged 80, he was the last surviving Welsh VC recipient. Lord Ashcroft purchased Lewis's service medals privately in 1999 and has since placed the collection on display at London's Imperial War Museum.

Written by Squadron Leader Malcolm Craig, RAF

Armed with service knowledge

Cohort plc is an independent technology group that helps small, innovative businesses to grow in the defence sector, with the help of ex-services personnel and the Armed Forces Covenant

www.cohortplc.com

For many people leaving the Armed Forces, it can be difficult to know what to do next. Few civilian professions seem to offer the same level of camaraderie, let alone the opportunity to provide a public service. That's where Cohort comes in. The group was founded in 2006 and now operates through six innovative defence technology companies, working across different areas of the defence sector, supplying the Ministry of Defence and the defence departments of other allied nations. Cohort is a signatory to the Armed Forces Covenant and, through the Covenant's Employer Recognition Scheme, employs former services personnel at all levels of the business.

"We are a group of responsive, agile small-to-medium-sized companies, providing high-technology systems and services for the defence sector," explains Andy Thomis, Cohort's Chief Executive. "We provide our companies with management and financial support without compromising their quick response and innovative culture. Across the group we employ a large number of people who come from the Armed Forces. They want to continue to make a contribution to the defence and security of the UK, and the benefit to us is that they understand our customers' needs and culture and talk their language. They can therefore make a real difference to our businesses."

One of the companies within the Cohort group is MASS, a data technology business that serves defence and security customers in the UK and around the world, providing hi-tech solutions, training and managed services in areas such as electronic warfare and cyber security. The company's Business Development Director is Rob Jones, who served in the Army for more than 25 years. "At MASS we provide a link for people coming out of the Armed Forces, utilising their skill set with our customers, but also as mentors and career guides to young graduates and academics," he says. MASS is currently working with former Royal Marines to amplify the message surrounding a career transition programme for serving personnel. "We want that to become a powerful message, not just at the end of a career but during it, so people can plan ahead," says Rob. "I am still passionate about solving the problems I experienced as a soldier. My physical fitness is no longer up to the demands of soldiering, so I am serving in the best way I can."

With so many ex-service people onboard, Cohort employees can easily maintain a connection to their military past. Some are reservists, one of whom was deployed to the Cabinet Office during the Covid pandemic to provide logistical support. The group also actively supports military charities such as the Royal British Legion and SSAFA.

Shane Knight is Managing Director of Cohort's Marlborough Communications Limited, a specialist supplier of advanced electronic communications and information systems to the UK defence sector. He emphasises how it important was for him to join a company where the experience of former Armed Forces personnel was so valued. "Around a third of our workforce is ex-services and it helps having other people around you," he says. "When you are dealing with military programmes, it's about having those guys who are used to going the extra mile. We also have plenty of non-services people who have bought into that ethos and we learn from each other. It's about that balance. We have people with business and commercial experience who can support us, and we bring the camaraderie and the experience and dedication of working in the military."

St Helena

St Helenian fishcakes with gurnard and red pepper

Flight Sergeant Chris Beavis, RAF

Located in the South Atlantic, roughly midway between Angola and Brazil, St Helena is well known for its fisheries and the abundance of fresh produce grown on the island. Sustainable fishing and simple ingredients are the staples behind the cuisine that I have highlighted in this traditional dish. Much of this recipe can be prepared in advance and kept in the fridge until you're ready to cook your fishcakes.

Preparation time: 45 minutes
Cooking time: 30 minutes

Serves 4

INGREDIENTS

For the fishcakes
1 large potato, peeled and diced
4 gurnard fillets, skinned and cut
 into 1cm dice
1 shallot, finely diced
20g parsley, coarsely chopped
20g coriander, coarsely chopped
Finely grated zest of 1 lemon
 and 1 lime
Salt and pepper
Vegetable oil to shallow fry

For the pepper and garlic sauce
4 red peppers
1 tbsp olive oil
50g white onion, finely diced
1 garlic bulb, cloves peeled
 and crushed
2 tsp lemon juice
1 small red chilli, finely chopped

To serve
Curly endive lettuce, picked

METHOD

To make the fishcakes
• Boil the potatoes in salted water until tender then drain, mash and cool.
• Bind the diced gurnard, mashed potato, shallot, parsley, coriander and citrus zests together, season and form into 12 equal portions and form into small fish cakes (you can cook a small patty of the mix in a little oil to check the seasoning).
• Transfer the fishcakes to a tray, cover and chill in the fridge until you're ready to cook them.

To make the pepper and garlic sauce
• Roast the red peppers over a naked flame or under a hot grill until charred and fully cooked through; peel or scrape the charred skin from the peppers, cut into quarters and remove the stalk, pith and seeds.
• Heat the olive oil in a small saucepan over a medium heat, add the onions and garlic and cook, stirring frequently, until caramelised; transfer to a blender, add the cooked peppers, lemon juice and chopped chilli, blend until smooth and season.

To cook the fishcakes
• Heat the oil in a frying pan over a medium heat and cook the fishcakes on both sides until well browned and thoroughly cooked through to the middle.

To serve
• Serve three fishcakes per portion, with the pepper and garlic sauce and a few picked curly endive leaves.

Major Edward Moss MC

Edward James Moss, affectionately known as Ted, was born at Woodlands West Farm Estate in St Helena in 1892, the son of the Honourable George and Edith Moss. His father worked for Solomon, Moss & Gideon, the largest shipping agent on the island, before taking up farming in 1885. His mother was one of the daughters of the Deason farming family.

Ted's childhood was spent learning to farm, shoot game and ride horses. After the British garrison left the island in 1906, the outlets for his father's farm produce became difficult to maintain and the family moved to Farm Lodge. At the outbreak of the Great War, Ted went to Britain to serve, and was commissioned as a Lieutenant into the Sherwood Rangers Yeomanry – a horse-mounted cavalry regiment based at Retford, Nottingham. After training, Ted was transferred to northern Greece, where his regiment was part of the Egyptian Expeditionary Force.

In Greece in 1918, Ted and three other soldiers had orders to capture a prisoner in the enemy trenches for interrogation. On reaching the enemy trenches, they were attacked by two companies of Turkish troops, around 200 men in total. Ted immediately opened fire with his Hotchkiss cavalry machine gun, providing covering fire and allowing his men to capture the prisoner and get back to their lines. He withdrew steadily, firing all the time, and managed to get back unscathed to the British trenches. This incident was witnessed by the Lovat Scouts who were in an observation post. For this brave act, Ted was awarded the Military Cross (which was presented officially by King George V in 1920).

Ted, now a Captain, would continue to serve in Egypt, Jordan and participate in the famous "push to Damascus", where the German and Turkish forces surrendered in November 1918. After the war, Ted spent another two years in the Middle East with the Sherwood Rangers, attempting to protect Armenians from Turkish aggression.

Back in England, Ted was demobbed and married Rebecca, a Scottish nurse whom he met on St Helena. Knowing the difficulties of farming on St Helena, the newlyweds decided to give Canada a try, where they stayed until 1925, during which time their son George was born. They then moved back to St Helena, where Ted worked as a manager for Solomon & Co in 1925. At the outbreak of the Second World War, he joined the St Helena Rifles as captain, and took command of a position in Longwood

famously known as Napoleon's final resting place. He was promoted to Major by the War Office.

After the war, he served as General Manager of Solomon & Co until retiring in 1965. He became deeply involved with the welfare of the St Helenian ex-servicemen, setting up a fund to help them and their dependants. He was also a founder member of the Chamber of Commerce and the Growers Co-operative Society, a senior Past Master of the Freemasons, and a Justice of the Peace for 27 years. In 1961, he was awarded the OBE. He represented St Helena at the Queen's Silver Jubilee celebrations in London and died a year later on 31 May 1978, aged 86. His ashes were sent to St Helena to be buried in the land of his birth.

Written by Squadron Leader Malcolm Craig, RAF, and the Museum of St Helena

The heart of glass

Ngwenya Glass uses the age-old art of traditional glassblowing, adding quirky designs to create exquisite tableware, ornaments and light fittings

www.ngwenyaglass.co.sz

It was a desperate search for glass elephants that took Chas Prettejohn and his parents to Swaziland. They had a collection of ornamental pachyderms marching halfway down their dining-room table but, in a search to complete the herd, they tried to find the company that made them. "We visited the Swazi Glass Craft factory in Swaziland and found it was derelict," says Chas. "I said to Dad, 'If we buy the place we can make as many elephants as we like!'"

Swazi Glass Craft had been founded in 1979 by a Swedish aid agency and then run as a quasi-governmental operation until its closure in 1985. The Prettejohn family relocated from South Africa to Swaziland to resuscitate the factory in 1987, renaming it Ngwenya Glass after the local mountain that looked like a basking crocodile. After tracking down some original staff and repairing the equipment with the help of master glass blower Sibusiso Mhlanga, Ngwenya Glass was literally breathing life back into the factory using 100 per cent recycled glass.

"When we started, we were advised not to talk about the recycled aspect as it wasn't considered hip," says Chas. "We have been sustainable a lot longer than it has been cool!"

Ngwenya Glass is isolated from the rest of the glassblowing world, so all training is done in-house and the company often has to manufacture its own tools. "We've done workshops with international glassblowers who have shared their knowledge with us," says Chas. "But they also leave having learned skills from our very talented Swazi glassblowers."

Today Ngwenya Glass, run by Chas and his wife Cathy Prettejohn, employs more than 70 people, and Sibusiso tutors the new apprentices. The company has started to gain international renown, not just for its ornamental African animals, but for its range of tableware, drinking glasses and light pendants. Ngwenya's designs often have a unique, quirky twist – one of the company's most popular products is a "crooked stem" wine glass that came from a doodle that Chas made during a telephone conversation.

"We're a company that has scored an 'A' when it comes to the circular economy, and we support the community in many different ways," says Chas. "We're handmade, sustainable, local and fair trade, and I think people appreciate that."

Bobotie

Corporal Aketa Babin, Army

South Africa

Bobotie, a South African dish pronounced "buh-BOOR-tea", is a type of casserole that dates back to the 17th century. Made with spiced minced meat (generally lamb, beef or pork) with a creamy egg-set topping, it's widely regarded as South Africa's national dish. Dutch traders discovered an Indonesian dish called "bobotok" in the Dutch East Indies and later introduced it to the Cape of Good Hope in South Africa, along with spices and cooking techniques from their journeys to Indonesia, where it was adopted by the Cape Malay community and eventually evolved over the years into the modern version of bobotie. It gets its unique flavour from the spices and bay leaves, which give it a real depth.

Preparation time: 20 minutes
Cooking time: 30–40 minutes

Serves 4

INGREDIENTS

75g sultanas
3 slices of white bread, crusts removed
  and torn into roughly 2–3cm pieces
350ml milk
2 tbsp olive oil
2 white onions, finely diced
6 garlic cloves, finely chopped
  or crushed
1 tbsp curry powder
1 tbsp ground cumin
1 tbsp dried mixed herbs
1kg best quality minced beef
6 bay leaves
2 tbsp Madras curry paste
2 tbsp mango chutney
4 tbsp tomato purée
1 lemon, juice and zest
2 large eggs
Salt and pepper

METHOD

- Preheat the oven to 190°C.
- Place the sultanas in a small bowl, pour over enough boiling water to cover and set aside for 15 minutes to steep.
- Place the torn bread pieces in a bowl, pour over 250ml of the milk and set aside to soak.
- Heat the olive oil in a skillet or oven-proof frying pan over a medium heat, add the onions and fry, stirring frequently, for about 5 minutes until they are soft and translucent.
- Stir the garlic, curry powder, cumin and mixed herbs into the onions and continue to cook for another minute.
- Turn up the heat to medium-high, add the minced beef, two of the bay leaves and the Madras paste; cook, stirring constantly, until the beef is lightly browned.
- Stir in the mango chutney, tomato purée, lemon zest and juice; season well with salt and pepper to taste, stir in the sultanas (including the soaking water), cover and simmer very gently over a low heat for 30 minutes. Stir occasionally and only add a little boiling water if the mix becomes very dry, set aside for 10 minutes to cool a little.
- Squeeze the excess milk from the soaked bread pieces (reserve the milk) and stir through the beef mixture to add texture and moisture to the mince filling.
- Pour the remaining 100ml milk and the milk reserved from soaking the bread into a mixing bowl, add the eggs, beat well until thoroughly mixed and season with salt and pepper.
- Press down the mince so it is flat and well compacted in the skillet, alternatively, transfer the mix to a shallow baking dish; pour the egg and milk mix over the tangy beef, allow to settle for a minute then garnish the top with the remaining bay leaves.
- Bake in the preheated oven for 30–40 minutes or until the savoury custard top is set and golden brown and the spiced mince is thoroughly heated through to the middle.
- Serve with some braised or boiled turmeric rice and a tomato and onion salad on the side.

Squadron Leader John Dering Nettleton VC

John Dering Nettleton was born on 28 June 1917 at Nongoma, Natal, South Africa. After school, Nettleton tried to follow in the footsteps of his grandfather (a Royal Navy admiral) but failed the entrance test. Nettleton joined the *General Botha* training ship as a cadet in 1930, as well as undertaking employment in the South African Merchant Marine and training as an apprentice civil engineer.

While on holiday in England in 1938, he decided to join the RAF, commissioning in December of that year. After successfully training as a pilot, he bounced around various squadrons before joining No. 44 Squadron, flying Hampdens out of RAF Waddington. He quickly rose to the rank of Squadron Leader, and was mentioned in dispatches following five months of concentrated raids on targets across Europe.

In April 1942, a daylight bombing mission was planned on a plant in Augsburg, Bavaria, responsible for the production of half of Germany's U-boat engines. It was the first major mission for the new Avro Lancaster, as well as the longest low-level penetration raid during the course of the war. Nettleton was placed in command of the entire mission. He led six Lancaster bombers from RAF Waddington in two flights of three, along with six Lancasters from No. 97 Squadron. As Nettleton's group crossed the Channel near Dieppe, German fighters shot down four of the Lancasters. Nettleton continued towards the target, and his two remaining aircraft attacked the factory, bombing it amid heavy anti-aircraft fire, but were hit as they flew away from the target. Nettleton's aircraft limped back on three engines, but his companion's Lancaster caught fire and crashed. For his bravery and actions during the raid, Nettleton was awarded the Victoria Cross, with a selection of DFCs, DFMs and DSOs handed to the other survivors.

Nettleton would unfortunately not survive the war; he was shot down on 13 July 1943 while undertaking a raid alongside 294 other Lancasters against targets in Turin. His body was never recovered. His death was officially presumed on 23 February 1944, just days after the birth of the son he never saw, John Dering Nettleton. Following the war, a new school was named after him in Braeside, Salisbury, Southern Rhodesia. On 2 March 1994, an accommodation block was formally opened at RAF Shawbury under the name of Nettleton, where a commemorative plaque is located inside detailing Nettleton's life and service.

Written by Emma Adams, widow of Major Gareth Rhys-Evans, Intelligence Corps, Army

"His death was officially presumed on 23 February 1944, just days after the birth of the son he never saw"

Somerset pork chop with cider sauce

Warrant Officer Catering Services Nige Ranger, Royal Navy

Pork chops with cider sauce is a dish that has been cooked and served for many years on Royal Navy ships. Of course, a specific recipe has never been followed or adhered to and, as with all dishes, a chef adapts and adjusts to every occasion or eventuality. So why is this dish of interest to me? Onboard, it was nice to get some Vat 69 cans of apples into the galley. These were usually purchased from the officers' mess and, of course, one can was always for the chef! Today, I live in North Somerset, the Thatchers distillery is four miles down the road and Cheddar Gorge is just 10 miles away, so I'm able to source fantastic local ingredients on my doorstep. These days, I prefer to shop locally and encourage people to do likewise, supporting our local growers, farmers, shops and markets, and to champion our regional dishes.

Preparation time: 20–30 minutes
Cooking time: 30–45 minutes

Serves 4

INGREDIENTS

4 pork chops, thick cut
35g butter
2 tbsp vegetable oil
1 onion, sliced
2 tbsp (level) plain flour
150ml chicken stock
200ml Somerset cider
2 tbsp wholegrain mustard
2 small eating apples, peeled, cored
  and cut into 12 wedges each
50g mushrooms, sliced
1 tbsp sage, shredded
1 tbsp parsley, coarsely chopped
200ml double cream
150g Cheddar cheese, grated
Salt and freshly ground black pepper

METHOD

• Lightly season the pork chops on both sides with salt and freshly ground black pepper.
• Heat the butter and oil in a frying pan over a medium-high heat and, when the butter is foaming, add the pork chops.
• Sear the pork chops until they're lightly browned on both sides.
• Transfer the pork chops to a plate, return the pan to the heat, add the onions and sweat, stirring frequently, until they're soft and translucent but without any colour.
• Reduce the heat, stir in the flour and cook, stirring constantly, for a minute or two.
• Gradually add the chicken stock and cider, bring to a simmer, stirring continuously, until the sauce is smooth and thickened.
• Preheat the grill to a medium-high setting.
• Stir the mustard, apples, mushrooms and sage into the sauce and continue to simmer for 10 minutes until the apples have softened; add a little more cider, stock or water if the sauce becomes too thick.
• While the sauce is cooking, grill cook the pork chops either side for 2–3 minutes until just cooked through to the centre; pour any pork juices collected on the plate into the sauce.
• Stir the chopped parsley and cream into the sauce, season to taste and continue to simmer gently.
• Cover the chops with the grated Cheddar, return to the grill for a couple of minutes, until the cheese is bubbling and starting to brown slightly.
• Transfer the chops to warmed plates, generously ladle over the sauce and, ideally, serve with mashed potatoes and fresh seasonal vegetables.

Odette Hallowes

Odette Hallowes, née Brailly, was born in Amiens, France on 28 April 1912, the daughter of a decorated war hero. As a child, Odette had an illness that blinded her for nearly four years, as well as polio; these early experiences would equip her with a singular determination and drive.

Odette – by then Odette Sansom – was living in Somerset with her three daughters, while her husband was at war, when she saw an appeal from the Admiralty for photographs of the French coast to assist in the forthcoming invasion. She felt compelled to help with images from her childhood in Boulogne, but mistakenly sent them to the War Office instead of the Admiralty – which resulted in her being scouted by Colonel Maurice Buckmaster's Special Operations Executive (SOE), who needed fluent French speakers.

As cover, Odette joined the First Aid Nursing Yeomanry, where she was described as "hasty and impulsive", but showing "a certain determination". On 2 November 1942, she landed in France to begin her first mission, to assist an SOE network in Cannes, alongside the resistance leader Captain Peter Churchill. As the pressure from the Germans increased, Odette and Churchill decided to move to Annecy in the French Alps. However, on 16 April 1943, after just six months in the field, Odette and Churchill were arrested by the German spy hunter Hugo Bleicher, after a tip-off by people in Paris. The next two years propelled Odette into folklore, after enduring appalling brutality at the hands of the Nazis.

Odette's love of Peter Churchill saw her take the brunt of the interrogations. She convinced her captors that she was the mastermind, that she and Churchill were married and that he was the nephew of the prime minister, a ruse that saw him reserved as a potential bargaining chip. It was recorded that Churchill was interrogated just twice, while Odette suffered some 14 instances of torture; she could barely walk due to injuries inflicted through interrogation. She was sentenced to death on two counts, famously saying: "Then you will have to make up your mind on what count I am to be executed, because I can only die once!" This infuriated Bleicher, who sent her to Ravensbrück Concentration Camp.

By 1945, as the Allies marched closer to Berlin, liberating as they progressed, they eventually reached Ravensbrück where the camp commandant took Odette with him to the Americans to surrender, hoping her "connections" to Winston Churchill

might save him; Odette had him arrested immediately, testifying at his trial. For her bravery and indomitable spirit, Odette received the George Cross (the only living woman so honoured), an MBE and the French Legion of Honour; making her the highest decorated woman in the Second World War.

Odette and Peter Churchill married in 1947, but divorced in 1956 when she married another ex-SOE officer, Geoffrey Hallowes. In 1951, Odette's home was burgled and her George Cross stolen. After an appeal it was returned with a note, which read: "God bless you and your children. I thank you for having faith in me. I am not all that bad – it's just circumstances. Your little dog really loves me. I gave him a nice pat and left him a piece of meat – out of fridge. Sincerely yours, A Bad Egg."

Odette lived until 1995, passing away in Walton-on-Thames, aged 82, leaving behind her a vast legacy. A film, *Odette*, was made about her in 1950 (starring Anna Neagle and Trevor Howard), a Royal Mail stamp of her was issued in 2012, and two biographies have been written, in 1949 and 2019. In March 2020, the Great Western Railway dedicated a train to Odette. It was unveiled by the Princess Royal. "We have heard details of Odette's remarkable story," said Princess Anne. "Her bravery was inspirational and her survival was extraordinary."

Written by Sergeant Jim Pullen, RAF (retired)

Inspired adventures

Adria specialises in sleek, functional caravans and motorhomes for a range of different family sizes and budgets

www.adria.co.uk

Whenever customers and clients visit the Adria factory in Slovenia, they inevitably come away with a sense of awe at the commitment and passion demonstrated by the people who produce Adria's award-winning caravans and motorhomes.

"We are agile and innovative and extremely passionate," explains Slavica Sterk, Managing Director of Adria's UK business. "This passion goes very deep and comes from the top. Whenever we speak to our dealers they say they never experience as much passion about a brand. This is because we know that our vehicle will bring joy to people's lives. They enable them to do what is in the DNA of each of us from historic times – to travel, explore and be close to nature. We feel as if we are selling dreams to people."

Adria was founded more than 50 years ago in Slovenia. The vehicles have been sold in the UK since the 1960s and the UK is now Adria's fourth largest market, with the sleek mid-range caravan Adora and the motorhomes Coral and Matrix being particularly popular. Adria is one of the largest manufacturers of caravans and motorhomes in the UK, its vehicles gaining a hard-won reputation for inspiring design and elegant style as well as durability and reliability. The company traditionally listens carefully to customers to understand and satisfy their needs, and then adapts its designs for different markets. One consistent theme is that Adria does not try to make vehicles look like a second home, but instead ensures that they are functional, open and light. It makes a range of vehicles for different family sizes and budgets, but all adhere to these central principles of imaginative, stylish but practical design allied with exceptionally high standards of manufacture.

"For a long time, we followed other manufacturers," says Slavica. "Then about ten or 15 years ago we decided to do things our way. There was a revolutionary change in the way we did our business and we began to offer something completely different: contemporary design with an obsession with quality. That made us very strong in the UK. Since then, we didn't follow, we lead."

Slavica is a caravan-user herself, so she understands exactly what customers need. She was born in Slovenia and started working for Adria in her home country before coming to lead the UK team in 2007. As a child, she toured Croatia and Slovenia and has fond memories of caravan holidays in Scandinavia and the Scottish Highlands. She believes these sorts of adventures are best enjoyed in an Adria vehicle. The company offers a range of innovations across their lines such as smart kitchens, hotel-style "Ergo" washrooms, a selection of sleeping solutions, optimised and flexible storage and panoramic windows that open a new view on the world. All have sleek and stylish exteriors matched with contemporary interior colour schemes and fabrics. These designs are constantly being refined, improved and updated to ensure Adria stays ahead of trends in their determination to give customers the perfect space for the holiday break.

The popularity of this continues to grow, and the 2020 range was launched in July and sold out by September. "We are constantly finding new customers, including people who used to travel abroad or go on cruises but now want to holiday at home," says Slavica. "These modern vehicles really appeal to this market."

Posh fish 'n' chips with cockle tartare

Paul Gayler MBE, food writer, TV chef and owner of Feedback Consultancy

Fish and chips are undoubtedly one of the most famous fish dishes eaten throughout the British Isles, yet it's not often cooked in the home, more usually bought from the local chippie, which seems a great shame. Here is my simple version of a more elevated dish, made with fish and shellfish from the east coast, including the wonderful renowned cockles.

Suffolk

Dairy-free
Preparation time: 30 minutes
Cooking time: 30 minutes

Serves 4

INGREDIENTS

For the fish and shellfish
Vegetable oil for deep frying
4 x 175g filleted and boneless white fish
  (haddock, cod, hake)
200g prepared squid, cut into 1cm
  thick rings
300g peeled large raw prawns
Salt, pepper and a pinch of curry powder

For the batter
225g self-raising flour, sieved
300ml cold lager (or stout)

For the cockle tartare
200g good-quality mayonnaise
  (homemade or purchased)
2 tbsp capers, chopped
2 tbsp gherkins, chopped
2 tbsp flat-leaf parsley, chopped
2 tbsp chives, chopped
120g brined cooked cockles, well drained
  (frozen and defrosted cockles are fine)
1 large hard-boiled egg, peeled
  and chopped

To serve
4 lemon wedges
Crispy fried chunky chips to serve

METHOD

• Heat the oil in a suitable saucepan or deep fryer to 180°C.
• Prepare the batter by simply whisking together the sieved flour and lager.
• Dry the individual pieces of fish and shellfish on kitchen paper, then season with salt, pepper and a pinch of curry powder.
• Coat the fish and shellfish in the batter, starting with the white fish; remove and lift from the bowl and carefully immerse in the hot fat.
• Cook for 4 minutes turning it over during cooking, before adding the batter-coated prawns and squid to the oil.
• Cook for further 3 minutes until all of the fish are golden and crispy.
• Remove all of the fish and drain on kitchen paper to remove any excess oil.
• Meanwhile fry your chips until golden and crispy.
• For the tartare sauce, simply stir everything together in a bowl and season to taste. Divide the tartare into four small ramekin-style dishes.
• Season the fish and chips with a little salt, place on four serving plates, place a dish of cockle tartare alongside and a wedge of lemon, then simply enjoy!

VEGETARIAN/VEGAN ALTERNATIVE
• Vegetarians can replace the fish with slices of halloumi, marinated overnight in yoghurt, then dried and passed through the batter. Remove the cockles from the tartare recipe and proceed as above.
• Vegans can replace the fish with slices of firm tofu, replace the mayonnaise with vegan mayonnaise, remove the cockles and egg from the recipe and proceed as above.

Sergeant Len Manning, Legion D'Honneur

Born in Paddington on 14 January 1925, Len Manning grew up in Chingford and left school at 15 knowing that he wanted to join the RAF. In 1942, he reached the minimum age and presented himself at the recruiting office in Regent's Park. Following gunnery training at RAF Bridgnorth, he was posted to 57 Squadron at RAF East Kirkby in Lincolnshire.

In July 1944, aged 19, Len participated in three missions as a tail gunner in the mighty Lancaster bomber. His first was a night raid over southern France during which he experienced his first enemy anti-aircraft fire, or "flak". A few days later he and his crew took part in a daylight raid on Caen in Normandy. After a 4am take-off, Len was greeted by the surreal sight of so many aircraft in formation it looked like a sky full of flying ants, visible to all, including the Germans who shot down or damaged many Allied bombers.

On their return, his crew prepared for another mission that night. After crossing the Channel in darkness, Len's Lancaster was picked out by searchlights and hit while it dived to evade anti-aircraft fire. Len bailed out of the burning plane in a damaged parachute and landed in France. He staggered eight miles through the night, with painful burns to his arms and face, before collapsing at a remote farmhouse. The farmer passed him on to the Resistance, who interrogated him to ascertain that he wasn't a German spy. Len was given a Luger pistol for his protection and was moved to various safe houses to avoid the attention of the retreating German Army. After VE Day, Len was taken to Paris by a US officer, before being repatriated back to Britain, where he learned that only two of his six crew members had survived the attack. In 1996, at a special event organised by RAF Duxford, he met the Luftwaffe pilot, Herbert Altner, who had shot down his Lancaster bomber.

Len was awarded the Legion D'Honneur by a grateful French government and in September 2013 was finally awarded the Bomber Command Clasp by the mayors of Sudbury and Ipswich. Registered as disabled due to his war injuries, Len worked in the plastics industry and became president of his Royal British Legion branch in Sudbury, Suffolk. He passed away with cancer on 1 September 2020, aged 95.

Written by Sergeant Scott Hill, RAF, and Sandra Bromley, RBL Membership Support Officer

"In 1996, Len met the Luftwaffe pilot who had shot down his Lancaster bomber"

Fermented genius

The world's market leader, Sarsons has become a byword for malt vinegar – both as a cooking ingredient, a condiment and a pickling agent.

www.sarsons.co.uk

For countless Britons, fish and chips just isn't the same without a splash of Sarsons. The company has been producing vinegar to the same recipe and using the same process since 1794, making it one of the country's longest-lasting brands, and one essential for the perfect plate of traditional fish and chips – as well as a handy store cupboard staple for numerous recipes.

"For more than 200 years, nothing has changed in terms of labels, manufacturing process and how we source our ingredients," says Michela Andrisani, Assistant Brand Manager for Sarsons Vinegar. "Our customers know that if you are making traditional fish and chips in the proper old-fashioned way, then you have to serve it with the best quality vinegar, which always means Sarsons."

That stamp of quality comes from the long history, which ensures that Sarsons tastes exactly the same today as it did when it was first invented in the 18th century. That's an extraordinary national thread, meaning somebody in the age of smartphones and the internet can enjoy exactly the same taste experience as an ancestor who lived through the French and American revolutions. The vinegar was first brewed by Thomas Sarson in London, but has been made in Manchester since 1968. In 2012, it was acquired by Mizkan – a 200-year-old vinegar manufacturer in Japan – who recognised Sarsons as an international leader in vinegar. Mizkan maintained the quality but extended the range, so the brand now produces flavoured vinegars, Worcester sauce, browning sauce for gravy and pickling vinegars for home pickling.

That longevity is down to the brewing process, which gives Sarsons its badge of quality. It all starts with malted barley, which is milled and transferred to a grist hopper. Hot water is added for the mashing process in the mash tun, which sees the grains "cracked" and "mashed" to extract the sugars. Next comes fermentation in the cooler – the liquid is allowed to cool and yeast is added. This process that is similar to how beer is made, except without the hops. After six days, the yeast will have converted the sugars to alcohol and is removed. Finally the liquid is transferred to an acetifier – this is where Sarsons introduces a naturally "good" bacteria called acetobacter in giant pine vats full of "wood wool", which is made from larch trees taken from the Leighton Estate in Wales. This turns the alcohol into acetic acid and gives vinegar its sharp flavour and "pave".

The finished vinegar is then standardised to 5 per cent acid and pasteurised before bottling. A staggering 15 million bottles are produced this way each year. The process takes seven days; most vinegars try to do the same in 24 hours, explaining the vast difference in taste. "What is important for Sarsons is the long heritage and the unique brewed process," explains Michela. "The recipe has basically not changed since the brand was born in 1794. The process and recipe is still the same after such a long time."

People trust Sarsons. They might not understand the method and craftsmanship that has gone into each bottle, but they appreciate the most important result – the taste. "Sarsons is known throughout the world," says Michela. "Our biggest hook remains fish and chips, especially if it is fried as the batter will soak up the vinegar without effecting the crispiness, and we always want to be here to support restaurants. We need each other as we share a belief in quality and tradition."

Mango chutney with kebabs

INGREDIENTS

For the seekh kebab
250g chicken or turkey mince
  (fat content approximately 7 per cent)
2 spring onions, greens finely sliced
2 tsp finely chopped coriander
1 tsp finely diced ginger
1 small green chilli, finely diced
1 garlic clove, minced
½ tsp fenugreek
½ tsp garam masala
Pinch of salt

For the malted mango chutney
1 mango
25g sugar
2 tsp Sarson's malt vinegar
¼ tsp cumin seeds
Pinch of salt

For the quick pickled cauliflower
½ small cauliflower
4 tbsp Sarson's Malt
  Pickling Vinegar
1 tsp sugar

To serve
4 small naan breads
Tomato and cucumber, diced (optional)
Coriander sprigs (optional)

METHOD

• For the malted mango chutney, peel the mango and remove the stone. Dice the flesh into small cubes, around 0.5cm.
• Combine the ingredients in a microwave safe jug or bowl. Cover the top with clingfilm. Microwave on full power for five minutes, stirring half way. Remove the clingfilm and leave to cool.
• For the quick pickled cauliflower, slice the cauliflower into thin sheets or cut into very small florets. Lay in a shallow dish.
• Sprinkle over the sugar then pour over the malt vinegar. Leave to soak.
• For the kebab, combine all the ingredients in a large mixing bowl.
• Knead with the hands until the mince holds together well. If the mix is too dry, add one teaspoon groundnut oil or one teaspoon flour if too wet.
• Preheat the grill to 200°C.
• With wet hands to prevent sticking, form the mince into lengths on two metal skewers. The kebabs should be around an inch thick. Lay the skewered kebabs over a rack with a tray underneath to catch any liquid.
• Grill for 10 minutes, or until meat is cooked through and beginning to brown on the outside. Turn regularly to ensure even cooking throughout. If preparing ahead, kebab meat can be mixed and left in a sealed container in the fridge for 24 hours, ready to be cooked.
• To serve, warm the naans according to packet instructions. Remove the kebabs from the skewers and lay in the naan.
• Layer in the chutney, pickled cauliflower, cucumber and tomato. Serve immediately.

Chimichurri with rib eye steak

INGREDIENTS

Bunch of parsley
½ tsp oregano, fresh or dried
2 garlic cloves
1 shallot, peeled and halved
½ tsp chilli flakes
2 ½ tbsp olive oil
Juice of ½ lemon
2 tbsp Sarson's Malt Vinegar
1 tsp sugar
2 rib eye steaks

METHOD

- For the chimichurri sauce, blitz the parsley, oregano, garlic, shallot and chilli in a blender with the oil, lemon juice, two tablespoons of Sarson's Malt Vinegar, sugar and a good pinch of salt.
- Blend until it's finely chopped and becomes a thick sauce, taste for seasoning. Refrigerate until ready to serve.
- Take the steaks out of the fridge one hour before cooking so that they come up to room temperature. Cook in a heavy-based frying pan or griddle pan to your taste then allow to rest on a warmed plate to rest for 5 minutes and serve with chimichurri sauce.

Traditional Scottish pie (with a twist)

Sergeant Fred Cooper, Army (retired)

My variation of the traditional Scottish pie has a light topping combining the traditional accompaniments of neeps (swede) and tatties (potatoes). A friend of mine, also ex-Army Catering Corps, has a food van in Florida called the Café Rouge and, once a year, he participates in the large Scottish festival there. Many years ago, he asked me for a recipe so I came up with this Scottish pie variation. Still, to this day, it is enjoyed by the American Scottish folk of Florida and beyond. Relished by many at those Scottish festivals it is equally as good at home for a hearty family meal or event.

Preparation time: 1 hour
Cooking time: 40 minutes

Serves 6

INGREDIENTS

For the pie filling
1½ tbsp olive oil
1 medium onion, finely diced
1 large carrot, finely diced
1 large stick of celery, finely diced
2 garlic cloves, crushed or finely chopped
750g coarse minced Angus beef,
  best quality you can get
40g plain flour
40g tomato purée
1 Oxo beef stock cube
125ml red wine
2 tbsp Worcestershire sauce
1 tsp dried thyme
Salt and pepper

For pie topping
1 large swede, peeled and cut
  into 1cm dice
1kg Maris Piper potatoes, peeled
  and cut into even pieces
1 large knob of butter
Salt and pepper

METHOD

For the pie filling
• Heat the oil in a casserole or heavy-based saucepan over a medium heat, add the onion, carrot and celery, season with a little salt and pepper and cook, stirring frequently, for 5 minutes until the vegetables have started to soften. Add the garlic and continue to cook for another minute.
• Turn up the heat to full, add the minced beef and cook until browned.
• Reduce the heat to medium, stir in the flour and tomato purée and cook, stirring constantly, for 2 minutes.
• Crumble over the stock cube and stir in the red wine, Worcestershire sauce and dried thyme; bring to a simmer and season with salt and pepper.
• Turn the heat to low, cover with a lid and simmer, stirring occasionally, for 30 minutes (add a splash of boiling water if the mix becomes too dry).

For the pie topping
• While the filling is cooking, bring a large saucepan of cold water to a boil with a generous pinch of salt, add the swede and potatoes and cook for 20–30 minutes until both are cooked through; drain through a colander, return the cooked swede and potatoes to the pan and shake over a low heat to dry them out.
• Mash the swede and potatoes (or pass through a ricer), mix in the butter, season with salt and pepper and set aside until you're ready to top the pie.

To cook the pie
• Preheat the oven to 180°C.
• Fill a suitable baking dish or shallow casserole with the filling and set aside to cool for 15 minutes.
• Spread the neeps and tatties over the top of the filling and cook in the preheated oven for 40 minutes until the top of the pie is golden brown.
• I recommend serving my Scottish pie with some seasonal greens such as tenderstem broccoli or spring greens; both go great together with the pie.

Colonel David Stirling KBE

The founder of the SAS, Archibald David Stirling was born on 15 November 1915 in Keir House, Perthshire, into an aristocratic Scottish family with a proud military heritage. As a child, he honed his skills as a hunter. Tall and athletically built, he had great confidence and social grace that resulted in him becoming a natural leader.

Yet he exhibited a spirit of adventure and a rebellious streak. After being thrown out of Cambridge University he was steered toward becoming a mountaineer and reservist in the Scots Guards. When war broke out, Stirling was in America, working as a cowboy while training to become the first man to climb Mount Everest. He immediately returned to Britain and re-joined the Scots Guards.

Stirling initially struggled with regimental discipline before joining the commandos. While in hospital after a failed parachute exercise, he began to plan a new parachute raiding force – one that would eventually become the Special Air Service (SAS). Using his connections and charm to get his Middle East headquarters endorsement (physically sneaking into the HQ while on crutches to speak to the commander-in-chief), he then drew in adventure-hungry recruits from the commandos. By November 1941, L Detachment SAS was ready for action. Its defining motto, "Who Dares Wins", was personally chosen by Stirling.

After an early failure, Stirling and his surviving men developed their partnership with another special force, the Long-Range Desert Group, and proceeded to wreak havoc behind enemy lines, destroying hundreds of aircraft in a string of hit-and-run raids. In September 1942, the SAS achieved regimental status. "The boy Stirling is quite mad, quite, quite mad," said his commander, Field Marshal Montgomery. "However, in a war, there is often a place for mad people."

In January 1943, Stirling was captured during a mission in Tunisia. By this time, he had become a legend, dubbed "the Phantom Major' by his German adversaries. After capture, he undertook many escape attempts, resulting in his eventual transfer to the supposedly escape-proof Colditz Castle in Germany.

After the war, Stirling was promoted to Colonel and made Deputy Commander of the SAS Brigade, where his role included tracking down members of the SS and Gestapo responsible for shooting Special Forces prisoners. He was knighted just before his death in 1990. Since 2002, the David Stirling Memorial has stood near his ancestral home, looking towards the Perthshire mountains.

Written by Warrant Officer Chris Campbell, Army (retired)

"The boy Stirling is quite, quite mad. However, in a war, there is often a place for mad people"

Home-grown singles

With a distillery based on a farm on the island of Islay, Kilchoman is pioneering a range of single-farm single-malt whiskies where all the barley is grown onsite

www.kilchomandistillery.com

When Anthony Wills decided to open the first single-malt Scotch whisky distillery on the Hebridean island of Islay for more than 100 years, people were sceptical. "They thought I was mad," chuckles Anthony, who came to whisky after several years' experience in the wine trade. "But I could see there was potential in the premium single-malt market and we started production at Kilchoman Distillery on Islay in 2005. People wondered why I came to Islay to open a distillery, but since we opened there have been 30 or 40 new distilleries in Scotland. I am very proud that we were the first on Islay, as it's allowed us to build a brand around the world."

Not only was Kilchoman one of the first of the new wave of craft distilleries to open in Scotland, it was also unique in its approach. Anthony wanted to locate the distillery on a working farm to gain immediate access to the barley and control over the malting process. That gave Kilchoman a unique selling point over its more established rivals, helping to establish a reputation for provenance and excellence. The Islay location is another boon, with the island having considerable standing around the world among the discerning single malt audience.

That sophisticated international customer base has allowed Kilchoman to come a long way in a short space of time. The brand exports to more than 50 markets around the world, with 80 per cent of sales coming from overseas. Anthony knew that the early days would be difficult – the long maturing period required for whisky means no profits for several years – but a change in drinking attitudes came at just the right time. "Other brands began to sell non-aged single malt which meant we could release our

first batch at three years," he says. "In 2009 we put out 8,000 bottles and they sold out in a few days. Over the following years, we have built up our stock but it was key to our success that the market become more accepting of younger single malts."

Kilchoman now sells a range of crafted single malts named after the locality. Machir Bay is matured in largely bourbon casks to create a distinct balance of classic Islay character with floral complexity, while Sanaig largely uses sherry casks to create a balance of dried fruit and dark chocolate with rich peat smoke. Loch Gorm has the spicy character of European oak, while the 100 per cent Islay is the world's only single farm single-malt Scotch. The distillery also offers a range of tours including the "Whisky And Wilderness Tour", which includes a walk around the local area to see the natural beauty that helps give Kilchoman its unique personality.

Anthony has since been joined by his three sons who, like their father, are captured by the beauty of Islay, the complexity of Scotch and the purity of the process that comes from having a distillery on a farm. Together, they intend to take Kilchoman into more international markets, while refining and improving the process even further. And, having shown that the single farm model can work for whisky, they are also interested in developing the concept. "It's now about leaving a legacy and we are discussing moving onto other spirits using a similar process, where we grow and produce everything on the farm," he says. "We believe we could do that now that we have developed a reputation and an expertise for our products."

Trinidad & Tobago

Pelau

Leading Aircraftman Seun Omisore, RAF

Trinidadian cuisine is a hybrid of many cultural influences, mainly West African, Indian, Creole and European, and pelau is no exception. Similar rice dishes exist all over the world, from the European pilaff and paella to West African jollof, St Helenian plo and Indian pilau, which in turn derived from the Persian polow. Pelau is a unique mix of several of these predecessors. It utilises fresh vegetables and coconuts from the islands and uses the African technique of browning the meat in sugar before adding the rice. In my recipe, I have marinated the chicken in Trinidadian green seasoning, which gives the pelau a good depth of flavour and adds a fresh herbal note.

Trinidad & Tobago

Preparation time: 35 minutes
plus 2–4 hours to marinate
Cooking time: 30 minutes

Serves 4

INGREDIENTS

For the green seasoning
2 onions, roughly chopped
2 celery sticks, roughly chopped
2 green chillies, roughly chopped
4 garlic cloves, roughly chopped
3 spring onions, sliced
50g parsley
50g coriander
1 lime, juiced
2 tbsp vegetable oil

For the pelau
400g boneless chicken thighs,
  cut into large dice
2 tbsp vegetable oil
4 tbsp dark brown soft sugar
2 onions, finely diced
2 carrots, finely diced
2 red peppers, finely diced
¼ pumpkin (or ½ butternut squash),
  finely diced
2 tomatoes, finely diced
550g long-grain rice, washed
300ml chicken stock
400g (1 tin) coconut milk
1 Scotch bonnet chilli
Salt and freshly ground black pepper

METHOD

To make the green seasoning
• Place all of the ingredients into a blender or food processor and blend to a smooth paste; drizzle in a little extra oil if necessary.

To marinate the chicken
• Place the diced chicken thighs into a mixing bowl, add three-quarters of the green seasoning and mix well, ensuring all of the chicken is covered with the marinade; cover and chill in the fridge for 2–4 hours, or preferably overnight.

To make the pelau
• Place a large saucepan or casserole over a medium-high heat, add the oil and when hot sprinkle over the brown sugar in an even layer; the sugar will start to melt then froth and bubble; as soon as the sugar starts to go dark around the edges add the chicken and stir immediately to coat it in the caramelised sugar.
• Cook the chicken, stirring frequently, for 5 minutes then add the onions, carrots, peppers, pumpkin and tomatoes and continue to cook for a further 5 minutes until everything is lightly coloured.
• Add the rice and continue to cook, stirring continuously, for a couple of minutes; pour in the stock and coconut milk, stir well, season with salt and pepper and let it simmer rapidly for about 8 minutes.
• Turn the heat to low, add the Scotch bonnet and remaining green seasoning, cover with a lid and cook for about 20 minutes or until all of the liquid has been absorbed.

To serve
• Remove the Scotch bonnet, check the seasoning and serve with sliced avocado and fried plantain.

Philip Louis Ulric Cross DSO DFC

Born on 1 May 1917 in the Port of Spain, Trinidad, Philip Louis Ulric Cross had dreamed of joining the RAF from the earliest age. Aged 14 he had written his name as "Flight Lieutenant P.L.U. Cross DFC" in two of his school books. "To me that was the height of anybody's ambition, to be a Flight Lieutenant in the Royal Air Force and to get the DFC," he said. "Most of my friends thought I was mad!"

By 1941, Cross had volunteered to serve in the RAF, along with 250 other Trinidadians, training as a navigator at RAF College Cranwell before joining No. 139 (Jamaica) Squadron. Excelling as an airman, Cross was selected to join the elite Pathfinder Force, tasked with the challenging and dangerous task of marking targets accurately for bombing raids.

In June 1944, he was awarded the DFC (Distinguished Flying Cross) for "exceptional navigational ability" and in 1945 was further awarded the DSO (Distinguished Service Order) for his "fine example of keenness and devotion to duty" having twice refused to be rested from flying. By the end of the war, Cross had completed 80 missions against targets in occupied Europe and Germany and had become one of the war's most decorated West Indian servicemen.

After the war, he left the service and studied law, passing the bar in 1949, practising in Ghana and Tanzania before eventually becoming a High Court Judge in Trinidad. Also actively involved in charity work, he co-founded the Cotton Tree Foundation (to combat poverty and unemployment in the Port of Spain) and served as the President of the Royal Air Forces Association Trinidad and Tobago Branch No. 1075.

He is survived by his two daughters, Nicola and Susan, and is held in high esteem in his home nation, with the local military airbase being renamed Ulric Cross Air Station. "Justice Ulric Cross was a man who not only served Trinidad and Tobago tirelessly, but dedicated his existence to the preservation of justice and democracy on an international scale," said Garvin Nicholas, Trinidad and Tobago's High Commissioner to London, in a 2014 ceremony. "Now more than ever, our society dearly needs role models like him."

Written by Flight Lieutenant Daniel Beechey, RAF

"By the end of the war, Cross had completed 80 missions against targets in occupied Europe and Germany and had become one of the war's most decorated West Indian servicemen"

Transforming young lives

Education Plus NE supports and educates young people in crisis to give them skills and confidence to realise their own potential.

www.educationplusne.co.uk

When the co-founders of Education Plus NE support young people, they often find ex-service men and women offer some of the greatest inspiration. "Peer-to-peer learning and individuals from outside traditional education have a real impact with our students" says co-director Kevin Wake. "We have signed the Armed Forces Covenant and work with the Forces to deliver training, education and career pathways. We also employ ex-servicemen in senior roles in the organisation alongside our teachers, sports coaches, mentors and support staff. This is something that has really helped a number of our young people, offering them the support in a different way to move towards real opportunities."

Education Plus NE was started in January 2017 by three professionals with considerable experience working in schools and youth services in the North East. They came together with the same ethos of giving students who faced challenges in mainstream education a better chance to succeed, by offering them quality education and a personalised support package. They set about developing a programme that would bring these children back into full-time education, ideally ahead of their GCSEs. "We started with one centre for 15 young people a week and now have provisions in Durham and Teesside that between them support 150 students a week," says Kevin. "These are often children with difficult personal and family situations who have had huge barriers to education."

The initial focus is to understand their individual situations, learning what motivates them and gaining their trust. Achievable goals are set as small steppingstones, restoring confidence and self-belief. The young people are introduced to students who have already turned their lives round thanks to Education Plus, as well as people from the Armed Forces and emergency services. Kevin believes the model can be rolled out to other areas of the UK to help children in crisis. "We have so many success stories," he says. "We take on some of the most challenging students in the region, including young people who have been permanently excluded. Time and patience are key to nurture the students, giving them an excellent blend of education and support to give them pride and real opportunities to achieve."

Mushroom bourguignon cobbler

The Hairy Bikers, aka TV chefs David Myers and Si King

Tyne & Wear

This is a really special dish with a rich, almost meaty, flavour. It's one of the recipes we couldn't quite decide on – should we make it a pie, a crumble or a cobbler? So we asked you on Instagram and you voted by a slim margin for a cobbler topping. We've used blue cheese in ours but, if you're not a fan, a veggie Cheddar would be fine too.

Vegetarian
Preparation time: 40 minutes
Cooking time: 55 minutes

Serves 4

INGREDIENTS

For the bourguignon
2 tbsp olive oil
12 button onions or shallots,
  peeled and left whole
300g carrots, cut into chunks
½ tsp sugar
25g butter
750g mushrooms (mix of portobello,
  chestnut, button, cremini), thickly sliced
1 large sprig of thyme
2 bay leaves
A few sage leaves, finely chopped
200ml red wine
300ml mushroom or vegetable stock
1 tbsp mushroom ketchup
1 tsp Dijon mustard
Finely chopped parsley, to serve
Sea salt and black pepper

For the cobbler topping
200g self-raising flour
1 tsp baking powder
½ tsp salt
1 tsp dried sage
50g blue cheese, crumbled
1 egg
75ml buttermilk

METHOD

• First make the bourguignon. Heat the oil in a large flame-proof casserole dish and add the onions or shallots and the carrots. Fry over a high heat, stirring regularly, until they are dappled with dark brown patches. Sprinkle over the sugar and continue to cook for another couple of minutes to help caramelise. Remove them from the dish and set aside.
• Add the butter to the casserole dish. When it starts to foam, add the mushrooms and cook over a high heat until they have reduced down. Put the onions and carrots back in the dish and season generously with salt and pepper. Add the herbs, then pour in the red wine. Bring to the boil and leave to bubble until the wine has reduced by at least a third. Add the stock, mushroom ketchup and mustard and stir until completely combined.
• Bring back to the boil, then turn down to a simmer and cover with a lid. Cook for half an hour, perhaps a little longer, until the vegetables are completely tender. Preheat the oven to 200°C.
• Meanwhile, make the cobbler topping. Put the flour and baking powder into a bowl and add half a teaspoon of salt. Add the sage and the cheese, then mix in the egg and buttermilk to make a fairly sticky dough. Form the dough into 12 small balls and space out over the top of the bourguignon. Cover and simmer for 10 minutes, then transfer the dish to the oven, uncovered, for a further 10–15 minutes until the cobbler topping has puffed up and is lightly browned. Serve in shallow bowls with a garnish of finely chopped parsley.

Kate Adie CBE OBE DL

Kathryn (Kate) Adie was born in Whitley Bay on 19 September 1945 and was adopted, as a baby, by a Sunderland pharmacist, Wilfred, and his wife Maude. She attended Sunderland Church High School before reading Swedish at Newcastle University, where she developed an interest in journalism and drama. Adie's broadcasting career started as a studio technician at BBC Radio Durham. After seven years she moved to Bristol as a producer, specialising mainly in arts programmes and farming, before being made an outside broadcast director, focusing on religion and sport. By 1976, she was a regional TV news reporter in Plymouth and Southampton, before moving to national TV news.

Fate helped to catapult her career in May 1980 when, as a duty reporter one evening, Adie was first on the scene to report the Iranian Embassy siege. She reported live and unscripted to one of the largest news audiences ever, as smoke billowed in the background and SAS soldiers abseiled in to rescue the hostages. Her career immediately took off and saw her report from around the world, visiting dozens of conflict zones including Northern Ireland, the Falklands, Kuwait, Afghanistan, Bosnia, Sierra Leone, Rwanda and Beijing's Tiananmen Square, gaining huge respect, especially among the Armed Forces. In Libya, she interviewed Colonel Gaddafi and was later shot by a drunk Libyan commander for refusing to act as an intermediary between the Libyan and British governments. Thankfully, the bullet nicked her collar bone and didn't cause permanent harm.

In 2003, she retired from BBC TV, where she had been chief news correspondent since 1989, and started presenting BBC Radio 4's flagship international news series, *From Our Own Correspondent*. Despite not being on our screens, Adie has kept herself busy as Chancellor of Bournemouth University (where she warned postgraduate students that confirming information and verifying news sources were critical in this climate of fake news), as well as being an ambassador for the charity SSAFA (Soldiers', Sailors' and Airmen's Families Association) and Skill Force. Her books include *Corsets to Camouflage*, which champions the role of women in the Armed Forces. She has won three RTS News Awards, two Monte Carlo International TV News Awards and two BAFTAs, and received a CBE in 2018.

Written by Cadet Tom Anderson, Sergeant Sean Henry, Corporal Alexander Turner and Flight Sergeant James Wise, Air Training Corps

"*In Libya she interviewed Colonel Gaddafi and was later shot by a drunk Libyan commander*"

Heard instinct

Boots Hearingcare uses cutting-edge technology and the nationwide reach of the Boots brand to improve hearing health for everyone

www.bootshearingcare.com

While people are now accustomed to getting their eyesight checked at the optician or their teeth checked at the dentist at least once a year, many members of the public seem unaware of the importance and ease of doing the same for their hearing. Boots Hearingcare is keen to normalise hearing screening and dispel any myths surrounding hearing loss and hearing aids.

Hearing instrument technology has advanced dramatically over the last few years, and the days of large, visible, whistling hearing aids are long gone. "The potential is vast, and the quality of the modern hearing instrument is extraordinary," says Rob Skedge, Managing Director of Boots Hearingcare. "They are so discreet and comfortable and come with a range of digital sound-processing abilities. Hearing loss is still something that is associated with age, but over time we have seen the age of onset lower and varying causes of hearing damage rise. It's also true that people, over the course of their life, want to stay active and connected, so we believe that helping people understand their hearing and the help available is a real priority."

Technology can help from the mildest of issues of mishearing odd words in noise to severe losses. Rob Skedge enjoys regularly using hearing devices himself. He says the background noise suppression and the superb sound quality he receives when direct-streaming his phone calls, radio, music and television directly to his ears reduces his listening effort and makes for a more relaxed experience. Rob, who doesn't have a significant loss, says he is comfortable using the hearing technology as it is discreet, modern, comfortable and demonstrates that technology can benefit a variety of needs.

"We have examples of people using first-time technology or upgrading current solutions and being brought to tears when they realise they can hear their loved ones and enjoy the fidelity in their favourite music again," he says. "Bringing this to people's lives is what makes our work so rewarding."

Technology continues to evolve, with customers now having control of how they want to hear via an app. During lockdown, Boots Hearingcare continued to provide a first-class service to thousands of customers with remote fittings. "As the devices are digitally programmable, and we held previous records online, we could respond to each customer's needs," says Rob. "Whether in-store or at-home, we concentrate on offering an exceptional experience. As technology continues to improve, we will expand the ways we can support customers to suit their personal situations. Digital signal processing in hearing aids today is so much better than the analogue tech of yesteryear, which simply made everything louder. Nowadays, hearing aids enable people through easier hearing to feel more confident, retain independence and enjoy more freedom."

Rob and his team are hopeful that a younger generation who have become accustomed to wearing ear pods may find the transition to hearing devices easier than their older relatives. "People of all ages can benefit from this technology," he says. "There are connections between hearing loss, listening effort, cognitive load and – in some cases – dementia, isolation, depression and risk of falls. Good hearing is vital for our sensory, mental health and overall wellbeing. We want to raise awareness of the importance of hearing health and early intervention, so people stay connected and age well."

Warwickshire faggots

Private Sophie Phillips, Army

This is my take on traditional Warwickshire faggots. Replacing the caul fat (the thin membrane that surrounds pigs' internal organs) with streaky bacon gives the dish a different look and taste, especially if you allow the bacon to crisp up in the oven. Faggots were created as a way of using up all the bits of the pig that would otherwise be discarded and consequently wasted, particularly the "pluck", which consists of the heart, lungs and liver. Faggots can be eaten hot or cold and, when served hot, are traditionally accompanied with mashed potatoes and peas. My faggots are served with braised peas as a nod to tradition, giving the dish a little more texture and overall flavour. Next time you're in the Black Country, be sure to visit one of the takeaways that serve fresh portions of faggots and peas with onion gravy, as they've been doing for almost 100 years.

Preparation time: 30 minutes
Cooking time: 45–50 minutes

Serves 4

INGREDIENTS

For the faggots
220g pork belly, cut into small pieces
150g pork shoulder, cut into small pieces
150g smoked bacon lardons
110g pork liver, cut into small pieces
1 medium onion, finely diced
2 garlic cloves, finely chopped
120g breadcrumbs
3 tbsp parsley, coarsely chopped
3 sage leaves, finely chopped
16 rashers streaky bacon
Salt and pepper

For the onion gravy
1 tbsp olive oil
2 medium onions, halved and thinly sliced
2 tsp caster sugar
800ml beef stock
175ml red wine
3 tbsp plain flour mixed with enough cold
  water to make a paste
Small handful parsley, coarsely chopped

For the braised peas
10g butter
2 tsp olive oil
1 tbsp flour
300ml chicken stock
6 spring onions, outer leaves removed
  and finely sliced
440g frozen peas
Sea salt and cracked black pepper

To serve
Creamy mashed potatoes
Flatleaf parsley sprigs

Warwickshire: Local hero

Corporal Arthur Hutt VC

Born in Earlsdon on 12 February 1889, Arthur Hutt was the first person from Coventry to win a Victoria Cross. When the textile factory he worked in formed a "Pal's Battalion" after the outbreak of war in 1914, Hutt joined up. It wasn't long before Hutt saw action at the Battle of the Somme, Ypres and in Italy as part of the 7th Battalion of The Royal Warwickshire Regiment.

On 4 October 1917, during the second battle of Ypres, the 7th Battalion were ordered to capture a building called Tweed House. They did so but, when they continued their advance, all the officers and non-commissioned officers in the platoon were hit. Private Hutt took command immediately, leading the platoon forward. After his platoon was held up by the enemy, he immediately ran forward alone, shooting the enemy officer and three men in the post and causing 40 or 50 others to surrender.

Realising that he had pushed too far ahead, Hutt withdrew his party, personally covering the withdrawal, killing a number of enemies before carrying back a comrade who had been badly wounded. After he had consolidated his position, he learned that some wounded men still lay out in the open. As no stretcher bearers were available, Hutt went out himself and carried in four men under heavy fire. For these acts of incredible bravery, courage and leadership, Hutt was awarded the Victoria Cross.

On his return to Coventry in 1918, Hutt was met at the station by the Mayor and driven to a civic reception, during which he received an extraordinary address and £500 from a fund set up for him by the city. Hutt was also awarded the Freedom of Coventry. After being discharged from the Army in early 1919, Hutt, like millions of others during the Great Depression, bounced between a number of jobs and unemployment. He eventually volunteered for the Auxillary Fire Service in November 1938 before joining the Home Guard during the Second World War, reaching the rank of Lieutenant in 13th Warwickshire (Coventry) Battalion. He died on 14 April 1954, at his nephew's home in Sewell Highway and was cremated at Canley Crematorium with full military honours. A year later, a Cornish granite memorial was erected in his memory in Coventry's War Memorial Park.

Written by Staff Sergeant Mark John, Queen's Royal Lancers, Army

METHOD

To make the faggots

- Preheat the oven to 170°C and line a baking tray with a sheet of baking parchment.
- Place the pork belly, shoulder, bacon and liver in a food processor and pulse until the meat is finely chopped; you just want to mince the meat and not turn it into a purée.
- Transfer the minced meat to a glass bowl, add the onions, garlic, breadcrumbs and herbs; season well with salt and pepper and mix all of the ingredients together until well combined.
- Split the mix into eight equal-sized portions and roll each into a ball; place the rashers of streaky bacon in eight cross shapes and wrap each of your faggots in the bacon.
- Place the faggots on the lined baking tray, with the bacon join-side down, and bake for 45–50 minutes until golden brown and thoroughly cooked through to the middle.

For the onion gravy

- Prepare the onion gravy while the faggots are cooking: heat the oil in a saucepan over a medium heat, add the onions and cook, stirring frequently, for 8–10 minutes until softened and starting to colour; add the sugar and continue to cook until the onions are lightly caramelised.
- Add the stock and red wine, bring to a boil, stir in the flour paste and simmer, stirring frequently, for a few minutes until the sauce has thickened; remove from the heat, stir in the chopped parsley, cover with a lid and set aside to keep warm.

To prepare the braised peas

- Prepare the peas 10 minutes before the faggots are ready: heat the butter and oil in a saucepan over a medium heat, stir in the flour and cook, stirring constantly, for a minute then gradually add the stock and cook until the sauce is smooth; increase the heat, bring to a boil, add the spring onions and peas, season well, cover with a lid and simmer for 5 minutes. Set aside to keep warm.

To serve

- Bring the onion gravy and braised peas to a simmer.
- Place a generous serving of mashed potatoes on four plates with two faggots per portion, spoon over the onion gravy, serve with a large scoop of the braised peas and garnish with a sprig of picked parsley.

Birmingham chicken balti

Corporal Lewis Rookyard, Army

West Midlands

Historically, "balti" is said to describe any food cooked and served in a balti pan (a wok-like pan) and, although there are various interpretations of its origin, most would claim that the modern balti was first invented and served in a Birmingham restaurant in 1977, after which many other restaurants, known as "balti houses", sprang up in the area to capitalise on the growing popularity of this style of cooking influenced by the Indian subcontinent. Balti curries offered a lighter and healthier alternative to popular Indian restaurant dishes such as korma or tikka masala; a true balti must be served in a balti bowl. Since the 1970s, balti has grown in popularity and can now be found both on restaurant menus and supermarket shelves across the country. The mixture of dry spices, garlic and chillies allow this dish to be modified to suit individual tastes and keeps the dish fresh and vibrant, and pack a punch if you want it.

Gluten-free
Preparation time: 20 minutes
Cooking time: 1 hour

Serves 4

INGREDIENTS

6 large garlic cloves, roughly chopped
20g ginger, peeled and finely chopped
3 chillies, finely shredded
2 tbsp vegetable oil
1 cinnamon stick
3 bay leaves
1 white onion, finely diced
500g boneless chicken thighs,
  cut into 2cm dice
1½ tsp garam masala
1½ tsp ground cumin
1½ tsp ground coriander
1 tsp paprika
6 large tomatoes, coarsely chopped
120g natural yoghurt
A large handful of fresh coriander,
  coarsely chopped
½ lemon, juiced

METHOD

- Pound the garlic, ginger, chillies and a pinch of salt to a rough paste with a pestle and mortar.
- Heat the oil in a suitable pan over a medium heat, add the cinnamon stick, bay leaves and onion and fry, stirring frequently, until the onions are soft.
- Add the chicken, turn up the heat and continue to cook for 3 minutes until lightly coloured all over; add the garlic, ginger and chilli paste, garam masala, cumin, coriander and paprika, stir well and continue to fry for another 3 minutes.
- Add the tomatoes, stir well, bring to a gentle simmer and cook for 10 minutes until the tomatoes are soft.
- Stir in half of the yoghurt, reduce the heat and simmer gently until the sauce has thickened.
- Add half of the chopped coriander, season with salt and pepper and stir in the lemon juice.
- Remove from the heat and, to keep it authentic, serve over some boiled basmati rice in balti dishes, spoon over the remaining yoghurt and garnish with the reserved chopped coriander.

VEGETABLE BALTI

- For a vegetarian version substitute the chicken for seasonal vegetables such as butternut squash, pumpkin, sweet potatoes, carrots, turnips, swede, parsnips, cauliflower, mushrooms, peppers, potatoes, spring onions, etc.
- For a vegan balti, prepare as above omitting the natural yoghurt or substitute with a dairy-free alternative.

Michelle Norris MC

Born in Stourbridge, West Midlands in 1987, Michelle Suzanne Claire Norris had always hoped to join the Army. Her childhood dream came true in 2005 when she signed up for the Royal Army Medical Corps. Shortly after completing her nine months basic training – where she acquired the nickname "Chuck Norris" – she was posted to Germany and volunteered for her first operational tour to Iraq.

She was attached to the 1st Battalion Princess of Wales Regiment as a combat medical technician aged just 19, only five feet tall and the only woman among 300 men. Eight weeks into her first deployment, on 11 June 2006, the largest and most intense battle in Iraq since 2004 took place. A search operation in the south-eastern Iraqi city of Al Amarah saw Norris's company group come under heavy, sustained and accurate fire from a well-organised enemy force of more than 200.

During the attack, Colour Sergeant Ian Page was shot in the mouth and badly wounded. While being heavily fired upon, Private Norris climbed up the side of the vehicle to rescue her vehicle commander and friend. Remaining calm in her first active combat treatment situation, she put all of her training into practice and administered first aid for three minutes with rounds of ammunition landing all around her. At this point, other soldiers joined her to help drag Page back into the vehicle. Norris and Page were then evacuated to safety by Lynx helicopter and Sergeant Page went on to make a full recovery.

Norris's commanding officer recommended that she receive a medal for her bravery, and the award of the Military Cross was gazetted on 15 December 2006. "Private Norris realised the severity of the situation immediately and, without thought or care for her own personal safety, she dismounted and climbed onto the top of the Warrior," reads the citation. "Despite the very real risks from sniper fire, heavy small arms fire and rocket-propelled grenade, she deliberately ignored the danger to her own life in order to administer live-saving first aid to the commander of the vehicle. Her actions were extremely courageous and outstandingly brave and have rightly earned her the Military Cross for actions to save the life of a comrade when under fire."

She was the first woman to be awarded that decoration and received it from Her Majesty the Queen at Buckingham Palace on 21 March 2007. The Military Cross is the third highest gallantry medal in the British Armed Forces, granted in recognition of "an act or acts of exemplary gallantry during active operations against the enemy on land to all members, of any rank in our Armed Forces". Michelle Norris is still serving in the Army today.

Written by Emma Adams, widow of Major Gareth Rhys-Evans

Wiltshire market-day dinner

Lance Corporal Chris Hamlet, Army

This is my version of a traditional Wiltshire market-day dinner, a slow-cooked West Country casserole, similar to a hotpot. Wiltshire is renowned for the outstanding quality of its outdoor reared pork and originally the dish would have comprised pork chops, kidneys, onions, apples and sage topped with potatoes. I have used pork shoulder, which lends itself to slow-cooking and gives the dish a great depth of flavour. I have also incorporated dry Wiltshire cider to bring out some contrasting flavours while maintaining its integrity as a simple one-pot dish. It can be easily prepared, placed in the oven and left to simmer for a few hours (traditionally while one would have nipped out to the market). It is best enjoyed with a modern twist of white and sweet potatoes to top off the dish.

Preparation time: 40 minutes
Cooking time: 3 hours

Serves 4–6

INGREDIENTS

3 tbsp olive oil
1kg good-quality pork shoulder,
  cut into large dice
1 white onion, peeled and cut into 1cm dice
2 leeks, halved lengthways and cut into
  1cm slices
3 garlic cloves, finely chopped
4 tbsp flour
500ml dry Wiltshire cider
4 bay leaves
350ml ready-made chicken stock
2 large carrots, peeled and cut into 1cm dice
1 large parsnip, peeled and cut into 1cm dice
220ml single cream
Small bunch of parsley, stalks discarded
  and leaves roughly chopped
4 sprigs of sage, stalks discarded and
  leaves shredded
400g white potatoes, peeled and sliced
400g sweet potatoes, peeled and sliced
25g butter, cut into small dice and chilled
Salt and freshly ground black pepper

METHOD

- Heat two tablespoons of the olive oil in a casserole or heavy-based saucepan over a high heat, add the pork and stir until browned, if necessary do this in a couple of batches to avoid overcrowding the pan; transfer the pork to a bowl with a slotted spoon and set aside.
- Return the pan to a medium heat with another tablespoon of oil, fry the onions, stirring frequently, for 2 minutes, add the leeks and garlic and continue to cook until the leeks have softened, adding a little more oil if necessary.
- Season the onion and leeks with a little salt and pepper, stir in the flour and cook, stirring constantly, for a couple of minutes.
- Gradually add the cider, stirring constantly, until everytohing is well combined and the sauce is smooth; add the bay leaves, chicken stock, seared pork (including any juices that have collected in the bowl), carrots and parsnips and stir well.
- Bring to a simmer then turn down the heat to low-medium, partially cover with a lid and simmer gently for 1½ hours, stirring occasionally.
- Pre heat the oven to 190°C.
- Remove the lid from the casserole and, if the sauce is still a little thin, simmer rapidly for a few minutes to reduce and thicken the sauce.
- Stir in the cream, parsley and sage, season with salt and pepper to taste and remove the casserole from the heat.
- Mix the sliced potatoes and sweet potatoes together in a bowl and season with salt and pepper.
- Layer the mixed potatoes across the top of the casserole in a fanning motion, placing them randomly to give the top a unique look once it is cooked, which will look fantastic when served at the table.
- Dot the cubes of butter across the top of the potatoes; this will help the top brown as it cooks in the oven.
- Cook on the middle shelf of the preheated oven for 1 hour 20–30 minutes until the potatoes are cooked through and have turned golden brown on top.
- Remove from the oven and leave to sit at room temperature for 10 minutes before serving.

Lieutenant Colonel Tom Edwin Adlam

Tom Adlam was born in Salisbury, Wiltshire on 21 October 1893. Originally training as a teacher, he was also a keen sportsman, playing for Salisbury FC in the second division. At the start of the Great War, Adlam enlisted in the 4th Battalion Hampshire Regiment before commissioning in November 1916.

He was serving with the 7th Bedfordshire Regiment in France when General Gough ordered an attack on 26 September 1916, initiating what became known as the Battle of Thiepval Ridge. At 5.45am on 27 September, the 8th Bedfordshire and 1/5th West Yorks were tasked with capturing the area to the northwest of Thiepval. Adlam, realising that time was important, rushed from shell hole to shell hole under heavy machine-gun fire, collecting men and grenades for a sudden rush. Despite being wounded in the leg he carried on, pushing the Germans back by hand-throwing bombs over 40 yards, capturing the enemy positions. His magnificent valour, and skilful handling of the situation, earned him a Victoria Cross.

After recovering from his wounds, Adlam was appointed to the Army Educational Corps (AEC) and continued with his duties as an instructor, before joining the Reserves in 1923 and becoming a teacher in Bedfordshire (as well as the first Chairman of the Sandy British Legion). In the years after the Great War, he became known simply as "The Salisbury VC". He was presented with a gold watch by Salisbury's mayor, as well as being invited to unveil the city's war memorial.

In 1939, Adlam again answered the call and served as a Staff Captain in the Royal Engineers (Movement Control Section). By war's end he had reached the rank of Lieutenant Colonel, and was involved in the organisation of the Normandy landings. Adlam later returned to teaching before passing away at Hayling Island, Hampshire, on 28 May 1978, aged 81.

There is a tablet and banner in his honour at Bishop Wordsworth's School, Salisbury, and a portrait of him at the city's Guildhall, where Adlam's VC and his other medals are on public display. In September 2016, 100 years after he earned his VC, a paving stone was laid in his honour by the Lord Lieutenant at the Guildhall. Adlam's life and actions are detailed in the book *My Dad: Colonel Tom*, written by his youngest son.

Written by Corporal Josua Taubale Vosakiwaiwai, Adjutant General's Corps, Army

"Adlam rushed from shell hole to shell hole under heavy machine-gun fire"

Pet sanctuary

Amesbury Pets has become a community hub for pet owners in Wiltshire and beyond, offering bespoke advice about animal nutrition and much more

www.amesburypets.co.uk

"My dog Rory comes to work with me most days," says Graham Eaton, owner of Amesbury Pets. "If he's feeling lively he meets and greets customers, though sometimes he prefers to stretch out by the counter and relax. Either way, it's a great way to break the ice."

When Graham came out of the Army in September 2019, he had some decisions to make after 22 years in the military. "It's tempting to go with something you know and many people with my background tend to get involved in intelligence of some kind," he says. "However, my interests lay in trying a totally new venture and I thought retail might appeal so as part of my resettlement I did a number of courses, including business."

He was quickly drawn to the idea of opening an independent pet shop in his part of Wiltshire, especially since the previous one had shut in 2018, leaving a gap in the market for local people wanting a high-quality personal service. "I found this shop in the centre of Amesbury, close to Stonehenge, and it's perfect for what I want," he says. "Easy to find and walk to, with plenty of room for all the products needed to help owners choose the best for their dogs, cats, rabbits, guinea pigs, birds, fish and reptiles."

Amesbury Pets quickly established a welcoming place in the community, which led to Graham's latest course in animal nutrition. "People like to come in and chat about their pets and many will ask advice," he says. "We specialise in natural feeding with a comprehensive range of biologically and naturally appropriate foods and treats along with an excellent variety of natural products for health and well-being. I always suggest people study the ingredients and decide what best suits their pet because we are truly independent and want to offer good quality in everything we sell."

The friendly atmosphere makes it the obvious place for new pet owners to come for a chat, and the delivery service is particularly helpful for customers who may not find it easy to reach the shop in person. "I think the personal touch is what has helped us thrive," says Graham. "Pets are part of the family and knowing we offer the best gives people confidence."

Chapter three

Puddings

This chapter includes doughnuts from Sierra Leone and pavlova from New Zealand, along with an assortment of regional British classics. Sweet sensations include tarts from Manchester, Yorkshire, Bedfordshire and Derbyshire; marmalade from Dundee; cakes unique to Hampshire, Hereford and Hertfordshire; and traditional favourites from Rutland, Northern Ireland, Worcestershire and Bristol.

Aberdeen buttery

Leading Catering Services James Coombs, Royal Navy

A once loved bakery product from Aberdeen, also known as "Rowies" by the locals, the buttery was a popular fisherman's snack and was a vast improvement on the unpopular hard biscuits that were issued as standard. A buttery could be taken to sea and wouldn't go hard; the mix of lard and salt meant it was relatively easy to preserve and could keep for up to two weeks. Butteries can be served at breakfast or lunch with either sweet or savoury items (traditionally, toppings must be spread on the flat side) or can be enjoyed instead of a bread roll with a bowl of soup, but be warned, they are fatty – very fatty!

Aberdeen

**Preparation time: 30 minutes plus
  2 hours proving and resting
Cooking time: 30 minutes**

Makes 16

INGREDIENTS

500g strong plain flour,
  plus extra flour for dusting
7g (1 sachet) fast-action dried yeast
  or 14g fresh yeast
1 tbsp soft light brown sugar
1 tbsp sea salt flakes
350ml room temperature water
Oil for greasing
275g butter
100g lard
Jam and butter for the filling

METHOD

- Sieve the flour into a mixing bowl and add the dried yeast, sugar and salt; if using fresh yeast mix with a little of the room temperature water, set aside until frothy and add with the rest of the water (see below).
- Make a well in the centre of the flour mix and gradually add the water (and yeast mix if using fresh) and mix until it comes together as a soft dough; you might not need to use all of the water.
- Lightly flour a worktop and knead the dough for 8–10 minutes, or until smooth and elastic.
- Place the kneaded dough into a clean, greased bowl, cover with clingfilm and set aside in a warm place to prove for one hour, or until it has doubled in size.
- While the dough is proving, cream together the butter and lard until well blended.
- Divide the fat mixture into four equal portions.
- Once the dough has proved, knead it for a further minute or two then roll out into a 40cm x 20cm rectangle of about 1cm in thickness.
- Move the dough so that the shortest edge is facing you.
- Spread one portion of the butter and lard mixture over two thirds of the dough, fold the remaining third over onto the fat then fold in half (you will have 2 layers of fat and three layers of dough).
- Repeat this rolling and folding process three more times until you have used up all of the fat mix, chilling the dough in the fridge for 20 minutes each time.
- Preheat the oven to 200°C.
- Cut the dough into 16 equal-sized pieces and roll each piece into a round or flat bun shape.
- Place the rolls on a lightly oiled baking tray, ensuring there is enough space in between them to rise, and leave for 45 minutes, or until they have doubled in size then cook in the preheated oven for 15–18 minutes, until golden brown and cooked through.
- Transfer to a wire rack to cool then serve, still warm, with butter and jam.

Marion Patterson

Marion Patterson, nee Chalmers, was born in Aberdeen on 26 August 1911. She spent her early years in Toronto, Canada before moving back to Aberdeen with her Dundee-born husband, Guthrie Patterson, and their two-year-old son Douglas in August 1939. On the outbreak of war, Marion enlisted as an ambulance driver to aid the war effort. She revelled in her role but, like many other parents in city centres across the UK, she was concerned about the effects of the war on her son so she made the difficult decision to send Douglas to live with her mother in Canada while she remained in Scotland.

In 1942, Marion became a Senior Fire Guard. While on duty in August that year, attending a burning building, she heard frantic cries from people trapped inside. With little regard for her own safety, she heroically burrowed into the burning building and located a trapped sailor. Using some loose timber as a lever, she lifted the burning wreckage sufficiently to free the trapped sailor's legs. After calling for help, a rope was lowered to them which she tied to the injured sailor, enabling her to get him out just before the building collapsed.

News of her courageous deed soon reached King George VI and she was invited to Buckingham Palace on 12 February 1943 where she became the first Senior Fire Guard to receive the George Medal for civilian gallantry. Marion was also told that she could visit Balmoral Castle as often as she wished for the remainder of her life, although it's unclear if she ever took up that offer. The King also commissioned the Scots artist Robert Sivell to paint her portrait (pictured, right), showing her standing in a bomb-damaged building. Originally on display at London's National Gallery, it now hangs in the Imperial War Museum, while a replica is in the Ottawa Canadian War Museum.

Marion was awarded another five medals during the war for her actions as a civil defence fire guard. After the war, she and her husband joined their son in Canada to raise their family. She enjoyed travelling, returning to Scotland and England numerous times until her death in 1993. Marion epitomises the local hero, selflessly risking her life for the benefit of her city and its occupants. Her medals, and a black-and-white sketch of Sivell's painting, are on display in Aberdeen Art Gallery.

Written by Kim Beechey

"With little regard for her own safety, she heroically burrowed into the burning building and located a trapped sailor"

Eton mess

Lance Corporal Lewis Smith, Army

Eton Mess is a traditional British cold dessert that dates back to 1893. It is generally accepted that it originated at Eton College, where it is still served during the tea break of the school's annual cricket match against Harrow. It was initially made with strawberries or other summer berries and mixed with cream or ice cream – the meringue is a later addition that gives a great texture to this light summer dessert. Quick and easy to make (especially if you use ready-made meringues), Eton mess is a real crowd pleaser.

Vegetarian, gluten-free
Preparation time: 25 minutes
Cooking time: 1 hour

Serves 6

INGREDIENTS

For the meringue
3 egg whites
1 pinch of salt
175g caster sugar

To assemble
500g strawberries, hulled; half chopped
  and half quartered
2 tbsp icing sugar
500ml double cream, well chilled
2 tsp vanilla extract

METHOD

To make the meringues
• Preheat the oven to 140°C and line a tray with baking parchment.
• Clean out a glass bowl and dry the inside completely ensuring any water or residue are removed and, in a stand mixer, whisk the egg whites with a pinch of salt until soft peaks start to form.
• Gradually add the sugar, whisking continuously for about 5 minutes until the meringue is thick with stiff peaks.
• Spoon mounds of the mixture onto the baking parchment and bake on the bottom shelf of the oven for 1 hour until the meringues are completely hard; ideally turn off the oven and leave the meringues in the oven to completely dry out overnight.
• Take the meringues out of the oven and place somewhere cool and dry.

To assemble
• Place the chopped strawberries in a blender or food processor with 1 tablespoon of the icing sugar, blend to a smooth sauce and set aside.
• Whip the cream, the remaining icing sugar and the vanilla extract in a bowl until soft peaks are just starting to form; be careful at this stage to not over-whip the cream as you want to keep the dessert light.
• Break the meringues into small pieces, place them into a large mixing bowl, add the quartered strawberries and gently fold in the cream.
• Fold two tablespoons of the strawberry sauce into the mix to create a marbled appearance.
• Divide the mix between six glasses or bowls, spoon the remaining strawberry sauce over the top and serve immediately.

Wally Harris MM

Born in London in 1921, Walter "Wally" Harris joined the Territorial Army (TA) as a craftsman aged 18 on 14 April 1939 and was one of the first soldiers to join the Royal Electrical and Mechanical Engineers (REME) on its formation in 1942. He was among 156,000 troops sent to Normandy on 6 June 1944 as part of the largest amphibious assault in history.

During the D-Day landings, Harris's fitter section had stopped to fit a replacement suspension wheel to a Sexton artillery vehicle in the village of Mons-en-Pévèle, when they were ordered to rejoin the main battery immediately. While running through the village, Harris saw a German tracked vehicle towing an 88mm flak gun, so he rushed back to get help.

As the main battery was busy covering the advancing troops, Harris had been instructed to take the anti-tank gun off the tank. He made the quick decision to instead cannibalise an M1919 Browning machine gun they had salvaged from a drowned Sherman tank during the initial D-Day landings. His colleague Corporal Swann immediately offered to assist. Harris carried the Browning as they backtracked through the village, watching for the enemy. After taking cover in the grass on high ground he opened fire on the enemy, some of whom immediately fell while others took cover. He then fired at the tracked vehicle carrying the ammo for the 88mm gun. It exploded.

The German troops immediately started to fire back. As Harris and Swann returned fire, more Germans started to appear. Harris, now standing, was pointing his gun at the German soldiers, who raised their hands and surrendered. Harris and Corporal Swann hurried back to their vehicle and set off for Brussels, in high spirits. For his bravery, Harris was awarded a Military Medal – although, when notified of this, he initially thought the letter was a summons to face charges for taking the Browning!

In 2009, Harris was awarded the freedom of the City of London, and in 2012 his story was made into a short TV film, *Above And Beyond: The Craftsman*. He remained an Honorary Mess Member of the REME until his death in June 2014, following which he was given full military honours, including a three-volley salute outside REME Corps and Garrison Church. Today, the Harris MM Warrant Officers' and Sergeants' Mess at MOD Lyneham is named in his honour.

Written by Captain Steve Blanks, Army

"Harris made the quick decision to cannibalise a Browning machine gun they had salvaged from a drowned Sherman tank during the initial D-Day landings"

Devonshire white-pot

Leading Catering Services Emma Keitch, Royal Navy

It is said that the name "white-pot" was given to this pudding due to its glistening white colour when going into the oven. Recipes for white-pot appear in most 17th century cookbooks; "pot" means "pudding" in Devonshire dialect and, over time, the pudding has also become connected to Devon in name. It would appear that, over the years, rice-based puddings have had applications other than just that of sustenance; the ancient Romans used rice pudding to settle an upset stomach and archaeologists have found evidence of a sticky rice, sugar and blood mixture being used as mortar on 2,000-year-old buildings. There are two versions of the Devonshire white-pot, one made with bread (an early form of bread and butter pudding) and the other made with short-grain rice. My recipe is based on the rice version and I've added apples in homage to the ancient Devon orchards.

Vegetarian, gluten-free
Preparation time: 15 minutes
Cooking time: 2 hours

Serves 4

INGREDIENTS

10g butter
300ml double cream
210ml whole milk
40g sugar
1 tsp sea salt
1 tsp rose water
1 medium egg
2 medium egg yolks
1½ tsp ground cinnamon
75g pudding rice
30g apples, peeled and cut
  into 1cm dice
20g currants
15g flaked almonds
2 tsp caster sugar
1 tsp water

METHOD

- Preheat the oven to 150°C and grease an ovenproof baking dish with the butter.
- Heat the cream, milk, sugar, sea salt and rose water in a saucepan over a medium heat, stirring continuously, until the sugar has completely dissolved then simmer for 3 or 4 minutes; remove from the heat and set aside.
- Mix together the whole egg, egg yolks and ground cinnamon until thoroughly combined then slowly whisk in the milk and cream mix; stir in the pudding rice, apples and currants ensuring they are fully coated.
- Pour the mix into the buttered baking dish and bake in the middle of the preheated oven for 2 hours; cover the dish with tinfoil if the top starts to get too dark.
- Meanwhile, heat a frying pan over a medium heat, add the flaked almonds and toast, stirring constantly, until golden brown.
- Once toasted move the almonds to the centre of the frying pan, sprinkle over the sugar, allow to melt slightly then add the water to form a syrup.
- Ensure all almonds are coated in the syrup, remove from the heat and place in a bowl to set.
- Once the pudding is cooked, sprinkle the crunchy almonds over the top to serve.

Chief Petty Officer Kate Nesbitt MC

Born 21 April 1988, Kate Nesbitt was raised in Whitleigh, Plymouth, into a military family. Her father was in the Royal Marines for 22 years, reaching the rank of colour sergeant, while her two brothers are also in the Armed Forces. After leaving school, she joined the Royal Navy in 2005, before undertaking her foundation medical training at the Royal Marines base in Arbroath, Scotland. She was posted to the Commando Training Centre in Lympstone, Devon and, on graduation, embarked on the Type 42 Destroyer HMS *Nottingham* before being deployed to Operation Herrick in October 2008, alongside 3 Commando Brigade.

It was in Afghanistan that Nesbitt demonstrated her courage and heroism. On 12 March 2009, her unit was patrolling in Nawa, near Lashkar Gah in Helmand Province, securing the area for the upcoming Afghan elections. During this patrol, mid-afternoon, Nesbitt's unit was ambushed by Taliban fighters and one of her patrol, Lance Corporal John List, was shot in the face.

Nesbitt, a 5ft Royal Navy medic, sprinted the 60–70 metres across open ground, with little regard for her own safety, to attend to him. "I just thought the quicker I got to him, the more chance I had to save his life," she said. "It was adrenaline." She found Lance Corporal List grievously injured with wounds from a bullet that had gone through his lip, ruptured his jaw and exited through his neck. She quickly stemmed the flow of blood with her bare hands, preventing him from bleeding, and ultimately saving his life. Bullets continued to tear up the ground around her as she worked to stabilise him before he could be evacuated. Her actions saved his life that day.

Kate was awarded the Military Cross by the Prince of Wales on 27 November 2009 at Buckingham Palace, the first woman in the Royal Navy to receive the award. Her citation recognised that "under pressure, her commitment and courage were inspirational and made the difference between life and death". Kate continues to tell her story to new recruits, both as a warning of the dangers they may face and to inspire the courage they may one day have to call upon in their duties.

Written by Lieutenant Dom Raeyen, Royal Navy

"*I just thought the quicker I got to him, the more chance I had to save his life. It was adrenaline*"

All this and Devon too

Sandridge Barton vineyard sits in a south-facing bowl on the edge of the River Dart, and its limestone ridge enables it to add a hint of Burgundy to its quality English wines

www.sandridgebarton.com

Sandridge Barton Wines may appear to be a new face on the rapidly expanding UK wine scene, but this Devon-based vineyard and winery has four decades of history and wine-making experience. The name Sandridge Barton marks a new era for the celebrated Dart Valley winery, Sharpham Wine, which has literally moved across the River Dart to create a new state-of-the-art winery, visitor centre and café. It sits next to the 32-acre Sandridge Barton vineyard which has been producing wine for over a decade.

"Despite the new name we are still the home of Sharpham Wine," says Duncan Schwab, the CEO and Head Winemaker. "We use the same crew, we grow the same grapes, operate the same machinery and we are very much in the same tradition of making wine from the Dart Valley but with some brand-new equipment and some exciting developments. Limestone is the soil of Burgundy and, rather excitingly, we have a limestone ridge, so new plantings this year will mean we can be the UK's answer to Burgundy." The team has already picked up multiple high-profile wine awards including, in

2020, Gold Medals for its Pinot Noir and Bacchus at the prestigious Wine GB Awards and best UK Traditional Method Sparkling Wine for its Sparkling Pink 2016 at the Bollicini del Mondo.

"Along with the longer ripening season, we have very iron-rich soil in the Devon region, with quite a bit of volcanic soil which imparts amazing flavours into the wine," explains Duncan. "We grow the very best grapes suited to the terroir and treat them kindly and gently to extract the best fruit flavours. Our wines are well known throughout the South West and the move gives us the opportunity to expand our production internationally, putting English wine firmly on the map."

The team already produces both natural and vegan wines, but this new stage means that Sandridge Barton can implement even more eco-friendly methods. "It is something we have been meaning to do for a while," says Duncan. "We can now be more environmentally conscious in growing the grapes and increasing the bio-diversity in our vines while still producing quality English wines in the most sustainable way."

Moving spirits

As well as creating its own unique grappas, dappas, devoncellos and sloe gins, Devon Distillery invites customers to create their very own bespoke gin, rum or vodka using their favourite botanicals

devondistillery.com

"Personalised spirit production should be accessible to anyone," says Cosmo Caddy, owner of Devon Distillery. "From a small village pub to an individual with an event, we want everyone to experience the joy and pride that comes with creating their own drink."

Devon Distillery is the first distillery of its kind in the UK. It produces bespoke, small-batch gin, rum, vodka and grappa, each one using local ingredients, as well as its own range of unique spirits, such as Dappa, Devoncello and SloeD Gin. Cosmo's connection to the alcohol industry goes back as far as he can remember. "My grandfather planted Sharpham Vineyard in 1982," says Cosmo. "One of only a few English vineyards at the time. I began picking and crushing grapes when I was four and spent my childhood going to fairs and markets."

Cosmo's first creation was a spirit inspired by an Italian grape-based digestif, grappa, which he rechristened as "Dappa". Unique to Devon, it went on to win several awards including a Great Taste Award in 2020 and an International Wine & Spirit Competition Quality Award. "I was taught how to make grappa by Marco, a ninth-generation distiller from Italy," says Cosmo. "He said that all the levers we pull and push while distilling the spirit, they are meant to be pushed with the feet. This means you can have a glass of champagne in your hands while you work."

A moment of inspiration saw Devon Distillery create a brand-new market in the spirits industry. "My sister got engaged and unfortunately wasn't a fan of Dappa," says Cosmo. "So I couldn't just give her a bottle. As an alternative, I decided to create a unique gin for the wedding day. I thought, why not take a still to the wedding and make the drinks there? She put some petals from her bouquet in with the botanicals and we distilled and bottled it there and then."

This was the beginning of "Still On The Move", a beautifully restored VW pickup van with full working distillery attached. "We want everyone to bring an ingredient that's special to them," says Cosmo. "All botanicals are welcome as long as they're not poisonous! It's a great way to bottle a moment in time – it can be sealed within the spirit forever. Or drunk on the night. We suggest a bit of both."

Devon Distillery has now opened its doors to anyone passionate about producing their own brand of gin, vodka or rum. "Working with the client to create their own recipe is a rewarding experience," says Cosmo. "Everything from the tastes, ingredients, bottles and labels can be customised. We use a collection of miniature stills and hold development days with customers to create their bespoke spirits. Members of the party can spend the day experimenting with us until they have something special. This is then scaled to as many litres as they need."

Clients have ranged from small village pubs to the Armed Forces. "The Royal Navy commissioned a Decommissioning Gin for HMS *Ocean*," says Cosmo. "Samples were made at the distillery and shipped out to the Caribbean during a hurricane – the ship's crew were rolling in high seas while trying the gins! By the time the vessel docked, we had made a bottling of their favourite flavours. A few weeks later we met them on the deck of the carrier for the official handover. Bottle number one went to Her Majesty – navy strength, of course."

Let them eat cake

Using elaborate ingredients and a sense of showmanship,
Georgia Green creates unique, opulent desserts for budding
cakemakers and global A-list celebs alike

www.georgiascakes.com

When it comes to cakes, Georgia Green, the founder of Georgia's Cakes, has every base covered. From baking opulent desserts for A-list celebrities to running sell-out workshops, while hosting a popular YouTube channel, she has become one of the world's most influential cake-makers.

"My cakes aren't, let's say, normal," laughs Georgia (pictured, right). "They're quite out-there and use a lot of different decorations. Things like chocolate drips, salted caramel popcorn, macarons and edible flowers." Georgia studied patisserie at the renowned culinary school Le Cordon Bleu, so her cakes don't just look stunning, they taste it too.

Her eye-catching creations led to her products being displayed in Harrods, and she has created cakes for supermodel Cara Delevingne and pop star Rihanna. "Someone found a blurry photo of Rihanna cutting into a cake at the anniversary of her Savage X Fenty lingerie label and sent it to me, asking if it was mine," says Georgia. "It was amazing that someone was able to see it and think 'That's a Georgia's Cake'!"

Following countless requests for cake tutorials, Georgia launched her YouTube channel in 2017, and her approachable style of teaching has earned it millions of views. "As my YouTube grew, I was asked to do a lot more in-person workshops, and I found myself enjoying those more than selling cakes to customers," says Georgia. Teaching offers soon came from all over the world, from places as far afield as New York, France, Australia and India.

Now based in both Tel Aviv and London, Georgia has shifted focus towards these workshops, setting up a baking workshop studio called Baker Street TLV with a fellow cake decorator. "There's no better feeling than giving a customer a beautiful cake and seeing the look on their face, but I fell in love with the idea of teaching," she says. "I love being surrounded by different people in the workshops and having a different experience each time."

She's been dubbed a "cake influencer", though Georgia politely bats aside the term. "My philosophy is to keep it real," she says, with a grin. "And that's personality-wise and ingredients-wise. I teach to the highest quality, but my cakes and I are always down to earth."

Bristol buns

Catering Services Darren Harris, Royal Navy

Bristol

Originally known as Colston buns after the controversial merchant, philanthropist and slave-trader Edward Colston – who is said to have created the initial recipe – Bristol buns were traditionally given out to children from impoverished backgrounds supported by charitable organisations in the Bristol area. The buns came in two sizes, the "dinner plate", which would be split into eight sections and shared with the family, and the smaller "ha'penny staver" bun, which was eaten to stave off hunger. In recent years, as the world has become aware of the extent of Colston's involvement in the slave trade, they are now generally referred to as "Bristol buns" and can still be found for sale in a select few local bakeries in and around the city. The recipe has been adopted by other towns and cities around the UK and adapted to create their own local buns, such as the caraway-scented Bath bun.

Preparation time: 2 hours,
 including proving time
Cooking time: 20–25 minutes

Makes 8

INGREDIENTS

For the buns
1 orange, juiced
30g dried apricots, finely chopped
75g mixed dried fruit
50g chopped mixed peel
450g strong white flour, plus extra
 for dusting
¾ tsp of salt
7g (1 sachet) fast-action yeast
50g golden caster sugar
1 tsp ground cinnamon
1 tsp ground ginger
½ tsp mixed spice
½ lemon, zested
250ml warm milk
40g unsalted butter, melted
1 egg, beaten

For the glaze
1 tbsp milk
2 tbsp caster sugar

METHOD

• Pour the orange juice into a small saucepan and bring to a simmer; meanwhile place the chopped dried apricots, mixed dried fruit and mixed peel in a mixing bowl.

• Pour the simmering orange juice over the dried fruits, mix well then leave to macerate for 20 minutes; strain (reserving any juice that hasn't been absorbed by the fruit) and set aside to cool.

• Sift the flour into a bowl; add the salt, yeast, sugar, spices and lemon zest.

• Whisk together the warm milk, melted butter, beaten egg and reserved orange juice; stir into the dry ingredients and mix well to form a dough.

• Turn the dough out onto a lightly floured worktop and knead for about 8 minutes until smooth and elastic; add the macerated dried fruit and continue to knead for a further 2 minutes.

• Place the dough into a bowl, cover with clingfilm or a damp cloth and leave to prove for about 45–60 minutes until the dough has doubled in size.

• Turn the dough out onto a lightly floured work surface and gently knock back.

• Preheat the oven to 180°C. Lightly butter a baking tray, or line with a sheet of baking parchment.

• Shape the dough into a smooth round ball, place on the baking tray and gently press down on the top to flatten slightly, creating a thick disc; score the top with a sharp knife with four lines to mark out eight equal-sized wedges. To make the ha'penny buns, divide the dough into eight equal-sized pieces, roll into balls, place on the floured baking sheet and flatten slightly.

• Cover the tray loosely with a damp cloth and allow to prove for 30 minutes.

• Bake in the preheated oven for 30–35 minutes (20–25 minutes for the ha'penny buns), until golden-brown on the top and cooked through.

• While the buns are cooking, warm the milk and sugar for the glaze in a small saucepan, stirring frequently, until the sugar has completely dissolved.

• Remove the buns from the oven, brush liberally with the glaze then transfer to a wire rack to cool; when ready to serve, break or cut the loaf into eight individual buns.

Squadron Leader George Leonard "Johnny" Johnson MBE, DFM

George Leonard Johnson was born on 25 November 1921 in Hameringham, Lincolnshire, the sixth and last child born to Mary Ellen and Charles Johnson. His mother died when he was three and, after growing up in poverty, he was sent to the Lord Wandsworth Agricultural College in Long Sutton, Hampshire, aged 11. He left school in 1939 to work as a park keeper in Basingstoke.

Known as Leonard to his family, he was nicknamed "Johnny" when he joined the RAF, a name that stuck. He volunteered in June 1940 as a navigator but was selected for pilot training before opting to become an air gunner. After a handful of operations he was retrained at RAF Fulbeck as a bomb aimer. He went on to complete a further 18 operations, ending his first full tour with 97 Squadron.

In March 1943, Johnson (pictured, far left) was selected for the 617 Squadron under the command of Wing Commander Guy Gibson. He began a rigorous six-week training programme to carry out Operation Chastise – a daring night raid to destroy three dams in the Ruhr Valley to disable Hitler's industrial heartland. On the evening of 16 May 1943, 19 specially fitted Lancaster Bombers took off from RAF Scampton, each carrying Barnes Wallace's famous "Bouncing Bomb". Johnny's Lancaster and others were detailed to attack the Sorpe Dam. Flying at over 200mph and at no higher than tree-top level to avoid enemy detection, they reached their target and released their payload at 12.45am having spent nearly an hour doing aborted dummy runs over the target. The drop was accurate but Sorpe was too solid to be damaged. 617 Squadron did, however, successfully breach two other dams – the Eder and the Möhne – which succeeded in damaging German production.

Only 11 Lancasters returned that night; 53 of the Dambusters lost their lives while three were captured. Johnson's actions earned him the Distinguished Flying Medal, and he was commissioned in November 1943, finally leaving the RAF as a Squadron Leader in 1962. He embarked on a teaching career before he and his wife Gwyn (who he met while training in 1941) retired to Torquay. Johnny now lives in Westbury-on-Trim, Bristol. In 2015 he was awarded the Lord Mayor of Bristol's Medal and in 2017 an MBE. "Glad to see the Dambusters are still here," said the Queen as she made the presentation. He was given an honorary membership of the RAF Club in Piccadilly, and in 2018 had a GWR train named after him. Johnson is the last surviving member of the Dambusters.

Written by Sergeant Paul Jon Higgins, RAF

"Only 11 Lancasters returned that night; 53 of the Dambusters lost their lives while three were captured"

Good sports

CSSC Sports & Leisure has been helping civil service and public sector workers enjoy the social and physical benefits of sport, leisure and exercise for 100 years

www.cssc.co.uk

The importance of wellbeing has come into sharp focus of late, especially around employees' health and happiness. For the Civil Service Sports Council (CSSC) wellbeing has been at the centre of its ethos since its conception, 100 years ago, and continues to be its driving force in looking after its members.

"We are a not-for-profit member organisation that provides sports, health, leisure and retail opportunities for public sector workers," says CSSC Group Chief Executive, Simon Lee. "We celebrate our 100th anniversary in November and we continue to live the values of our founders, of using sport, competition and camaraderie to unite and celebrate the public sector."

CSSC has always had close ties with the Armed Forces, with "Representative Sports" being played between the forces and civil service departments. This relationship remains strong, with CSSC signing up to the Armed Forces Covenant in 2019. CSSC provided services throughout the Second World War and, in 1946, its sports ground in Chiswick was visited by King George VI and Queen Elizabeth.

Some CSSC athletes have been world-beating in their field. Middle-distance runner Joy Jordan was the first world record holder the civil service ever had, setting a new 800 metres record in 1960. In 1981, a young Linford Christie represented the Inland Revenue at the CSSC Festival of Sport. CSSC also has strong links with the Civil Service Football Club (CSFC), dating back to 1863: CSFC is now the sole surviving member of the 12 clubs that formed the Football Association. In 2013 CSSC set up a football match at Buckingham Palace, hosted by the Duke of Cambridge, to mark the 150th anniversary of both the CSFC and the FA.

To reflect the growing and wide variety of interests, in 1995 for its 75th anniversary, CSSC was rebranded as CSSC Sports & Leisure. It now has a membership in excess of 150,000, all of whom can enjoy more than 2,200 different sports, savings, days out, experiences, entertainment, clubs, activities and opportunities.

"Whatever your interests are," says Simon, "whatever sport appeals to you, whatever leisure activities you are passionate about, wherever you may live, the unique part of CSSC is our community and the number of ways we help our members to explore their hobbies, live their best life and give back to those who give so much of themselves."

CSSC may be a national organisation but its real heart is at the local level, where volunteers in "Area Associations" hold events for regional members. "To help bring communities together and celebrate our centenary, we've planned a series of events throughout 2021 and beyond, locally and nationally," says Simon. "We were founded on the spirit of togetherness and unity, and that's where our principles will always stand."

As the civil service moves towards working in local hubs throughout the UK, CSSC is using its established network and expertise to support that change. Everyone who joins CSSC is either a civil servant, a public-sector worker or a member of the Armed Forces. "Our members spend their days looking after people," says Wendy Eley, CSSC's Group Operations Director. "And, by taking care of those who look after others, we are all helping the nation to thrive. We like to think of ourselves as the people who look after the people who look after people."

Bedfordshire

Chocolate "toothpaste" tart

Senior Aircraftsman John Britten, RAF

This unusual Bedfordshire delicacy is basically a sweet-pastry tart filled with a chocolate mousse, topped with whipped cream. Named chocolate "toothpaste" because of its creamy yet grainy texture, it's not confirmed when or where this tasty pastry popped up. However, when questioned, many Bedfordians reminisce fondly about their school dinners and it is still found in some smaller bakeries in and around Bedford to this day. Inspired by my love for chocolate tarts and the dish's affectionate nickname, my interpretation provides a richer, but equally sweet and simple, tart that mimics the minty freshness of toothpaste.

Preparation time: 30 minutes
 plus 45 minutes setting time

Serves 12

INGREDIENTS

For the base
430g dark chocolate digestives
150g butter, melted

For the ganache
100g hazelnuts
360g dark chocolate, finely
 chopped into small pieces
250ml double cream
25g unsalted butter, at
 room temperature
1 tsp peppermint extract

For the garnish
200ml double cream
Peppermint extract
10g toasted hazelnuts
 (reserved from the filling)
Mint leaves

Bedfordshire: Local hero

Observer Captain Joyce Shrubbs MBE

Despite being crucial to the defence of Britain during the Second World War, little is mentioned of the Royal Observer Corps (ROC). Consisting of a core of civilian volunteers, trained and led by a small cadre of full-time officers, the ROC wore similar uniform to the RAF and was responsible for the visual detection, identification, tracking and reporting of aircraft over Britain.

Born in 1927, Joyce Shrubbs was inspired to join the military after seeing her brother, who was serving in the Royal Navy, shot down by a German bomber while playing a game of football against the Army near the white cliffs of Dover. Joyce was only 13 at the time. Rather than waiting until she was 18 to join the Women's Auxiliary Air Force, she spotted an advert for the Royal Observer Corps, which would take girls aged 17, leading to her change in career path in 1944.

Throughout the war, Shrubbs mainly served in the Group Headquarters in Bedford, and was responsible for plotting the course of both allied and "hostile" aircraft over the airspace of the UK, including the infamous V1 "doodlebug" flying bombs. After the war, following a brief period of disbandment in 1945, the ROC was revived but with a different goal and change of command, now working directly for the Home Office. Its mission was now providing a service that it hoped would never be used – to report and measure active fall-out in the event of a nuclear attack.

Shrubbs served as the Group Commandant in Bedford during this period, rising in both responsibility and rank until she was in charge of the airspace of approximately a fifth of the country, and reached the rank of Observer Captain (Group Captain equivalent). She served in the ROC for 48 years until March 1994, aged 67, becoming the only female officer in the history of the ROC to achieve the rank of Observer Captain. As a result of her work for the RBL she was awarded the National Certificate of Appreciation, the RBL's highest award, in 2015. Furthermore, as the President of the ROC Association she was made an MBE. Shrubbs continued to work in the farming industry in Bedfordshire, retiring only recently.

Written by Sergeant Scott Hill, RAF (1st RBL Serving Ambassador) and Sharon Turton, Membership Support Officer for Beds and Herts RBL

METHOD

To make the base

- Crush the dark chocolate digestives into fine crumbs either by putting them into a food bag and crushing with a rolling pin or pulsing in a food processor.
- Transfer the biscuit crumbs to a mixing bowl and mix with the melted butter until thoroughly combined.
- Spoon the mixture into a lightly buttered loose-bottomed tart tin and spread over the base and up the sides, making sure to press it down and into all the edges, until you have a thin, even layer over the base and sides of the tin; place in the fridge for about 30 minutes to set.

For the ganache filling

- Place the hazelnuts into a food processor and pulse until they're coarsely chopped into small pieces; alternatively crush them with a pestle and mortar.
- Lightly toast the chopped hazelnuts in a small frying pan over a medium heat until they're lightly coloured then tip them onto a plate and set aside to cool.
- Tip 90g of the toasted hazelnuts into a large mixing bowl with the dark chocolate; set the reserved 10g of toasted hazelnuts aside for the garnish.
- Pour the double cream into a saucepan, add the peppermint extract and then bring to a simmer; taste the cream mixture and add a little more peppermint extract if necessary.
- Pour the hot cream onto the dark chocolate and hazelnuts; allow this to stand for 20 seconds then add the butter and gently stir until the mixture is combined.
- Quickly but carefully pour the ganache into the set base; if the mixture is too stiff, tilt the base slightly to fill the whole tart evenly then leave it to set in the fridge for about 15 minutes.

To garnish and serve

- Once set, whip the cream with a dash of peppermint extract and pipe or spread onto the tart.
- Remove the tart from the tin (this will take patience and a gentle hand).
- Finally, sprinkle with the reserved toasted hazelnuts and decorate with mint leaves.

GLUTEN-FREE ALTERNATIVE

- Exchange the digestives for a gluten-free biscuit; preferably with chocolate as it helps the base to set and harden.

Steep by steep

Family-run Hampshire company Ahmad Tea has achieved international success, combining a passion for great blends with commitment to community values

www.ahmadtea.com

When it comes to tea, family business Ahmad Tea is a textbook British success story. Starting life as a small teashop in Southampton in 1986, it's now one of the biggest tea companies in the world, with a full-flavoured presence in more than 80 countries worldwide. Despite this global success, the man who set up that teashop 35 years ago still pays a vital, hands-on role.

"We're proud that our chairman Rahim Afshar is still the head tea-taster," says Tracey Wakelin, Head of Global Marketing. "He comes in at least once a week to taste the tea – his promise is that he would never sell anything he wouldn't drink at home. This means every cup of tea is tasted seven times before he approves it for sale."

This dedication to quality means Ahmad Tea has won many times over at the world's largest and most trusted food and drink awards, and its name has become a byword for quality. "One of our mantras is 'the highest quality tea at an affordable price'," says Tracey. "And over the last five years, we've won a number of Great Taste awards, which gives us the right to call ourselves a Great Taste Producer."

Ahmad Tea is also streets ahead when it comes to the environment and charity work. "The family don't talk much about it publicly – but corporate responsibility is in our DNA," says Tracey. "Everything we do is based around giving back, we dedicate a large percentage of our profits to charitable and sustainability causes, encouraging our international partners to do the same." This also includes a clean-water project, through a partnership with Oxfam and scholarships for young people in countries such as Niger, carefully set up so they can go ahead with or without the involvement of Ahmad Tea.

Ahmad Tea might not have been around quite as long as the Royal British Legion but they share similar community-oriented principles, providing valuable help to the areas where they work. "We've been on an incredible journey over the last 35 years," says Tracey. "Every community that supported us, we've supported back; it's a beautiful brand with a beautiful story."

Cambridge burnt cream with poached plum compote

Senior Aircraftsman John Jones, RAF

The origins of this popular dessert have, for many years, been contested by England, France and Spain, all three countries claiming that they were the first to produce – respectively – Cambridge (or Trinity) burnt cream, crème brûlée or crema Catalana. It would appear that, after more than three centuries, the jury is still out. My version is based on Trinity College's burnt cream recipe using regional, seasonal produce.

Preparation time: 45 minutes
Cooking time: 30–45 minutes

Serves 4

INGREDIENTS

For the burnt cream
1 vanilla pod
9 egg yolks
350ml double cream
120g caster sugar

For the plum compote
300ml boiling water
150g caster sugar
500g plums, halved and stones removed
2 cinnamon sticks

For the tuile (langue de chat) biscuits
100g plain flour
100g caster sugar
3 egg whites

METHOD

To make the burnt cream
• Preheat the oven to 110°C.
• Split the vanilla pod lengthways and scrape out the seeds with the blade of a small knife.
• Whisk the egg yolks and sugar until pale.
• Pour the cream into a saucepan, add the scraped vanilla pod and seeds, place over a moderate heat and bring to a simmer; remove from the heat and allow to stand for 10 minutes to infuse.
• Pour a quarter of the infused cream over the egg and sugar mix, stir well with a wooden spoon (avoid whisking the mix to prevent froth settling on the top of the custard), then stir the egg mix into the remaining hot cream.
• Transfer to a clean pan and cook gently over a low heat, stirring constantly until the mixture starts to thicken and coats the back of a spoon.
• Strain the mix through a fine sieve and pour into ramekins.
• Transfer the ramekins to a roasting tray, with the base lined with a folded tea towel to prevent direct heat, and pour in enough boiling water to come half way up the sides of the ramekins.
• Place in the preheated oven and cook for approximately 30–45 minutes until barely set and with a slight wobble in the centre when gently shaken from side to side.
• Remove the ramekins from the water bath and allow to cool at room temperature before chilling in the refrigerator.
• Cover the top of each set cream with a thin, even layer of the remaining caster sugar; use a blow torch to caramelise the sugar then set aside until the melted sugar has hardened.

To make the plum compote
- Pour the boiling water into a saucepan, place on a high heat, add the sugar and allow the mixture to bubble for around 30–40 seconds before adding the halved plums and cinnamon sticks.
- Simmer over a low-medium heat for 10 minutes, remove from the heat, set aside to cool then chill for 20 minutes.
- Remove the cinnamon sticks then pulse to a coarse purée in a food processor.

To make the biscuits
- Preheat the oven to 160°C.
- Whisk together the flour, sugar and egg whites to a smooth paste.
- Line a baking tray with a silicone non-stick mat or a piece of baking parchment.
- If you have a stencil you can use this for the shape of the tuiles, if not place a spoonful of the mix onto the mat and flatten and spread to an elongated oblong shape with the back of the spoon or small palette knife to a thickness of about 2mm.
- Bake for about 8 minutes until golden brown around the edges.
- Once the biscuits are cool enough to hold their shape transfer them with a palette knife to a wire rack to cool then store in an airtight container until needed.

To serve
- Serve the burnt creams with the compote and tuile biscuits.

Cambridgeshire: Local hero

Flight Sergeant Charles WH Cox MM

Charles William Hall Cox was born on 3 September 1913 in Cambridgeshire. After completing his education, he joined the RAF and became a specialist in the newly invented radar, serving in various coastal units during the Battle of Britain. His skills led to him being summoned by the Air Ministry in February 1942, when Air Commodore Victor Tait, Director of Radar, told Cox that he had been "volunteered for a dangerous mission". He was deployed to C Company 2nd Parachute Battalion to take part in a raid on the French coast to seize components of German radar – codenamed Operation Biting.

Following the increased loss of RAF bombers, British intelligence suspected that the Germans had developed advanced radar capabilities. Leaked German documents, Enigma decryptions and the interrogation of German prisoners showed that high-frequency radar signals were being transmitted from two radar sites, "Freya" and "Wurzburg". It was the latter that Cox and C Company were tasked with infiltrating. Cox, as the top radar specialist with classified knowledge that would prove useful to the Nazis if he were captured, was assigned a "bodyguard" for the operation – though, unbeknown to him, this "bodyguard" was also there to "despatch" Cox in the event of capture.

As C Company and Cox parachuted in, a number of crucial tools were lost or damaged. Cox entered the station with gunfire whizzing past him, having to rip components from the station with whatever tools he could find, including chisels, hammers and crowbars. What would have taken anyone else hours, Cox managed in minutes, and his actions later earned him a Military Medal. During Operation Biting, C Company lost two paratroopers, with another eight wounded and six captured. But it was a huge intelligence success, providing a wealth of information on German radar in the run-up to D-Day. It also highlighted the effectiveness of airborne operations, resulting in the creation of the Parachute Regiment.

Following the war, Cox started a small electrical shop in Wisbech, living in the town until his death in November 1997. His Military Medal is now at the Imperial War Museum in Duxford. In his book on Operation Biting, *Night Raid*, author Taylor Downing explains how Cox wasn't trained for anything like this operation, but he pulled it off. "What he achieved was remarkable," says Downing. "An absolutely brilliant feat."

Written by Lieutenant Terry Griffin, Royal Navy

Jersey wonders

Flight Sergeant Stu Harmer, RAF (retired)

As with many traditional dishes, there are varying opinions on the preparation of Jersey wonders (also known as les mervelles), especially when it comes to flavourings and shape. The most common shape is the simple single twist, as in my recipe below, and the general consensus of opinion appears to be "less is more" when it comes to flavourings, so no spices in the dough, no filling and no sugar coating. Although compared to doughnuts, they are not made with a yeast dough so have a slightly crumbly texture that is more akin to cake than a doughnut. A traditional story is told that the Jersey housewives would make their wonders as the tide was going out as, if they cooked during the incoming tide, the cooking fat (usually lard) would overflow the pan while the wonders were frying.

Channel Islands: Local hero

John Louis "Bonnie" Newton

John Louis "Bonnie" Newton – so named in his early years by a Scottish lady who thought him a particularly "bonnie lad" – was born in Alderney in 1901. From the outset, he took to the sea and was well known as a sailor, fisherman and small-time smuggler; he was physically diminutive, and envied, admired and distrusted for his energy and resourcefulness.

In June 1940, as France was falling, Newton joined the Royal Navy and was soon a leading seaman on a minesweeper in Scapa Flow. Ambrose Sherwell, the Guernsey Procurer, sent a telegram to the Admiralty asking for his release from the Navy as "he was the only man who might be able and ready to smuggle food into the island during the impending German occupation". However, by the time Newton was found, the Channel Islands had fallen.

Newton soon came to the attention of Ian Fleming, who went on to create James Bond. Fleming was working for naval intelligence and immediately recognised Newton as a resourceful and skilled ship's pilot who could navigate the Channel Islands. He recruited him into the Special Operations Executive (SOE) to skipper the French fishing vessel *Mutin* to carry out clandestine missions in France. For the next two years, Newton and his crew went back and forth to German-occupied Brittany, rescuing Allied airmen, landing agents and taking supplies for the French Resistance. In September 1942, Newton was part of the raiding force that spectacularly captured the entire seven-man German crew of Casquets Lighthouse. Later that year he received the Distinguished Service Cross in recognition of his bravery and undaunted devotion to duty.

In December 1942, Newton relocated to the Mediterranean where he set up a new SOE cloak-and-dagger sea-transport service to enemy-occupied France and Corsica, delivering weapons to the French Maquis, Italian Partisans and resistance fighters in Corsica. At the end of the war, the French awarded him the Croix de Guerre and Silver Star for outstanding courage and the Italians awarded him the Italian Star, issued to Partisans and volunteers for liberty.

After the war, Bonnie and his wife Ellen made their home in Guernsey, running a guest house at Les Banques, but the sea was his love. In 1962, he collapsed as he was climbing aboard a motor cruiser and died as he had lived, on board a boat.

Written by Squadron Leader Jon Pullen, RAF (retired)

Preparation time: 20 minutes
Cooking time: 20 minutes

Makes about 20

INGREDIENTS

600g self-raising flour, sifted
1 pinch of salt
100g butter, cut into small dice
200g caster sugar
5 large eggs, beaten
Vegetable oil for deep-frying

METHOD

For the dough
- Sift the flour into a mixing bowl with a pinch of salt, rub in the butter with your fingertips to fine breadcrumbs then mix in the caster sugar.
- Gradually add the eggs and mix to bring the dough together.
- Lightly dust your worktop with flour and knead the dough for a couple of minutes until smooth.

To shape the wonders
- Divide the dough into about 20 even-sized pieces, about 55–60g each, and roll each one into a ball; cover with a tea towel while you shape each one.
- Roll out each ball into a cylinder shape, about 8cm long, between your hands then, on a lightly floured surface, press flat with your palm and fingertips to a flat oval about 10cm long by 6cm wide.
- Cut a slit down the centre of the length of each oval and tuck the top tip of the oval 360° through the slit, pulling through to the other side to make the twist, press down gently with you palm to flatten slightly; repeat with the remaining balls of dough.

To cook
- Heat the vegetable oil in a suitable pan (ensuring there's enough oil to cover the wonders) to 180°C; to test if the oil is hot enough drop in a small piece of bread – it should sizzle and start to brown in a few seconds.
- Deep fry the wonders a few at a time (I cook them in a wok, five at a time), making sure they don't stick together, and turning occasionally for about 4 or 5 minutes until golden brown on each side; drain on kitchen paper to absorb any excess oil.
- Eat the Jersey wonders while they're still warm or store in an airtight container until you're ready to eat them.

Choc therapy

Montezuma's takes inspiration from the elaborate chocolate culture of South America, adding a distinctly British spin and a strong ethical sensibility

www.montezumas.co.uk

Helen and Simon Pattinson co-founded Montezuma's in 2000 after experiencing the chocolate culture of South America. They wanted to create a company that explored great chocolate in a fun and creative way but which had an ethical underpinning in the tradition of great British chocolate companies.

"We are very proud to be a British company making British chocolate, and doing business properly," says Helen. "We're also resolutely ethical in everything, from the sourcing of ingredients – cocoa, vanilla, milk, nuts – to packaging, and we've helped to raise more than £100,000 for a local charity, Children On The Edge."

Montezuma's now has six shops with three more to follow. It continues to develop exciting new flavours, such as Butter Nutter (milk chocolate with a peanut butter truffle centre) and Happiness (milk chocolate with salted caramelised hazelnuts), while hardcore fans adore the Absolute Black: 100 per cent cocoa with no added sugar.

Any of these can be used in Montezuma's unique spin on the quintessential British classic, bread and butter pudding. "I'd recommend using 100g of our 74 per cent Fitzroy organic dark chocolate," says Helen. "After that you'll need 575ml milk, 150ml double cream, 65g butter, 8 slices of bread, 3 eggs, 40g caster sugar, 1tbsp of demerara and 50g of our Smooth Operator milk chocolate.

"Cut the bread into halves or triangles, butter on both sides and place in an greased ovenproof dish, measuring about 20cm x 20cm. Slowly melt the chocolate, milk and cream in a pan. Whisk the eggs and caster sugar into the chocolate mix and pour over the buttered bread. Leave the bread to soak up the mixture for 15 minutes, then sprinkle over the demerara sugar

and chopped-up chocolate pieces. Bake at 160°C for 45–50 minutes – you will get better results if you sit the dish in a big roasting tray filled with hot water. This will help prevent the lovely chocolate custard doing the curdle trick and spoiling the party."

Montezuma's products are available at its own stores as well as in supermarkets, delis and farm shops around the UK, and are also exported to the US, the Middle East, the Far East and Australia. "We try to retain the artisan feel in whatever we do," says Helen. "For us it's all about having interesting flavours, fun ingredients and doing things the right way."

Taking care

From its branches around London, Surrey and Sussex, Carepoint Services delivers a very personal level of care and companionship to clients who live in their own homes

www.carepointservices.co.uk

Few working relationships can be as close as that between a client and their caregiver. That's why staff at Carepoint Services – who look after more than 200 clients around the South East aged 18 and upwards, including ex-military personnel – strive to ensure they match the right client with the right careworker. "If you find somebody you click with, you are more likely to share with them," explains Head of Care Joan Bothma. "We want both client and careworker to look forward to seeing each other every day. That's what our person-centric specialist provision is about."

Both Joan and Carepoint Services' Managing Director Yousuf Hingah have care in their blood. Joan's mother was a nurse and, from the age of ten, Joan would test her grandparents' blood pressure on the family farm in South Africa. Yousuf's father was a nurse, specialising in mental health, and Yousuf himself started his career as a care worker. These experiences fed into the development of Carepoint Services, with its careful focus on teaching staff to listen to clients and learning about their

individual stories. The learning begins in the recruitment process and is embedded into every stage of training. The company's 150 or so professional caregivers are asked to listen to clients to ensure that specific needs are understood and met, whether it's for short daily drop-ins or end-of-life care.

"The carers have to become part of the family, while maintaining professional boundaries, to ensure they get the care they want and need, and get it in the way they want and need," says Joan. "That's the crux of it. We talk to the client and the family about everything, such as how they like their tea. It's a simple thing but, nine times out of ten, clients won't tell the carer and then they have to sit there and drink so many horrible cups of tea they'd rather have a glass of squash. We listen to their life stories as they are important, and we want to make them proud of what they achieved. Each person is a unique individual and we want to treasure that story while allowing them to maintain their independence and dignity at home surrounded by their friends and families."

Treacle tart with Derbyshire treacle stout custard

Sergeant Stefan Sewell, RAF

Derbyshire

I have dedicated this recipe to the Derbyshire town of Milford, also known as the "Treacle City". Milford was home to a huge gas works industry that dated back to 1822, which produced coal tar and treacle sweets. The latter were issued to the workers to moisten their dry throats, something caused by the dusty atmosphere. It's said that when the mill was demolished, some of these sweets were found under the floorboards and that, during a delivery, a barrel of treacle spilled its contents over the road, enabling Milford to live up to its name of the Treacle City. The earliest recipe for treacle tart has been found in a cookbook by Mary Jewry, published in 1879, and consists of alternating layers of black treacle and pastry. The original recipe has gradually evolved over the years and in 1885, after much research and development, Lyle's first marketed golden syrup in its iconic metal tins, which led to the creation of treacle tart as we know it today. I was born and bred in Suffolk and still live close to the Lyle's sugar refinery; I can remember, as a child, smelling the sugar beet burning on the frosty winter morning air as I walked to school. Little did I know then that I would be using the sugar products they produced throughout my culinary career, especially in this treacle tart recipe, which is a simplified version of the one I made in the final of the National Chef of the Year in 2018.

Preparation time: 45 minutes
Cooking time: 45 minutes

Serves 4

INGREDIENTS

For the pastry
200g plain flour
1g bicarbonate of soda
120g salted butter, chilled and diced
50g hazelnuts, blended to a powder
1 egg, beaten
60g caster sugar

For treacle tart
1 egg, beaten
38g double cream
114g salted butter
338g golden syrup
1 vanilla pod, split
95g sourdough, blended to fine crumbs
Sea salt

For the salted hazelnuts
25g hazelnuts
1.5g salt
2.5g hazelnut or vegetable oil

For the stout custard
300ml double cream
150ml Derbyshire Treacle Stout
75ml milk
½ vanilla pod
2 egg yolks
88g caster sugar

METHOD

To make the pastry case

- Crumble the flour, bicarbonate of soda, butter and hazelnuts together, make a well in the centre, add the egg and sugar and bring it all together to make a soft, pliable dough.
- Knead the dough briefly until smooth, shape into a ball, flatten with the palm of your hand; wrap it in clingfilm and place in the fridge for 30 minutes to rest.
- Preheat the oven to 180°C.
- Roll out the chilled pastry to the thickness of a one pound coin; line a small lightly buttered cake tin or flan ring; blind bake until lightly browned and set aside to cool.

For the treacle tart

- Mix the egg and cream together in a bowl.
- Place the butter, syrup and vanilla pod into a pan and warm over a medium heat until simmering.
- Take the pan off the heat, pick out the vanilla pod, stir in the breadcrumbs then whisk in the egg and cream mix; allow to cool slightly then pour into the pastry case.
- Bake in the oven, still set at 180°C, for about 30 minutes until the filling is golden brown on top and just set.
- Sprinkle the top with sea salt and allow the tart to rest at room temperature.

For the salted hazelnuts

- Mix all of the ingredients together, spread out on a baking sheet and bake at 180°C until golden brown; cool slightly, gently pulse in a food processor to coarse crumbs then set aside until ready to serve.

For the stout custard

- Place the cream, stout, milk and vanilla pod in a saucepan and, over a medium heat, bring to a simmer.
- Meanwhile, whisk the egg yolks and sugar until pale, pour in the hot cream and stout mix, stir well and strain through a fine sieve into a clean saucepan.
- Place the saucepan over a low heat and gently cook, stirring constantly, until the custard coats the back of a spoon (about 80°C).

To serve

- Cut the warm tart into four portions, sprinkle with the toasted hazelnuts and serve with the stout custard.

Derbyshire: Local hero

William Gregg VC DCM MM

William Gregg was born on 27 January 1890 at Tag Hill, Derbyshire, attending the Mundy Street School in Heanor before becoming a miner at Shipley Colliery and marrying his childhood sweetheart, Sarah, in 1910, aged 20. His peaceful life was disrupted with the outbreak of the Great War and his enlistment in the 13th Battalion of the Rifle Brigade on the 24 November 1914. Though wounded during the Battle of the Somme in 1916 he would go on to become the first British soldier of the war to win three separate gallantry awards.

On 26 March 1917, while stationed in the Hulluch Sector near Loos, Gregg received the Military Medal for crawling between the opposing lines to identify a dead German soldier, retrieving his shoulder straps, ID discs and pay book, which all provided vital intelligence for the Allies. Eight months later, he was awarded the Distinguished Conduct Medal for carrying messages between different sections of his battalion while under heavy machine-gun fire.

On 8 May 1918, Sergeant Gregg took command of his company, at Bucquoy, when all his officers had been hit during an attack. He rushed an enemy post, killed the entire machine-gun team and captured the gun and four men located in the next dug-out. Despite the heavy casualties his company had experienced, Gregg pushed on, rushing another gun-post, killing two men and capturing a third. Gregg's party was later driven back by an enemy counter-attack. With reinforcements arriving, he personally led the counter-offensive, re-capturing the enemy guns. Gregg displayed conspicuous bravery and leadership under heavy fire, earning him the Victoria Cross. "He was completely fearless," said one of his platoon corporals. "A fine fighting man and one we would follow." Gregg received his VC personally from King George V on 9 August 1918 at the British Army HQ at Doullens in France.

After the war, Gregg returned to his wife Sarah and the colliery but answered the call to war in 1939, joining the National Defence Company of the Sherwood Foresters. "If the country was worth living in, it was worth defending," he said. On 10 August 1969 Gregg passed away in Heanor, receiving full military honours. A local leisure centre is named after him, while a trophy, the William Gregg VC Cup, is given to the winner of a local schools football tournament.

Written by Corporal Becky Croker, RAF

Portland pudding

Leading Catering Services Emma Keitch, Royal Navy

In the late 18th century, King George III visited Weymouth in Dorset several times, exploring the Isle of Portland, and during his visits he made the Portland Arms his headquarters. The king was said to have a sweet tooth and never failed to order the landlady's famous Portland pudding; due to his love of this dish he advertised it in the Dorset County Chronicle and christened it the "Royal Pudding". My recipe incorporates the traditional citrus flavours with a chocolate twist.

Preparation time: 15–20 minutes
Cooking time: 25–30 minutes

Serves 4

INGREDIENTS

Pudding mix
75g lightly salted butter, softened
75g caster sugar
2 eggs, separated
1 tsp orange extract
75g self-raising flour
25g glacé orange and lemon peel
15g dark chocolate chips

Orange sauce
75g caster sugar
75g lightly salted butter
2 oranges, zest and juice
75ml fresh orange juice
3 tsp orange extract or 25ml Cointreau
40ml double cream

METHOD

For the pudding mix
- Preheat the oven to 180°C and grease four 8.5cm pudding moulds.
- Cream together the softened butter and sugar until pale and fluffy.
- Slowly beat in the egg yolks and orange extract, continuously mixing until combined.
- Fold in the sieved flour and the glacé orange and lemon peels, mixing thoroughly.
- Whisk the egg whites until they form stiff peaks and slowly fold into the batter mix until fully incorporated.
- Fold in the chocolate chips and half fill each mould with the pudding mixture.
- Bake the puddings in the preheated oven for 25 minutes or until a skewer comes out clean when inserted into the middle.
- Once cooked, remove the puddings from the oven and turn out onto a plate.

For the orange sauce
- Add the sugar to a pan and, over a medium heat, cook, without stirring, until the sugar has dissolved and formed an amber colour.
- Add the butter and the juice and zest of the two oranges then stir until incorporated.
- Once the butter has melted, add the fresh orange juice and orange extract or Cointreau.
- Simmer for 4–5 minutes ensuring it doesn't burn.
- Add the double cream, pour over the warm puddings and serve.

Dorset: Local hero

Louis Arbon Strange, DSO, OBE, MC, DFC & Bar

Louis Strange was born in Tarrant Keyneston, Dorset on 27 July 1891 and educated at St Edward's School in Oxford. Seeing military aircraft flying over his family farm as a child, he vowed to become a pilot and joined the Ewen School of Flying in July 1913 and, in October that year, was commissioned as a Second Lieutenant in the Royal Flying Corps. His determination was evident, as was his ability to envision ways to improve his aircraft for warfare. He pioneered aerial warfare, experimenting with bombs on wing racks. A successful attack on Courtrai railway station in 1915's Battle of Neuve Chapelle won him the Military Cross. After a year of serving on the front line, Strange was awarded the Distinguished Flying Cross (DFC) and the Distinguished Service Order before being ordered by the then Major Trenchard to return to the UK, where he went on to establish air gunnery schools in Kent and Turnberry. After the war, Strange was granted a commission in the newly formed Royal Air Force before retiring due to ill health in 1921.

At the start of the Second World War, the 48-year-old Strange was too old for regular service, but joined the RAF Volunteer Reserve as a pilot officer. While posted in France, his squadron was tasked with saving what they could from an abandoned airfield littered with cannibalised aircraft. With no pilot available he took off in the only serviceable aircraft remaining, an unfamiliar Hurricane, with no armament and barely any instruments in the cockpit. Anti-aircraft fire forced him higher and higher to then be attacked by several Bf 109s. He dived the aircraft to near tree-top height and successfully escaped, later being awarded a bar to his DFC.

Strange retired from the service in June 1945 and was made an OBE; he was also awarded the American Bronze Star Medal in early 1946. He returned to farming but kept his love for aviation; buying light aircraft and flying in competitions. In the 1950 Daily Express Challenge Air Trophy he was, at the age of 59, the oldest of the 76 competitors. He continued flying for many years, and died peacefully in his sleep on 15 November 1966. His legacy lives on in the RAF: in 1997, the 23 Squadron briefing room was named "The Strange Room" in his honour.

Written by Petty Officer Aircraft Engineering Technician (Mechanical) Hollie Hill, Royal Navy

"His determination was evident, as was his ability to envision ways to improve his aircraft for warfare"

A baker's best friend

From cake toppers to stencils, scrapers to cutters, LissieLou provides bakers with all the necessities needed to complete the perfect baking creation

www.lissielou.com

LissieLou started life as a passionate hobby for Verity Scott. After designing decorations for her sister's wedding, Verity began producing cake decorations for weddings and parties from her bedroom, with increasing help from her mother, Ann. As their interest and commitment grew, a formal company was born and Verity gave up her corporate career to commit herself full time with Ann. Steady growth has seen the company expand in support of the wider baking industry and was enough to entice Verity's brother, Henry, to come on board. He similarly left the relative security of a corporate role.

LissieLou produces a wide range of high-quality cake preparation and decorative products – cake toppers, scrapers, biscuit cutters, embossers, stamps, stencils and boards – aimed equally at home bakers and many of Britain's best professional bakers. Overseas customers are a strong component too. "In the past decade, baking has become a huge part of British culture and it's a lovely industry to be in," says Ann. "There's so much community spirit, trust and loyalty. It's amazing to see people using our products and learning and sharing their passion for baking."

The company is now based in offices in rural Oxfordshire and regards the staff from the local community as an integral part of the LissieLou family. "We simply couldn't do what we're doing without our fabulous team and we are privileged to have such dedicated individuals," says Henry. "We are supported too by a superb group of brand ambassadors; they are absolute masters of their craft and we love witnessing their own individual journeys. We are also very fortunate in having so many loyal and enthusiastic customers."

Verity has her eye on the future. "We are looking forward to the many exciting opportunities and challenges ahead, supporting the growing number of baking enthusiasts," she says. "All of us at LissieLou are thrilled to be a small part of this wonderful cookbook celebrating the Royal British Legion's centenary milestone in support of so many of the Armed Forces community. We will enjoy many of the exciting recipes!"

The Old Granary
HALL & WOODHOUSE

Riverside Pub

THE CRANBORNE POACHER
RICH & FRUITY
RUBY ALE

The GOLDEN CHAMPION
Golden Ale

THE BLANDFORD FLY
SWEET & SPICY
GOLDEN ALE

The HOPPING HARE
Pale Ale

The Legendary TANGLE FOOT

The FURSTY FERRET
Amber Ale

Beer fit for Wellington's troops

The family-owned brewer Hall & Woodhouse has been running pubs throughout the south of England and brewing award-winning beers for more than 244 years

www.hall-woodhouse.co.uk
www.badgerbeers.com

The 244-year-old family-owned brewery, Hall & Woodhouse, is famous for its award-winning Badger beers and a high-quality estate of beautiful pubs. What is less commonly known, is that the company's long history was founded on a military connection. Founder Charles Hall opened his first brewery in Ansty, Dorset in 1777 as a means of using unsold corn. A few years later he spotted an opportunity in the nearby coastal town of Weymouth.

"Wellington's troops moved to Weymouth in around 1795 during the Napoleonic Wars, and Charles got the licence to supply their beer rations" says Mark Woodhouse, the seventh-generation family director, of his canny great-great-great-great grandfather. "His comment was, 'beer is better than boredom, so trade was brisk'. Charles was savvy enough to know they wouldn't be there forever, and he immediately reinvested the profits into the business, and started to buy pubs." This ethos of reinvesting is one that has been followed down through the generations and has helped ensure that the company has not only prospered in the good times, but survived through 14 recessions, three world wars and two pandemics.

Today the company is still fully privately owned, predominantly by the Woodhouse family (George Woodhouse joined the business in the 1800s, marrying into the Hall family and becoming a partner in the newly formed Hall & Woodhouse). The military connection remains firm: Mark's grandfather, father and uncle all served in the military, with his uncle Jock receiving a Military Cross. Uncle Jock then joined the SAS, for whom he developed the regiment's infamously rigorous selection process, after which he joined the family business, creating the popular children's soft drink brand Panda Pops.

But it is Badger beer – brewed in a new brewery (the third one built in 244 years) in Blandford, Dorset – and its beautiful pubs that Hall & Woodhouse is famous for. It currently operates over 180. "Of our pubs, we manage 55 ourselves and we have 130 tenanted pubs which we call 'Business Partnerships'," says Mark. "These tend to be the smaller pubs, but no less fantastic. We are constantly evolving our estate depending on the market."

Although in 2020 the pub estate was hampered by Covid-19, Hall & Woodhouse's brewery has been running at full tilt, increasing bottled beer sales by 50 per cent and winning several accolades at the 2020 World Beer Awards. Badger's Golden Champion was the UK winner in the Pale Beer category, with four other Badger beers – Twice Tangled, The Cranborne Poacher, The Fursty Ferret and The Blandford Fly – all taking home awards too.

Hall & Woodhouse is looking forward to celebrating its 250th anniversary in 2027. "The pandemic has raised questions about what sort of state your business was in when you went into it, how you managed the crisis and showed resilience, and what your plans are now coming out of it," says Mark. "We went into it with modest levels of debt, backed by high levels of freehold property, a product of great long-term business decisions from previous generations. We have also used the time to retrain our team and gear up to hit the ground running when the pubs can reopen."

The 2020/21 pandemic is the first time Hall & Woodhouse has had to close the doors of its pubs in its 244-year history. However, it has shown the resilience needed to not only survive but to thrive, and is well placed to continue its journey for the next 250 years.

Nan's marmalade and Scottish oatcakes

Murray Chapman, Director at Young Pastry Chef of the Year, Master Chefs of Great Britain

The first marmalade was made in Dundee in 1791 by the Keiller family. I was brought up by my Nan, who sadly passed away in April 2020 at the ripe old age of 106½, and this is a modern version of her recipe. Living in Broughty Ferry in the late 1960s was a great time; we had fish from the sea and, more importantly, we were surrounded by fields of strawberries and loganberries. I used to spend hours making jams and marmalades with my Nan and this oatcake recipe has been in my family for over a century. It dates back way before the First World War, probably to the mid-1850s. There are some recipes you can update and some that are so good and simple it would be a crime to try and change them and this is one of those – just a simple addition of sea salt and milled white pepper.

Dundee

Preparation time: 45 minutes
Cooking time: 3 hours

INGREDIENTS

**For the Seville orange, honey and
whisky marmalade**
1.5kg of Seville oranges
1.2 litre water
500g clear honey
500g granulated sugar
4 nips of 10-year-old Laphroaig whisky

For Nan's Scottish oatcakes
125g unsalted butter
500g Scottish oatmeal
250g plain flour, sieved
Sea salt
Milled white pepper
A touch of hot water

METHOD

For the marmalade
- Cut off the tops and bottoms from the oranges; make sure they are all of an equal height then cut each into eight segments and cut out all the flesh.
- Roughly chop the tops and bottoms of the oranges and place, with all the flesh, in a deep pan with the water; bring to a boil and simmer for 1½ hours.
- When the flesh has broken down, pass the mixture through two layers of muslin.
- Cut the orange peel lengthways into thin slices, place in the liquid and cook until they are soft, approximately 1 hour, then pass the liquid through a sieve into a clean saucepan reserving all of the orange peel.
- Place the saucepan over a medium heat and reduce the liquid to 1.2 litres.
- Mix the honey and granulated sugar with the liquid, bring to a boil and cook for 10 minutes.
- Add the orange peel and continue to cook until the setting point is reached; a good idea is to have a small plate in the freezer to help test for the setting point. Continuously skim while it is cooking.
- When setting point is reached, remove from the heat and gently stir in the whisky.
- Pour the marmalade into sterilised preserving jars and cover.

For the oatcakes
- Preheat the oven to 190°C.
- Chop the butter and allow to soften.
- Mix together the oatmeal and flour and rub through the butter by hand.
- Lightly season with the salt and pepper.
- Add the hot water to form a dough (it will be warm to touch).
- Roll out the mixture to desired thickness and cut into discs with a pastry cutter.
- Bake on a sheet of baking parchment or on a non-stick tray in the preheated oven for about 15 minutes (depending on thickness).
- Remove from the oven and place on a cooling rack and, when cool, enjoy with the marmalade.

Private Thomas Beach VC

With 12 Victoria Cross medals awarded in a single day, the Battle of Inkerman, commonly known as the "Soldiers' Battle", was a bloody and vicious affair that took place on 5 October 1854 between British, French and Ottoman allies and the Imperial Russian Army. It is often said to have broken the spirit of the Russians, who never made any large-scale efforts to field troops for the rest of the Crimean War. The 8,500 strong British Army suffered 2,357 casualties, of whom 635 died of their wounds.

Thomas Beach VC, born 24 January 1824 in Dundee, joined the 92nd Regiment of Foot at the age of 16. He spent almost his entire adult life within the ranks, serving his country in numerous locations, including the West Indies and the Greek islands. At the start of the Crimean War in 1853 he was posted to Gibraltar as part of a garrison force, but courageously volunteered to fight in the Crimean peninsula and was placed with the 55th Regiment of Foot.

During the Battle of Inkerman, Beach single-handedly went to the aid of a wounded officer, Lieutenant Colonel Carpenter, who was being set upon by five Russians, all attempting to stab him with their bayonets. Beach immediately attacked the Russians, killing two and holding off the other three until assistance arrived. His heroic actions earned him a Victoria Cross for bravery in the face of the enemy.

Leaving the British Army in 1863, Thomas Beach VC fell on hard times and turned, like so many veterans before him, to alcohol. Without the support of charities like the Royal British Legion he had no means to deal with his addiction and died on 24 August 1864 at the age of 40, less than a year after leaving the Army. Dundee Royal Infirmary recorded his death as a result of alcohol poisoning.

He was buried in an unmarked pauper's grave in Dundee's Eastern Necropolis. His VC was sold to the Maharaja of Patiala in the 1920s where, following India's independence from the UK, the medal was gifted by the Maharaja's son to the people of the Punjab. Beach's VC is still held in the Sheesh Mahal Museum, Patiala, India to this day. In 2003, a commemorative bench was installed at the cemetery in Dundee, near his unmarked grave, in honour of his outstanding gallantry.

Written by Squadron Leader Andrew Mortimer, RAF

"During the Battle of Inkerman, Beach single-handedly went to the aid of a wounded officer who was being set upon by five Russians"

Cask masters

VCL Vintners offers long-term savers the chance to invest in the burgeoning market for bottles or casks of single malt whisky

www.vclvintners.london

Most people regard whisky as something to drink, a chance to appreciate a drop of something special at the end of a meal or on special occasions. But whisky can also be approached as a particularly palatable investment opportunity – this is an asset that is made with labour and love; something that spends decades maturing and acquiring value before it's ready for bottling. London-based firm VCL Vintners has specialised in this market over the past decade, allowing clients to invest in a unique asset class. VCL Vintners is therefore uniquely positioned to guide clients both new and experienced through the various opportunities to invest in whisky, be that through individual and collectable bottles or entire casks.

"We basically provide private individuals with an opportunity to invest into single malt casks of whisky from Scotland," explains Benjamin Lancaster, who is a co-owner of VCL Vintners alongside Timothy Ashley and Stuart Thom. "Fundamentally, people come to us when they are looking to re-allocate capital, often from portfolio and cash areas that aren't performing too well. We then give individuals the chance to invest into some of the biggest distilleries in operation in Scotland, as well as some of the silent and highly collectable ones. Whisky is an ageing asset so casks can have a shelf life of anything up to 50 years and, as the maturation goes on, the value increases. Whisky of that age becomes rarer, so the investment becomes more valuable." According to the *Knight Frank Wealth Report*, whisky was the best performing alternative investment of the last decade, achieving a 586 per cent rate of interest.

The company works with around 30 distilleries in Scotland, focusing on those that fulfil certain financial criteria – the need to have a significant market share, have a solid business model, and a great reputation. For the distilleries, this is a chance to gain financial support ahead of bottling and distribution, essentially allowing them to take an advance today against future sales. Accessing this market can be difficult owing to the extensive networks required when acquiring the best casks, and VCL has an exceptional track record in portfolio selection, asset management and client care. Cask whisky investment is low cost, hassle free and very secure.

"Whisky production takes a lot of labour and time and quite a bit of financial investment for a return you might not see for decades, so distilleries want to recoup some of that cost to set against future production," explains Benjamin. "We also provide a bridge between the public and the distillery because most of the distilleries aren't really geared up to be public facing; they are run by very small teams and dealing with the general public isn't one of their skills."

The chance to invest in something as interesting and unusual as whisky has seen VCL Vintners attract clients from a wide demographic, including many from the 18-to-25-year age bracket. "It's definitely a break from the norm," says Benjamin. "It's a lot more interesting than most investment opportunities and we get a lot of feedback about that. It's secure, it's physical, it isn't on paper, and it's one of the best performing investments of the past decade. As it is a consumable, clients develop an affiliation with their cask. You can have samples drawn and we can arrange visits for bottlings. You can even request a bottle at the end of the process, so you have something to enjoy and drink as well as having the potential for large profit."

Fifteens

Corporal Daniel Holt, RAF

These no-bake treats are very popular and can be found in many cafés around Northern Ireland; you will rarely find these anywhere else and it appears that they are not so popular in the Republic of Ireland. They get their name because they are made with three main ingredients of which you need 15 each. I chose this recipe because of its simplicity and, as there's no baking, it's perfect for getting kids involved in the kitchen.

VEGETARIAN

**Preparation time: 20 minutes
  plus 2 hours chilling time**

Makes about 20

INGREDIENTS

15 digestive biscuits
15 large vegetarian marshmallows
  (quartered)
15 glacé cherries, halved
200ml condensed milk
75g desiccated coconut

METHOD

- Either blitz the biscuits to a crumb in a food processor or crush them in a food bag using a rolling pin.
- Mix the crumbed biscuits with the glacé cherries, marshmallows and condensed milk until thoroughly combined.
- Lay out a sheet of clingfilm on the worktop and sprinkle with the desiccated coconut.
- Shape the biscuit mix into a fat sausage about 20cm long and sit it on of the coconut, once you have an even shape, roll it in the coconut to evenly coat and wrap it tightly in the clingfilm.
- Put it in the fridge for at least 2 hours (preferably overnight) and once set cut into 1cm thick slices and enjoy. The log will keep in the fridge for up to a week.

Alternatives
- You can use any of your favourite biscuits in this recipe; a personal favourite of mine is Biscoff.
- You can also add dried fruit, chocolate chips or your favourite chocolate bars cut up into small pieces.

Eric Norman Frankland Bell VC

Eric Norman Frankland Bell was born on 28 August 1895 in Enniskillen, County Fermanagh. His father, an officer in the Royal Inniskilling Fusiliers, was posted to Cheshire and the Bell family relocated to join him, eventually settling in Hill Street, Liverpool. At school Eric excelled at art and eventually attended the School of Architecture at Liverpool University. He trained as an architect and worked as an "office boy", working in oils, pen and ink. He was also a talented musician and spoke French and German fluently.

When war broke out, Eric's father was recalled to the Army, serving as the Quartermaster and then Adjutant of 9th Battalion, Royal Inniskilling Fusiliers. Eric was commissioned on 22 September 1914, initially joining the 6th Royal Inniskilling Fusiliers, transferring to 8th Battalion then 9th Battalion on 12 November 1914, joining his father and his two brothers, Alan and Haldane. After being sent to France on 15 October 1915, he attended a trench mortar course and was promoted to Lieutenant before being attached to 109th Brigade Trench Mortar Battery. It was on 1 July 1916, at Thiepval in France, that Eric made the ultimate sacrifice during the first day of the Battle of the Somme.

When his fellow soldiers were pinned down by machine gun fire from a German position, Captain Bell crept forward and eliminated the machine gunner. Later, on no less than three occasions when bombing parties were unable to advance, Eric went forward alone and threw trench mortar bombs among the German positions. When he had no more bombs available, Eric stood on the parapet, under intense fire, and used a rifle with great coolness and effect on the advancing enemy. As he was rallying and reorganising infantry parties that had lost their officers, he was killed. All of these actions were far outside the scope of his normal duties with his battery. He was only 20 years old.

Eric Bell was posthumously awarded the Victoria Cross, which was presented to his father by King George V at Buckingham Palace on 29 November 1916. A source of immense pride within the family, Captain Bell's medal was eventually passed down to his nephew, Air Marshal Sir Richard Bolt KBE CB DFC AFC RNZAF (retired). Sir Richard gifted the medal to the museum of the Royal Inniskilling Fusiliers on 15 February 2001, where it is proudly displayed today.

Written by Sergeant Scott Turner, RAF

"Eric made the ultimate sacrifice during the first day of the Battle of the Somme"

Nana knows best

Nana Lily's luscious puddings, condiments and sauces are reminding enthusiastic customers around the world – including the US President – of the very best home-made treats

www.nanalilys.com

Nana Lily's decadent, fruity Christmas pudding goes back four generations, all the way to Ellen Halpin-Bwarnett's Irish great-grandmother. The recipe was passed down to Ellen through her grandmother and mother – both of whom were called Lily – and her festive puddings won acclaim from family and friends, who eventually convinced her to start selling them. Her mouth-watering, traditional recipe has even captured the interest of the US Congress.

"The puddings go back to the West Coast of Ireland, to my great-grandmother, and they remain unchanged," says Ellen, who now resides in Worcester. "They would originally have been steamed over an open peat fire. My mother remembers sitting by the fire to make sure the pot did not boil dry. Using 21st century methods, the puddings are still steamed and retain their amazing flavour, especially after soaking up Kilbeggan Irish whiskey for four days."

Nana Lily's launched in August 2016 and Ellen's Christmas puddings quickly went on to win one of the Guild of Fine Food's Great Taste awards. They are now stocked at a range of farm shops and delicatessens; Ellen also sells her products on QVC and through her website, and has a global client base, including connections with the highest levels of US government. "President Joe Biden's great-grandfather grew up not far from my great-grandmother in County Mayo," says Ellen.

The Christmas puddings soon led on to a range of condiments and sauces, including double award-winning Whiskey Butter, Ham Glaze and Autumn Chutney. Moreover, in 2020, Ellen began developing a range of sponge puddings: one flavoured with lemon, another with limoncello, a sticky toffee pudding and a sticky toffee with Irish cream. "They have been selling phenomenally!" says Ellen. "During lockdown, people craved indulgent treats that tasted homemade." In just a few short years Nana Lily's has grown from a kitchen-table endeavour to an international business. And, while Ellen is delighted that she can share her recipes with so many people, she remains committed to the principles of home cooking that began all those years ago with her great-grandmother.

Logistics as a mantra

From its base in Manchester, Mantra Learning helps to provide training for people in the logistics industry, from HGV drivers to digitally savvy fleet managers

www.mantralearning.co.uk
www.logisticsacademy.co.uk

Over the past year, the importance of the distribution industry – whether it's food, clothes, personal protective equipment or vaccines – has never been more apparent. But the UK is facing a logistical crisis thanks to a lack of qualified HGV drivers. This is something that Manchester-based Mantra Learning is striving to overcome by providing training for people from all walks of life, including former military personnel, to achieve their goods vehicle and fork-lift truck licences. "The clear mission we have is to make logistics a career of first choice," explains Mark Currie, Mantra Learning's CEO. "We have set up The National Logistics Academy, which utilises its 53 HGV training locations across the country. Our strategy is to address the driver shortage to support the UK's biggest logistics companies."

Among those that Mantra Learning is seeking to recruit as trainees and instructors are former members of the Armed Forces. The company has signed the Armed Forces Covenant, pledging to support the services, and Mark emphasises the value of employees with the skills taught by the Army and other services. "We have links to the Royal Logistic Corps and a number of people come from the Armed Forces to be instructors," says Mark. "They make very good instructors as well as good drivers. They are very valued employees and former members of the Armed Forces should see there are huge opportunities – we would love to support their training. The important thing to remember is that logistics isn't just about driving a truck. We also need people to manage the vehicle fleets. There's a whole raft of opportunities, from creating digital reports to building mechanised sorting systems."

Mantra Learning was founded in 1968 to tackle the HGV driver shortage and its purpose-built site was opened in 1978 by the Duke of Kent. When Mark arrived at the company in 1999 the company was in poor health, and shortly after he joined it received a dismal rating from Ofsted, but Mark was able to engineer a complete turnaround so it achieved an Ofsted Grade 1 in 2005. Mantra now offers the full range of logistics skills training for both new recruits and existing staff.

In response to the introduction of the apprenticeship evy, Mantra launched The National Logistics Academy in 2015, offering innovative, high-quality training and apprenticeships throughout the UK. In 2019/20 The Academy and Mantra had successfully achieved 32 per cent market share of the HGV apprenticeship marketplace. The National Logistics Academy was also well placed to tackle the national HGV driver shortage. Things got worse in 2020, when the Covid pandemic made it impossible to train new drivers. Currie estimates there is a shortage of at least 100,000 drivers across the country, compounded by an ageing workforce with the average age at nearly 50 and only 1 per cent of drivers under 25.

"We have two thrusts," says Mark. "One is driver training driven by need but we also want to have more digitally aware transport managers, which is a great opportunity for younger people. Things we take for granted, like same-day delivery, take a lot of technology and we want to improve the skills and knowledge of those going into the sector. This is a sector where you can start at the bottom and get to the very top on your own merits."

Manchester tart

Catering Services James Hopkinson, Royal Navy

The humble Manchester tart used to be a firm favourite for school dinner puddings in Lancastrian family homes (Manchester was part of Lancashire until 1974) and was even popular onboard naval warships. Nowadays, it is rarely ever mentioned. This simple recipe brings it up to date with a historical nod to Manchester's heritage. The added honeycomb represents the Manchester worker bee – a symbol that has adorned anything associated with the city, including litter bins, road signs and locally brewed beer; indeed, until 2011, it was part of the crest of HMS Manchester. The bee is also a visible symbol of Mancunians' work ethic and the city's sense of unity.

Preparation time: 60 minutes
Cooking time: 20 minutes

Serves 4

INGREDIENTS

For the honeycomb
200g caster sugar
5 tbsp golden syrup
2 tsp bicarbonate of soda

For the sweet pastry
240g plain flour
120g butter
60g caster sugar
1 egg

For the tart filling
200g raspberry jam
3 tbsp desiccated coconut
2 heaped tbsp custard powder
500ml whole milk
175g caster sugar
A few drops of vanilla essence
5 free-range egg yolks
400ml double cream,
 whipped to soft peaks

To serve
3 tbsp desiccated coconut,
 toasted in a dry frying pan
 until golden brown

Greater Manchester

METHOD

To make the honeycomb

- Butter a 20cm square, shallow roasting or baking tray.
- Stir the caster sugar and golden syrup together in a deep saucepan over a gentle heat until the sugar has completely dissolved.
- Once completely dissolved, turn the heat up a little and simmer until you have an amber coloured caramel (this won't take long), then as quickly as you can, turn off the heat, tip in the bicarbonate of soda and beat in with a wooden spoon until it has all disappeared and the mixture is foaming.
- Scrape into the greased tin immediately – be careful, the mixture will be very hot.
- The mixture will continue bubbling in the tin; simply leave it and, in about 1–1½ hours the honeycomb will be hard and ready to crumble on top of your tart.

To make the tart case

- Preheat the oven to 200°C. Butter a 24cm loose-bottomed tart tin.
- Sieve the flour into a bowl and rub in the butter to a sandy texture.
- Mix the sugar and egg together in a bowl, add to the flour and mix to a soft dough, try not to over-work the mixture; wrap the dough in clingfilm and rest in the fridge for 30 minutes.
- When the pastry has chilled, roll out on a lightly floured worktop and line the tart tin ensuring an even thickness throughout; trim off the excess pastry leaving a small overhang to allow for shrinkage during cooking.
- Place a disc of baking parchment into the pastry case and half fill with ceramic baking beans or rice. Blind bake the pastry case in the preheated oven for 15 minutes, remove the baking beans and parchment and return the tart case to the oven for a further 5 minutes or until pale golden-brown; trim off any excess pastry and set aside to cool.

For the tart filling

- Spread the raspberry jam onto the pastry base in an even layer; sprinkle over the three tablespoons of non-toasted desiccated coconut and set the tart case aside.
- Mix the custard powder with a little of the milk in a mixing bowl to make a thick paste; pour the remaining milk into a saucepan, bring to a simmer, sprinkle in 50g of the sugar and stir in a few drops of vanilla essence.
- Pour the hot milk over the custard powder mixture while continually stirring.
- Return the mixture to a clean saucepan, bring to a boil, reduce the heat and simmer for 30 seconds stirring constantly; remove the pan from the heat.
- In a bowl, beat together the egg yolks and the remaining 125g of caster sugar until well combined.
- Pour the custard over the egg and sugar mix, whisking continuously, until the mixture is smooth and well combined; pour the mixture into a clean saucepan, place over a medium heat and cook, stirring continuously, until the mixture is thick enough to coat the back of the spoon.
- Transfer the custard to a clean bowl, cover the surface with a piece of clingfilm (this prevents a skin from forming on the surface of the custard), set aside to cool, then chill in the fridge for 30 minutes.

To fill and serve

- Fold the whipped double cream into the chilled custard mixture until well combined.
- Spoon the custard and cream mixture into the pastry case in an even layer and sprinkle over the toasted coconut and crumbled honeycomb to serve.

Sergeant John Hogan VC

Born on 8 April 1884, John Hogan was educated at Waterhead Church Day School in Oldham before following in his mother's footsteps and working in the textile industry. Only 5 ft 3½ inches tall, Hogan enlisted in 6th (Militia) Battalion, Manchester Regiment on 5 December 1902 before transferring to the regular service the following year. He served in India, reaching the rank of Corporal in 1911, before returning to the UK in 1912. Hogan transferred to the reserves while working as a postman in Heyside.

Following the outbreak of war, Hogan received a promotion to sergeant and embarked to France with the Manchester Regiment in August 1914. His 5th Division supported the British Expeditionary Force's retreat following the Battle of Mons, as well as engaging in the brutal battles of Marne, Aisne and Ypres. On 29 October 1914 he was fighting outside Festubert in France where an Allied trench-line had been captured by German troops. Hogan and 2nd Lieutenant Leach volunteered to recover the trench by themselves, undertaking bloody close-quarters fighting. Against overwhelming odds they succeeded, killing eight enemy soldiers, wounding two and capturing 16 prisoners.

For this he was awarded a Victoria Cross – something he was informed of in December 1914 while recovering in an English hospital from a shrapnel injury. In 1915, Hogan was posted to the 11th Battalion, who were destined to fight at Gallipoli, but in 1916 he was demoted to private for being drunk on active service. In 1917, Hogan was sent back to France with the 11th Battalion as well as being made acting unpaid sergeant, where he survived the rest of the war. He was discharged from the Army in 1919 and struggled to find work, selling matches on the streets of Manchester and working as the valet to the music hall star Benny Ross. Hogan was part of the VC Guard at the interment of the Unknown Warrior in 1920 and was briefly an in-pensioner at the Royal Hospital Chelsea from 1932–33. Too old for active service in the Second World War, Hogan started work in a munition factory in 1939 before passing away on 6 October 1943, aged 59.

His gravestone is in Chadderton Cemetery in Oldham, and his name is on the Victoria Cross plaque in Oldham's Church Terrace and on a VC Memorial paving stone in Royton Park. There is also a street just north-east of Manchester city centre called John Hogan VC Road.

Written by Commander Antony Laycock MSc, Royal Navy

"Hogan volunteered to recover the trench, undertaking bloody close-quarters fighting, killing eight enemy soldiers, wounding two and capturing 16 prisoners"

Electric dreams

Fischer Future Heat offers an eco-friendly energy alternative with a heating system that is tailored for each individual room in your home

www.fischerfutureheat.com

It was when Keith Bastian started working for a German heating company in 1997 that he began to appreciate how inadequately British homes were heated. For 12 years he worked for that company in the UK before deciding to go it alone and create Fischer Future Heat, a company based in Leicester that brings the Fischer heating system directly to the UK.

"The whole ethos of the business comes from the great desire I have to help fulfil the issues people have when it comes to heating their homes," he explains. "Our product is very well received wherever we take it and that didn't surprise me because, as soon as I saw what was possible, I ripped out my own central heating and installed this system. The problem with central heating is that it is inefficient. In our system, every room has its own controller and programmer so there is no wastage of energy."

The Fischer Future Heat system is powered by electricity rather than gas. That makes it more efficient in the long term, with no need for maintenance, as well as better for the planet. Keith's father was in the air force in India and, after he died, Keith's family were supported by a military benevolent fund. He now believes that many of the future battles facing humanity will be environmental rather than military. "The future is electric," he says. "It's essential for climate change. In the future, we won't be fighting traditional wars, we will be fighting viruses and climate change. People need to realise that the future is electric and the road to zero carbon starts now. It's something we can all do and it is something that will make a better world for everybody."

As Keith points out, a large and increasing amount of the UK's daily energy needs are now met by renewable sources. He runs Outfox The Market Energy, which offers 100 per cent renewable energy generated by UK-based wind farms. "People like gas because it is cheap but just because something is cheap doesn't mean you should waste it," he says. "For 15 years we have been telling people the future is electric and that's true for everything from cars to heating. With Outfox The Market, we sell electricity to homes which is completely generated offshore by wind. The new turbines are absolutely huge: one rotation can power several hundred homes. That sort of technology is getting bigger and better and more efficient."

The electricity-powered Fischer Future Heat system takes full advantage of this efficiency. The system can be installed in a day and is easily controlled and programmable. Users can set different temperatures for each room, adjusted for personal preferences and needs at different times of day, creating the perfect environment with the minimum amount of waste. "Most people come to us because they want rooms that are warm and comfortable all year round," he says. "There is nothing to maintain, it always works at the click of a button. It's not like a gas boiler that needs servicing every year and never works at the start of winter because it's been off all year. Some people are so fixated on gas, which is a fossil fuel and does a lot of harm to the environment. We have been a pioneer in this for years because we want people to be comfortable and we don't want them to waste energy."

Lardy cake

Sergeant Andrew Ngugi, Army

This recipe is an old classic. Lardy cake is a speciality of the Southern English counties, although looking back through old cookbooks Hampshire was the first to create this delicacy. Lardy cake is made from rendered lard (essentially clarified pig fat) and sugar layered in a dough. During the Second World War clarified beef dripping was used and, unofficially, you could also make lardy cake using butter, but that would make it buttery cake, not lardy cake! Lardy cake is fine cold but wonderful hot and straight out of the oven, when it is delightfully soft, squidgy and rich; eating it involves a lot of enthusiastic finger licking. I have lived in Hampshire for over 20 years and this has been a regular baking staple among my wife's family for years.

Hampshire

Preparation time: 30 minutes plus about 2 hours resting/proving time
Cooking time: 35 minutes

Serves 10 good-size portions

INGREDIENTS

500g white bread flour
1 tbsp salt
14g (2 sachets) instant yeast
105g lard, at room temperature
220ml milk
100g unsalted butter,
  at room temperature
220g mixed dried fruit such as raisins,
  currants and sultanas
140g sugar

METHOD

- Mix together the flour, salt and yeast in a bowl.
- Using your fingertips, rub 30g of the lard into the flour until it's well incorporated.
- Add three-quarters of the milk and mix to form a soft dough; add as much of the remaining milk as you need to get a dough that is soft and leaves the sides of the bowl clean when pulled away.
- Rest for 15 minutes to allow the dough to relax.
- Preheat the oven to 220°C.
- Tip the dough onto a lightly floured surface and knead for 10 minutes until the dough is smooth.
- Place in a clean bowl, cover and leave to rise until doubled in size; the time it will take for this to happen will depend on the room temperature but be patient as it will be worth it.
- Once the dough has doubled in size, place it onto a floured surface and roll into a rectangle about 20cm x 50cm and about ½cm thick.
- With the short edge facing you, dot a third of the remaining lard and a third of the butter over the surface of the dough.
- Sprinkle over a third of the fruit and a third of the sugar.
- Fold the top third of the dough down and the bottom third up so that the dough is folded in three and roughly square.
- Turn the dough a quarter turn.
- Roll out and repeat the process twice more, using up all the lard and fruit, just as if you were making fresh puff pastry if you have done so before.
- Line a 23cm x 23cm square loose-bottomed tin with baking parchment. Roll out the dough to fit the tin and place it inside.
- Cover with clingfilm, and leave to rise for 45 minutes.
- Bake for 30–35 minutes, or until golden brown.
- Leave to cool slightly before removing from the tin.
- Cut into portions and serve to your waiting guests; with the aroma of the dried fruit now in the air they will be itching to try it.
- Traditionally served warm, spread with butter, but it goes equally well with some ice cream or warm custard.

Sergeant Joshua Leakey VC

Joshua Leakey comes from a rich military family history, the son of retired Air Commodore Mark Leakey (current director of the Armed Forces Christian Union). He is the second member of his family to be awarded the Victoria Cross – his cousin, Nigel Leakey, was posthumously awarded the medal during the Second World War – and he is also related to Lieutenant General David Leakey, the former Black Rod and former senior British Army officer.

Leakey was born in Horsham, Sussex and his family moved around before eventually settling in Hampshire. He joined the Army and the Parachute Regiment in 2007, and was subsequently posted to 1st Battalion. In May 2013, he was deployed to Afghanistan as part of a task force to disrupt insurgent safe havens in Helmand province.

On 22 August 2013, he was part of a combined UK/US assault led by the United States Marine Corps into a Taliban stronghold to disrupt a key insurgent group. After dismounting, the patrol came under heavy enemy fire, pinning the command group on the exposed slope of a hill. They attempted to extract from the killing zone for an hour, resulting in a Marine Corps captain being shot and wounded and communications put out of action. Leakey, on the opposite side, realised the seriousness and dashed across a large area of hillside under machine gun fire. Approximately 20 enemy had surrounded two friendly machine gun teams, rendering them ineffective.

Fearlessly, Leakey gave first aid to the wounded officer, taking control of the situation and initiating the casualty evacuation. Moving under enemy fire, he got one of the suppressed machine guns into action and returned fire. Again working under enemy fire, he carried 60lbs of equipment and ran to the second machine gun and back up the hill to re-site the gun and return fire. Leakey handed over control of the gun and led the wounded officer to safe evacuation. Throughout this battle, 11 insurgents were killed and four wounded.

On 26 February 2015, Leakey was awarded the Victoria Cross. Announcing the award, the Chief of the General Staff, General Sir Nicholas Carter, broke with tradition to hug him. Leakey also received the City of London's highest honour, Freeman of the City. He is still serving and recently presented his medals on loan to the Imperial War Museum Duxford.

Written by Corporal Chris Swift, Parachute Regiment, Army (retired)

"Fearlessly, Leakey gave first aid to the wounded officer, taking control of the situation and initiating the casualty evacuation"

Chocs away

Using the expertise of classically trained naval chef Mark Raynor, T&M Artisan Chocolates is creating award-winning luxury confectionery using a startling list of exotic ingredients

www.tmchocolates.co.uk

Not many people would dare brace the sort of radical career change that takes somebody from working on Her Majesty's submarines to producing luxury chocolates, but for Mark Raynor such a switch would have been almost unimaginable without the support of the Royal Navy. Mark had been a chef for 10 years before he joined the Royal Navy in 2001, serving aboard submarines in the communications department and as a chef. After leaving the service 15 years later, he needed a new direction and found inspiration in confectionery, founding T&M Artisan Chocolates in 2019, with essential support from his former employers.

"I did a small-business course in Oxford with the international chocolate manufacturers Barry Callebaut while on my Royal Navy resettlement and that was fantastic," says Mark. "It was about the science of chocolate, how to temper and mould the ingredients. It also gave me an understanding of how to run a small business, the paperwork, the accounts and dealing with suppliers for ingredients and packaging."

T&M Artisan Chocolates is located in a converted barn on a farm in rural Hampshire. Here Mark creates exotic combinations in eye-catching designs, selling products over the internet as well as via regional delicatessens, farm shops and food markets. Mark favours vivid designs and bold flavours. His peppermint fondant has been described as an "after-dinner mint on steroids", while he also produces a chilli and smoked paprika ganache in dark chocolate, and a mango and cardamom creation in white. These are sold alongside more traditional chocolates – hazelnut praline, coconut crème, coffee fondant, salted caramel – in the company's signature box of 12. The peppermint fondant

and old English chewy toffee both collected awards at the Great Taste Awards, while the smoked paprika wins converts for whoever samples it.

The company can also produce bespoke designs, such as the chocolates it created for a local school decorated in the school colours, or those designed for a cruise company that travelled to Spain and the Nordic coast. "We made the smoked paprika and chilli in the colours of the Spanish flag, and we made a liquorice and blackberry for the Nordic cruise that was designed to look like the Northern Lights," says Mark.

With partner Hannah Southon working on marketing and helping with paperwork, Mark continues to explore the science and possibilities of chocolate, utilising the skills he developed in the Royal Navy. He reached the rank of Leading Hand before leaving the forces early, having developed post-traumatic stress disorder following a tour of Afghanistan. But he gained so much from his experience. "From day one in basic training you are part of a disciplined service and that stands you in good stead for civilian life," he says. "You develop that team mentality, where it isn't about you as an individual but working together and the camaraderie that comes with that. Plus you get to see the world."

T&M Artisan Chocolate uses Fairtrade ingredients and biodegradable packaging and also tries to support local businesses. Forthcoming lines include a hot honey, which uses chocolate from a British chocolate company, as well as locally produced honey and chilli. "We are providing a product that we think is extraordinary but affordable," says Mark. "A lot of people don't have a lot of money right now, so we want to offer them a little bit of luxury at a competitive price."

Hereford cider cake

Sergeant Lewis Day, Army

Hereford cider cake rose to fame as a local delicacy during the second half of the 19th century and, in 2007, Herefordshire cider gained Protected Geographical Indication (PGI) status, which specifies that, to bear the name, it must be pressed using only locally grown cider apples. The use of Herefordshire cider (if available) helps to keep this recipe authentic and complements the fresh apple in the sponge perfectly; I used Colcombe House's Mischief on the River, although you can, of course, substitute it for any good-quality apple cider. The cake has a beautiful speckled colour to the crumb that is unique to this cake and looks great when sliced and served to your guests. The combination of baking soda and cider (I use a little more cider in my recipe than most) helps the cake to rise and stay light and airy; I like to sprinkle mine with caster sugar mixed with a little cinnamon to give this great cake a fantastic finish.

Vegetarian
Preparation time: 20 minutes
Cooking time: 30–40 minutes

Serves 8

INGREDIENTS

125g butter
125g light brown soft sugar
2 medium eggs, lightly beaten
220g self-raising flour, sifted
1 tsp bicarbonate soda
½ tsp ground cinnamon
1 dessert apple, peeled and finely chopped
200ml Herefordshire cider
Caster sugar and cinnamon to finish

METHOD

• Preheat the oven to 170°C and grease a shallow, 20cm square cake tin.
• Beat the butter and sugar together in a large mixing bowl until light and fluffy.
• Add the beaten eggs, flour, bicarbonate of soda and cinnamon and mix thoroughly.
• Without beating, gently mix in the apples and cider until thoroughly incorporated.
• Pour the batter into the prepared cake tin, level the top and cook for 30–40 minutes or until the top of the cake is golden, firm to the touch and a skewer comes out clean when inserted into the middle.
• Allow the cake to completely cool in the cake tin before turning out onto a serving board or plate.
• Sprinkle the top with caster sugar mixed with a little cinnamon to perfectly finish your cider cake.
• Serve on its own or with a splash of cream if you're feeling really naughty. Enjoy!

Reg Robins

Reg Robins was born in Hereford on 27 March 1922, but he always said he had two birthdays. When he tried to join the Army, aged 16, he was asked his age several times by the recruiting sergeant before the penny finally dropped. Reg added two years to his age to make him old enough to join up.

He was the youngest of four brothers who all ended up joining the 1st Herefords. "Having four brothers in the same regiment and in the same action was a bit of a worry, especially for my widowed mother," he said. "You were anxious about one another the whole time, especially me, being in command." Robins was a platoon sergeant when they left to fight. By 1942, the First Battalion had been selected along with the Fourth Battalion Kings Shropshire Light Infantry and the Third Battalion Monmouthshire Regiment to form the 11th Armoured Division. When called to war, the four brothers had to cross the Channel on different ships because they were not allowed to travel together.

Reg was wounded in France in 1942 but was back in action within 24 hours. In 1944, just after D-Day, he landed on Juno beach and recalls passing the graves of Allied troops from the first landing and thinking, "when will it be my turn?" In 1944, on the borders of Germany, he was hit again, as was his brother Bill. A week later they were flown home. The nerves in Reg's arms were damaged and, despite numerous operations, he never fully recovered. Incredibly, all four Robins boys made it home safely at the end of the war. On 21 March 2015, Lady Darnley, Her Majesty's Lord Lieutenant for Herefordshire, presented the Legion of Honour to Reg in recognition of his part in the liberation of France.

Up until his death Reg still visited Hereford Cathedral every month to pay his respects to the men he served alongside in the 1st Herefords who didn't come back. When asked if he would ever return to the beaches of Normandy he would answer: "I don't need to go back there to remind me – it's all in here," tapping the side of his head. "Every day." A staunch member of the Royal British Legion, Reg was serving as President of the Hereford North branch when he passed away on 29 December 2017.

Written by Emma Wilding, Help for Heroes

> *"Having four brothers in the same regiment and in the same action was a bit of a worry, especially for my widowed mother"*

Ahead of the curve

Barefoot Caravan's stylish, curved and aerodynamic living spaces are not only ideal for exploring but also draw a crowd at festivals and promotional events

www.go-barefoot.co.uk

When solicitor Cathy Chamberlain attended festivals and outdoor events with her friends, she often wished that she could stay in style and comfort. In 2012, she decided to do something about that and began to design her dream caravan. Teaming up with established sidecar manufacturers Watsonian Squire, she came up with Barefoot Caravan: a classic-looking curved caravan made of leakproof fibreglass, designed and fitted to the highest standards. The first Barefoot Caravan was completed in 2015 and made an immediate impact.

"It seems to make people smile," she says. "I wanted it to be easy-to-tow, aerodynamic and charming. It's a timeless design. We weren't intentionally trying to be retro but we wanted to be classic with a modern twist. It is comfortable, light and bright and inside it has lots of space. It's like a Tardis!"

Designed and manufactured in Britain, the caravan is also selling well in the United States, South Korea and Australia. Each Barefoot Caravan is made-to-order and looks unique, with customers able to choose from a range of exterior colours and different upholstery designs. The idiosyncratic curvaceous design means some elements – notably the door hinges and curved front window – have to be made bespoke, while the interior elements are tailored and fitted especially for the curved design to maintain the sense of flow. The Barefoot packs in a sitting area, large bed, kitchen, shower room and lots of storage.

The Barefoot Caravan's distinctive appearance makes it instantly recognisable. This sees it being used by companies for promotional events and has led to a shared sense of community among owners. "We have an owners' group set up by one of our customers and there is a strong community building around the caravans," says Cathy. "They love the fact we are manufacturing in Britain. We often sell to people who haven't been caravanning before. I think that is because it is narrow and easy-to-tow and it has a level of quality in the design and finish they haven't seen in caravans before. People love the fact they can go to outdoor events and festivals in luxury and have a home-from-home experience."

Critical infrastructure

HS Infra provides critical and secure infrastructure for governments and military clients around the world, always using the knowledge and expertise of ex-forces personnel

www.hsinfra.co.uk

There can't be many companies in the UK whose staff have almost five centuries of military experience between them, but that's something the personnel of HS Infra can boast with pride. The firm is headed by CEO Steve Hutchinson, who founded the company in 2015 after 30 years in the Royal Corps of Signals. When Steve joined the Army direct from school as a teenager, he was working with Morse code but by the end of his Army career he was an officer dealing with high-security data, radio and satellite networks. This was where he developed the knowledge and expertise he was able to put into HS Infra, a company that provides end-to-end solutions for critical infrastructure in IT and construction, working closely with the Ministry of Defence and UK government.

"Essentially, we deliver secure and critical infrastructure to the MoD and we have some very exciting contracts lined up over the coming years," explains Steve, enigmatically. "It's an expansive area. We do secure data, as in fibre and copper networking, secure IT systems and mechanical services – for instance, cooling and electrical services. We have also stepped into construction, taking on contracts to build secure facilities for the UK and overseas governments. That gives us quite a wide portfolio which we define as critical infrastructure – essentially, we help the government and military protect their data. The people we work with understand what we do and come to us based on our reputation, which is something that gives us enormous pride."

HS Infra's senior management has extensive experience of delivering outstanding results in demanding situations, planning and delivering secure infrastructure globally and delivering high-end infrastructure projects in austere environments, meeting the high MoD standards at all times. The company recently acquired its own office space in Herefordshire and is now looking to expand internationally via its connection to the MoD and UK government. "Most of our contracts are UK-based," says Steve, "but we have a number of overseas contracts in the UK MoD space and in 2021 we will be visiting a number of countries to deliver some of our projects, which will give us more of an international presence."

As the company has grown from a skeleton staff to around 30, Steve recruits directly from the Armed Forces, often former soldiers who he served alongside in his previous role. His wife Debbie (pictured opposite, above, with Steve), who served for 24 years, is one of the company directors and is responsible for developing the company's long-term strategy. HS Infra is part of the Armed Forces Covenant and Steve admires fellow former service personnel for their agility, adaptability and effectiveness. A shared vocabulary also helps. "All of our client base is military and government," he says. "We speak their language and know exactly what is needed, which has created a very strong relationship. We pride ourselves on our reputation and relationships with the users and we have a very good rapport with our clients."

For Steve and his employees, the essential work they do to support the nation's critical infrastructure feels to them like a continuation of their military service and HS Infra remains a vital part of the country's secure infrastructure. "That ties in very much with who we are as people and what we want to achieve," he says. "We also support a number of military charities to maintain the bond with our military heritage."

Lemon posset with poppy seed shortbread

Chef Siobhan Kent, Royal Navy

Posset dates back to the 1400s. It was originally a drink made from curdled milk enriched with sugar and alcohol (the most popular being sack, a sweet ale similar to sherry). Popular among our kings and queens, its exact origin has been lost in the mists of time but was said to have been consumed to celebrate special occasions. Posset sets, used to mix and serve the possets, were popular gifts, so much so a posset set from the Spanish ambassador, made of gold, crystal and precious gems, was given to Queen Mary I of England and King Phillip II of Spain when they became betrothed in 1554. This set is on display today in Hatfield House, Hertfordshire. The modern posset – sweetened cream, set with an acidic fruit – can be found on many a high-street restaurant's menu.

Hertfordshire

Vegetarian
Preparation time: 30–40 minutes
Cooking time: 30 minutes,
 plus 6 hours setting time

Serves 4

INGREDIENTS

For the posset
400ml double cream
100g caster sugar
1 large lemon, zest and juice
10ml limoncello
4 tbsp lemon curd

For the shortbread
125g plain flour
20g ground almonds
40g cornflour
160g unsalted butter, diced
60g icing sugar
¼ tsp almond essence
50g poppy seeds

METHOD

To make the possets
• In a small saucepan bring the cream and sugar to a boil over a low heat, let it simmer for 4 minutes and then set aside to cool.
• Whisk the lemon zest, lemon juice and limoncello into the cream mixture until well incorporated.
• Spoon one tablespoon of lemon curd into each of four wine glasses, level out, pour even amounts of the posset on top of the lemon curd and place in the fridge to chill for 6 hours or overnight.

To make the shortbreads
• Preheat the oven to 180°C and line a baking tray with baking parchment.
• Sift the flour, ground almonds and cornflour into a bowl.
• Cream the butter and sugar together in a mixing bowl until light and fluffy, mix in the almond essence and poppy seeds until combined then fold into the flour and almond mix to form a stiff dough.
• Wrap the biscuit dough in clingfilm and rest in the fridge for 15 minutes.
• Remove the dough from the fridge, roll it out on a lightly floured surface to about 5mm thick and cut into biscuits with a 5cm round cutter.
• Place these onto the prepared baking tray, leaving a 2cm gap between each shortbread biscuit, then place in the fridge to rest for 15 minutes.
• Bake for 10–12 minutes or until lightly browned and transfer to a wire rack to cool.

To serve
• Serve the chilled possets with the poppy seed shortbreads.

Lieutenant Colonel Arthur Martin-Leake VC & Bar, VD

Arthur Martin-Leake was born on 4 April 1874, the fifth son of eight children, at High Cross, near Ware in Hertfordshire. He studied medicine at University College Hospital, eventually qualifying in 1893. He was initially appointed to the District Hospital in Hemel Hempstead but, following the onset of the Boer War, he joined the Hertfordshire Yeomanry in 1899.

After serving his year as a trooper, where he was involved in the surrender of Prinsloo (a key Boer officer), Leake stayed in South Africa as a civilian surgeon in the Army before joining the South African Constabulary (formed by General Baden Powell). It was on 8 February 1902 when the 27-year-old Leake, a surgeon captain still serving with the South African Constabulary, would win his first Victoria Cross. During action outside the town of Vlakfontein, Leake attended to a wounded man, despite being under fire from approximately 40 Boers only 100 yards away. He then rushed to the next wounded soldier, an officer this time, and continued to deliver medical assistance despite being shot himself three times. By this point all eight in the patrol were wounded, but Leake refused water until all of his patients had been tended to. He was repatriated back to Britain due to his wounds, where he received the VC for his selfless commitment and devotion.

Leake returned to the medical profession and, by 1903, was a Fellow of the Royal College of Surgeons, despite still recovering from his wounds. He then served in India as the Administrative Medical Officer with the Bengal-Nagpur Railway until 1912, when he returned to England on leave – just in time for the start of the Balkan Wars. Leake again volunteered for active service, this time with the British Red Cross as part of the Montenegrin Army, receiving the Order of the Red Cross from Montenegro's King Nicholas.

He returned to India, but again volunteered for service on the outbreak of war in August 1914, this time as a lieutenant. Between 29 October and 8 November 1914, aged 40, Leake won the first ever Bar to a VC, during the First Battle of Ypres, after rescuing a large number of Allied wounded while under heavy fire; again his citation mentions devotion to duty and conspicuous gallantry. Promoted to major in 1915 he ended up in charge of the whole of the 46th Field Ambulance in April 1917, ending the war as a lieutenant colonel.

> *"Aged 40, Leake won the first ever Bar to a VC, during the First Battle of Ypres, after rescuing a large number of Allied wounded while under heavy fire; his citation mentions devotion to duty and conspicuous gallantry"*

Leake left the Army after the Great War and returned to India, before retiring to the family home in Ware in 1937, aged 63. However, on the outbreak of war in 1939, he again volunteered, this time as a surgeon in a mobile medical unit. After the war, Leake returned to retirement before passing of lung cancer in June 1953, aged 79.

This incredible individual is commemorated with a plaque and a tree dedicated to his memory in the National Memorial Arboretum in Alrewas, Staffordshire. There is also an Arthur Martin-Leake Way named in his memory in Ware, as well as a memorial paving stone. His medals are displayed in the Museum of Military Medicine at Keogh Barracks in Mytchett, Surrey.

Written by WREN Telephonist Tania Murray, Royal Navy (retired)

Highland berry verrine

Senior Aircraftsman Darren McLellan, RAF

Scotland produces over a third of the UK's soft fruit and has been famous for the quality of its produce for well over 100 years. Raspberries, strawberries, blueberries, blackberries, blackcurrants and gooseberries thrive in the long summer days of the cool Scottish Highlands where the farmers protect the crops from the elements by growing them in long polytunnels, pollinating them with swarms of bees. This dessert uses berries from an Inverness-shire farm famous for its selection of delicious berries. These verrines (named after the small glasses in which they are served) are simple to make, but are a very tasty and attractive way to present your dessert and impress your friends and family.

Preparation time: 20 minutes plus 4 hours to set

Serves 4–6 (depending on the size of your verrine glasses)

INGREDIENTS

For the berry compote
800g mixed red berries
4 tbsp brown sugar

For the mousse base
175g caster sugar
50ml water
3 egg whites
250ml double cream

To garnish
Mixed berries
Mint leaves
50g dark chocolate

METHOD

To make the berry compote
• Place the berries and sugar in a heavy-based pan over a low heat, bring to a simmer and let the fruit cook, carefully stirring occasionally, for about 20 minutes until soft; set aside to cool.

To make the mousse
• Boil the sugar and water to 120°C (using a sugar thermometer).
• Meanwhile beat the egg whites to stiff peaks in a stand mixer then slowly pour in the sugar syrup, in a steady stream, whisking continuously.
• Continue whisking at a medium speed for 10–15 minutes until the mixture has cooled.
• Beat the cream in a separate bowl to soft peaks, fold in half of the cooled compote, mix in a third of the meringue then carefully fold the remaining meringue into the mousse; spoon into a piping bag fitted with a plain 1cm nozzle.

To assemble
• Spoon a little of the remaining compote into the bottom of your chosen glasses, pipe a layer of the mousse on top and repeat with as many layers as you like.
• Cover the verrines and leave to set in the fridge for at least 4 hours or ideally overnight.
• Garnish with berries and mint leaves with a little grated dark chocolate over the top to finish.

Able Seaman John "Jackie" MacLennan, Royal Navy

John "Jackie" MacLennan (pictured, right, with his brother Charles) was born 19 January 1926, one of five siblings raised in Hilton Village, Inverness. His father died when he was young. "My mother had to do it all on her own and times were hard," Jackie recalls. "We didn't have much growing up." When the Second World War broke out Jackie's older brother Alistair, 11 years his senior, was drafted into the Army. When Jackie turned 17 in 1943, he volunteered to join the Royal Navy and, after his training, found himself aboard HMS *Kimberley*, a K-class destroyer.

In July 1944, *Kimberley* commenced special duties during the planned Allied landings in the south of France as part of Operation Dragon. That August, Winston Churchill boarded and embarked on a trip to the assault area – Jackie remembers the prime minister posing for photos on deck with the crew. A few months later, HMS *Kimberley* joined Operation Olive, in support of the Italian campaign, and started bombarding the coastal city of Rimini on 1 September 1944. "I was on the guns and we fired everything we had at them," says Jackie. "We even had air support that radioed the ship to inform us if we were on target or if adjustments needed to be made." The attack lasted until 13 September, by which time Rimini had been hit by over 1,470,000 rounds, and only 2 per cent of its buildings were left undamaged.

At the end of 1944, HMS *Kimberley* landed in Piraeus, the port of Athens. Jackie went ashore and noticed soldiers wearing a red eagle badge, the sign of his brother Alistair's division, the 4th Indian Infantry. "I asked one of them if they knew my brother, so they drove me out to where he was staying. One of them called out: 'Mac, you've got a visitor'. It had been so long that Alistair didn't recognise me!" It turned out that Alistair's division had watched the intense bombardment at Rimini, but had no idea that young Jackie was leading the attack.

HMS *Kimberley* was one of only two K-class destroyers to survive the war. It was later broken up for scrap in March 1949. After the war, Jackie and Alistair returned home to Inverness. Jackie (who now lives in Nairn) became a painter and decorator, while Alistair was a mechanic who worked on the buses. Many other brothers across the world were not so lucky to survive the war.

Written by Flight Sergeant Katrina Harries, RAF

> *"We fired everything we had at them. We even had air support that radioed the ship to inform us if we were on target or if adjustments needed to be made"*

Clean thinking

From decontaminating transport infrastructure to cleaning up oil spills, Ambipar Response is helping to keep the environment clean and safe

www.ambipar.com

Whenever a hazardous event occurs – a chemical accident or an oil spill – Ambipar Response springs into action. This crisis management and counter-pollution specialist is responsible for maintaining the country's coastal areas through a contract with the Maritime and Coastguard Agency, and works with everybody from Network Rail to the Environment Agency to clean up crisis sites. The company also works with counter-terrorism agencies and is called in for response to biological, chemical and radiological incidents.

"We do significant work around critical national infrastructure such as power stations, refineries and railway lines, ensuring they stay in operation in the event of an incident," explains Chief Executive Officer Zäl Rustom. "We provided Covid decontamination for the railway infrastructure to ensure that food, PPE and key workers could move up and down the country, and we carried out the first decontamination of flights repatriating travellers from Wuhan."

The company was formed in 1948 by Danny Vernon Howells and it was asked to clean up one of the country's first oil spills a few years later. It has had several names and different owners over the years but is now owned by the Ambipar Group, a Brazilian company that specialises in crisis response worldwide. Over the years, Ambipar Response has developed a unique capability to respond quickly and flexibly to any problem, deploying trained personnel from more than 150 worldwide locations to deal with anything from a small local oil spill to an international maritime disaster. Much of this is down to the staff, a significant number of whom are drawn from the military and merchant navy.

"That is something I am looking to grow as ex-service personnel have an excellent grounding," says Zäl. "They are the can-do crowd. They understand change, they are flexible and they can deliver. That's an essential part of our success. We will throw ourselves at novel tasks because we can do some good and make some money. As a company, this is our focus."

The art of blending

With a recipe that dates back 300 years, Usquaebach uses a blend of the finest single malt and grain whiskies to create a quintessential Scotch whisky

www.usquaebach.com

When one handles a beautiful porcelain flagon of Usquaebach's "Old-Rare" Blended Scotch Whisky, it is like holding a vestige of precious history. This exceptional Scotch whisky brand, with over 225 years of tradition, is a tribute to the intricate art of blending. Usquaebach's flagship "Old-Rare" blend is a unique combination of 41 carefully selected single malts and two of the finest grain whiskies.

"This is a very elegant and smooth whisky," says American owner Sean Perry, who acquired the brand in 2005. "In the 1800s, people enjoyed complex, mellow whiskies. With its porcelain flagon, 'Old-Rare' is like a time capsule of whisky past – very authentic."

Sean is fiercely protective and proud of Usquaebach, which wears the badge of honour to be "The First Name in Scotch Whisky". The modern-day word for whisky is derived from this ancient word meaning "water of life" in Scottish Gaelic. Memorialised by Robert Burns in his 1790 poem "Tam o' Shanter", Usquaebach was a common term for whisky in the late 18th century. During the Victorian era, the word was trademarked and, centuries later, ownership of the company moved to America. Usquaebach gained a strong reputation in the United States, where it was proudly served at the White House during two inaugural dinners in 1969 and 1989. Today Usquaebach is highly acclaimed by scotch connoisseurs around the world.

Like most Scotch whiskies – single malts included – Usquaebach prides itself on skilfully bringing together whiskies of many ages and various casks, and, in Usquaebach's case, many distilleries, to create outstanding Scotch whiskies. Blended whiskies like Usquaebach offer complex and diverse flavour profiles thanks to gifted master blenders, who build whiskies using superior single malts and grain whiskies.

In addition to "Old-Rare", Usquaebach offers three distinctive expressions, all comprised of premium whiskies strictly from the Scottish Highlands. "The Reserve" is a classic blend comprised of more than 50 per cent quality single malts aged between 16 and 18 years; "15 Year" blended malt, which is a marriage of single malts aged for a minimum of 15 years; and finally, its limited-edition "An Ard Ri" ("The High King") cask-strength blended malt is an expertly crafted blend of 20 single malt whisky casks aged up to 21 years. This expression is finished in sherry casks and, despite being cask strength, it is exceptionally smooth, making it a dram suitable for the most special occasions. "An Ard Ri" is also served in porcelain flagons to honour tradition and emphasise quality.

"It would be much less complicated to bottle in glass, but we are dedicated to bottling these expressions in handcrafted porcelain flagons," says Sean. "That is how whisky was traditionally bottled, and we are determined to keep that tradition alive." This belief chimes with Usquaebach's refreshing approach to its craft. In an era when the premium spirit market is dominated by novelty, Usquaebach offers the promise of tradition, consistency and authenticity. "I consider Usquaebach to be innovative considering today's marketplace," says Sean. "We are committed to core values of quality, tradition and authenticity, over profitability and gimmicks. Expert master blenders and longstanding relationships with many distilleries allow us to create timeless whiskies. Our plan is to keep doing just that."

Lincolnshire plum bread and butter pudding

Corporal Chris Scotting, RAF

My love affair with Lincolnshire began in 1990 when my father was posted to RAF Scampton, and over the past 30 years I have become an honorary "Yellowbelly" (a native of Lincolnshire). I have spent time all over the county, including Cranwell and Nettleham, and now reside in Sleaford. The familial link to the RAF was a major factor in my decision to join the military and the inspirational stories of the Dambuster raids and the bravery of Guy Gibson and his crew have always stuck in my mind. Picking a dish to represent this magnificent county was no easy feat, given that everyone associates Lincolnshire with sausages. This dish, however, is warming and comforting and reminds one of being by a blazing fire in one of the county's village pubs.

Vegetarian
Preparation time: 30 minutes
**Cooking time: 1 hour for the bread
 and 40 minutes for the pudding**

Serves 6

INGREDIENTS

For the plum bread
225g butter
340g caster sugar
450g mixed dried fruit
1 cup of cold tea
2 medium eggs, beaten
450g self-raising flour
Butter, at room temperature

Custard mix
3 whole medium eggs
3 medium egg yolks
75g caster sugar
1 vanilla pod, split lengthways
 and seeds scraped out
500ml double cream

To serve
Custard, double cream
 or vanilla ice cream

Lincolnshire: Local hero

Vivian Hollowday GC

To willingly enter a crashed and burning aircraft in an attempt to rescue the crew once is a significant act of bravery; to do so twice, is outstandingly so. For these two separate acts, Vivian Hollowday was awarded the George Cross, the first non-commissioned member of the RAF to receive the decoration.

Aircraftsman Vivian (Bob) Hollowday was born 13 October 1916 at Ulceby, near Grimsby, in North Lincolnshire. Joining the RAF Volunteer Reserve at the outbreak of World War Two, he was posted to 14 Flying Training School at RAF Cranfield, near Bedford.

On 2 July 1940 he was returning to camp and saw an aircraft crash and burst into flames. Rushing through burning debris, he entered the aircraft and found the pilot, Sergeant Noel Davies, on fire. Hollowday used his bare hands to extinguish the flames. Unfortunately, his endeavour was in vain; Davies, aged 20, had been killed instantly in the crash.

A month later, again returning to his unit, Hollowday witnessed a further aircraft accident, where ammunition had exploded. Borrowing a gas mask and using sacking as rudimentary protection, he entered the wreckage no less than four times before he was able to extract the first occupant. He then re-entered the fire to remove a second crew member. Despite all his efforts, again, the three-man crew had all been killed in the crash. For these two incidents of incredible gallantry, Hollowday was awarded the George Cross on 21 January 1941, receiving it the next year at Buckingham Palace.

He served in both the European and North African theatres, achieving the rank of Corporal. Postwar he was able to find work at a company called Quenbey Price in Bedfordshire with the help of Mr Church, with whose family he had been billeted in 1940.

In later life, Vivian became President of the Military Medallists League, a supporter of the Royal Chelsea Hospital, was actively involved with the Royal Society of Saint George, and was a member of the Legion of Frontiersmen. He was also an active Committee Member of the Victoria Cross and George Cross Association before passing away on 15 April 1977 in Bedford. His medal group – which also includes the 1939–45 Star, Africa Star, Italy Star, France and Germany Star, Defence Medal 1939–45, War Medal 1939–45 with oak leaf and 1953 QEII Coronation Medal – is held in the RAF Museum collection. Hollowday's "unofficial" medals include the Cross for European Confederation, Australian Bronze Medal and the Belgian Albert 1st Merit Cross. He was also given the Freedom of the City of London in 1966.

Written by Warrant Officer Kevin Morley, RAF

METHOD

For the plum bread
- Preheat the oven to 140°C and lightly butter two 900g loaf tins and line with baking parchment.
- Mix together the butter, sugar, dried fruit and tea in a saucepan and stir over a low heat until the butter is melted.
- Mix together the beaten eggs and flour in a large mixing bowl.
- Gently mix the warm butter mixture into the flour and eggs a little at a time.
- Divide the batter between the prepared loaf tins and bake in the preheated oven for an hour or until a skewer or small knife comes out clean when inserted into the middle; if necessary cook for a further 10 minutes.
- Leave the loaves to cool for a few minutes in the tins then transfer to a wire rack and leave to cool completely.
- Thickly slice the cooled plum bread, butter generously then fill a baking dish with multiple layers of the delicious bread.

For the custard
- Whisk together the eggs, egg yolks, sugar and vanilla seeds.
- Heat the cream to scalding point then whisk into the egg mixture.

To bake the pudding
- Pour the custard over the layers of plum bread and leave to soak for 20 minutes.
- Meanwhile, preheat the oven to 160°C.
- Bake in the preheated oven for 35–40 minutes or until the custard has just set.

To serve
- Let the pudding sit at room temperature for 10 minutes then serve with your choice of custard, double cream or vanilla ice cream.

Mix masters

From its base in Lincoln, Cocktail Delivery can dispatch high-end, professionally mixed cocktails within 24 hours, nationwide

www.COCKTAILDELIVERY.co.uk

The night the UK went into its first lockdown in March 2020, Jim Claffey and Mat Graham had been looking forward to sharing a few Old Fashioned cocktails in their favourite bar. Instead, they set up a video call and by the end of evening had formed Cocktail Delivery, offering a menu of around 20 professionally mixed cocktails in personalised packaging for next-day delivery anywhere in the UK.

"To have that high-quality bar-finish cocktail in your home wasn't possible before now – we were the first people to offer that," says Jim. "These are pre-batched, prepared the way the best bartender would, and packaged in premium bottles. All the customer needs to do is add ice, shake and pour. Through this period, people wanted to send cocktails to their friends and family, and we helped people connect through lockdown."

Online videos help with preparation, while there are mixology masterclasses for those who want to learn how to produce the perfect cocktail. The shake is essential – "every great cocktail you have ever had has been shaken" – and Cocktail Delivery is able to create exciting cocktails using a wide range of ingredients and premium artisan spirits. As well as classics like the Old Fashioned and Espresso Martini. The team – Jim, Mat, mixologist Sophie Bradley and sales manager Hannah Price – enjoy inventing new cocktails such as an Earl Grey Mar-tea-ni and Margarita Picante with infused chili and coriander.

All cocktails come with an air-dried garnish and are created, mixed and bottled in Lincoln. They make popular gifts and can be used for weddings, birthday and corporate events, while hotels and restaurants have started to use the service, attracted by the speed, consistency and exceptional quality. "It's hard to make a great cocktail at home," says Jim. "You need knowledge and a deep pocket to have the range of ingredients required. We have ingredients you'd never think of using and we know how to balance a cocktail so it's not too strong or too weak. We have the experience, we understand taste and we love making brilliant cocktails."

Pavlova

Sergeant Chris Nicols, Army

Pavlova is a meringue-based dessert named after the eminent Russian prima ballerina Anna Pavlova. It's claimed that the head chef at the famous Wellington Hotel created the dessert after being inspired by the dancer's tutu. Pavlova essentially comprises a meringue, cooked with a crisp shell and soft marshmallow-like interior, topped with whipped cream and filled with fresh berries. Although it has been heavily debated whether Australia was the first to claim pavlova as a national dish, evidence suggests that New Zealanders were the first to make it after receiving packages of corn starch imported from America, which included simple recipes for meringue bases. These were tried, tested and tweaked, and so the pavlova was born.

Vegetarian, gluten-free
Preparation time: 35–40 minutes
Cooking time: 1 hour 10 minutes

Serves 4

INGREDIENTS

For the meringue
4 large egg whites
210g caster sugar
½ tbsp cornflour
1 tsp white vinegar
1 tsp vanilla extract

For the fruit and cream topping
200ml double cream
2 tbsp icing sugar
1 tsp vanilla extract
Fresh berries, such as blueberries,
  strawberries or raspberries
Sprigs of mint for decoration

METHOD

• Preheat the oven to 140°C and ensure there is a shelf in the middle of the oven.
• Line a baking tray with baking parchment and draw a circle around a plate roughly 18cm in diameter; this will be used as a guide for the meringue base.
• Wipe a mixing bowl and whisk attachment with a clean tea towel to remove any traces of grease.
• Whisk the egg whites to soft peaks; you can use an electric mixer or whisk by hand, but again ensure they are dry and free of any grease.
• Gradually add the sugar, whisking continuously, until all of the sugar is incorporated and the egg whites form stiff glossy peaks; fold in the cornflour and vinegar (this will help with that marshmallow-like texture you want for the meringue centre) and finally whisk in the vanilla extract.
• Spoon the meringue onto the lined baking tray, keeping it within the circle and level the top; ensure the sides are slightly higher to create that small dip you want for that lovely cream and berry topping.
• Place the tray in the middle of the preheated oven for 1 hour 10 minutes or until the meringue is starting to colour and has a crisp shell.
• Turn the oven off and leave the pavlova in the oven with the door open for 20 minutes then leave to cool for a further 10 minutes at room temperature.
• Whisk the cream, icing sugar and vanilla to soft peaks.
• Wash the berries and place in a colander to remove any excess water.
• Once the meringue has completely cooled, spoon the cream into the middle, leaving a border around the edge, arrange the fresh berries on the cream and decorate with a few sprigs of mint.
• Cut into four large portions and serve immediately with any leftover berries.

Moana Nui a Kiwa Ngarimu VC

Moana Nui a Kiwa Ngarimu was born on 7 April 1919 in Whareponga on New Zealand's North Island, the son of Hamuera Meketu Ngarimu and his wife Maraea. After being schooled in Whareponga and Ruatoria, Ngarimu attended Te Aute College, where he excelled in rugby, before starting to work on the family farm. As the Second World War broke out, Maori MPs requested that the New Zealand government allow Maori to serve overseas; on 4 October 1939 the 28th New Zealand (Maori) Battalion was established, organised on a tribal basis. Ngarimu signed up on 11 February 1940.

On 1 May 1940 the Maori Battalion left for England, where Ngarimu was chosen to undertake intelligence duties, becoming a second lieutenant and platoon leader in the battalion's C Company. The Maori Battalion encountered heavy fighting during the African Campaign in Greece, Crete, Libya and the battle of El Alamein. By March 1943, the 22nd Division (of which the Maori Battalion was a part) was moved to Tunisia. As part of the Battle of the Mareth Line, Ngarimu and C Company were tasked with taking Point 209, a fortified German position that the Maori soldiers called Hikurangi, after their mountain at home.

Lieutenant Colonel Bennett, Battalion Commander, wrote of Ngarimu: "Displaying courage and leadership of the highest order, he was himself first on the hill crest, personally annihilating at least two enemy machine-gun posts. Wounded in the shoulder and leg, he stayed with his men." On 27 March 1943 the enemy counter-attacked. Ngarimu was killed this time. Even his enemies testified to his outstanding courage, and the Germans later surrendered that day. Apparently, Ngarimu had just written to his parents describing a dream of his great grandmother Hana Maraea who was beckoning him.

For his bravery, determination and outstanding leadership Ngarimu was awarded the Victoria Cross. It was presented by the governor general to his parents in Ruatoria on 6 October 1943. The ceremony was attended by 7,000 Maori and recorded by the National Film Unit. His grandmother, Makere Ngarimu, died the night his VC was presented. His citation was published in English and Maori in a booklet entitled *The Price of Citizenship*. He is commemorated in the Ngarimu VC and 28th (Maori) Battalion Memorial Scholarship Fund, set up in 1945 to promote Maori education and the maintenance of Maori language and culture.

Written by Captain Steve Blanks, Army

> *"Displaying courage and leadership of the highest order, he was himself first on the hill crest, personally annihilating at least two enemy machine-gun posts"*

Keeping the forces up to date

D3A Defence uses its extensive Armed Forces expertise
to serve as an essential intermediary between the military
and defence-sector contractors

www.d3a.co.uk

When Craig Haslam joined the military aged 17, he told his parents, "I'll stay as long as I'm enjoying it." Nearly three decades later, after 17 years in the Marines and a further 10 as a Special Forces soldier, he was still convinced he'd found his vocation. This came to an abrupt end in 2015, however, when he sustained life-changing injuries after being knocked off his pushbike by a car. "I was medically discharged, but I left kicking and screaming because I wasn't finished," says Craig. "My devotion remains to the military, and to all who serve."

That hunger took Craig (pictured, opposite, top right) into working for the defence industry, where he soon spotted gaps in the market that could benefit from his military expertise. He set about forming his own company to fill those gaps and, in 2019, D3A Defence was born. Taking its name from the military acronym for "Decide, Detect, Deliver, Assess", the business operates as an essential go-between for the military and the many companies competing for equipment and training contracts across the Armed Forces.

"The defence industry has been very quick to push products on its end users," says Craig. "Unfortunately, this doesn't always plug the capability gaps. For example, the training on offer hasn't always been at the right level. The UK military is changing quickly, and I want to help them understand those gaps and how best to fill them."

Ninety per cent of D3A's staff share military backgrounds, with an average length of service of more than 20 years, and 70 per cent of them remain reservists. "We sign the Armed Forces Covenant and stick to it like glue," says Craig. "I want to ensure we're still giving back." This means that the company has ongoing access to the most up-to-date military requirements, a wealth of individual experience and an ever-expanding personal network to underpin their products. These range from specialist training – everything from camera and software techniques to tactical strategy – to bid and acquisition support for both the military creating industry reports for tender, and the companies competing for business. "Essentially, we're independent interpreters between the military and industry," Craig explains. "We're here to help both."

One of the company's specialities is providing simulation support, training the military to use different software, as well as maintaining and operating existing systems. "Importantly, we can gauge the level of expertise required for every aspect of training," he adds. "After all, we've all been there."

In fact, at the heart of every D3A project are those men and women Craig used to serve alongside. "We believe the furthest forward soldier needs to be the biggest beneficiary of everything we do," he says. "Whether it's equipment or training, whether it's for a junior private or a colonel, everything revolves around them."

In just two years, the company has won a significant number of contracts and already seen its workforce expand, despite the huge challenges presented by lockdown occurring only a few months after it formed. "We were lucky, we had enough work to keep everyone busy," recalls Craig. "No one was furloughed and the staff were extraordinary in their efforts."

As D3A Defence continues to grow, he is determined to maintain the ethos that has been with him since he embarked on his career aged 17. "The furthest forward soldier will always remain our biggest beneficiary. We're here for the long haul, and it'll always be him or her we're thinking of."

Yorkshire curd tart

Lance Corporal Pete Frettingham, Army

Yorkshire curd tart is Yorkshire's rustic version of the modern cheesecake but, in my opinion, it trumps a cheesecake every time. In this recipe the sweet pastry beautifully complements the curd cheese filling, resulting in a rich and full flavour. Originally, this would have been made with curd from the farm but these days curd cheese is readily available from supermarkets. Curd tart is often seen in tea and coffee shops across Yorkshire, filling the bellies of walkers, tourists and those out wanting to experience local food, much of which has been modernised while retaining the great original and traditional flavours. I particularly love that this recipe is rarely made outside of Yorkshire, preserving its unique Yorkshire heritage; it's a real treat for visitors.

Preparation time: 15 minutes
Cooking time: 30 minutes

Serves 6–8

INGREDIENTS

For the sweet shortcrust pastry
150g plain flour
2 tbsp icing sugar
75g cold unsalted butter,
 cut into 1cm dice
1 egg yolk
½ tsp lemon juice

For the filling
50g caster sugar
225g curd cheese
2 whole eggs
2 egg yolks
1 lemon, zest only
1 tsp rosewater (optional)
25g unsalted butter, melted
50g currants
Sprinkle of nutmeg

METHOD

For the pastry
- Preheat the oven to 200°C.
- Mix the flour and icing sugar together in a bowl, add the butter and rub it in with your fingertips until it resembles fine breadcrumbs.
- Mix the egg yolks, lemon juice and a tablespoon of water together and mix into the flour mixture; the best way to do this is to create a small well in the flour before bringing it all together with a small spoon or knife. If the mixture is too dry, add in small amounts of water until the dough comes together.
- Wrap the dough in clingfilm and chill in the fridge for at least 2 hours.
- Butter the base and sides of a 20cm loose-bottomed sandwich cake tin.
- Take the pastry out of the fridge and roll out between two sheets of baking paper until you have a disc that measures about 15cm across.
- Remove the top sheet of baking parchment and quickly place your hand under the pastry and carefully flip onto the tin, remove the bottom piece of baking parchment and line the cake tin, ensuring you push the pastry into all the corners.
- Cut away any excess pastry ensuring you leave about 1cm to allow for shrinkage during cooking; return to the fridge to allow it to firm up.
- Tip: when handling the pastry, try to work quickly so it doesn't warm up too much. If this does happen, return it to the fridge and allow it to firm up – this will allow it to be handled with ease.

To blind bake
- Once chilled, prick the base of the pastry with a fork ensuring you don't pierce the whole way through.
- Line the pastry case with baking parchment and fill with ceramic baking beans or uncooked rice.
- Blind bake for 15 minutes, then remove the parchment and beans and return to the oven for a further 5 minutes until lightly coloured.

Mix for the curd filling
- Lower the oven temperature to 180°C.
- Beat the curd cheese and sugar together until smooth and mix in the melted butter, egg yolks, whole eggs and lemon zest, stir in the currants and, if you're using it, the rosewater.
- Pour the filling into the baked pastry case and bake for 20 minutes until it's just set, it will continue to cook once it is removed from the oven; set aside to cool on a wire rack.
- Once cooled remove the tart from the tin, cut into wedges and either serve on its own or with some ice cream or lightly whipped Yorkshire cream.

North Yorkshire: Local hero

Edna Holland

Anyone cutting down a big tree today would make light work of it with a chainsaw. However, in the 1940s, powered chainsaws were incredibly rare. The only tools available were axes and saws – even if you were one of the thousands of women in the Women's Timber Corps, the Forestry Section of the Woman's Land Army during the Second World War.

On the day Britain declared war on Germany, 3 September 1939, all males between 18 and 41 had to register for service, so women had to perform many roles previously carried out by men. Aged 17, Edna Holland (née Lloyd) from Beverley in the East Riding was one of some 9,000 "lumberjills" employed during the war. "The Forestry Commission men taught us everything they knew," she said. "They were going into the forces and wanted to pass on their knowledge of how to fell a tree and to make sure we knew how to do it properly so we could carry on their good work when they were gone. They were not prejudiced at all. They always accepted us and treated us well. Some of the younger men that went to war had worked in the forests from the age of 14 after finishing school. It was hard work, but we learned such a lot. We started off by learning to fell a tree. Then we were taught how to measure different sized pit props. My goodness, we got muscles everywhere! But it made us feel really good."

Edna carried out her training in Wetherby and was then stationed at Boltby, where she felled trees across the North Yorkshire Moors. This timber was a vital asset and was used to make telegraph poles, roadblocks, packaging boxes and gun butts for the war effort, and even crosses for war graves. Edna spent three years as a lumberjill, and her comrades provided vital support when her brother Bill was killed during the invasion of Italy in 1943. "We were all devastated," she says. "I was very close to him and he was very popular with all the girls."

Ray Lonsdale's steel sculpture in recognition of the lumberjills stands in Haygate Bank, Dalby Forest, near Pickering. The Women's Timber Corps was only part of the vast troop of women across the UK who took up roles previously undertaken by men, making a significant contribution to the war effort.

Written by Flight Sergeant Katrina Harries, RAF

Yorkshire terroir

For the gin producers behind Spirit of Harrogate, it's the access to high-quality spa water and local botanicals that makes their award-winning gins and spirits so memorable

www.spiritofharrogate.co.uk

The proud and beautiful Yorkshire jewel of Harrogate has been celebrated for its natural spring water since 1571, when William Slingsby first uncovered its unique health-giving properties. These waters include high quantities of salt, iron and some of the highest sulphuric content in Europe. For decades, the water was prescribed as a health cure but now it can be experienced through Spirit of Harrogate's Slingsby gin, which launched in 2015 and has already won dozens of national and international awards.

"My business partner Mike Carthy and I wanted to do a series of products that reflected the heritage of the town where we live and work," explains co-founder Marcus Black. "Gin is like wine, with a degree of terroir, and Harrogate has its water and access to other local ingredients that we use, like heather, nettle and primrose. We felt we could combine these ingredients to capture the essence of Harrogate."

After cycling through several recipes, Spirit of Harrogate's Slingsby London Dry was ready to launch in August 2015. Black describes it as a pre-war-style gin, reflecting an era before smaller distilleries were asked to stop making spirits and instead help with the war effort, something that led to the decline in gin's popularity and a focus on larger juniper-heavy gin brands. However, in the past decade, there has been a firm resurgence in gin thanks to artisan companies such as Spirit of Harrogate, who make softer, fruity gins that utilise botanicals grown in the kitchen garden of a local hotel or are sourced from the local countryside and moorland. This is supplemented by grapefruit and juniper sourced abroad – although Spirit of Harrogate has already planted juniper bushes at a local golf course so it can have its own supply of this key ingredient.

The company has forged links with other local businesses, producing bespoke gins for Michelin-starred venues in Leeds and working with the famous Bettys Tea Rooms to create a gin-infused chocolate and gin cookery experience. One early collaboration was with a local farm that produced Yorkshire rhubarb which Mike and Marcus (pictured, opposite) began adding to their London Dry gin. "We started it as a limited edition, offering customers to our Harrogate store a sample and it was extremely popular and then became an unbelievable success so it is our best seller by a considerable margin," says Marcus. "The rhubarb we use is paler in colour, sweeter and less sinewy and when we put it through our distillation process, we get an incredible taste. We have since added a gooseberry variant and we source the fruit just outside York."

The pair continue to innovate, combining their expertise – Marcus is an accountant and Mike a chemist – and deep love of the area to produce these stylish, distinctive and authentically Yorkshire gins. There's a Slingsby marmalade gin that uses a local marmalade preserve, an Old Tom made with Yorkshire liquorice, a barrel-aged gin, seasonal specialities like the Christmas Pudding Gin and also vodka, rum, pre-mixed drinks and spritzers. "Gin is a matter of personal taste but in Harrogate we have great water and that's such an important part of gin," says Marcus. "Between 58 and 63 per cent of gin is made of water and Harrogate water is something we have over other areas that produce a lot of gin. We are now in most of the major retailers and are growing our presence overseas. We want to be a global brand, taking the essence of Harrogate to the world."

Peach and marmalade hollygog pudding

Senior Aircraftsman George Finch, RAF

Hollygog pudding originates from the small village of Kiddington in Oxfordshire. It is a traditional farmhouse pudding that has been passed down through generations of farming families. The traditional pudding recipe consists of golden syrup rolled in shortcrust pastry then baked in milk. A classic home comfort food, my take uses Frank Cooper's traditional Oxfordshire marmalade with fresh peaches served with crème anglaise (fresh egg custard) flavoured with orange.

Preparation time: 50 minutes
Cooking time: 25–30 minutes

Serves 4

INGREDIENTS

For the pudding
2 ripe peaches
180g butter
4 tbsp caster sugar
50g cornflour
250g plain flour
60ml cold water
150g Frank Cooper's marmalade
Milk for baking
Demerara sugar for sprinkling

For the crème anglaise
150ml milk
150ml double cream
35g caster sugar
1 tsp cornflour
4 egg yolks
2 tsp orange extract
Zest of 1 orange, finely grated

METHOD

To make the pudding
- Preheat the oven to 200°C.
- Score a cross at the bottom centre of the peaches, bring a saucepan of water to a boil and poach the peaches until just tender.
- Drain the peaches, place into a bowl of cold water and, once cold, carefully peel off the skin, halve, remove the stone and finely slice.
- In a bowl, add the butter and sugar then sift in the cornflour and flour.
- Rub the mixture with your fingertips until the mix resembles breadcrumbs.
- Add the water and mix until a soft dough is formed (add a little extra water if necessary); wrap the pastry in clingfilm and leave to rest in the fridge for 20 minutes.
- Roll out the pastry to a 1cm thick square and trim off any uneven edges.
- Evenly spread the marmalade over the pastry, evenly scatter over the sliced peaches and roll the pastry into a cylinder tucking each end underneath.
- Place the roll into a buttered ovenproof dish, add enough milk to come up to halfway up the sides of the roll, brush the top with milk and sprinkle over a little demerara sugar; place in the preheated oven and bake for 35–45 minutes.
- Remove the pudding from the oven, cover with a piece of foil and set aside to rest for a few minutes while you make the custard.

For the crème anglaise
- Pour the milk and cream into a saucepan and gently heat until nearly simmering.
- Place the sugar, cornflour and egg yolks into a bowl and whisk until the mixture thickens and becomes pale yellow in colour.
- Slowly add the hot milk and cream to the egg mixture, whisking constantly, until well combined into the egg.
- Pour into a clean saucepan and slowly heat, stirring continuously, until the custard has heated through; add the orange extract and continue to cook until the custard is thick enough to coat the back of the spoon.
- Cut the pudding into four even portions and serve in a bowl with the crème anglaise and scatter over the orange zest.

Major John Howard DSO

The son of a London barrelmaker, Reginald John Howard's humble beginnings make him something of an anomaly among officers. Born on 8 December 1912, he was a promising maths student and was awarded a scholarship to a secondary school but, due to financial hardship, he had to turn to full-time work at 14. In 1932, he enlisted in the Army as a common soldier, receiving his basic training at Shrewsbury with the King's Shropshire Light Infantry. He was made company clerk, and also honed his physical skills to become a physical training instructor. Due to lack of education his application to become an officer was rejected, but he made Corporal before the end of his six-year enlistment period.

After the Army, he joined the Oxford city police, marrying Joy Bromley in 1939 prior to raising two children. With war looming, Howard was called back to the King's Shropshire Light Infantry as a Corporal and quickly rose through the ranks, to Company Sergeant Major and, in April 1940, Regiment Sergeant Major. A month later, the Brigade Commander offered Howard the chance to commission; he joined the Oxfordshire and Buckinghamshire Light Infantry, rising to the rank of Captain by the end of the year.

When his battalion was marked for conversion to airborne in early 1942, Howard volunteered for the transition, rising to the rank of Major in 1942 and commander of "D" Company, which he proceeded to train and drill for the next two years. During the planning phase of D-Day, Major Howard's company was selected to perform a surprise gliderborne raid to seize two key bridges, the Bénouville and Ranville, to ensure transfer of supplies from Sword Beach.

Howard honed techniques from numerous pre-invasion exercises, using a spot near Exeter that was geographically similar to the French bridges. On June 1944, three gliders containing 90 men in total from "D" Company were released at 8,000 feet over the Normandy coast. Howard's constant training paid dividends; all gliders landed almost on top of their targets with the assault troops engaging their objectives immediately. Howard proceeded to set up a command post inside a trench, while his platoon continued to hold their objectives. By the time the German command realised what had happened, Howard's forces had been bolstered by the 7th Parachute Battalion and a detachment of commandos from the 1st Special Service Brigade, who marched over the bridge to the sound of bagpipes. With these reinforcements, they

"Howard's constant training paid dividends; all gliders landed almost on top of their targets, with the assault troops engaging their objectives immediately"

were able to hold Pegasus Bridge against the attacks of the 21st Panzer Division, securing the success of D-Day. Howard was nominated for the Distinguished Service Order.

A car accident forced Howard out of the Army, resulting in him taking a job in the Ministry of Agriculture. On the tenth anniversary of D-Day in 1954 he was awarded the Croix de Guerre avec Palme by the French government, while a road over Pegasus Bridge was named in his honour. In June 1959, a book about "D" Company's assault on the bridges was published entitled *The Longest Day*; it was turned into a film in 1966, with Howard serving as a consultant. Howard retired in 1974, settling in Burcot, Oxfordshire; he returned to lay a wreath at Pegasus Bridge every year until his death on 5 May 1999, aged 86.

Written by Flight Lieutenant Daniel Beechey, RAF

Collective security

The Steadfast Group offers bespoke security services – from mobile patrols and surveillance to CCTV and fire alarms – all the time guided by military-standard operating procedures

www.steadfastsecurity.co.uk

Even as a youngster Mike Harbord, the founder of The Steadfast Security Group, had an entrepreneurial mindset, raising money in his spare time by cleaning windows and selling fish. He credits his late grandfather with his business sense, with Mike spending his weekends working at the family's butcher shop. After leaving school, however, the prospects of a career in the British Army took precedence and, after his basic training, he was deployed around the world. Mike (pictured, opposite top) was engaged in training and exercises in Canada, Germany, India, Sri Lanka, the Middle East and the Himalayas, and took part in operational tours of Northern Ireland. He was soon promoted to sergeant and became popular with his comrades, displaying a formidable personality, a will-to-win attitude and some often unconventional training techniques.

During his time in Northern Ireland, he suffered a helicopter drop and later a grenade explosion on exercise which cost him the sight of one eye. His injuries finally saw him discharged, with a war pension and 40 per cent disability. Never one to rest on his laurels and with little prospects of work, he turned his attention to business and started Steadfast Security in the early 1990s. Thirty years later that company, Steadfast Security, has expanded to offer a range of bespoke security solutions for personal business and domestic needs while continuing to maintain close connections with the military.

"I believe the success and longevity of Steadfast is underpinned by maintaining the high standards of the military," says Mike. "I'm a strong advocate of recruiting ex-military service personnel throughout the business and we support veterans with employment opportunities and sponsoring charity events in the community. We've signed up to the Armed Forces Covenant and we contribute to a range of military charities."

Both Mike's son Paul and daughter Natalie joined the board of directors after serving time in the military. "I'm obviously very proud of my kids serving the country in the way they have," says Mike, "and to have them join the company was great."

Mike's enthusiasm for future success lies with new technologies and innovative work methods. "As the security industry has evolved over the years, we have seen welcome legislation that has vastly improved standards that our customers now enjoy," he says. For instance, as CCTV (closed-circuit television) monitoring became a standard for the industry, Mike invested heavily in a 21st century control room. "This gives us the ability to monitor CCTVs throughout the country," he says, "expanding our operations nationally."

The company offers superior security service to businesses and individuals across the north-east and increasingly in London. "As a company we do mobile patrols, alarm systems, fire systems, close quarters, reconnaissance, cameras – we cover the whole security spectrum – and we are guided by military-standard operating procedures. We don't always talk about the support we provide as it is simply part of our mindset. We help people who need help because we would expect that for ourselves – it's the military attitude."

Mike currently has no plans for retirement. "I'll be on the ground until my boots wear out," he says, with a wry smile, "and maybe then Natalie and Paul can take the helm."

Rutland plum shuttles

Senior Aircraftsman Ryan Bennett, RAF

The plum shuttle is more of a folk tradition, rather than a signature dish of Rutland, that dates as far back as 1809. They were given to loved ones and potential love interests on St Valentine's Day instead of flowers or gifts. They are called shuttles because their shape resembles that of a shuttle used by handweavers and, while not as common in the modern day, they're still a tasty dish that's easy to prepare. My recipe, inspired by the traditional plum shuttle, has been tweaked slightly. It has a richer dough and a touch of added sweetness from the jam and cream filling – perfect for serving with tea and coffee or indeed giving to a potential date on Valentine's Day because, at the end of the day, who doesn't enjoy a nice bun?

Preparation time: 45 minutes
Cooking time: 30 minutes

Serves 12

INGREDIENTS

For the shuttles
450g plain flour
½ tsp salt
40g caster sugar
16g fresh or 8g dried active yeast
50ml warm water
100g butter
100ml warm milk
2 eggs, plus 2 beaten eggs for glazing
25g each of dried apricot, raisins, sultanas,
  cranberries and banana chips
100g tinned plums drained and diced
  (reserve 2 tsp of the juice)

For the filling
100ml double cream
10ml vanilla essence
250g strawberry jam

METHOD

For the plum shuttles
• Heat the oven to 200°C.
• Sift the flour and salt into a bowl.
• Cream the sugar and yeast together and mix with the water; leave to stand for a few minutes until frothy.
• Melt the butter in a pan, add the milk and warm through until tepid; remove from the heat, pour into a mixing bowl and beat in the eggs.
• Pour both the yeast and the milk mixtures into the flour and mix in the dried fruit and drained plums, with 2 tsp of the juice.
• Mix to a smooth dough and knead well for 5–10 minutes on a floured worktop until smooth; cover with a damp cloth and leave to rise until double in size, this can take up to 20 minutes.
• Knock back the dough by kneading again for 2 minutes.
• Divide the dough into 12 even-sized pieces and shape each into a small oval by rolling into a ball with your hands and then carefully rolling two opposite sides of each ball to form an oval with slightly tapering ends.
• Place on a greased baking tray, or one lined with a sheet of baking parchment, cover with a damp cloth and leave to rise for 15 minutes in a warm place.
• Brush with beaten egg and bake for 25–30 minutes until golden and they make a hollow sound when you give the bottom a light tap; transfer to a wire cooling rack.

To serve
• While the shuttles are cooling, add the vanilla essence to the cream and whip to stiff peaks.
• Once cooled, slice the shuttles down the middle from end to end to make a slit, spoon some strawberry jam down the middle and pipe or spoon the cream on top.

Wilf Hamit

Born on 16 October 1918 in Collyweston, Northamptonshire, Wilf Hamit spent most of his life living and working in the Rutland area. His mother passed away when he was only 11, and he and his four siblings were raised by their father. Wilf joined the Army aged 21, having just become engaged. Over the next six years – as part of the 7th Armoured Division, the fabled Desert Rats – he saw active service in several of the war's pivotal moments. He also lost his brother Marcus in the North African campaign.

Wilf was involved in the Dunkirk evacuation, El Alamein and the invasion of Italy. He came ashore at Arromanches in Normandy as part of the D-Day landings, and was then part of the liberation of France and Germany. But, like many soldiers, he didn't often talk about his service life. "He was shot at a few times," says his daughter Barbara, who lives in Cottesmore, Rutland. "He said that El Alamein was horrific. There was 40 minutes of gunfire, which is why he ended up so deaf. Dad said he was driving through the desert as part of a mission and they stopped to have a cup of tea. Within minutes they were machine-gunned down. Dad and one other soldier were the only survivors."

To have survived through so many key battles that shaped the Allied victory is an extraordinary achievement. "Dad was like the cat with nine lives," says Barbara. In 2019 he was visited by Lieutenant Colonel McCombe, the Joint Regional Liaison Officer for 7th Infantry Brigade and Headquarters East, who spoke to Wilf about his service memorabilia and swapped stories.

"It has been a great privilege to meet Wilf," said McCombe. "He is one of a group of extraordinary people that played a pivotal part in World War Two. They're our forefathers who laid the foundations for today's modern-day infantryman – who continue to serve all over the world, with the same commitment and professionalism. I've got a copy of his memoirs that I'm looking forward to reading and sharing with the younger members of the regiment. It's quite rare to meet someone who was in all the key places during the Second World War. He's a very impressive man." Wilf passed away on 20 December 2019 at the grand old age of 101.

Written by Flight Lieutenant RAJ Wells, RAF

> "*Wilf was involved in the Dunkirk evacuation, El Alamein, the invasion of Italy, the D-Day landings, and the liberation of France and Germany*"

Sierra Leone

Banana akaras with dipping sauces

Corporal Spencer Monaghan, Army

Sierra Leone

Doughnuts, in various shapes and forms, from around the world date back to the beginning of the 19th century and have been popular ever since. My version is a twist on an African doughnut or fritter, which I've served with chocolate and caramel dipping sauces. Africans have many names for fritters – in Sierra Leone they are called akaras and are sometimes referred to, colloquially, as "pofpofs". For Sierra Leoneans, rice is the essential staple food, eaten at every meal. It is used instead of flour in the batter for my recipe, alongside their favourite fruit, the banana. Akaras can be enjoyed as a dessert, snack or at lunchtime with friends; just make sure you get your share of the sauces!

Vegetarian, gluten-free
Preparation time: 40 minutes
Cooking time: 20 minutes

Serves 4

INGREDIENTS

For the akaras
4 large bananas, thickly sliced
½ tsp nutmeg
80g caster sugar
1 tsp vanilla extract
160g rice flour
80–100ml hot water
Icing sugar, to coat

For the chocolate dipping sauce
120ml double cream
80ml whole milk
3 tbsp (heaped) golden syrup
200g good-quality dark chocolate,
  broken into small pieces (not too bitter)

For the caramel dipping sauce
30g butter
80g light brown soft sugar
3 tbsp milk
60g icing sugar

To cook the akaras
Vegetable oil to deep fry

METHOD

For the akara batter
• Mash the bananas in a mixing bowl, add the nutmeg, caster sugar and vanilla extract and mix until well combined.
• Add the rice flour to the bowl and mix thoroughly to bring all of the ingredients together.
• This next stage is really important to make the dish a success; slowly mix in the hot water until the correct consistency is obtained, you want a thick batter that will hold its shape while frying; set aside to cool completely.

To make the chocolate sauce
• Put all of the sauce ingredients into a saucepan and gently melt over a low heat, stirring frequently, until your sauce is smooth and shiny; turn off the heat and leave the pan on the hob to stay warm.

To make the caramel sauce
• Place the butter, brown sugar and milk in a small saucepan and bring to a rapid simmer, stirring continuously, over a medium heat. Turn down the heat to low and simmer for a minute; set aside and allow to cool for 5–10 minutes then whisk in the icing sugar to finish the sauce.

To fry the akaras
• Heat enough vegetable oil to deep-fry the fritters in a suitable pan over a medium-high heat.
• Check oil is hot enough by testing with a small ball of batter; if it bubbles straight away the oil is ready, if not continue to heat.
• Drop heaped spoonfuls of the batter into the hot oil, cooking four at a time and ensuring they don't touch; carefully flip them over with a heatproof spatula or spoon so they cook evenly and get that lovely golden-brown colour on the outside.
• Drain the fritters on absorbent kitchen paper to soak up any excess oil, fry the rest of the batter and dust with icing sugar to finish.

To serve
• Serve warm, piled on a plate with bowls of both dipping sauces.

Pilot Officer Adesanya Kwamina Hyde DFC CBE

Adesanya Kwamina Hyde – known throughout his career as Ade Hyde – was born in Freetown, Sierra Leone in September 1915. Although born into the Kroo (a West African ethnic group known for their maritime skill, who were traditionally fisherman), Ade grew up in a Sierra Leone Creole (or Krio) house. After his education in Freetown, Ade saw an advert in the local paper for volunteers to join the Royal Air Force. True to his adventurous spirit, he enlisted in 1941 and, after arduous training, qualified as a navigator. He subsequently took part in more than 31 operations for Bomber Command, which included the D-Day operations over Normandy in 1944.

On 9 August 1944, Hyde (then a Flight Sergeant) and his crew set off to bomb a German V1 flying-bomb site in Les Chatelliers in northern France. However, as they neared their target under heavy enemy fire, a German anti-aircraft shell exploded close to Hyde's Lincoln Handley Page Bomber, which sent shrapnel piercing through the aircraft fuselage. A large piece of shrapnel struck Hyde and lodged in his right shoulder. The routine procedure following such a serious and painful injury during an operation was to administer a morphine injection. Ade knew that this would render him incapable of navigating back and therefore put the lives of the whole crew at risk. He refused the injection and navigated back to England in extreme pain. He only accepted the morphine when the pilot spotted the white cliffs of Dover and was sure he could find his way back to base unaided. In November 1944, Ade Hyde was awarded the Distinguished Flying Cross for this act of valour, courage and devotion to duty. After spending the next three months in hospital, he was promoted to Pilot Officer.

After demobilisation from the RAF, Hyde returned to Sierra Leone and joined the Colonial Service where he served for over 20 years, culminating with the role of Sierra Leone Ambassador to the United States. However, it was during Hyde's penultimate role as Secretary General of the National Reformation Council that he was awarded the CBE in Her Majesty's New Year's Honours list in 1968. Ade Hyde retired from public duties in 1969 and passed away in 1993, aged 78.

Written by Warrant Officer Guy Davies, Royal Corps of Signals, Army (retired)

"Ade knew that a morphine injection would render him incapable of flying home and put his crew at risk, so he refused it"

A global connection

Avanti is a British-based company that is connecting the world with satellite technology, using the expertise of ex-services personnel to help NGOs, governments and the military

www.avantiplc.com

The modern world thrives on communication. It was this knowledge that brought the two founders of Avanti together in the early 2000s – one an expert in satellites, the other an expert in finance. Both implicitly understood how rapidly the world was changing and both shared an audacious vision to design, build and launch pioneering satellite technology to help connect the world. "They had an idea in common but they came at it from different angles," says CEO Kyle Whitehill. "They managed to raise some money and then spent over $1 billion investing in satellite technology."

This British-based company now has offices with more than 200 staff across sites in the UK, Cyprus, Turkey, Kenya, Tanzania, South Africa and Nigeria as well as a fleet of geostationary-orbit high-throughput satellites (HTS) that provide secure voice and data communication across Africa and support the British and American military. As you'd expect, technology and innovation is the beating heart of Avanti. This was the first British company to launch a Ka-band satellite, HYLAS 1, and the first satellite operator to provide Ka-band services across the UK and Europe. Today, Avanti owns and operates a fleet of five high-throughput satellites covering Europe, the Middle East and Africa and a fully resilient and secure extensive ground network.

In addition, Avanti is a trusted provider of COMSATCOM to armed services and global government agencies, offering large capacity and very high throughputs. Technological capabilities include steerable beams in civilian or military parts of the electromagnetic spectrum, military-grade encryption and the ability to provide obfuscated positioning – all geared towards the needs of the military end user. It's this military connection

that has led to Avanti's work with military charities such as Walking With The Wounded. Kyle always had a strong interest in the military and almost joined the Royal Marines before moving into telecommunications, spending 17 years at Vodafone. He joined Avanti as CEO in April 2018, replacing co-founder David Williams.

"When I joined Avanti I wanted to build a military business working with armed forces in the US and the UK," he says. "We provide connectivity to them to ensure that they can get contact in very difficult terrain. I was then invited to a charity dinner and sat next to a young guy who had been injured on active service. As a company we then became very interested with that as an issue and agreed to support former service personnel. We want to help ex-veterans return to the civilian world and have started hiring ex-service people when we can. They make excellent employees as the military gives people enormous responsibility at a very young age."

As well as the military work, Avanti remains fully engaged with communication in Africa. Most of its satellite capacity – what Kyle describes as "the heart of the company" – is located above Africa. Avanti is the largest supplier to the continent's biggest mobile phone group, and the company plays an essential role in connecting rural communities. "That was the original mission and we now provide coverage across all of sub-Saharan Africa," says Kyle. "We have invested our time and effort into providing connectivity into schools in a number of different African countries, particularly supporting girls' education, which in Africa is a real challenge, bringing them content and contact through broadband."

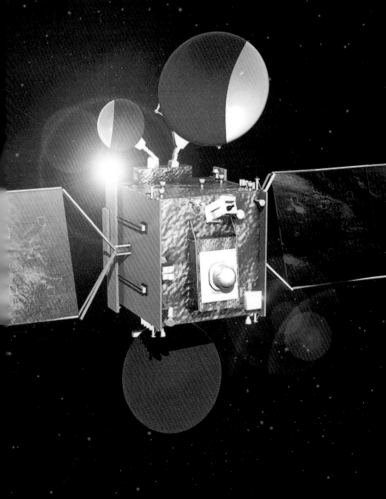

Ernest Shackleton-inspired mince pies

Leading Catering Services Simon Hopkins, Royal Navy

An inspirational 20th century character, Sir Ernest Shackleton, knighted by King Edward VII, was famous for his Antarctic missions and adventurous spirit. On his final expedition to the Antarctic in 1922, Shackleton suffered a fatal heart attack in South Georgia and, at his wife's request, was buried there in the Grytviken cemetery. During his expeditions, nutrient-packed foods such as mince pies, biscuits and jackfruit were eaten by the crew, all of which I have included in my Shackleton-inspired recipe. I have added a contemporary twist to the traditional mince pie by cooking a shortbread case, filling it with my homemade mincemeat and serving it with a Cointreau sauce and citrus-marinated jackfruit garnish.

Vegetarian
Preparation time: 1 hour,
  including pastry resting time
Cooking time: 45–50 minutes

Serves 4

INGREDIENTS

For the mince pie filling
2 Bramley apples, peeled, cored and diced
4 oranges, grated zest and juice
100g sultanas
100g raisins
100g currants
75g light brown soft sugar
1 tsp mixed spice
10ml Cointreau

For the shortbread biscuit
150g plain flour, sifted
75g caster sugar
100g butter, chilled and diced

For the Cointreau sauce
100ml milk
10g butter
10g plain flour
¼ tsp ground nutmeg
100ml Cointreau
50ml clear honey
10ml double cream

For the jackfruit garnish
1 jackfruit (you can use canned
  if fresh is unavailable)
2 oranges
1 lemon
50g caster sugar

METHOD

For the mince pie filling
- Mix all of the ingredients together and store in a sealed jar until ready to use.

For the shortbread biscuit
- Preheat the oven to 160°C and lightly butter four muffin tin moulds.
- Place the flour and sugar into a large mixing bowl, rub in the butter until it starts to bind together then knead lightly to form a smooth dough.
- Roll out the dough on a lightly floured worktop to the thickness of a one pound coin and, using pastry cutters, cut out four discs large enough to line the moulds and four discs to fit the top.
- Carefully line the muffin moulds with the four large discs, place the four smaller discs on a baking sheet lined with parchment paper and chill both in the fridge for 30 minutes.
- Cook in the preheated oven for 15–20 minutes until golden brown; allow the shortbreads to cool and harden in the moulds then transfer them to a wire rack to cool completely.

For the Cointreau sauce
- Pour the milk into a saucepan and bring to a simmer over a medium heat; set aside.
- Melt the butter in a heavy-based saucepan over a medium heat, stir in the flour and cook, stirring constantly, for a couple of minutes then gradually add the hot milk, stirring continuously, until smooth.
- Stir in the nutmeg, Cointreau and honey and cook on the lowest setting, stirring frequently to ensure the sauce doesn't catch on the bottom, for 20–30 minutes.
- Remove from the heat, stir in the cream, taste and add a little more honey if required; set aside to keep warm.

For the jackfruit garnish
- Preheat the grill to medium-high.
- Prepare jackfruit by removing the core and pips.
- Grate the zest of the oranges and lemon, mix with the jackfruit, dust with caster sugar and grill until the jackfruit is cooked and golden brown.

To serve
- Fill the shortbread biscuit cases with the mince pie filling and place a lid on top.
- Dress the jackfruit garnish in the centre of four plates, place a mince pie on top and spoon over the warm Cointreau sauce.

South Georgia: Local hero

Lieutenant Commander Ian Stanley DSO

One of the first acts of the Falklands War was to re-take South Georgia. The plan was to insert elite SAS troops by helicopter onto Fortuna Glacier and march down the spine of the South Georgia mountains, taking the occupying Argentinian force by surprise. However, as three Wessex helicopters inserted the task force during the night of 21–22 April 1982, an enormous 100mph storm engulfed the glacier. Freezing temperatures and low visibility forced the SAS troop commander to radio back for rescue.

Ian Stanley was the mission commander, leading the rescue formation in the radar-equipped anti-submarine Wessex 3 helicopter. In close formation with him were two troop-transporting Wessex 5 "Junglies". The three cabs crept up the glacier towards the SAS team to land next to them, but a snow squall wiped out all visibility and a Wessex 5 crashed into the glacier, rolling onto its side and throwing debris everywhere. Stanley landed next to the wrecked Wessex 5 and managed to load up the crashed SAS troops and aircrew, including one injured soldier. With ten people in Stanley's cab and 14 in the other, they rose again. But, barely ten seconds after launch, another ferocious snowstorm hit the formation, causing the other Wessex 5 to crash. Faced with no other option, Stanley returned to HMS *Antrim*, to load up with medical supplies and blankets. They returned to where they thought the wreckage was but were unable to locate the survivors on the glacier through the thick cloud and blizzards.

Later that afternoon, Stanley had one last crack at recovering the survivors. Instead of creeping slowly up the glacier, he flew high above to see if they could find a gap to spot the survivors. Unbelievably, they saw a single orange life raft, and Stanley spiralled down to land his Wessex 3 beside it and load up the survivors. He squeezed 14 large passengers into his tiny cabin and back towards HMS *Antrim* in atrocious conditions. He still had to safely land back on a moving ship, and his heavy payload left him with no margin for error. His incredible skill saved what could have been a total disaster. Ian Stanley was awarded the Distinguished Service Order (DSO) for his actions and has been the subject of many books. He now has a mountain on South Georgia – Stanley Peak – named after him.

Written by Lieutenant Matt Le Feuvre, Royal Navy

Rhubarb and custard

Leading Chef Lee Calver, Royal Navy (retired)

I have loved rhubarb from a young age. This, along with the fact that some of my biggest chef influences now own Michelin-starred restaurants in Yorkshire, gave me the inspiration to create this recipe. A seasonal fruit, Yorkshire rhubarb is known for being the best in the world; forced rhubarb is grown quickly and produces a great flavour. In this dessert I have recreated a twist on the popular rhubarb and custard sweet.

South Yorkshire

Gluten-free
Preparation time: 30 minutes
 plus 2½ hours setting time
Cooking time: 20–30 minutes

Serves 4

INGREDIENTS

For the custard panna cotta
1½ sheets bronze leaf gelatine
350ml double cream
100g caster sugar
1 tbsp vanilla extract
4 large egg yolks

For the poached rhubarb
200g Yorkshire rhubarb, peeled and trimmed
2 tbsp grenadine syrup
50g caster sugar
700ml water

For the grenadine syrup jelly
5 sheets bronze leaf gelatine
530ml rhubarb cooking liquid

METHOD

To make the custard panna cotta
• Soak the gelatine in cold water, place the cream, sugar and vanilla into a saucepan and bring to a boil over a medium heat.
• Place the egg yolks into a mixing bowl and whisk in about a third of the boiled cream; pour the egg and cream mix back into the hot cream, return to the heat and stir, but do not boil.
• Once the custard is hot, squeeze the water out of the gelatine, stir into the custard until dissolved, then strain through a fine sieve and pour into four wine glasses, dividing the custard evenly between them. Put the glasses into the fridge to set.

For the rhubarb
• Cut the rhubarb into lengths small enough to fit into a saucepan, add the caster sugar, grenadine syrup and water, bring to a boil then turn the heat down and simmer, checking the rhubarb regularly.
• To check if the rhubarb is cooked, gently pierce with a small knife and once the knife goes through with little resistance, turn off the heat and allow the rhubarb to carry on cooking in the liquid.
• Once cooled slightly, carefully remove the rhubarb from the liquid, place onto a cutting board to cool and strain the cooking liquid through a fine sieve.

To make the grenadine syrup jelly
• Soak the gelatine in cold water.
• Measure out 530ml of the rhubarb cooking liquid, pour into a saucepan and bring to a simmer; squeeze the water out of the softened gelatine and stir into the hot liquid until completely dissolved.
• Strain the jelly through a fine sieve, pour into a shallow baking dish and chill in the fridge for about 2 hours until set.

To assemble
• Cut the rhubarb into 1cm slices, remove the jelly from its container and cut into small cubes.
• Place five pieces of poached rhubarb on top of the set panna cotta and top with three cubes of jelly, you can add micro lemon balm or lemon zest to finish.

Lieutenant Commander Eugene Esmonde VC DSO

Born near Sheffield on 1 March 1909, Eugene Esmonde came from a military family. His brothers served in the Great War and his great uncle was awarded the Victoria Cross in the Crimean War. Esmonde was raised a Catholic and initially wanted to become a priest but applied to join the RAF in 1928. He was awarded his pilot's wings in December 1929 and served in several squadrons before leaving the RAF in 1931. After a spell as a commercial pilot with Imperial Airways, Esmonde was offered a 15-year commission and promotion to Lieutenant Commander if he resumed his career as a military pilot with the Fleet Air Arm. He accepted in April 1939, taking command of 754 Naval Air Squadron (NAS), flying Walruses and Seafoxes before being moved to 825 NAS in May 1940. Esmonde led his squadron of Swordfish in anti-submarine, anti-shipping strikes and ground-attack sorties from RAF Detling. Two embarkations aboard the carrier HMS *Furious* saw the squadron operating in Norway and the Mediterranean.

In May 1941, Esmonde and 825 NAS embarked on HMS *Victorious* and were immediately involved in the hunt for the Bismarck. Esmonde led nine Swordfish in atrocious weather to strike the gargantuan German warship but failed to sink it. Despite this, he was personally awarded the Distinguished Service Order from King George VI on 11 February 1942.

The next day, Esmonde was ordered to attack three German capital warships that were audaciously attempting to return home through the English Channel. Braving terrible weather, the six Swordfish were promised an escort of six squadrons of RAF Spitfires. After only a single squadron of Spitfires arrived, Esmonde pressed on with the attack regardless, his six biplanes facing the anti-aircraft fire of three warships and their escorts. All the RAF planes were shot down, with only five men out of 18 surviving. Eugene Esmonde and his crew were killed. His bravery resulted in the award of one of only two naval aviation Victoria Crosses of the war. He was even mentioned in Churchill's speech of 13 May 1945.

Esmonde's body later washed ashore in the Thames Estuary and he was buried in Woodlands Cemetery in Gillingham, Kent. He is still a hero of the Fleet Air Arm; his photo and VC citation are on the wall of the main briefing room at the Merlin MK2 training squadron (824 NAS) and he has a road named after him at RNAS Culdrose in Cornwall.

Written by Lieutenant Commander Mark Barber, Royal Navy

"His bravery resulted in the award of one of only two naval aviation Victoria Crosses of the war"

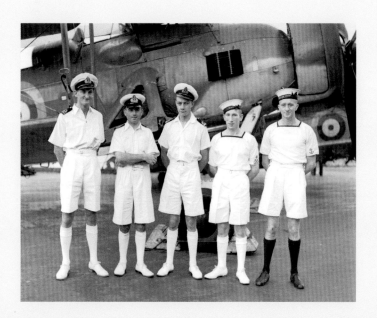

The finest cut

Pantera Carpentry works on high-rise building developments around the south-east of England as well as providing upscale joinery for furniture and interiors

panteracarpentry.com

When Pete Mills and Robert Farquhar co-founded Pantera Carpentry in 1998, the pair had no idea their partnership would one day evolve into a business with a turnover of £20 million and a history of producing outstanding work for some of the country's largest developers. As Pantera has grown it has introduced apprenticeship and management trainee schemes to maintain its high standards, while contributing to a range of national charities.

"Charity work is very important to us," says Pete Mills. "With this company, it's not just about making a profit – it's about giving something back. That can be our charitable work or it can be our apprenticeships. There is something very rewarding about seeing young people who come into the business who want success and work so hard. Seeing them grow is better than any paycheck."

Employees include former members of the Armed Forces, who are hired through the Armed Forces Covenant scheme. "They often go into site management and project supervisor roles as they have very transferable skills," says Pete. "As we've grown, the issue has always been bringing in the right people. We started an apprentice scheme and mentored them so that every apprentice has a mentor who is a board member or senior management, who meets with them and reviews their progress every three months. We then started a management cadet programme, taking school and college leavers and putting them through a relevant degree on a three-to-five-year programme."

Pantera's major projects include large-scale and complex developments such as One Tower Bridge and Wood Wharf in Canary Wharf, as well as general housebuilding. The company offers a range of services, working with housebuilders to provide the carpentry for roofs, doors, porches and floors and interiors such as wardrobes, stairs and bathrooms. For major projects, it concentrates on entrance and communal areas such as the reception, concierge, gym and spa.

The turning point for Pantera came when the company reached a certain size and Pete realised they needed what he describes as "some grey hairs" to help them move to the next level. He brought in a chairman, Paul Healey, who remains essential to the Pantera story. "Paul said we had a great company and we could push to become a bigger outfit, or we could stay where we were and still do very well," says Pete. "We decided we wanted to be the best and we never looked back. Paul then mentored me in networking, building relationships and charity work. He organises an event every year for Marie Curie that raises £400,000 from this single event and he does a lot of charity cycle treks. I accompanied him on a trek for his 65th birthday and I've completed one each year since."

Pete is proud of not just what Pantera has achieved but also the way they've done it. "We worked very long hours, we spotted talent and we kept the right people around us," he says. "Some of the carpenters have stayed with us, gone to college and are now directors in the business. We have always tried to be different. As we started as carpenters ourselves, we care about the people who work for us and have won numerous awards for our health and safety standards. We care about our guys and make sure they are properly equipped and looked after."

Surrey scrum

Emma Kennedy, comedian, writer
and Celebrity MasterChef winner

*Here's my take on a classic Portuguese custard
tart – that mainstay of posh bakeries, known as
the pastéis de nata – but here using the fabulous
raspberry as a surprise centre.*

Surrey

Vegetarian
Preparation time: 30 minutes
Cooking time: 25 minutes

Makes 24 small or 12 large

INGREDIENTS

For the filling
2 large egg yolks
1 whole egg
100g golden caster sugar
2 tbsp cornflour
400ml single cream
1 vanilla pod (or a couple teaspoons of
  vanilla extract to your own taste)

For the cases
One sheet ready-made puff pastry

METHOD

To make the filling
- Mix together your egg yolks, egg and sugar in a saucepan (don't put it on the heat yet) until they turn a lighter colour. I use Burford Brown eggs – their almost orange yolks are wonderful. Then whisk in your cornflour. Take your cream and slowly whisk it in. Add the vanilla, if you're using a pod, scrape out the seeds and throw the whole pod in as it cooks. Your mixture should be silky and smooth.
- Put your pan on a medium heat and stir or whisk constantly until the mixture thickens. Be careful your mixture doesn't catch on the bottom. I prefer to whisk rather than stir with a spoon, I find it stops clumps forming. As soon as your mixture comes to the boil, remove from the pan and pour immediately into a bowl. Cover it with clingfilm and let it cool. You can leave the vanilla pod in – all it's doing is adding taste.

To make the cases
- Take one sheet of puff pastry, cut it in half and lay one half on top of the other. Then roll the sheets in a tight tube. Using a sharp knife, cut 24 discs (don't worry if they don't look like discs, you're going to flatten them in a minute). If you prefer larger versions, cut 12 discs.
- Lightly flour a board and using a rolling pin, roll each disc into a round.
- Lightly butter a muffin tin – I use the 24 ones but if you can use a 12-muffin tin if you want the larger versions. Press your rolled discs into each muffin hole. Make sure you haven't got any holes.

To cook
- Spoon in the cooled filling, popping one raspberry (add 2 or 3 if you're making larger ones) into the filling then cover over with more custard filling.
- Place into a pre-heated oven (200°C, 180°C fan, Gas mark 6) and cook for around 25 mins or until they're golden brown on top. Let them cool in the tin for 5 minutes and then move them to a cooling rack.
- Your Surrey scrums are ready. They can be eaten warm but I prefer them cold. Delicious with a dollop of clotted cream. Enjoy!

Lord Henry Manvers Percy VC

Lord Henry Hugh Manvers Percy was born in 1817 at Burwood House in Cobham and was the third son of Louisa Harcourt and George Percy, Lord Lovaine (later the fifth Duke of Northumberland). Percy obtained his commission in the Grenadier Guards as an ensign on 1 July 1836. After a spell serving in Canada, he was appointed adjutant to the 1st Battalion in 1947.

As captain and lieutenant-colonel in his regiment, Percy served in the Crimean War, during the Eastern Campaign of 1854–55, where he was wounded twice, at the battles of the Alma and Inkerman. He also fought at Balaclava and at the siege and fall of Sevastopol. The Crimean War was a particularly brutal conflict, famous for the Charge of the Light Brigade and the rise of Florence Nightingale.

During the battle of Inkerman, the Grenadiers found themselves some distance from the Sandbag Battery. Percy decided to charge single-handed into the battery, followed immediately by the guards. Later that day, he found himself, with many men of various regiments who had charged too far, nearly surrounded by Russians, and without ammunition. Despite being wounded, Percy managed to evacuate more than 50 of his men, leading them through the terrain under heavy Russian fire. For his actions, he was recognised on the spot by Prince George, the Duke of Cambridge, and was later awarded the Victoria Cross.

Furthermore, for his gallantry in the Crimea, Percy was promoted to Colonel and appointed an aide-de-camp to Queen Victoria (1855–65). The French awarded him the Legion of Honour; the Turks gave him the Order of the Medjidie, 4th Class. He was also awarded the Crimea Medal with four clasps, and the Turkish Medal.

As well as a period in parliament as a Conservative MP for North Northumberland, Percy continued his service after the Eastern Campaign, eventually rising to the rank of general on 1 October 1877. Sadly, the promotion was short-lived; on 3 December 1877, Percy died suddenly at his home in Eaton Square, Belgravia. He was buried in the family vault in St Nicholas Chapel, Westminster Abbey, his coffin adorned with his plumed hat, sword, Victoria Cross and Order of the Bath. His VC is held by the Royal Northumberland Fusiliers Museum, Alnwick Castle.

Warrant Officer Class 2 James Hawker, Army (retired)

> *"Despite being wounded, Percy managed to evacuate more than 50 of his men, leading them through the terrain under heavy Russian fire"*

Making catering a piece of cake

Crane Patisserie London provides high-end bespoke desserts,
first-class catering for events and a gourmet home-delivery
service, with flavours that speak for themselves

www.cranepatisserie.com

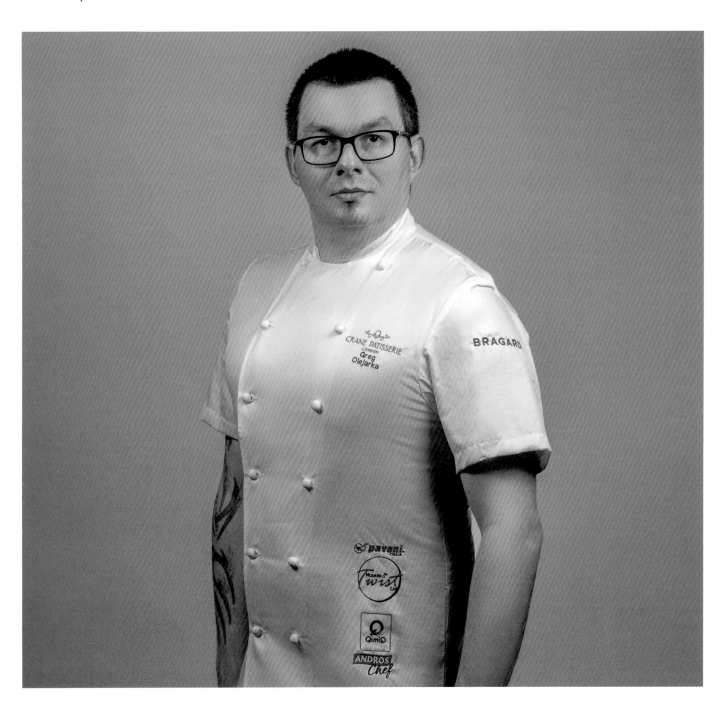

The spectacular rise of Crane Patisserie London since its launch in 2019 reflects what can be achieved through sheer dedication and drive. It also represents a triumph for its international founders – chef Grzegorz Olejarka and business owner Lucanus Wijeyesekera.

Fuelled by Grzegorz Olejarka's passion for patisserie, Crane Patisserie has become renowned for its bespoke desserts and pastries. "We stand out from the crowd because we create things that are handmade and bespoke to the client's needs, not the other way round," says Grzegorz. "Clients come to us with an idea and a date and a budget and we come up with a solution. At present nobody else in the UK can create cakes of this quality in such volume and at a price to match your budget." Corporate clients include several major hotel chains, while Crane Patisserie also supplies private customers who need a cake for a special occasion, whether for a birthday or anniversary. While most bespoke cake companies require up to three months' notice for this sort of service, Grzegorz prides himself on delivering at short notice, sometimes in as little as 48 hours.

As well as high-end cakes, the company also provides first-class gourmet catering. "We can provide full three- or four-course gourmet catering for events, or custom menus planned around our customers' needs," says Grzegorz. The 2020/2021 pandemic has also shown Crane Patisserie's ability to think outside the box and use its skillsets creatively. It now offers a home-delivery service that Grzegorz hopes will continue even as lockdown draws to a close. "We began to do gourmet meals, five or six courses with the ingredients and instructions or how to cook it," he says. "That has been very

popular. It's all pre-packed and part-cooked so you just need to heat, assemble and serve with the instructions as if you were in a restaurant. That is something different, something exciting and unusual, and we want to continue this after lockdown. Our online portfolio is growing daily. We keep lifting the bar higher with something different, something exciting and unusual to tempt most palates."

Born in Poland with mixed Polish and Italian heritage, Grzegorz benefits from the influence of two distinctive cultural cuisines as well as a powerful work ethic imbued by his military-trained grandfather. He worked his way through the ranks in some prestigious establishments in Poland, France and the UK, from Michelin-starred restaurants to five-star hotels, ending as head chef at the world-renowned Mandarin Oriental London. His co-founder Lucanus was born in Sri Lanka and educated in Italy and has also worked his way through some renowned UK establishments to become an expert in catering and hospitality.

Crane Patisserie makes a point of using seasonal produce, taking full advantage of its excellent location in Alton, Hampshire, surrounded by rich and diverse farmland and close to the coast. "We will always use whatever is in season," says Grzegorz. "I really enjoy cooking with the English seasons. If something is in season, you have to use it. You don't export strawberries in the winter when you can get things like blood orange as they are in season – there are so many fruits you can use. That access to great seasonal produce is one of the great things about working in the UK." From timeless classics to novel dishes, Crane Patisserie London has it all.

Warm Welsh cakes with honey-baked plums

Sergeant Ian Mark, RAF

Popular since the 19th century, Welsh cakes are a very simple but delicious dish to make. This is my modern twist, making the traditional Welsh cake almost pancake-like and serving it with one of Wales's most popular fruits and vanilla ice cream.

Vegetarian
Preparation time: 10 minutes
Cooking time: 25 minutes

Serves 4

INGREDIENTS

For the honey plums
8 plums, destoned and quartered
50g clear honey

For the Welsh cakes
450g self-raising flour
2 tsp baking powder
⅓ tsp mixed spice
⅓ tsp ground cinnamon
⅓ tsp ground nutmeg
170g caster sugar
225g margarine
160g sultanas
2 medium eggs, beaten with
 a splash of milk
1 tsp vanilla extract

To serve
Vanilla ice cream

METHOD

For the plums
• Preheat the oven to 180°C.
• Place the plum quarters onto a small baking tray, pour over the honey and place in the preheated oven for 15 minutes, basting with the honey and juices every 5 minutes.
• Remove the plums from the oven, cover with foil and set aside to allow the plums to steep in the liquid.

For the Welsh cakes
• Sift the flour into a mixing bowl and mix in the baking powder, spices and sugar.
• Rub the margarine into the flour mix to a sandy texture, mix in the sultanas and make a well in the centre; add the beaten eggs and milk and, using your hand, bring the mixture together to a dough, but don't overwork.
• Lightly flour a worktop and roll out the dough to 5–7mm thick and, using a round 8cm cutter, cut into discs.
• Cook the cakes in a non-stick frying pan over a medium heat until golden brown on both sides.

To serve
• Stack two Welsh cakes on each plate and spoon over the plums and juices.
• Serve with vanilla ice cream.

Wing Commander Frederick "Taffy" William Higginson RAF DFM DFC OBE

The son of a Welsh-speaking policeman, Frederick Higginson was born in the Gorseinon district of Swansea in 1913. He was educated at Gowerton County School before joining the RAF in 1929 aged just 16, where he was immediately nicknamed "Taffy". Initially trained as a fitter and air-gunner, his life was changed when he was accepted for flying training in 1935.

By May 1940, he was a seasoned frontline pilot having flown Gloster Gauntlets during the Battle of France. On 17 May 1940, now flying the Hawker Hurricane with 56 (Punjab) Squadron, Higginson achieved his first kill, a Dornier Do 17. By 30 September 1940, he had survived the Battle of Britain, been awarded the Distinguished Flying Medal (for demonstrating greatest determination in the face of the enemy, and cool and courageous leadership), been commissioned as an officer and had increased his personal score to 12 enemy aircraft. One of Higginson's crash landings came after an engagement with a Messerschmidt fighter, which resulted in the aircraft shooting each other down and both crash-landing in the same field.

In June 1941, he was shot down and captured over Dunkirk. Higginson was bundled into the sidecar of a motorcycle by a German soldier and took advantage of a momentary distraction from a low-flying aircraft, grabbing the handlebars and tipping the motorcycle. After a year of evasion, re-capture and escape he finally reached safe territory in Gibraltar in September 1942, disguised as a priest.

On his return to No. 56 Squadron, Higginson re-trained on the Typhoon as a tactics instructor. In 1943, Higginson was awarded the Distinguished Flying Cross for his consistent participation in his squadron's operational activities, displaying great skill and courage in combat with the enemy throughout. He spent the remainder of the war in various staff posts. Outside of work, Taffy was a keen rugby player, playing for London Welsh, Richmond and Surrey until he was 40. Higginson left the RAF in 1956, having risen to the rank of Wing Commander, and spent the rest of his working life with Bristol Aircraft Ltd, for which he was awarded an OBE for service to industry in 1964.

In his later years, Higginson returned to Wales to live in Carmarthenshire with his wife. He died in 2003 and in 2010 was memorialised in Gowerton County School with a plaque unveiled in his honour.

Written by Lieutenant Commander Richard Lewis QVRM RNR

"After a year of evasion, re-capture and escape, he finally reached safe territory in Gibraltar in September 1942, disguised as a priest"

"TAFFY"

O. F.W. HIGGINSON. D.F.M.   56 SQUADRON

In the line of fire

Every day, staff at North Wales Fire & Rescue Service use their training and expertise to deal with a variety of emergency incidents across a vast geographical area

www.nwales-fireservice.org.uk

"At the heart of everything is prevention," explains Stuart Millington, Assistant Chief Fire Officer at North Wales Fire and Rescue Service. "If we need to attend a dwelling fire, in some ways we have failed, as it's far preferable to prevent the fire in the first place. Around 50 per cent of fires start in the kitchen and that's because it's easy to become distracted if the doorbell or phone rings, it only takes a few seconds for a fire to develop when your back is turned."

The best way to keep people safe is through education, says Stuart. "It's about changing behaviour," he says. "That means getting into the habit of turning appliances off when leaving the room. And certainly don't cook if you have been drinking. It's also very important to have working smoke alarms."

The landscape in North Wales is one of the most beautiful in the UK, making it a great place to work and visit, but this diversity can present a challenge in itself. "We cover a large geographical area with vastly different requirements," says Stuart, "from heavy industry to coastal, urban and rural localities and large expanses of moorland. During dry weather the number of wildfires has increased in recent years. In these rural areas we rely heavily on our on-call firefighters."

On-call firefighters are key to protecting the communities in which they live and work. "This is particularly true in rural locations, where the majority of on-call firefighters also have other jobs," says Stuart. "The service they provide is a testament to their own commitment as well as that of their employers who allow them to respond to incidents at a moment's notice."

North Wales Fire and Rescue Service is keen to recruit on-call firefighters at stations across the region. "As proud signatories of the Armed Forces Covenant we are keen to help veterans reintegrate into local communities by providing on-call firefighter opportunities that will utilise their existing skills and following additional training, prepare them for whatever they may face," says Stuart. "Like the military, it's certainly a job that can be testing at times. I am immensely proud of the service that all of our staff provide to their communities."

Some bunny loves you

White Rabbit Chocolatiers in East Yorkshire has created a chocolate wonderland, proving that ethical chocolates can also be ravishingly desirable

www.whiterabbitchocolatiers.co.uk

Based in the scenic Yorkshire market town of Beverley, near Hull, White Rabbit Chocolatiers is a family business that blends artisan chocolate-making techniques with firm principles when it comes to sourcing produce. "Each piece of chocolate is unique, as each is crafted by hand," says Amy Fenner, one of the co-directors of the business, along with her brother, Ed Hawkes, and their mother, Sally Hawkes. "And we take great care in selecting ingredients. We work with ethical producers, sourcing most of our beans from co-operatives and farms in South America. Along with quality, family and indulgence, sustainability is one of our big mantras."

The company was established by Sally Hawkes in 2004 as a shop selling fine confectionery. In 2007 Sally – a Master Chocolatier with training in London, Burgundy and Vancouver – acquired larger premises and started to make her own chocolate, and by 2009 she was winning awards. Her blackcurrant and juniper dark truffle won three stars at the Great Taste Awards in 2014, received a sought-after Top 50 Foods award and was then nominated for a Golden Fork. White Rabbit has since won 21 Great Taste Awards, and four from the prestigious Academy of Chocolate. Its products have also been a hit on social media. "We had a viral video of our hot chocolate bomb, which melts in milk and explodes, revealing mini marshmallows inside," says Amy. "Each one has 'boom' handwritten on it, which is the kind of finishing touch that mass-produced confectionery can't have."

The company was named after a 14th-century stone carving of a pilgrim hare in the church opposite

its first shop, a carving that inspired the rabbit character in Lewis Carroll's *Alice In Wonderland*. Since 2018, White Rabbit Chocolatiers has been based in a bigger building, with a café and shop. The aim is to bring luxury chocolate to all. "We want our chocolate to be accessible for everybody to enjoy," says Amy. "We do workshops, one-off events and let people up into the kitchen for chocolate parties. Everything is made by hand, so visitors can sit and watch the traditional chocolate-making process up close. Our aim has always been to create a chocolate wonderland!"

Sticky Bramley apple and date pudding

Corporal Gareth Williams, RAF

Tyrone

With its highly fertile soil, Tyrone is justly famous for its Armagh Bramley apples, which have been given Protected Geographical Indication (PGI) status. This means that they can only be grown in the Archdiocese of Armagh in Northern Ireland, which covers the counties of Armagh and Tyrone. The addition of the Armagh Bramley apple gives this British classic a hint of tartness that works extremely well to cut through the richness of this pudding.

Vegetarian
Preparation time: 35 minutes
Cooking time: 30–35 minutes

Serves 4–6

INGREDIENTS

For the pudding
125g unsalted butter, softened
150g whole Medjool dates, stoned
150ml boiling water
3 Bramley apples, peeled and cut into
 ½cm dice
1 vanilla pod, split and seeds scraped out
140g self-raising flour
¾ tsp bicarbonate of soda
120g dark muscovado sugar
2 medium eggs, at room temperature
2 tbsp black treacle
65ml full-fat milk
Clotted cream (optional)
Apple crisp (optional)

For the toffee sauce
150g dark muscovado sugar
50g unsalted butter
175ml double cream
1 tbsp black treacle

For a vegan toffee sauce
75g golden syrup
125g vegan butter
150g dark muscovado sugar
75ml soya cream

METHOD

For the pudding
• Preheat the oven to 175°C and grease four mini pudding tins with 25g of the softened butter.
• Put the dates in a heatproof bowl, pour over the boiling water and soak for 20 minutes.
• Melt 25g of the butter in a saucepan over a medium heat and cook the diced apples with the vanilla pod and seeds, stirring frequently, until soft but still holding their shape; remove the vanilla pod then set aside.
• Drain the soaked dates, reserving 50ml of the water, then blend the dates with the reserved soaking water to a purée in a food processor and set aside.
• Mix the flour and bicarbonate of soda together in a mixing bowl then, in a separate bowl, cream the remaining 75g of softened butter and the muscovado sugar together using a plastic spatula or similar until they are light and fluffy.
• Beat in the eggs one at a time, making sure you combine well after adding each egg.
• Mix in the black treacle and then gently fold in the flour and bicarbonate of soda mix a quarter at a time.
• Fold in the puréed date mixture, milk and cooked diced apples; it should now resemble a soft, thick batter.
• Spoon into the prepared pudding tins and bake, ensuring there is enough space between the tins to allow even cooking, for 30–35 minutes or until firm and risen.

For the sauce
• Meanwhile, put all of the ingredients for the sauce into a saucepan, place over a medium heat and bring to a boil, stirring constantly, then simmer for a couple of minutes until smooth and thickened.
• Once your puddings are cooked and cooled slightly, loosen them from the sides of the tins with a small knife or palette knife and turn them out of the moulds.

To serve
• Put a pudding on each of four plates and spoon over the toffee sauce.
• I have decided to serve mine with a quenelle of shop-bought clotted cream and an apple crisp but this would be fantastic just served with a scoop of vanilla ice cream.
• To make the apple crisp; peel and thinly slice a Bramley apple and bake on a non-stick baking mat at 120°C for 2 hours until crisp; cool and store in an airtight container.

VEGAN ALTERNATIVE
• For a vegan version of the pudding, make the following substitutions: replace the eggs with one mashed banana, the butter with vegan butter, the milk with almond milk and the clotted cream with oat crème fraiche.
• Put the syrup, butter and sugar into a saucepan and simmer over a medium heat for 5 minutes without stirring then allow to cool slightly before stirring in the soya cream.

Sir John Gorman MC

John Gorman was born at Mullaghmore in County Tyrone on 1 February 1923, the eldest son of the district inspector of the Royal Ulster Constabulary (RUC), who himself had served with distinction in the British Army during the First World War. Gorman attended the Imperial Service College, Windsor, and joined the British Army when the Second World War broke out, commissioning into the Irish Guards in December 1942.

He received a baptism of fire with his first posting – part of the latter stages of the Normandy Landings. On the morning of 18 July 1944, while taking part in the Battle for Caen, Gorman was commanding a group of M4 Sherman tanks as part of the Guards Armoured Division. Crossing a stream, he saw four German tanks 200 yards away, the largest of which was a Tiger II – a huge vehicle that completely outclassed the Sherman. Shells simply bounced off the Tiger II armour and, when the Sherman's gun jammed, Gorman ordered the driver to ram the enemy tank at full speed. The German crew scrambled out with their hands up, but fire from the other three enemy tanks set light to the Sherman. Unable to extract his tank, Gorman ordered his crew into a ditch, then commandeered a nearby British Firefly tank, mounting a 17-pounder gun to deal with the remaining Germans.

Gorman was awarded the Military Cross and the driver (Lieutenant Corporal Baron) received the Military Medal from General Montgomery in the field. Later, during the liberation of Brussels, Gorman discovered a stash of Piper Heidsieck champagne, hidden by the Germans in railway arches; he filled up a truck and the whole crew celebrated in style.

On leaving the Army in 1945, Gorman followed in his father's footsteps into the RUC, becoming district inspector in Antrim and then Armagh. He left the RUC to become head of security for the BOAC, and for his work he was appointed CBE in 1974. Gorman entered politics as chairman of the Northern Ireland Forum for Political Dialogue in 1996, and left with a knighthood in 1998. He served as Deputy Speaker from 1999 until 2002. He passed on 26 May 2014; at his wake, his friends and family remembered him with the same champagne, Piper Heidsieck, that he had "liberated" from the Germans around 70 years previously.

Written by Warrant Officer First Class Richard Kavanagh, Army (retired)

> *"During the liberation of Brussels, Gorman discovered a stash of Piper Heidsieck champagne, hidden by the Germans – the whole crew celebrated in style"*

Kings of the kitchen

A fixture of British kitchens for more than 150 years, Swan creates high-quality homeware products, from kettles and toasters to espresso machines and fridges

www.swan-brand.co.uk

There are few things more quintessentially British than a cup of tea, and British brand Swan have been helping to support the nation's tea-drinking needs since the 1930s. During the Second World War, the company sold 300,000 of its iconic teasmades a year, while supplying tea urns and kettles to the nation's war-struck homes and workplaces even as its huge factory in Birmingham was requisitioned to make munitions for the war effort. Today, Swan continues to produce a huge range of coordinated products for kitchens, making everything from kettles and toasters to homeware, microwaves, espresso machines, sandwich makers and fridge freezers.

"The heart of the business is small domestic appliances but we offer coordinated product ranges right up to fridges," says Managing Director Rob Wileman. "We are continuing to grow in terms of turnover, staff and products. We are very much a British brand and there is a hunger for British brands right around the world. Social media marketing gives us a massive international reach and our passion truly appears to resonate on a worldwide scale."

Appropriately enough, Rob's first job at Swan was as a tea boy. That was in 1986 when the company occupied a vast factory in the centre of Birmingham where it had been located for decades. While the Swan brand was born in the 1930s, the company could trace its origins right back to 1868 when it started life as Bulpitt & Sons Ltd, a brass foundry that produced a range of polished aluminium products such as frying pans, kettles, tea sets and jelly moulds. In the 1920s, Bulpitt began to produce electric kettles, creating one of the first to use an immersion element. Another masterly innovation was the distinctive safety cut-out for kettles, which meant the immersion would disconnect if the element overheated.

Swan went through various changes of ownership before it was purchased by Littlewoods, for which it began to produce unique and notable products. Rob was then producing a range of traditional small appliances at the old Swan factory for a new company, which he called Cygnet – "son of Swan" – before he and business partner Paul Simpson acquired the Swan brand from Littlewoods. Swan was relaunched with a stylish modern version of the classic teasmade, manufactured to mark the 150th anniversary of John Lewis. Since then, Swan has extended its range but maintained the focus on coordinated products, so everything in the kitchen will match, from a stand mixer to mug tree. Popular styles include the spartan Nordic and the bold Gatsby, as well as the sleek new Stealth range. This streamlined design offers a range of products designed to help improve health through low-fat cooking while mastering quick and easy food preparation. Although renowned for its kettles and tea urn, Swan has also moved into coffee-making, with the new espresso machine making an immediate splash on launch.

With a global distribution centre in Stoke-on-Trent, Swan supports numerous regional charities such as the Alice Charity, which is involved with helping countless disadvantaged families in the local area. Rob is hugely optimistic about the future of the company. "The reincarnation of Swan has really caught the imagination," he says. "We are moving into China, North America, South Africa and Australia, where there is huge interest in our brand, and we wholeheartedly feel this is something we can take even further."

Banoffee cream pie

Tim Anderson, MasterChef winner, owner of Nanban Brixton

Banoffee pie sounds and tastes like something that I would have eaten growing up in America – but it turns out it was actually invented in Jevington, East Sussex (though inspired by an American recipe). This version combines a classic British banoffee pie, with its biscuit crust and caramel sauce, with a traditional American banana cream pie, with shortcrust pastry and custard. It's a special relationship, in pie form.

Vegetarian
Preparation time: 45 minutes
 plus 5 hours chilling time
Cooking time: 50 minutes

Serves 8

INGREDIENTS

For the toffee sauce
50g dark brown sugar
15g butter
½ tbsp vanilla bean paste or vanilla extract
20g miso (optional)
100ml double cream

For the pie
350g pre-made all-butter shortcrust pastry
50g white chocolate
50g butter
50g banana chips
3 digestive biscuits
40g plain flour
150g plus 1 tbsp golden caster sugar
¼ tsp salt
500ml milk
3 egg yolks, beaten
15g butter, melted
½ tbsp vanilla bean paste
6 ripe (but not brown) bananas,
 cut into 3mm-thick coins
300ml double cream
25ml dark rum

METHOD

To make the toffee sauce
• Melt the brown sugar and butter together in a pan over medium heat, then whisk in the vanilla and miso. Add the double cream and whisk to combine, bring to the boil, and leave to cool. Keep at room temperature for serving.

To make the pie
• Roll the pastry out to 3mm thick. Place into a 20–22cm diameter pie tin (preferably with a removable base), prick the bases all over with a fork and transfer to the freezer for at least a half hour until frozen solid. Blind-bake at 180°C, covered with greaseproof paper and baking beans or rice, for 20 minutes, then remove the beans or rice and continue to bake for another 20 minutes until golden brown.
• Meanwhile, melt the white chocolate and butter together in a microwave or bain-marie and transfer to a food processor along with the banana chips and biscuits. Process until a paste is formed.
• While the pie crusts are still warm, spread the paste onto the bases of the crusts in a thin layer, then transfer to the fridge, uncovered, to cool and set.
• Combine the flour, 150g sugar, salt and milk in a deep saucepan. Cook over a medium heat, stirring frequently, until the mixture boils. Boil for two minutes, then remove from the heat. Whisk a little bit of the milk mixture into the eggs, then add the egg mixture to the saucepan. Cook over a medium heat for 3 minutes, stirring constantly.
• Add the butter and vanilla, stir to combine, and remove from the heat. Toss the banana coins with the remaining 1 tbsp sugar and leave to sit until they become slightly sticky then tip the banana slices into the pie crust and spread out in an even layer. Pour over the custard and chill for at least 2 hours.
• Whip the double cream and rum together into soft peaks, then pipe or spread onto the top of the custard and chill again for about 1 hour.

To serve
• Slice in eight portions and serve with the toffee sauce.

Colonel Charles Michael Sweeny

Charles Michael Sweeny was born in 1882 to a wealthy mining family. He started his education at West Point Military Academy in New York in 1900 and was twice expelled for demerits or bad behaviour. On his final expulsion in 1904 he was free to embark on a new life as a "soldier of fortune", despite the fact that it was illegal for US citizens to join foreign armed forces at that time. Sweeny found no shortage of conflicts in which to serve, scraping through revolutions in Mexico, Venezuela and Nicaragua.

As war broke out in 1914, Sweeny enlisted in the French Foreign Legion. He became a decorated officer, the first American to receive the highest medal for valour, though he was also injured by a bullet to the lung, which required extensive surgery and weeks of recuperation. In 1919, aged 27, he was made a brigadier general in the Polish army, fighting the Soviet Union, before becoming a military advisor to the Turkish leader Kemal Ataturk during the Greco-Turkish war. It was in Turkey in 1922 that Sweeny first met Ernest Hemingway, the start of a lifelong friendship. Sweeny was the war hero that Hemingway longed to be, while Hemingway was the acclaimed writer that Sweeny would have liked to have been. Sweeny was an honorary pallbearer at Hemingway's funeral in 1961.

By 1939, America's neutrality laws prohibited nationals enlisting overseas. Sweeny, however, was undeterred by the threat of $1,000 fines and prison. Inspired by the pilots of Lafayette Escadrille (the French squadron manned by US volunteers in the Great War) he embarked on an audacious campaign to recruit US pilots to fight the Nazis. He left his family in Paris and returned to America, recruiting and smuggling 50 American volunteers to Europe via Canada. Following the fall of France in 1940, Sweeny teamed up with his nephew, a successful London-based businessman, also called Charles Sweeny, and obtained permission from the British Air Ministry to enlist American pilots in the RAF. His volunteers formed three squadrons within the RAF, which became the legendary Eagle Squadrons – the first of millions of US volunteers who fought fascism in Europe.

After the war, Sweeny, estranged from his wife, settled in Salt Lake City, where he died on 28 February 1963, aged 81. His death was front-page news across America.

Written by Squadron Leader Simon Stafford, RAF and Mrs Ali Stafford

"America's neutrality laws prohibited nationals enlisting overseas but Sweeny was undeterred by the threat of $1,000 fines and prison"

Miles of style

For the ultimate road trip, RP Motorhomes leads the field with its
luxury range of motorhomes built on Mercedes-Benz Sprinters

www.rpmotorhomes.com

It started as a dream on a driveway. Steve and Jaye Young desired a motorhome for their family of four that was safe, comfortable and offered decent storage capacity. With nothing on the market fitting the bill, they designed their own – and now they do the same for their customers, taking a special-order Mercedes-Benz Sprinter van and remodelling it to create a spacious, luxurious and capable motorhome. "We finished our first one in 2014 and used it as a family," says Jaye. "Since then, each year we have something new and improved. That's the thing about this industry – you have to evolve, as there will always be new innovations, ideas and materials."

Innovation is central to RP Motorhomes. The company, located in Yorkshire, was one of the first in the industry to use lithium batteries, and it also uses materials that ensure that the vehicle is lighter and has more payload. In some models, the bathroom takes the form of a slide-out pod, which creates two separate living areas. Steve and Jaye are also monitoring the development of electric vehicles, waiting for a battery that has the sort of range their customers require. "Steve is a perfectionist in making sure the kit is the best we can get," says Jaye. "He won't commission a motorhome for manufacture until he is happy with the performance and the finish – that is how he operates and that is what has given us our reputation."

All RP Motorhomes are built using Mercedes-Benz Sprinters, a vehicle that provides a reliable base. Three models are available: the 6-metre Rebel, 7-metre Explorer and 7.4-metre Phantom. "Within each model there are three levels of conversion, starting with the Premium, the Exclusive with more tech and the AWD 4X4 for the overland market," says Jaye. "They have different layouts including the new elevated rear lounge, and we work with customers to refine their personal habitation requirements – so they get exactly what they want. We understand that each customer has unique habitation requirement. Each motorhome isn't quite bespoke but there is a lot of customisation involved."

The all-wheel-drive models have become particularly popular, with this now making up a significant proportion of the market. "People have an appetite to take control of their leisure time," says Jaye. "They want their own facilities and don't want to rely on communal facilities. Our motorhomes can go anywhere and be off-grid, and that's what people are really looking for – maybe 70 per cent of our business is that off-road market now."

As motorhome users themselves, Steve and Jaye are always mindful that these vehicles serve as people's homes. That means they need to be comfortable, but also functional, reliable, adaptable and durable. In giving customers what they want, the company has continued to grow. "This started as a hobby but we could immediately see there was potential," says Jaye. "We have since built a very strong reputation as a company that will always go the extra mile for our customers and try to do things a bit differently. Because of that, we have grown from being a little dream on a drive to becoming quite a force within the motorhome industry."

Yorkshire ruby ale ginger parkin with rhubarb and custard

Senior Aircraftsman Matthew Strickland, RAF

Yorkshire forced rhubarb is grown out of season; it is initially cultivated outside for two years, the exposure to frost toughening the roots, then lifted from the ground and placed into forcing sheds in November where it is kept in complete darkness. Traditionally, the pickers pull the stalks in candlelight, as any exposure to strong light will impair the rhubarb's growth. The cultivation method for forced rhubarb was developed in the early 19th century and was originally practiced by many hundreds of West Yorkshire small farmers, smallholders and market gardeners. I have paired the rhubarb with its traditional counterpart, custard and a rich ginger parkin, a traditional Yorkshire cake. This would be great to eat on Bonfire Night, for a perfect autumnal dessert.

Vegan and gluten-free version below
Preparation time: 2 hours (the parkin is
  best prepared a day or two in advance)
Cooking time: 1 hour

Serves 6

INGREDIENTS

For the parkin
50g unsalted butter
60g black treacle
60g golden syrup
75ml dark ruby Yorkshire ale
125g plain flour
75g rolled oats
7g baking powder
10g stem ginger, grated
1 egg
125g dark brown soft sugar

For the whipped crème Ànglaise
235ml double cream
4 egg yolks
65g caster sugar

For the poached rhubarb
200g rhubarb
250ml grenadine or water
150g caster sugar
125g treacle

**VEGAN AND GLUTEN-FREE
PARKIN INGREDIENTS**

75g golden syrup
200g dairy-free margarine
250g dark brown soft sugar
70ml water
160g gluten-free flour, self-raising or plain
280g gluten-free oats, chopped fine
  in a food processor
1 tsp gluten-free bicarbonate of soda
2 tsp ginger, ground
½ lemon, zest and juice

METHOD

For the parkin

The Parkin is best if made a few days in advance as this allows the texture to become sticky and the flavours to develop.

- Preheat the oven to 160°C.
- Gently melt together the butter, treacle, syrup and ruby ale.
- Mix the flour, oats, baking powder and stem ginger in a bowl.
- Beat the egg together with the dark brown sugar until light and airy (this makes for a lighter and softer finish to the cooked cake) and beat in the melted mixture.
- Gently fold the dry ingredients into the combined wet ingredients, trying to keep as much air in the mixture as possible; take care not to over-work the mix, as this can tighten up the gluten in the flour resulting in the batter stiffening and producing a heavier, dense cake.
- Pour the batter into either six small, buttered pudding moulds or a baking tin lined with baking parchment and bake in the preheated oven for 25 minutes (about 10 minutes longer if cooking in a baking tin) or until a skewer comes out clean when inserted into the centre of the cake.

For the whipped crème Ànglaise

- Heat the cream in a saucepan over a low heat.
- Whisk the egg and sugar until pale in colour, whisk in the hot cream, pour back into the saucepan and return to the heat.
- Cook, stirring constantly, until the mixture thickens and can coat the back of a spoon.
- Strain the custard into a clean mixing bowl, cool then chill in the fridge until completely cold.
- Whip the cold mixture until light and airy, this can be done in an electric mixer, but for a small amount it can easily be done with a hand whisk.

For the grenadine rhubarb

- Wash the rhubarb, peel the outer layer and cut into thumb-size pieces.
- Bring the grenadine or water and sugar to a boil in a saucepan over a medium-high heat, add the rhubarb, reduce the heat and gently poach until just soft.
- Set aside and allow the rhubarb to cool in the liquor.

To serve

- De-mould the parkin or cut into rounds with a 5cm cutter and serve with the poached rhubarb, with some of its poaching liquid, and pipe or spoon over the whipped crème Ànglaise.

VEGAN ALTERNATIVE

- Preheat the oven to 160°C.
- Melt the treacle, syrup, margarine, sugar and water in a microwave or in a saucepan.
- Mix the flour, oats, bicarbonate of soda, ginger and lemon zest together, combine with the wet mix and lemon juice.
- Grease and line a 23cm square baking tin, pour in the parkin batter and bake for about 45 minutes; the cake needs to be dry on top and have a little bit of spring (it won't ever be very springy due to the oats).
- Serve with your favourite dairy-free ice cream and the poached rhubarb.

Captain Sir Tom Moore

Captain Sir Thomas Moore, affectionately known as "Captain Tom", was born in Keighley, West Yorkshire on 30 April 1920. He was educated at Keighley Grammar School before starting an apprenticeship in civil engineering. As war broke out, his apprenticeship was cut short and he was conscripted in the 8th Battalion, Duke of Wellington's Regiment in May 1940, before being selected for officer training and commissioning as a Second Lieutenant on 28 June 1941.

In October 1941, Moore transferred to the 146th Regiment Royal Armoured Corps and was subsequently posted to India later that year to set up a training programme for Army motorcyclists in Mumbai and Kolkata. He was promoted to Captain in October 1944, and survived an unfortunate bout of dengue fever. In February 1945, Moore returned to the UK to take a course on the workings of the Churchill tanks and became an instructor. He never returned to the regiment, remaining an instructor and Technical Adjutant of the Armoured Vehicle Fighting School until he was demobilised in 1946. After leaving the Army, Moore worked as a sales manager for a roofing company before becoming a managing director for a concrete manufacturer.

On 6 April 2020, aged 99, he began a sponsored walk around his garden in aid of NHS Charities Together during the Covid-19 pandemic. His goal was to raise £1,000 by his 100th birthday. However, news of his sponsored walk went viral and, by the time he was done, he had raised over £32 million – and captured the hearts of a nation during a year of crisis. His biography, *Tomorrow Will Be A Good Day*, was a bestseller. He was granted the Freedom of Keighley and Freedom of the City of London. He received a Pride of Britain award, after thousands of nominations were received, and was appointed the first Honorary Colonel of the Army Foundation College in Harrogate and the Yorkshire Regiment Medal for his "outstanding contribution to our military effectiveness and military reputation". Moore even became the oldest man to top the UK singles chart, collaborating on a rendition of "You'll Never Walk Alone". After his 100th birthday on 30 April, 800,000 people signed a petition calling for Moore to receive a knighthood and, after a special nomination by the Prime Minister, Moore was knighted on 17 July 2020 by Her Majesty the Queen. His death, from Covid-19 and pneumonia on 2 February 2021, prompted millions of tributes from around the world.

Written by Sergeant Richard Street MC, Army

"*Moore even became the oldest man to top the UK singles chart, collaborating on a rendition of 'You'll Never Walk Alone'*"

Kings of the scone age

Founded in Yorkshire on family values, the Haywood & Padgett bakery now exports its delicious scones all over the world, by the million

www.haywood-padgett.co.uk

Scones have an appeal all of their own, quintessentially British and the heart of afternoon tea, and yet the perfect snack at any time of day. When David Haywood and Wayne Padgett started working together in South Yorkshire in 1985, their main aim was to establish a high quality, traditional family bakery – so, producing the perfect scone was always high on their agenda. Determined and ambitious as they were, neither could have imagined that 36 years on, that two-man enterprise would be employing 180 staff as the world's largest specialist baker of scones.

"Back then, we were hand-rolling and cutting 100 scones an hour," says Managing Director, Wayne Padgett. "Now, we produce 6 million scones a week and it would be easier to list a couple of supermarket giants who don't stock our scones, rather than detail all those who do. We export to Australia, America, the Middle East and Europe, and scones are what we're renowned for, they're our specialty," says Wayne. "Everything in the business is based around the consistency and quality we provide."

When Haywood and Padgett started the business they quickly realised that none of the supermarket giants at that time stocked scones, and that prompted their move into wholesale. "It's all about guaranteeing the best," says Wayne. "That was the premise the firm started on – best ingredients, best expertise and best experience – and it's the ethos we work to. It's a family firm, and my three daughters and son have followed me into the business."

The company is well known within the retail trade for producing the finest scones, a reputation that's enhanced by a workforce who feel a real pride in what they are achieving. "We always want to live up to customers' expectations, which can vary," says Wayne. "We have a huge market in France on the back of *Downton Abbey*, for example, and in Spain there's a large expat community. Australia actually has a long history with its own recipes and likes to try ours, and Americans enjoy British traditions such as afternoon tea. *Bake Off* is also good for us – it makes scones seem so easy while proving that only a few of us make them perfectly."

Logical logistics

The Clipper Group is a retail distribution specialist who has managed to successfully adapt to the changing digital landscape, always finding routes to market

www.clippergroup.co.uk

When the UK government needed a logistics specialist to help liaise with the military to distribute PPE to front-line NHS workers during the Covid pandemic, it turned to The Clipper Group, long-standing specialists in retail distribution. The company was founded in 1992 by Steve Parkin, who remains executive chairman, and between 2006 to 2021 it expanded in size from £60 million to £600 million by focusing entirely on retail. "We realised the space we were operating in was changing as online retail expanded," explains CEO Tony Mannix. "We didn't choose to diversify. Instead, we wanted to focus on the sector and be very collaborative with our customers."

Clipper operates in more than 50 locations across Europe – largely in the UK, but also in Ireland, Poland and Germany. Its policy is to use the same site for several clients. That allows staff to work across different accounts depending on demand, with the client only paying for the labour they have used. It's an approach that means a small retail start-up can share a site with a major player like John Lewis, receiving the same standard of service and greatly benefiting from the economies of scale. "It allows us to invest in things like automation and robotics and staffing," says Tony. "We can meet our clients' demands as they change and grow, without saddling them with cost before they need it."

This created a culture of collaboration between retailers that proved beneficial during Covid, as all retailers were faced with new challenges at the same time, often requiring co-operative solutions. Clipper was also rapidly able to adapt its services to the distribution of PPE in March 2020, creating an operational distribution system within five days and ultimately delivering more than one billion pieces of equipment during the first few months of the pandemic. This was helped by the company culture – Team Clipper – which is about developing a shared attitude of continuous improvement across all sites. "That team culture is everything," says Tony. "We really care about the detail and we have great people who care just as much as we do."

Those people include 1,100 who have been employed via the charity sector. Clipper anticipated that Brexit would cause shortages among its traditional sources of temporary workers, which drew heavily on European students. The company therefore decided to look for sectors of the population who were typically overlooked. "We then reached out to ex-offender charities, homeless charities and mental health charities," says Tony. "Now 10 per cent of our workforce comes from this route. Mencap estimates that around 80 per cent of people with a learning disability have mild or moderate levels of disability but only 20 per cent are in employment. Some of our Mencap employees are regularly our best-performing. That has been a fantastic experience for us and it's made great business sense. We also offer training at every level as we want to promote from within."

Clipper hopes to build on recent successes by expanding geographically and through tactical acquisitions within the retail sector, particularly looking at new technologies that it can bring under the Team Clipper umbrella. "We have looked at the things our customers require that lie outside our skillset and then acquiring the talent," says Tony. "That allows us to expand while remaining in retail, as our success and our ability to understand the principles of logistics comes down to us being specialists rather than generalists."

Pershore plum and apple cobbler

Private Amir Gurung, Army

The Worcestershire market town of Pershore is renowned for the abundance and variety of plums prevalent in the area. These plums are available all year round but are best in mid-July, especially the Pershore purple and Pershore yellow egg plums, which have been a local delicacy for more than 200 years. Using the main ingredient sourced from the heart of Worcestershire, I have created a dessert that I think really showcases the plums. Put it in the oven to cook while you and your family enjoy a Sunday roast as a perfect pudding to round off your lunch.

Worcestershire

Vegetarian
Preparation time: 30 minutes
Cooking time: 40 minutes

Serves 8

INGREDIENTS

For the plum and apple filling
750g Pershore plums, each
  stoned and cut into six or eight wedges
50g caster sugar
1 tsp ground cinnamon
1 vanilla pod, seeds scraped out
3 medium apples, peeled, cored and diced
100g butter

For the cobbler topping
275g plain flour
1 tbsp baking powder
Pinch of salt
150g cold butter, diced
½ tsp ground cinnamon
150g caster sugar
100ml milk
1 medium egg
2 tbsp demerara sugar

To serve
Cream, custard or ice cream

METHOD

• Preheat oven to 170°C.

To make the filling
• Put all of the ingredients for the filling into a large saucepan, place over a medium heat and stir continuously until the butter has melted and the sugar has completely dissolved.
• Continue to simmer gently, stirring occasionally, until the fruit has released it juice and just started to break down, take off the heat and tip into a baking or pie dish and allow to cool.

To make the cobbler topping
• Sift the flour, baking powder and salt into a mixing bowl and rub in the butter with your fingertips until it resembles coarse breadcrumbs, add the sugar and cinnamon and mix well.
• Whisk the milk and eggs together, make a well in the centre of the flour mix, pour in the liquid and mix to thoroughly combine.

To cook
• Top the plum and apple filling with large spoonfuls of the cobbler topping leaving small gaps between each spoonful to allow them to expand slightly during cooking.
• Sprinkle the top with a little demerara sugar to help the cobbler turn golden brown and form a crust.
• Place in the preheated oven and bake for 40 minutes until the cobbler is cooked and the fruit filling is bubbling – perfection!
• Let the cobbler sit at room temperature for 5–10 minutes then serve with some fresh cream, custard or ice cream to melt over the top of the piping-hot pudding.

Colonel Henry Walton Ellis

Henry Walton Ellis was born on 29 November 1782, the son of a Worcester MP, Lieutenant Corporal John Joyner Ellis. At this time, commissions in the British Army could be bought by gentlemen wishing to give their sons a lifelong career; John Ellis purchased such a commission for his infant son, in his own 89th Regiment of Foot.

The 89th disbanded when Ellis was still a baby, and he was put on half pay until he was transferred to 41st Foot. Aged nine, bizarrely, he was made a lieutenant, and at 11, a captain. Aged 14, Ellis served in the British Expedition to Ostend in 1798, and was wounded in the 1799 Anglo-Russian invasion of Holland. He also served in the Channel, at Ferrol and in the Mediterranean in 1800. Following injury in Egypt, in 1801, Ellis was promoted to major and received an Army Gold Medal.

By the time he was 25, Ellis was a battle-hardened veteran of 11 years; in 1808, he was given command of the first battalion of his regiment in Nova Scotia. He fearlessly led his men in the invasion of Martinique in 1809 and through campaigns in the south of France, during which he repeatedly distinguished himself. He was again wounded, at the Siege of Badajoz in 1812 and in the pass of Roncesvalles, Pyrenees, 1813. In recognition of his service, Ellis was promoted to colonel and appointed Knight Commander of the Order of the Bath in January 1815.

On 18 June 1815, Ellis's regiment joined the Duke of Wellington's army on the field of Waterloo the night before the battle, to be brought forward on the following day. After withstanding several French charges, Ellis received a musket-ball through the right breast. Despite his wound, he calmly rode out of the defensive position, before falling off his horse, sustaining further injury. He was placed in an outhouse and his wounds were dressed. Disastrously, the hut caught fire and Ellis succumbed to his injuries and burns on 20 June 1815.

Ellis never married but left two sons, who both received commissions from the Duke of Wellington as a token of their father's sacrifice. There is a plaque in the courtyard of the Wellington Museum in Waterloo, and a monument in Worcester Cathedral depicting the moment Ellis was shot, commissioned from funds raised by members of his regiment in his honour.

Written by Corporal Gill Knox, Royal Military Police, Army (retired)

> *"By the time he was 25, Henry Walton Ellis was a battle-hardened veteran of 11 years"*

Ever since the original Teepol cleaning product was first produced in 1942, it has had a military application. As one of the first synthetic detergents, Teepol was used by soldiers and sailors during the war to clean barracks and military equipment, and even today it is used around the world to clean helicopters, planes and other military items. Customers include the Ministry of Defence, the RAF and BAE Systems as well as the NHS. But soldiers haven't always put Teepol to its intended use.

"We have this story from one of the London newspapers with the headline 'The Day Nelson Got Soap in His Eye'," says Sue Moon, whose company now manufactures Teepol. "Some squaddies thought it would be a good idea to add Teepol to the fountains at Trafalgar Square. There were bubbles everywhere and the photos (pictured, above) are fabulous."

Teepol is currently made in Orpington but was originally developed by Shell as a by-product formed when refining crude oil. Shell realised that this surfactant could be used as a detergent as it was far more effective than soap, and began producing four products under the Teepol name – a multipurpose detergent, hand soap, disinfectant and bleach. Over time, the brand was passed between various companies until it was bought by London Soap & Chemicals (LSC). LSC had been formed by Sue Moon's father, Sydney, after the Second World War. He had worked for BP during the war and then started a business in Bermondsey making detergent and floor polish. As a former BP man, he always had a desire to own Shell's Teepol brand, eventually acquiring it in the early 2000s. The company now produces many different products that proudly carry the Teepol name, celebrating the history and high quality of a trusted brand.

The company employs around 15 people at its factory in Orpington, which it has occupied since 1968. It produces Teepol and other products for the domestic market but also exports worldwide, to all countries that value the Teepol name. "We are on a small industrial estate that was set up specifically to take businesses that were being pushed out of London to allow the redevelopment of bomb sites," says Sue. "It's a purpose-built trading estate with long leases for all the companies asked to relocate. We came here in 1968 and I believe we are the last original business still here. Teepol remains a well-known brand in the oil and gas industry and we export significant volumes to Africa, Asia and the Middle East. We get international enquiries because the products have military specification clearance – a Teepol product is exactly what you need if you want to wash down a helicopter."

While Teepol products were traditionally used for industrial purposes in institutional markets like schools and council offices, Sue is expanding into the domestic retail market while also streamlining and simplifying the range. "I am taking us back to our roots, manufacturing professional quality cleaning products available to the retail market, as shown on our website," she says. "I am keeping the industrial look and larger bottles – which means less waste – and emphasising the multi-use aspect. This is out of fashion but it remains true that one liquid can remove many stains from almost any surface. I hope people will go back to buying one big bottle of a single product rather than ten small ones as it's more ecological and better value."

Lemon and poppy seed cake

Sergeant Ian Mark "Bear", RAF

During the First World War, huge areas of the French and Belgian countryside were blasted, bombed and fought over repeatedly. Previously beautiful landscapes turned to bleak, barren and muddy scenes where little or nothing could grow. There was a notable and striking exception to the bleakness – the bright red Flanders poppies. These resilient flowers flourished in the middle of so much chaos and destruction, growing in their thousands upon thousands. For 100 years, the poppy has been worn as a show of support for the Armed Forces community and remains a humble, poignant symbol of remembrance and hope. Our cake pays homage to the simple poppy with the red of the raspberries and use of poppy seeds. It also uses thyme, which often grows close to poppies.

Preparation time: 15 mins
Cooking time: 35–40mins
Allergens: gluten, egg, dairy

Serves 16

INGREDIENTS

For the cake
5 lemons
3 limes
340g margarine
675g caster sugar
825g self-raising flour, sifted
4 tsp baking powder
12 eggs, beaten
335g olive oil
75g poppy seeds
12g (1 tbsp) fresh thyme, finely shredded

For the Italian buttercream
170ml water
555g granulated sugar
12 egg whites
385g unsalted butter, cut into small cubes
3 tsp vanilla essence
2 punnets of fresh raspberries

METHOD

• Preheat oven to 180°C, grease and line three 24cm cake tins with baking parchment.
• Juice and zest lemons and limes, keeping the juice and zest separate.
• Using a hand whisk or spatula, cream together the margarine and caster sugar.
• Slowly mix in the self-raising flour and baking powder, then add the beaten eggs and citrus juice, thoroughly incorporating with each addition, to form the base mixture.
• Beat in the olive oil in stages – this will make the sponge rich and moist.
• Using a spoon, fold in the citrus zests, poppy seeds and fresh thyme.
• Evenly distribute the batter between the three 24cm cake tins (just over halfway full).
• Bake in the pre-heated oven for approximately 35–40 minutes or until the mixture has come away from the sides of the cake tin and springs back when lightly pressed in the middle.
• Leave to cool in cake tins. Then place upside down on baking wire and, once cool, turn out and remove the baking parchment.
• For the buttercream, combine water and sugar in a pan and place on a low heat. Once the sugar has dissolved into a clear syrup, increase to a medium heat and bring to the boil.
• Meanwhile, whisk the eggs whites until they are doubled in size and form soft peaks. This can be done by hand but is best done with a stand mixer with a whisk attachment.
• Cook the syrup to 112°C, remove from the heat and, whisking continuously, slowly drizzle into the whisked eggs, taking care to avoid pouring onto the whisk attachment.
• Once all the syrup has been added, keep whisking until the bowl is cool to the touch.
• While still whisking, add a few cubes of butter at a time and allow to fully incorporate well before adding anymore. Once the butter is fully mixed in, add the vanilla essence.
• Keep whisking until the buttercream comes together and is smooth and silky looking.
• To assemble, place a third of the buttercream into a piping bag with a medium round piping nozzle. Pipe the buttercream in a spiral motion starting from the centre onto two of the cakes. Put a generous amount of raspberries evenly into the buttercream.
• Place one layer on top of the other, with the un-iced cake on the top.
• Using a palette knife, smear the remaining 2/3 of buttercream evenly around the outside and top of the cake. Allow to set. This is now a blank canvas for decoration.

The Tomb of the Unknown Warrior

The First World War witnessed loss of life that had never been seen before, with millions across the world making the ultimate sacrifice. With so many loved ones not returning from the war, there was a need to provide families at home with an outlet for their grief. It is thought that the idea behind an anonymous memorial to represent the one million British and colonial troops that had died or were missing as a result of the conflict came in 1916 from Reverend David Railton when he stumbled across a grave on the Western Front in the French town of Armentieres: on the tombstone he saw the words "an unknown soldier of the Black Watch".

In order to allow families to mourn in the belief that the grave could represent their loved one, strict anonymity needed to be maintained selecting the serviceman. On 7 November 1920, four bodies from the battlefields of the Somme, Ypres, Arras and the Aisne were brought to a Chapel in Saint-Pol-sur-Ternoise in northern France and placed in four plain coffins, each covered by Union Flags: the two officers did not know from which battlefield any individual soldier had come. Brigadier General Louis John Wyatt, General Officer commanding British troops France and Flanders, was given the task of selecting one of the bodies. With closed eyes, he rested his hand on one of the coffins before it was then transported to London.

On the morning of 11 November 1920, the coffin was placed on a gun carriage drawn by six black horses. It then began its journey through the crowd-lined streets, as King George V unveiled the Cenotaph. The King placed his wreath on the coffin and a card, which read: "In proud memory of those warriors who died unknown in the Great War. Unknown, and yet well-known; as dying, and behold they live". The coffin was laid at the west end of the nave of Westminster Abbey "amongst the kings", filled in with 100 sandbags of earth from the battlefields.

On 11 November 1921, the present black Belgian marble stone was unveiled; on it is the following inscription: *"Beneath this stone rests the body of a British warrior, unknown by name or rank, brought from France to lie among the most illustrious of the land, and buried here on Armistice Day 11 November 1920, in the presence of His Majesty King George V, his ministers of state, the chiefs of his forces, and a vast concourse of the nation. Thus are commemorated the many multitudes who during the Great War of 1914–1918 gave the most that man can give life itself. For God, for*

King and country, for loved ones home and empire, for the sacred cause of justice and the freedom of the world, they buried him among the kings because he had done good toward God and toward his house."

When the Duke of York (later King George VI) married Lady Elizabeth (later Queen Elizabeth, The Queen Mother) in Westminster Abbey, she paused on her way down the aisle to lay her wedding bouquet on the grave as a mark of respect. Her spontaneous act of remembrance spawned a beautiful tradition that has seen many other royal brides follow her example, including Her Majesty Queen Elizabeth II, the Princess Royal and the Duchess of Cambridge.

Today, the grave of the Unknown Warrior is one of the most visited war graves in the world, a place of pilgrimage for the families of servicemen and women. He represents all those who have given their lives in defence of the nation. In the words of the poet Laurence Binyon: "At the going down of the sun and in the morning, we will remember them".

Written by Squadron Leader Jon Pullen, RAF (retired)

Appendices

Cooking conversion tables

Volume

Metric	Imperial	US cups
15ml	½fl oz	–
30ml	1fl oz	⅛ cup
60ml	2fl oz	¼ cup
75ml	2 ½fl oz	⅓ cup
120ml	4fl oz	½ cup
150ml	5fl oz	⅔ cup
180ml	6fl oz	¾ cup
250ml	8fl oz	1 cup

Oven temperatures

Metric (fan assisted)	Imperial	Gas mark
140°C (120°C)	275°C	1
150°C (130°C)	300°C	2
170°C (150°C)	325°C	3
180°C (160°C)	350°C	4
190°C (170°C)	375°C	5
200°C (180°C)	400°C	6
220°C (200°C)	425°C	7
230°C (210°C)	450°C	8
240°C (220°C)	475°C	9

Weight

Metric	Imperial
15g	½oz
30g	1oz
60g	2oz
90g	3oz
110g	4oz
140g	5oz
170g	6oz
200g	7oz
225g	8oz
255g	9oz
280g	10oz
310g	11oz
340g	12oz
370g	13oz
400g	14oz
425g	15oz
450g	1lb

Spoons

Teaspoons	Tablespoons	Metric	US cups
1 tsp	–	5ml	–
2 tsp	–	10ml	–
3 tsp	1 tbsp	15ml	1/16 cup
–	2 tbsp	30ml	⅛ cup
–	3 tbsp	45ml	–
–	4 tbsp	60ml	¼ cup
–	5 tbsp	75ml	⅓ cup
–	6 tbsp	90ml	–
–	7 tbsp	105ml	–
–	8 tbsp	120ml	½ cup
–	16 tbsp	250ml	1 cup

US cup measures

1 US cup	Metric weight	1 US cup	Metric weight
Almonds, ground	110g	Rice, uncooked	200g
Butter/margarine	225g	Sugar, brown	220g
Cheese, grated	120g	Sugar, caster/granulated	200g
Currants	150g		
Flour	125g	Sugar, icing	125g
Honey/treacle/syrup	340g	Sultanas/raisins	170g
Milk	225g	Vegetable oil	220g
Oats	85g		

Acknowledgments

By Squadron Leader Jon Pullen, RAF (retired)

At its heart, *Cooking With Heroes* is a wonderful collaboration of individuals from across the military family and beyond, all pulling together to support the amazing Royal British Legion, who have supported us for a century. We started off 18 months ago as a small group of 11 and grew to an amazing team of 156 chefs, engineers, pilots, administrators, logisticians, soldiers, sailors, airmen and women, veterans, reserves, mums, dads and cadets – every facet of what we refer to as the military family. It is simply fantastic to think that this many people volunteered their time and talent for free in order to make this amazing project a reality.

So what would a cookbook be without any recipes? We'd like to thank our team of talented and creative chefs, led by ex-Flight Sergeant Stu Harmer, who have given their time and talent to present a quite stunning array of recipes. Our Royal Navy chefs led by WO1 Jason "Dixie" Deane and Chief Petty Officer Russell Keitch: WO1 CS Nige Ranger, CPOCS Darren Cross, CPOCH John Potts (Retd), Sgt Tristan Merrick RM, POCS Russ Aitken, LCS Bunama Bojang, LCS James Coombs, LCS Troy Dorsette, LCS Charlie Hall, LCS Simon Hopkins, LCS Emma Keitch, LCS Chris Maxwell, LCS Kenron Mercury, LCH David Bulpitt (Retd), LCH Lee Calver (Retd), LCH Ashley Gilham, LCH Aaron Lee, LCH David Phillips (Retd), CH Siobhan Kent, CS Alyon Adams, CS Gessan Alexander, CS Kevin Cordice, CS Darren Harris, CS James Hopkinson, CS Laura Hultberg, CS Carlos Kalowekmo, CS Mourika O'Garro, CS Lasarusa Tuimanu and RFA CH James Higgins. The Army chefs led by Staff Sergeant Sam Coote: Sgt Fred Cooper, Sgt Lewis Day, Sgt Adi Nayacatabu, Sgt Andrew Ngugi, Sgt Chris Nicols, Sgt Ben Wallace, Cpl Aketa Babin, Cpl Rajesh Babooram, Cpl Purja Gurung, Cpl Spencer Monaghan, Cpl Lewis Rookyard, LCpl Christina Davies, LCpl Pete Frettingham, LCpl Chris Hamlet, LCpl Ben Smith, LCpl Lewis Smith, LCpl Ben Stewart, Pte Simbai Akomba, Pte Richard Darboe, Pte Amir Gurung, Pte Carly Hawsden and Pte Sophie Phillips. And our Royal Air Force chefs led by Sergeant Stefan Sewell: WO Si Jacobs, FS Chris Beavis, FS Jonathan Smith, FS Sharon Smart,

> *"We grew to a team of 156 chefs, engineers, pilots, administrators, logisticians, soldiers, sailors, airmen and women, veterans, reserves, mums, dads and cadets – every facet of what we refer to as the military family"*

Sgt David Bradley, Sgt David Davey-Smith, Sgt Andy Epps, Sgt Ian Mark, Sgt Cpl Karla Wickham, Cpl Lee Coxon, Cpl Robert Donnelly, Cpl Peter Farrington, Cpl Jamie Fisher, Cpl Mark Harrison, Cpl Daniel Holt, Cpl Andy McClurg, Cpl Jamie Mcfee, Cpl Chris Scotting, Cpl Gareth Williams, SAC Joseph Barlow, SAC Ryan Bennett, SAC Joshua Billingham SAC John Britten, SAC Jack Capel, SAC Scott Colvin, SAC George Finch, SAC Ross Haynes, SAC Jody Huteson, SAC John Jones, SAC James Kerr, SAC Prem Lama, SAC Clint Lashley, SAC Connor Mackie, SAC Darren McLellan, SAC Phoebe Mitchell, SAC Kai Nudds, SAC Seun Omisore, SAC Josh Pulham, SAC Sam Shepheard, SAC Nicole Short, SAC Christopher Simpson SAC Sam Smith, SAC Matthew Strickland, SAC Abbie West and SAC Yu-Ting Yau. To dedicate your own time and money to create these recipes is hugely appreciated and we hope you enjoy seeing your recipes within the book and them being used to raise money for such a worthy cause.

We, of course, have to thank our celebrity chefs who also gave their time and effort to create recipes for this incredible cause, we hope you enjoyed the challenge – Paul Ainsworth, Tim Anderson, Arlene Betts, Patti Boulaye, Murray Chapman, Phil Daniels, Paul Gayler, Ainsley Harriott, Melissa Hemsley, Emma Kennedy, James Martin, Jamie Oliver, Rick Stein, The Hairy Bikers, Sophie Thompson, Cyrus Todiwala and Graeme Watson. We wouldn't have the honour of these chefs being part of our team without the help of Teresa Greener and Trudy Baddeley, for that we thank you.

These recipes wouldn't have come to life without support from outside the team, including Kate Hale at the IOS Museum and all those involved in creating the cookbook *Holy Mackerel: Recipes from the Friends of St Martin's Church*. The Isles of Scilly recipe would not have been anywhere near as authentic without you.

Of course, the other half of the book was the research and writing of the stories of our astonishing local heroes, which was led by Flight Lieutenant Daniel Beechey, our writing director. The Royal Navy team led by Lt Cdr Andrew "Tank" Murray AFC supported so ably by his

"Thank you to our volunteer writers. Your writing is both emotional and powerful, with so many worthy heroes being celebrated within this book"

team of writers: Cdr Anthony Laycock, Lt Cdr Mark Barber, Lt Cdr Alex Kelley, Lt Cdr Richard Lewis QVRM, Lt Terry Griffin, Lt Matt Le Feuvre, Lt Dom Raeyen, Lt Seb Sheppard, Lt Aren Tingle, WO1 George Edwards, CPO AET Ryan Barnett, PO AET Hollie Hill, WREN Tel Tania Murray (Retd), Mrs Amanda Edwards and Mrs Joan Murray. The Army team of writers led by Captain Steve Blanks: Maj Matthew Pittaway, WO1 Alun Evans, WO1 Richard Kavanagh (Retd), WO2 Chris Campbell (Retd), WO2 Guy Davies (Retd), WO2 James Hawker (Retd), SSgt Mark John, Sgt Richard Street, Cpl John Drummond (Retd), Cpl Gill Knox (Retd), Cpl Chris Swift (Retd), Cpl Josua Taubale Vosakiwaiwai, Mrs Emma Adams, Mrs Claire Teague and Mrs Emma Wilding. And the Royal Air Force writing team led by Squadron Leader Malcolm Craig: Wg Cdr Manjeet Ghataora, Sqn Ldr Andrew Mortimer, Sqn Ldr Simon Stafford, Flt Lt RAJ Wells, Fg Off Katie Leonard, WO Kevin Morley, WO Stephen Perham, FS Katrina Harries, Sgt Paul Higgins, Sgt Scott Hill, Sgt Jim Pullen (Retd), Sgt Scott Turner, Cpl Rebecca Croker, Cpl Matthew Lockwood and Mrs Ali Stafford, along with Cdt Tom Anderson, Sgt Sean Henry, Cpl Alexander Turner and FS James Wise from Air Training Corps in Chester-Le-Street. Your writing is both emotional and powerful, with so many worthy heroes being celebrated within this book, I hope that when you finally get to see your words in print you will feel as proud of your efforts as I am.

To complete the editorial team we were fortunate to have Flight Lieutenant Samantha Broderick (Retd), who led our marketing push and our team manager Kim Beechey who made sure we were all in the right place at the right time. Thanks to you both for your constant efforts to get the team moving together.

But of course, the team had help from many sources, from the families of the heroes themselves, museums, researchers and – of course – RBL members. We'd like to thank you for all your help and support throughout the process of creating this content: 626-Squadron.co.uk, Nigel Allison, AncientFaces, the Australian War Museum, Terry Avann, Gloria Bagley, Battle of Britain London Monument, Francis Brancato, Kate Brett, Tom Brown, Carolton Nursing Home, Carol Clark, the Commander C Clouston Family, Ray Coutu, Sadie Crowe, Jackie Daly, Stuart Duncan, Peter Eldridge, William Higginson, Gordon Hill, Tyson Holmes and the Holmes Family, the Imperial War Museum, Jean Kelsick, Sue Laker from the Priaulx Library, Jean-Francois Lomenech, Alanna Meharg, the *Stamford Mercury* and Alan Walters, Hakki Müftüzade, Paradata.org.uk, Gabriella Peralta, Stephen le Provost, RAF Museum London, the Regimental Museum of The Royal Welsh, Alec Ryan, Adria Seccareccia and the McGill University Library, Bill Sergeant, Margaret Sheard and Chris Elliott from the CyprusScene.com team, Adam Sizeland and Liam Yon from the St Helena Museum, Mark Seaman, David Horsley, Michelle Smart, Jeff Street, Kevin Tobin, Sharon Turton, VC Online and Michael Zavacky.

Particular thanks go to the Royal British Legion team, who have supported us throughout the project. Big thanks to Rob Hogg-Thompson and Emily Prestidge, who held countless meetings with us making sure our book met the very high RBL standards. Thank you for your trust, support, guidance and for allowing us to be part of your centenary. And, of course, thanks to the team at St James's House for once again believing in us and turning the ramblings of idiots into this most beautiful book, allowing us to show our support to the Legion in such a special way. Special thanks go to our editor John Lewis, to designers Jochen Viegener, Anton Jacques and Richard Seymour, to Royal Editor Robert Jobson, to writer Peter Watts, to Garry Blackman for his guidance throughout, to Claire Godeaux for spreading the word and, of course, to the CEO of SJH, Richard Freed, for his trust, belief and commitment to supporting our Armed Forces charities.

And finally, we need to thank our families who, for a year, have put up with us disappearing to our bedroom offices, sheds and other lockdown hiding places to put together the content for the book you hold. Without the combined efforts of you all this book wouldn't exist and with it the opportunity to not only spread the word about the talents and courage of the Armed Forces but the opportunity to raise much needed funds for the Royal British Legion on this their centenary.

A message from the publisher

Our company, St James's House – an imprint of the SJH Group – is a UK-based publisher that specialises in commemorative albums for major events that have included The Queen's 90th Birthday Celebration at Windsor Castle, the RAF's centenary and VE Day 75.

For 2021, we were honoured to partner with the Royal British Legion (RBL) to co-publish *Cooking With Heroes: The Royal British Legion Centenary Cookbook*. Researched and written by the Armed Forces and a wide range of their supporters, this publication will serve as a unique culinary resource and a lasting tribute to the work of the RBL.

On behalf of the RBL, we would like to thank everyone from the military family who has helped to create and promote this book; we would like to thank our bestselling celebrity chefs for their editorial contributions and ongoing support; and we would like to thank our sponsor organisations – without whom this project would not have been possible.

Thanks to the generosity of our sponsor organisations, our company has been able to provide publishing and marketing services for this book at no cost to the RBL. We have also been able to support the RBL financially through media licence fees and by donating all net retail profit to them.

We would, of course, also like to thank you, our reader, for your support of this project, and we hope that you will use and enjoy this book for years to come.

Credits

Publisher

St James's House
298 Regent's Park Road
London N3 2SZ
(St James's House is an imprint of the SJH Group)

T: +44 (0)20 8371 4000
E: publishing@stjamess.org
W: www.stjamess.org

Richard Freed, Chief Executive
richard.freed@stjamess.org

Stephen van der Merwe, Managing Director
stephen.vdm@stjamess.org

Garry Blackman, Group Commercial Director
garry.blackman@sjhgroup.com

Richard Golbourne, Sales Director
r.golbourne@stjamess.org

Anna Danby, Publishing Director
anna.danby@stjamess.org

Stephen Mitchell, Editor-in-Chief
stephen.mitchell@stjamess.org

John Lewis, Editor
john.lewis@stjamess.org

Robert Jobson, Royal Editor

Anton Jacques, Art Director
anton.jacques@sjhgroup.org

Richard Seymour, Senior Graphic Designer
r.seymour@sjhgroup.org

Elayna Rudolphy, Food Stylist

Neil White, Food Photographer

Publishing partner

The Royal British Legion
Haig House, 199 Borough High Street
London
SE1 1AA

T: 0345 845 1945
E: info@britishlegion.org.uk
W: www.britishlegion.org.uk

Charles Byrne
Director General

Robert Lee
*Assistant Director of Remembrance and
National Events*

Teresa Greener
Head of Special Events and Celebrity Liaison

Ben France
Head of Corporate Partnerships

Robert Hogg-Thompson
Corporate Partnerships Officer

Emily Prestidge
Public Relations Officer

*And thanks to everyone else at the Royal British
Legion who has contributed to the making of
this book*

Photography

Alamy
Getty Images
Imperial War Museum

Boatwork Ltd photo: Richard
Langdon/Ocean Images (p. 170)
EBB Limited: Images courtesy of
Brett Trafford Photography (p. 108)
Nana Lily's: Paul at
paulmatthewsphotography.com (p. 365)

All photography for recipes by Neil
White, food stylist Elayna Rudolphy

Other images are the copyright
of individual organisations

Index

SPONSORS INDEX

Printed in the UK by DG3 Leycol on 130gsm Essential Silk. This paper has been independently certified according to the standards of the Forest Stewardship Council® (FSC)®.

ISBN: 978-1-906670-91-7

The endpapers of this book feature portraits of 140 volunteers from across the Armed Forces family and beyond, all of whom gave of their time and expertise to help create this book.